ZIMBABWE

Kruger
National
Park

MOZAMBIQUE

NORTHERN TRANSVAAL

Pietersburg

Nylstroom

GUATENG

Pretoria
Tembisa
Johannesburg
Krugersdorp
Germiston
Katlehong
Soweto
Heidelberg
Vereeniging
Sebokeng

Kempton Park

dorp
tchefstroom
sdorp

Nelspruit

MPUMALANGA

SWAZILAND

REE STATE

Ulundi

KWAZULU NATAL

LESOTHO

DRAKENSBERG Mts

Pietermaritzburg

Durban

Aliwal North

Indian Ocean

Queenstown

Umtata

N CAPE

Bisho

n's Town

0   200miles

0   200km

The Last Trek – A New Beginning

F.W. DE KLERK

The Last Trek – A New Beginning

THE AUTOBIOGRAPHY

MACMILLAN

First published 1998 by Macmillan

an imprint of Macmillan Publishers Ltd
25 Eccleston Place, London SW1W 9NF
and Basingstoke

Associated companies throughout the world

ISBN 0 333 73264 2

1 3 5 7 9 8 6 4 2

A CIP catalogue record for this book is available from
the British Library.

Typeset by SetSystems Ltd, Saffron Walden, Essex
Printed and bound in Great Britain by
Mackays of Chatham plc, Chatham, Kent

To all those who made the last trek with me
and who share my hope for the success of
our new beginning

Contents

List of Illustrations

Aged six months with my mother. (*Private*)
At the age of three years. (*Private*)
Family photograph, circa 1940. (*Private*)
With my father, Jan de Klerk. (*Private*)
Aged sixteen. (*Private*)
With friends at Potchefstroom University. (*Private*)
On my engagement to Marike, 18 April 1958. (*Private*)
Our wedding day, 11 April 1959. (*Private*)
A family photo from 1974: Willem, Susan, Marike, me and Jan.
    (*Private*)
My inauguration as a member of Parliament, Cape Town, February
    1973. (*Private*)
Inauguration as minister of post and telecommunication affairs,
    3 April 1978. (*Private*)
With ex-President P. W. Botha. (*The Argus*)
With Dr Mangosuthu Buthelezi, 1990. (*The Argus*)
With President Sam Nujoma at the celebration of Namibian
    independence, 12 March 1990. (*The Argus*)
With Revd Allan Hendrickse and Marike at a Labour Party meeting,
    December 1990. (*Private*)
Meeting with President François Mitterrand, Paris, May 1990. (*South
    African Government Communication and Information Service*)
With President Yeltsin, the Kremlin, June 1992. (*South African
    Government Communication and Information Service*)
A meeting of Codesa at the World Trade Centre, Kempton Park,
    December 1991. (*South African Government Communication and
    Information Service*)
Visiting a victim of violence in Tembisa, 1 August 1993. (*South
    African Government Communication and Information Service*)
With Ambassador Henry Swarz, Marike, and Dave Steward, director-
    general in the Office of the State President, after receiving the
    Philadelphia Peace Medal, Philadelphia, 4 July 1993. (*Private*)

Preface

I have discovered that writing a book is not a simple undertaking. It has been an enriching experience, but one which has once again made me aware of my own limitations.

Although this is an autobiography, I have tried to look beyond myself and not to make it a typical autobiography. With this book, and with the De Klerks and myself as prototypes, I wish to help create perspective on the motivating forces behind the development of political attitudes – particularly within the National Party and among Afrikaners. I hope that this will contribute to a more discerning view of our country's stormy history than at present prevails.

I thank everyone who has assisted me with the writing of this book. Professor David Welsh and Mr Alf Ries have provided invaluable contributions. My office staff and former political colleagues also deserve special mention. I should also like to thank our publishers – and Catherine Whitaker, in particular – for their professional advice, guidance and enthusiasm. Special thanks should go to my cousin, Estelle Crowson, who has overseen the Afrikaans translation.

Finally, this book would never have become a reality had it not been for Dave Steward's key role. He worked just as hard as I did. His research and contributions were indispensable and it would not be out of place to give him recognition as co-author.

Introduction

The new South Africa was born on 10 May 1994, the day that Nelson Mandela was inaugurated as president of South Africa. Late in the autumn morning, six Impala aircraft of the South African air force roared across the eggshell blue skies above the Union Buildings in Pretoria, trailing the colours of the new South African flag. Minutes earlier Nelson Mandela had taken the oath of office as the first democratically elected president of South Africa. For the first time in its history our country had a government that was truly representative of all its people.

I sat with the other honoured guests and participants in this historic occasion on a specially built platform above the amphitheatre of the Union Buildings, the seat of the South African government almost since the creation of the Union of South Africa on 31 May 1910.

Nelson Mandela had chosen the site for his inauguration well. The Union Buildings are set just below the crown of one of the three parallel ridges of hills between which Pretoria was built. They were designed by the great British imperial architect, Sir Herbert Baker, and could have been built in any of the capitals of the former British Empire. (In fact, they closely resemble the parliament buildings in New Delhi.) They comprise two long wings of honey-coloured sandstone under terracotta tiles linked by a gracious colonnaded amphitheatre. On either side of the amphitheatre there are elegant clock towers, whose chimes had measured the comings and goings of generations of public servants and cabinet ministers. Its dark halls, its tranquil courtyards and high-ceilinged offices had, until that day, been the sole preserve of South Africa's white rulers and administrators. It had been – more than any other building – the symbol of state power. From where I was seated on the inauguration platform, I could see the president's office, which I had just vacated, and beside it the closed shutters and balcony of the cabinet room, where the edifice of apartheid had been erected, law by law, and where, law by law, during my presidency and that of my predecessor, President P. W. Botha, it had been dismantled.

The new president stood before me, tall, slightly bent with age, beaming with goodwill in the silver sunshine of the brilliant autumn day. We were – and are – political opponents. Although we respected each other, there was little warmth in our relationship. I could not forget his bitter and unfounded attacks on me, and he could not shake off his deep suspicions concerning my role and intentions. Nevertheless, I did not begrudge him his moment of triumph. This was the realization of the dream that had sustained him for the twenty-seven years of his imprisonment. It was the culmination of the struggles and aspirations of generations of black South Africans. It was the day that many white South Africans had dreaded for centuries, the day that my party, the National Party, had for most of its existence done everything in its power to avoid. It was the moment for which I had worked day and night since I became president of South Africa in September 1989.

Beside me, was my wife Marike. She had been with me, and had supported me, in all the major episodes of my career – when I first entered politics in 1972; when I became a cabinet minister in 1978; when I was elected as the leader of the National Party in the Transvaal in 1982; again when I was elected leader of the National Party in 1989 and when I made the speech on 2 February 1990 that set in motion the process that was finally reaching its culmination in the amphitheatre before the Union Buildings.

Also seated with me on the podium was Archbishop Desmond Tutu, resplendent in his purple robes. The diminutive priest had goaded us for years over the sins of apartheid – but he had also wept and threatened to leave South Africa if his comrades in the United Democratic Front continued to necklace their enemies. He was referring to the particularly brutal form of execution by which the revolutionaries had burned their victims to death by fastening petrol-filled tyres around their necks and setting them alight. Somehow Winnie Mandela had also managed to make an appearance on the main platform, despite her estrangement from her famous husband. As always, she was a centre of attention. She had promised to free the people of South Africa with her matchboxes and necklaces. In the end they were liberated not by violence after a devastating racial war, but through peaceful negotiations and compromise. Also around us were the chiefs of South Africa's security forces, General Johan van der Merwe, the commissioner of the South African police; General Georg Meiring, the chief of the defence force accompanied by the chiefs of the army, navy and air force. Their uniforms, crisp and smart, bore rows of military decorations for campaigns waged primarily against the ANC and its allies. Until a week earlier Nelson Mandela and many of the key ANC leaders feared that they would mount a *coup d'état*, rather than surrender power to their erstwhile enemies.

The funeral of Dr Verwoerd – the architect of apartheid – had been held in this same amphitheatre. Now, twenty-eight years after his death, it was witnessing the final burial of his vision of an ethnically compartmentalized commonwealth of southern African states. It was filled with an assembly that would have been quite unthinkable during his lifetime. He had doggedly preferred international sporting isolation to the prospect of accepting Maori players in the rugby teams of our traditional arch-rivals, New Zealand. While he was in office visas were granted to black American diplomats only after weighty consideration by the cabinet. Now the amphitheatre was filled with South Africans and foreigners of all colours and races, mixing freely and happily together. Senior office bearers of the African National Congress mingled easily with National Party cabinet ministers whom they had come to know quite well during the tortuous negotiations that had preceded our first fully democratic elections on 27 April. Dr Mangosuthu Buthelezi, the leader of the Inkatha Freedom Party, found himself in the same audience as ANC leaders from Natal. For years members of his party had been locked in a murderous struggle with the ANC for the control of the province of KwaZulu-Natal.

The amphitheatre was also filled with numerous international guests for whom the idea of any public contact with South Africa would have been anathema during the long decades of our international isolation. Vice-President Al Gore and Hillary Clinton, Robert Mugabe and numerous heads of government and state were seated together in the sharp morning sunshine, shielding their eyes with their programmes as the ceremony proceeded. Among them was Fidel Castro and a senior representative of the Russian Federation. Less than seven years earlier our army had been locked in battle with Russian- and Cuban-led Angolan troops on the Lomba River, in southern Angola. It was probably one of the largest land battles in Africa since the Second World War. We had convincingly won that battle – but it had shown us how precariously isolated we had become.

The moment arrived when the chief justice called upon me to take the oath of office as one of the two executive deputy presidents in the Government of National Unity, which was about to take over the government of South Africa. The other executive deputy president was

Thabo Mbeki, widely regarded as the ANC leader who was most likely to succeed Nelson Mandela.

I was no longer president. I would be moving from the president's office behind the impressive colonnaded portico to my left to a mirror image office to my right. I had never had any illusions that this would be the outcome of the reform process that I began on 2 February 1990. I had equally few illusions about the difficulty of the task that lay ahead and about the problems and frustrations that would accompany the loss of power.

Judge Corbett administered the oath to me in my own language, Afrikaans. I made a point of swearing it in the name of *Drie-enige God* – the Afrikaans for the Holy Trinity. I did so because of the concern among Christians – and particularly the Afrikaans churches – about the ANC's approach to religious matters. I wished to illustrate my commitment to Christian values, within the framework of religious freedom.

I was deeply aware of my responsibility for assuring the best possible future for my own people – as well as for all the other peoples of our incredibly complex society. If I turned in my seat and looked out through the bullet-proof glass that had been erected around the ceremonial platform I could see the square mass of the Voortrekker Monument silhouetted against the southern sky. Out beyond the terraced gardens and sweeping lawns – now covered in festive marquees, huge public announcement systems and tens of thousands of eager South Africans – it was a stark reminder of my heritage. My people had erected the monument some fifty years earlier to the Afrikaner Voortrekkers – pioneers in Afrikaans – who had opened up the interior of South Africa with their flint-lock muskets and trains of lumbering ox wagons. The marble bas-reliefs that adorned its interior walls bore silent testimony to the tribulations that they had suffered in their quest to establish their own free republics in the interior of the sub-continent. The people depicted in the murals were the heroes of whose deeds I learned at my mother's knee. The dream that they had dreamt of being a free and separate people, with their own right to national self-determination in their own national state in southern Africa, had been the dream that had motivated the ancestors who stared sternly at me from our old family photographs. It had been the central goal of my own father, who had been cabinet minster during the 1950s and 60s. It was the ideal to which I myself had clung until I finally concluded, after a long process of deep introspection, that, if pursued, it would bring disaster to all the peoples of our country – including my own.

Immediately after the conclusion of the formalities President Mandela, Deputy President Mbeki and I appeared on the terrace above the crowd on the lower lawns of the Union Buildings. Mandela, standing in the centre, lifted my and Mbeki's hands above our heads to the roar of the masses below. He referred to me as one of Africa's greatest sons. I remembered his many attacks on me and marvelled at the ambivalent nature of our relationship. I wondered how long his new-found respect for me would last.

A magnificent pavilion had been erected in the grounds of the Presidency, about two kilometres away, where the new president was to host a lunch for five or six hundred foreign and local guests. Unfortunately, the arrangements to transport the guests from the amphitheatre to the grand marquee collapsed in a snarl of luxury coaches unable to move backward or forward through the jubilant crowds at the Union Buildings. It took some of the guests more than two hours to cover the short distance. Others, like Britain's representative, Prince Philip, almost did not make it at all. Instead, he donned a panama hat to protect himself from the sharp autumn sun and philosophically made his way to one of the lesser marquees on the upper lawns of the Union Buildings, before he found his way at last to the main reception. He later told me that he had had a wonderful time. It was that sort of day. Princes mixed with peasants; statesmen with sightseers; soldiers and guerrilla fighters with their former enemies. Those who finally arrived at the grand pavilion – in urgent need of liquid refreshment – were ushered in between lines of singing and laughing flower-decked schoolgirls from all of our different communities.

It was a day of joy. It was a day of liberation – not only for black South Africans but also for us white South Africans. Suddenly, the burden of three hundred and fifty years had been lifted from our shoulders. For the first time we could greet all our countrymen without guilt or fear as equals and as fellow South Africans. When I awoke that morning I was still the president of South Africa. When I went to bed the mantle had passed from me to Nelson Mandela. Few heads of government could ever have laid aside their high office with a greater sense of accomplishment, regardless of the uncertainties of the future.

Five months earlier, when Nelson Mandela and I had received the Nobel Peace Prize at the City Hall in Oslo, I had quoted a verse from the foremost Afrikaans poet, N. P. van Wyk Louw. Freely translated it reads as follows:

> Oh wide and woeful land, alone
> beneath the great south stars.
> Will soaring joy ne'er rise above
> your silent grief?
>
> Will ne'er a mighty beauty rise
> above you, like the hail-white summer clouds
> that billow o'er your brooding peaks
> and in you, ne'er a deed be wrought
> that over the earth resounds
> and mocks the ages in their impotence?

On 10 May 1994 I felt that I had witnessed such a beauty. On that day I felt that we had wrought such a deed.

1

Roots

If there was a beginning for me and my family to the long trek that led to that day in Pretoria on 10 May 1994, it may be found in a corner of the Netherlands in the late seventeenth century.

At the end of 1995 Marike and I were invited to visit Zeeland in the Netherlands. We were taken by the governor of the province to the little town of Serooskerke-on-Walcheren, a small Dutch community with an old red-brick church that could have been taken from a painting by Vermeer. Schoolchildren sang for us and the whole community made us feel specially welcome. We also visited the vestry where we were shown the church's seventeenth-century parish records in which there were several references to the De Klerk family. On one occasion two De Klerk brothers had become involved in such an intense dispute that they had been forbidden to take communion. In all my travels, my visit to Serooskerke has a special place for me because it was there that my ancestor, Abraham de Clercq, was born on 11 October 1671.

Abraham was the son of Pieter and Sara de Clercq whose own forefathers had fled to the Netherlands from France to escape religious persecution at the hands of French Catholics. Indeed, the Le Clercq family had played a prominent role in the French Protestant church and some Le Clercqs had been burnt at the stake as a result of their adherence to their beliefs.

Abraham was six when his father died and sixteen when his thirty-six-year-old mother Sara, his sister Jannetje and his brother Joos, set sail for the Cape aboard the *Oosterland*, a ship belonging to the Dutch East Indies Company. They were part of a group of some 280 French Protestants – or Huguenots – who decided to settle at the Cape in 1688, three years after religious freedom was curtailed in France by King Louis XIV's decision to revoke the Edict of Nantes.

One can imagine the sense of excitement – and trepidation – with which the De Clercq family embarked upon the three-month voyage to what must have seemed to have been the end of the earth. Sara was going with a clear purpose: she had been asked to marry another Huguenot, Guillaume du Toit, who had settled at the Cape two years earlier. They had met before Guillaume's departure and were married on 16 May 1688, less than a month after her arrival at the Cape.

Cape Town at that time was a tiny community of thatched cottages and white-washed buildings, huddled in an amphitheatre between the ramparts of Table Mountain and the sea. The town was clustered around a castle that the Dutch had built in 1666 to protect the trade route to their empire in the East Indies. Cape Town was founded in 1652 by an official of the Dutch East Indies Company, Jan van Riebeeck, as a rest and recuperation station for the Dutch trading fleets en route to and from the Indies. Its main purpose was the provision of fresh vegetables and water to the passing fleets. One of Van Riebeeck's first acts was to establish a garden for the cultivation of fruit and vegetables and a little dam to capture the water from the streams that tumbled down from Table Mountain, especially during the rainy winters. There was also a small hospital where the scurvy-ridden crews of the Dutch East Indies Company ships could recover before continuing on the second leg of their arduous journeys to or from the Netherlands.

The gardens established by Jan van Riebeeck still exist today as a beautiful park in the heart of Cape Town. Our parliament buildings – where many of the events that are related in this book occurred – are situated beside them. The offices of the president, where Nelson Mandela first met President Botha and where my first meeting with him took place, are still called the Tuynhuys – the Garden House – because they were originally built as a storehouse for the company's gardens. The remains of the storage dam now lie beneath one of Cape Town's modern shopping centres where my offices are now situated.

By the time the De Clercqs arrived in the Cape, settlers were beginning to leave the immediate vicinity of the castle and were establishing farms up to eighty or ninety kilometres into the interior. Guillaume du Toit was one of them. He had started a farm called Aan't Pad (on the road) at the little village of Stellenbosch, some fifty kilometres to the east of Cape Town. Apparently he was doing quite well, and it was to this farm that the De Clercqs moved after their arrival at the Cape.

Even so, life at the Cape must have been very hard. The Du Toits' residence probably consisted only of a few rooms with polished cow-dung floors and reed ceilings. The surrounding countryside was still extremely wild. A Danish traveller, some eighteen years earlier, had described how he had had to climb into a tree beside the banks of a 'great salty river' some four miles from the Cape to escape from wild animals. While he was in the tree he watched 'huge lions and other animals fighting ferociously over a carcass on the other side of the river, roaring loudly enough to make a heart of steel tremble'. Today Salt River is an industrial suburb and railway centre almost in the heart of Cape Town, and the nearest wild lions are over 1,000 kilometres away.

Apart from the threat posed by wild animals, the early settlers also had to contend with raids by the Khoi (or Hottentots) and San people (or Bushmen) who had been the original inhabitants of the Cape. They resented the arrival of the strangers from across the great sea. The settlers brought smallpox. Their cattle presented tempting targets. The relationship was often bitter – and increasingly the San were forced further and further into the interior. The Khoi people gravitated more toward the new settlements established by the settlers. They suffered the fate of many other indigenous peoples throughout the world at that time: servitude, disease and the loss of their land.

In May 1709 – when he was thirty-eight – Abraham de Clercq married Magdalena Mouton, the daughter of another Huguenot family. Little is known of their history, except that they appear to have been fruitful, but not prosperous. They had ten children, but little or no property. In 1734 the governor of the Cape, Jan de la Fontaine, took pity on them and granted them a farm at a place called Vogelvallij – or Bird Valley – about a hundred kilometres north of Cape Town. He is reported to have done so because of Abraham's 'poverty and large family'. By that time Abraham was already sixty-three. He died eleven years later at the ripe old age – for those days – of seventy-four.

For the next two hundred years or so, the story of the De Klerks was the story of the emerging Afrikaner nation. Indeed, Hendrik Bibault, the half-brother of one of our ancestors, Susanna, was the first settler to call himself an Afrikaner – or an African. When soldiers of the despotic Dutch governor, Wilhelm Adriaan van der Stel, threatened him, he shouted; '*Ik ben een Afrikaander.*' (I am an African.) It was a seminal moment in the history of South Africa and was, perhaps, the first indication of the emergence of a new community with its own identity on the continent – a predominantly Dutch-speaking community with its roots in Europe, but with its heart in Africa and its eyes set on an independent future as a nation in its own right in the vast and open spaces of the sub-continent.

It is, perhaps, also interesting to note that this same Susanna was the daughter of Diana of Bengal, an Indian slave who was sold to one Augustin Boccart in 1667. Nevertheless, Susanna was raised with her father's (Detlef Bibault) legitimate (and white) children by his Dutch wife Willemyntjie de Wit, apparently without any problem or discrimination. Susanna married Wilhelm Odenthal in 1711 and was the mother of Engela Odenthal, who married my direct ancestor, Barend de Klerk, on 7 April 1737.

This was part of my genealogy of which we did not speak – and of which I did not know – when I was a child.

What I did learn of was the role that the De Klerks had played in the history of our people. I learned about Theunis Christiaan de Klerk, who was one of five Dutch burghers who were hanged for treason after a failed rebellion against the British in 1815. The British occupied the Cape for six years in 1795 during the Napoleonic Wars. They finally took over the colony in 1805. The independent-minded Dutch settlers had found them even more objectionable than they had found the despotic Dutch East Indies Company. In 1815 a fracas between the burghers and the colonial government escalated into a mini rebellion. Five of the ring leaders, including Theunis Christiaan de Klerk, were sentenced to death. Theunis was allowed to attend the christening of his youngest child before he was hanged, and used the opportunity to write a very moving poem which ended with the following verse:

> I thank you Lord for all this good
> that You still do me every day.
> God has always done me good
> What my God does is always good.

The five burghers were hanged at a place called Slagtersnek on the eastern frontier of the colony, but the executions were bungled when four of the five ropes broke. Slagtersnek joined the litany of the Afrikaners' growing bitterness toward the British.

Some twenty years after Slagtersnek the anti-British sentiment of the Dutch settlers had reached such proportions that a large part of the population decided to leave the Cape and migrate into the uncharted wilderness. Their migration has become known as the Great Trek.

Many De Klerks participated in the Trek. One of them, Lourens de Klerk, wrote a chronicle of the experiences of the Voortrekkers as they entered the hinterland of southern Africa. He recorded the hardships and disasters that they encountered, but also the pleasures and excitement of entering new lands and camping beside uncharted streams and mountains.

The De Klerk family was also well represented at another critical moment in the history of the Afrikaners. In 1837, the Voortrekker leader, Piet Retief, led his column of ox-wagons over the mighty Drakensberg Mountains into the lush green valleys of Natal. In February, he went to the capital of the Zulu king, Dingane, to negotiate a treaty that would grant the settlers land rights in Dingane's kingdom. After the treaty was signed Dingane invited Retief's party of sixty-six men to join him in celebrations in his great kraal at Mgundgundlovu (which means the place of the Great She-elephant), a circle of hundreds of beehive huts surrounding a large parade ground. They were told that protocol required them to leave their weapons outside, while they enjoyed the singing and dancing of the Zulu warriors and maidens. Suddenly, in the midst of the festivities, Dingane shouted out, '*Bulalani Abathakathi!*', which means, 'Kill the wizards!' Retief and his party – which included three De Klerks – were clubbed and stabbed to death and their corpses were dragged to a nearby hill where they were devoured by vultures. Afterwards, the Zulu regiments, known as *impis*, attacked the unsuspecting wagon trains where Piet Retief and his men had left their women and children. Ninety-seven men and women and 185 children were slaughtered along the banks of the Bloukrans and the Bushmans rivers. The Voortrekkers subsequently called one of the massacre sites '*Weenen*' – or the place of weeping.

As a child, I was brought up on stories of Piet Retief and the treachery of Dingane; of the massacres of the Voortrekker women and children; of how Dirkie Uys, a fourteen-year-old boy, died defending his fallen father; of how the Voortrekkers swore a solemn oath, that if God gave them victory over the Zulus, they would build a church in His honour and remember the day as a sacred holiday for ever; of how the Voortrekkers then wrought vengeance on the Zulus at the battle of Blood River in 1838, so-called because the river flowed red with the blood of the Zulu warriors. There was not a single fatality among the 500 or so Voortrekkers.

The other stories on which I was weaned as a child dealt with our struggle against the British. I was taught how we had been forced to leave the Cape because of the repression of the British; of how we finally succeeded in establishing our own republics in the Transvaal and the Orange Free State; of how we managed to regain our independence after the First Freedom War in 1881, after the great victory of Majuba (which actually involved only a few hundred men); of how we subsequently lost our independence again after what we called the Second Freedom War and what the British referred to as the Anglo-Boer War (1899–1902).

The Anglo-Boer War burnt itself into the collective consciousness of my people, the Afrikaners, like no other event in our history. Perhaps, the experience of the southerners after the American Civil War comes close to the anguish that our people suffered. But it was worse. Like General Sherman, the British carried out a scorched earth policy that destroyed our farms and killed our livestock. Unlike him, they interned our women and children in what became known as concentration camps. According to Thomas Pakenham, in his epic work on the Boer War, 'no one knows how many Boers – men, women and children – died in the concentration camps. Official estimates vary between 18,000 and 28,000' – out of a total population of a few hundred thousand. When I grew up, there was hardly a family in our community that had not suffered some or other loss during the Anglo-Boer War. Many of the older people still had firsthand memories of the conflict.

I mention all these events because they are essential to any understanding of the influences that shaped my early attitudes and beliefs.

My own direct ancestors on my father's side did not participate in the Great Trek. By 1825, Johannes Cornelis de Klerk (Abraham's grandson) had moved to the Burgersdorp district of the Eastern Cape Province. The family acquired a beautiful farm called Spioenkop (Spy Hill) with a strong spring – an important asset in the dry Karoo. My great-grandfather and his brother farmed there and lived in homes about a hundred yards from each other. Then they argued. The feud became so bitter that, there, in the great expanse of the Karoo, they built a fence between their homes. Despite the fact that they had no neighbours for miles around, they never spoke to one another again. Today they lie buried together at Spioenkop in the same small family cemetery.

The issue that divided them was religion. Throughout their history and wanderings in southern Africa, the Afrikaners had remained rigidly devoted to the Reformed faith of their forefathers. Those in the outlying districts often experienced great difficulty in obtaining the services of trained ministers – or dominees – to attend to their spiritual welfare. Their needs were met, in due course, by Scottish missionaries, whose Presbyterianism belonged to the same Calvinist religious family as their own Dutch Reformed Church. The foremost among these was the Reverend Andrew Murray, who is today revered among Afrikaners as one of the founders of the Dutch Reformed Church. However, some of the Scottish ministers introduced evangelical and methodist tendencies – including the singing of hymns – into the traditionally austere litanies of the Afrikaans congregations. This deeply disturbed many of the more conservative congregations in the eastern Cape. They had traditionally sung psalms and believed that many of the new hymns deviated from the written word of the Bible. They were also suspicious of the indirect influence that they believed the British colonial administration of the Cape enjoyed over the Dutch Reformed Church. Ultimately, in 1847 the Cape Synod of the Dutch Reformed Church in Cape Town rejected the protests of the conservatives that the hymn book was idolatrous, which left them isolated, alienated and angry.

One of the leading conservatives was my great-grandfather, Barend de Klerk. He, and others who shared his convictions, sought the support of like-minded Christians in the Netherlands. In response to their call, the Reverend Dirk Postma of the Christian Reformed Church in the Netherlands came to South Africa and helped the conservatives to found their own church. It was called the Reformed Church (as opposed to the Dutch Reformed Church) and became known among Afrikaners as the Dopper Church. Barend's brother remained a loyal member of the Dutch Reformed Church. It was over this issue that they fought and refused to speak to one another for the rest of their lives.

The nine congregations of the Reformed Church that existed by 1860 had a serious problem: they had only one minister, the Reverend Dirk Postma. There was an urgent need for the training of additional pastors for the growing Reformed flock. Accordingly, in May 1869 the General Synod of the newly founded church decided to establish a theological college at Burgersdorp. Its purpose would be to train ministers of religion and teachers in accordance with the doctrines of the Reformed Church.

By 1895 the Theological School of the Reformed Church of South Africa had twenty-four students, one of whom was my grandfather,

Willem Johannes de Klerk. The subject to which they soon turned their attention was, however, not theology. It was the growing threat of war between the British Empire – of which Burgersdorp was a reluctant part – and the two Afrikaans republics to the north, the Orange Free State and the Transvaal, which the Voortrekkers had established some forty years earlier.

The ostensible cause for the war was the refusal of the Transvaal Republic to grant unrestricted franchise to the thousands of white immigrants who had streamed to the Witwatersrand after the discovery of gold in 1888. In reality, the Boer Republics were a bothersome obstacle to the plans of British imperialists in London and the Cape to expand their influence northwards across the continent.

Naturally, the students at the Theological College sympathized with their fellow Afrikaners across the Orange and Vaal rivers. Many of them, including my grandfather, rushed to join the Boer forces – particularly in the ambulance corps. My grandfather was captured at an early stage. As a British subject from the Cape Colony he faced a charge of treason. He might have been hanged, had the British not changed their policy. Instead, he was twice imprisoned because, as the British put it, he was one of those 'who had not distinguished themselves by their loyalty to us'. On the second occasion he spent six months in the King William's Town jail in the Eastern Cape Province.

When not in prison he continued with his studies at the Theological College. The college was regarded, probably quite rightly, as a nest of pro-Boer sympathizers. The principal, Professor Cachet, was charged with high treason for having preached that God was with the Afrikaners and their cause was righteous. Ironically, pro-British Afrikaners from the Burgersdorp community were among his main accusers. The charges were later dropped.

In 1896 Joseph Chamberlain, the British colonial secretary, had predicted that a war in South Africa would be one of the most serious wars that could possibly be waged. He said that it would be in the nature of a civil war and would be a long war, a bitter war and a costly war. He added that it 'would leave behind it the embers of a strife which I believe generations would hardly be long enough to extinguish . . .'

Chamberlain's prophecy in 1896 was right: the war was the most serious conflict in which the British were involved since the defeat of Napoleon Bonaparte. It did take on the character of a civil war – and it did leave behind it embers of a strife which took generations to extinguish.

After his imprisonment by the British, my grandfather, Willem de Klerk, returned to the Burgersdorp Theological College, from which he graduated as a minister of religion in 1902. He later served as a minister for the Reformed congregations in Heidelberg, in the Transvaal, Aliwal North in the Cape and, in 1911, at Potchefstroom in the Transvaal. After Potchefstroom he served the Church in Johannesburg until his death in 1943, when I was seven years old.

In the intervening years he had retained his strong ties with the Theological College in Burgersdorp. In 1905 the college moved to Potchefstroom in the Western Transvaal. Potchefstroom was to play an important role in the history of my family and in my own life. It was founded on the banks of the Mooi River in 1838 by the Voortrekker leader, Andries Hendrik Potgieter. It was the oldest town in the Transvaal and was the capital of the young republic until 1854, when the seat of government moved to Pretoria. Later it developed as one of the main commercial and agricultural towns of the Western Transvaal and was also a prominent educational centre and the main centre of the Reformed Church. It was accordingly a natural choice for the new site of the Reformed Theological College. In 1919, after many years of struggle, the college was amalgamated with the Potchefstroom Gymnasium – or High School – to form the Potchefstroom University College for Christian Higher Education. In the early fifties the college attained full university status.

My grandfather played a prominent role in the establishment of the University College and, while continuing his duties as a Reformed minister, became its first registrar – or head of administration. He held the post until 1928 and served for many years on the council of the University College.

In 1910, after the Anglo-Boer War, the two British colonies in South Africa (Natal and the Cape Colony) and the two old Afrikaner republics (the Transvaal and the Orange Free State) came together to form the new Union of South Africa. Almost from the beginning there were sharp differences within the coalition that won the first general election. On the one hand there were those, including many Afrikaners led by General Louis Botha and General Jan Smuts, who wished to work for a united white nation of Afrikaners and English-speaking South Africans within the British Empire. They subsequently formed the South African Party. Opposed to them, there were those led by General Barry Hertzog, including my grandfather, who still cherished the ideals of Afrikaner nationalism. In 1914 they formed the National Party.

My grandfather had always had a keen interest in politics. In 1914 he became a founder member of the National Party. He stood in Potchefstroom as a National Party candidate for Parliament in 1915 – and lost. In 1933, the South African Party under General Smuts and the National Party under General Hertzog agreed to form a coalition to deal with the national crisis created by the Great Depression. The following year the two parties formally merged to create the United Party. Many Afrikaners, led by the Cape leader, Dr D. F. Malan, felt betrayed and established a breakaway purified National Party. My grandfather supported them together with his son-in-law, Hans Strijdom, who later was to become prime minister of South Africa. In 1934 they signed a manifesto that called on Afrikaners 'to strive for freedom until South Africa has been separated from the British Crown and Empire, to become a free republic – the historical and most desired state and form of government for South Africa'. In 1938 – when I was two years old – he stood as a candidate for the Purified National Party in one of the constituencies in Johannesburg. Once again he lost.

The following year, the United Party government split over the issue of whether the Union of South Africa should declare war against Germany – as General Smuts wanted – or whether it should remain neutral – as General Hertzog wanted. General Smuts fervently believed in South Africa's role as one of the dominions in the Great British Commonwealth of Nations. General Hertzog remembered the embers of bitterness against Britain that still smouldered in the hearts of his Afrikaans supporters. The cabinet and the Parliament chose war and General Hertzog led his followers out of the government.

These then were my roots. On 18 March 1936 I was born into a family that had been closely involved in the whole historic development of the Afrikaner nation and its struggle for freedom. My family had a long history of involvement in politics. My great-grandfather, Jan van Rooy (the father of my grandmother De Klerk), had served in the senate for the first five years after the establishment of the Union of South Africa. My grandfather on my mother's side, Frederik Willem Coetzer, after whom I had been named, had served for a full term in the Provincial Council of the Orange Free State. My grandfather, Willem de Klerk, was a deeply committed Afrikaner nationalist, and had twice stood unsuccessfully for Parliament. My uncle, Hans Strijdom, was a leading figure in the National Party and would later become prime minister. My own father, Jan de Klerk, had a long and distinguished political career, as a cabinet minister under three successive prime ministers and as president of the senate. Politics was in my blood.

2

My Childhood

My very earliest memory is of being carried on my father's shoulders surrounded by a mass of people. It was on the occasion of the laying of the cornerstone of the Voortrekker Monument in Pretoria in December 1938, when I was two and a half years old. The monument was built to mark the centenary of the Great Trek and was the occasion of a great revival of Afrikaner nationalism.

This first memory is appropriate. My father was to become one of my main mentors and role models during my formative years. Throughout my life I would share his deep commitment to the cause of Afrikaner nationalism and to the Afrikaans culture, language and heritage. Later in my career I would, however, develop a very different approach to the manner in which Afrikaner interests – together with those of South Africans of all races – could best be accommodated in an inclusive and non-racial society.

My father, Jan de Klerk, was born in 1903, the second of twelve children. His father, Willem Johannes de Klerk, married three times. He had one son by his first wife, who died in childbirth, seven children by his second wife and four by his third wife. My grandmother was his second wife, Aletta Johanna van Rooy, whom he married in 1902, and who died in 1918 during the great influenza epidemic. My father grew up in an environment that was encompassed by my grandfather's adherence to the Reformed religion; by his active involvement in Afrikaner nationalism; by his deep commitment to Afrikaans culture – and specifically to Potchefstroom University – and by the bonds that develop within large families.

The young Jan de Klerk went to school in Potchefstroom. Even though it was an overwhelmingly Afrikaans community, the policy of the Transvaal education authorities at that time was to assimilate Afrikaners into the English culture and language. On his first day at school he was punished for speaking Afrikaans. He went on to study at Potchefstroom University where he played an active role in student politics and served as the chairman of the Student Council. He qualified with a BA degree and a teaching diploma.

On 11 April 1927, my father married my mother, Hendrina Cornelia Coetzer, who had been born in Reddersburg in the Orange Free State in 1904. Her father, Frederik Willem Coetzer, had been a law agent – someone who did much the same work as an attorney, but without formal university training. Throughout his life he was also a farmer. In addition to this, he served as a member of the Provincial Council of the Orange Free State. So, as I have already pointed out, I had strong political influences from both my paternal and maternal grandfathers.

After graduating, my father became a teacher – to start with, in the sleepy Transvaal town of Nylstroom. Later he taught at a farm school near the town of Benoni, east of Johannesburg, and then in Johannesburg itself, where I was born. He was subsequently appointed as the principal of the Primrose East Primary School near Germiston, just outside Johannesburg. In those days, schoolteachers enjoyed a special status in the Afrikaans community. Afrikaners had not yet established themselves in the business sector and in the professions to the degree that they have now done. In most communities, the dominee (the pastor) and the school principal were regarded, almost *ex officio*, as the leaders of society.

In 1945 my father left teaching and took up the post of organizing secretary of a new organization, called the White Workers Protection Union. The organization was established by a group of Afrikaners on the East Rand to counteract growing communist influence in the trade union movement – and to protect the interests of white workers. They were particularly concerned about moves at that time to replace female Afrikaner workers in the clothing industry with black workers. The movement had very limited funds and my father had to do the rounds of church councils and Afrikaans cultural organizations to collect money for their operations. The National Party in the Transvaal gave him a small office from which to work.

My father's sister, Susan, was married to Hans Strijdom, who at that time was leader of the National Party in the Transvaal. He was a powerful and charismatic figure and was known as the Lion of the North – because he lived in the Northern Transvaal. In the run-up to the 1948 election, he invited my father to become a full-time party worker. My father accepted the offer and was put in charge of election planning and organization for the whole of the Witwatersrand, the most populous part of the country. He introduced new organizational approaches and control mechanisms which later had a considerable influence on the methods and structures of the National Party in the Transvaal – and throughout the country. His contribution assisted the National Party to develop a formidable electoral machine.

On 26 May 1948, when I was twelve years old, the National Party won a surprise victory in the national elections. General Smuts, who had emerged as a world figure after World War II, was defeated in his own constituency of Standerton in the Transvaal. Nobody could have been more astounded by the result than my uncle, Hans Strijdom. At first he refused to believe it. The main causes for the National Party's victory were white concerns over the enormous influx of blacks into the cities during the war; the disillusionment of returning soldiers; and perhaps even the simple promise made by the Nats that they would restore the right to buy white bread, after several years of war rationing during which only brown bread could be legally sold.

The National Party's slogan during the election campaign had been apartheid, a word best translated as separateness, which had only recently been introduced into the South African political lexicon. During and immediately after World War II there was a large influx of blacks into the urban areas, drawn by the jobs offered by South Africa's rapidly growing industries. Large shanty towns developed around most of South Africa's major cities and a new generation of street-wise urban blacks began to emerge. Under the pressure of this influx of more sophisticated and articulate black South Africans, the traditional distinctions between the races began to blur. Whites felt threatened and blamed the laissez-faire approach of the ruling United Party for this state of affairs.

The National Party promised that its policy of apartheid would put a stop to the confusion caused by the influx of blacks into the cities. It did so. During the fifties it codified and entrenched the existing ramshackle laws and practices that governed the daily lives of black South Africans. It firmly applied the pass laws that made it an offence for blacks from the rural areas to visit cities for longer than seventy-two hours without special permission. All blacks were forced to carry passes that contained a full record of their employment and of the places in which they were entitled to reside. They were required to produce their passes whenever they were approached by an official or a policeman. Failure to do so resulted, over the years until the abolition of the pass laws in 1986, in the arrest, prosecution and humiliation of more than sixteen million South Africans.

The National Party had not invented racial discrimination. Segregation laws had been firmly in place throughout most of South Africa since the nineteenth century. Apartheid, by whatever name, had been applied almost as a matter of course by the former British colonial administrations and Boer Republican governments alike. However, the new government applied segregation much more methodically and systematically than any of its predecessors. During the years following its election victory, it passed, or refined, laws governing virtually every aspect of the lives of black, coloured and Indian South Africans. All South Africans were strictly classified according to their race. Their race, in turn, determined where they could live; where they would be educated; where they could work; where they could travel; whom they could marry and with whom they could have sexual relations; where they could go for entertainment; and, ultimately, where they could be buried.

My own father was part of this. He was a member of the Parliament and the government that adopted and implemented these policies. I supported apartheid as a young man.

Why?

My father was a good and a kind man. All his life he was a devout and practising Christian. So were all – or most – of his colleagues that came to our home while I was growing up, whose children I knew at school and university. How could he – how could we all – have supported policies that we now regard as unjust and repressive?

The answer, I think, is that, like any other people in the world at any time in history, we were the products of our times and circumstances. Much of human history has been a tale of discrimination and exploitation. Most nations throughout the centuries have been prepared to pursue their own interests at the expense of others. Nearly always they have found some means of rationalizing their actions by cloaking them in some self-justifying doctrine. Until the middle of the century, racial discrimination was more the norm than the exception that governed the interaction between peoples of different races throughout the world. For most of its existence the British Empire openly and unashamedly applied a colour bar against most of its non-white subjects. The early settlement of the United States, Latin America and Australia was characterized by conflict with the original populations that sometimes led to the extinction of whole peoples. Slavery continued in the United States until the Civil War. Segregation was legally practised in the South until the Brown decision of the Supreme Court in 1954. The idea of separate but equal was supported by many respectable citizens in the South who today would regard themselves as mainstream Democrats or Republicans.

There were a number of motivations for apartheid, some of them selfish, some idealistic; some acknowledged, some unspoken. Foremost among these was our conviction that without apartheid, our people would be swamped by the vast black majority – and that this would inevitably lead to the extinction of our own hard-won right to national self-determination. Also, in 1948, most Afrikaners were small farmers or blue-collar workers. We were concerned about the threat to white workers and miners posed by competition from cheaper black labour.

There were other, more worthy, motivations: our desire that indigenous black cultures should be nurtured and developed and that they should not be swamped by the more powerful economic and technological forces of the Western materialistic culture.

Ultimately, we feared that if blacks and whites were to remain within the same system they would, sooner or later, become involved in a struggle for supremacy that would lead to a devastating race war. We saw separatism as the only means of avoiding the conflict that had been the cause of so much inter-ethnic violence in so many other plural societies throughout the world. It was within this framework that the National Party originally proposed its own policy of separatism.

Another factor in the National Party's surprise victory in the 1948 election was identified by some observers as its unexpected wins in a number of key urban constituencies in which my father's electoral methods may have played a decisive role. After the election my father became secretary for the National Party throughout the Transvaal.

At that time South Africa was divided into four provinces, each of which had an elected provincial council and a provincial executive responsible for certain aspects of government, including education, roads and hospitals. In March 1949 my father was elected as member of the Transvaal Provincial Council for Krugersdorp. The National Party had once again become the majority party in the council and my father became a member of the Provincial Executive. He also continued to serve as chief secretary of the National Party in the Transvaal on a part-time basis.

In 1954, the eighty-year-old Dr Malan retired as prime minister and was replaced by my uncle, Hans Strijdom. He invited my father to serve in his first cabinet as minister of labour and public works.

My father accepted the offer and was soon appointed as a non-elected member of the Senate – the upper house in the two-chamber Parliament that South Africa had at that time. For the whole of his subsequent political career he was a member of the Senate and never became a member of the lower house, the House of Assembly. His appointment to the cabinet was bitterly criticized in some quarters as nepotism – particularly by those who had more senior positions in the party. My parents consequently had a very hard time during his first year in office. My brother and I were close to them and shared their hurt during this period of rejection by their colleagues in Parliament. My father soon proved himself to be a competent minister and won the respect of his colleagues by the manner in which he participated in the debates on the first controversial legislation that he piloted through Parliament.

His ministerial career, like my own twenty years later, involved a variety of portfolios. Apart from the first two – labour and public works – he was subsequently responsible for home affairs, immigration and education, arts and science. After Prime Minister Strijdom's death in 1958, he served in the cabinet for the full term of Dr Verwoerd's premiership and also for the first years of the term of office of his successor, John Vorster.

In 1967 my father almost became state president. At that time the state president acted as a ceremonial head of state – while power rested with the prime minister, who was head of the government. He was defeated after an insidious campaign in which his membership of the minority Reformed Church played a central role. His detractors also mounted a smear campaign against him, which included the distribution of an anonymous letter. Although our family was hurt by these activities, we braved it out and in due course the dust settled – but my father's chances of becoming state president had been destroyed. In 1969 he was appointed as president of the Senate and, in this capacity, acted as state president during the absence overseas of President Fouché in 1971. He retired from politics in 1974, two years after I was elected to Parliament for the first time in November 1972, and died in 1979 at the age of seventy-five.

Throughout his career, he was unashamedly conservative when it came to the protection of Afrikaner interests. He was a staunch supporter of his brother-in-law's ideal of the re-establishment of an Afrikaner republic; he was a fervent Afrikaner nationalist throughout his life; and in his early years he believed that apartheid was the best solution to South Africa's racial problems. Later, when he was a senior minister he supported the kind of reformist approach that my brother Willem had begun to advocate as editor of one of the leading Afrikaans newspapers, *Die Transvaler*. I am convinced that he would also have supported the reform initiatives that I took during my presidency.

Ironically, during my ministerial career and later when I became president, it was my task to repeal many of the laws that he had placed on the statute book. I was also able to build on some of the foundations that he had laid – especially with regard to the development of a national education policy that encompassed all of the different ethnic education systems that then existed in South Africa.

My parents had only two children, my brother, Willem – known in his younger years as Wimpie – who was eight years old when I was born, and myself. When I was four Willem went to boarding school and came home only for weekends. I looked forward to his visits home. Because of the differences in our ages, I regarded him almost as a father figure. A special bond developed between us, which was strengthened when he came home for long holidays from school and later from university. But nevertheless, in a sense, I grew up almost as an only child.

Because of my father's career changes, I had a very unsettled childhood. We moved several times. For most of the time we lived on a smallholding outside the town of Krugersdorp – which is situated some thirty kilometres to the west of Johannesburg. For a while we rented a house in the northern suburbs of Krugersdorp and at one stage, while my father was working for the National Party during the 1948 election campaign, we stayed in a boarding house in Johannesburg. There my parents had a large room which they shared, and I had a small one to myself.

For long periods, we lived on our 200-acre farm outside Krugersdorp. My mother had inherited it from her father, along with a heavy mortgage. While my father was a schoolteacher, and while we were living in other parts of the Transvaal, we could not afford expensive holidays so we spent most of our holidays on the farm. We went to live there permanently when I was about ten years old. The old farm house was fixed up and over the years, whenever there was some spare money, additions were made to the house until it could be described as sprawling. Nevertheless, for most of my childhood our family was quite poor. We had to count our pennies and my father struggled to make ends meet on his small income. It was only later, when he held the dual posts of member of the executive committee of the Provincial Council and Transvaal secretary of the National Party, that his financial situation began to improve.

After we moved to the farm my father came home only twice a week – once in the middle of the week and then for the weekend. I had to accept his absence because I knew that he was working for the National Party and for the Afrikaner people. My father's career, like my own later, meant that our families did not lead normal lives. For most of the time my mother and I were alone – and she consequently played a major role in my upbringing. She took great care to develop my, and my brother's, self-confidence. She made us feel special and encouraged us to believe in ourselves – but without allowing us to become swollen-headed. She was a very refined woman and placed a great deal of stress on teaching us the social graces. She taught us the importance of being considerate to other people and, in particular, to those who were less privileged than us. She did not shout at us – but instead had her own special way of getting her message across. For example, on one occasion while I was still at primary school, when my table manners were particularly atrocious, instead of giving me a lecture, she simply stood up, fetched a mirror and without saying a word, placed it in front of me while I ate. All she said was, 'Just take a look and see how your are eating.' It was much more effective than a long sermon! She was very artistic and cultivated in us an appreciation for beauty – whether it was showing us a pretty garden, or how to dress well or to appreciate the decoration of a room. She had a great sense of balance and proportion. One of her greatest delights was gardening and she laid out a beautiful garden, with large lawns, pergolas and rockeries.

From Standard 2 onwards – when I was eight years old – I never had a continuous settled rhythm to my life until I got married. I could not say goodbye to my father every morning when he went to work or greet him when he returned every evening or sit around the same table with him for dinner every night. From my high school days I was at boarding school. Because there were no longer any children at home, my mother also began to travel more and more with my father – as all political wives have to – and played an active supporting role in his political career.

Notwithstanding all of this, I was a happy child and did all the normal things that children do. I played in the same kind of fantasy world as other children. I often pretended I was a famous detective and loved riding around on an imaginary motor cycle, consisting of a bent tree branch. From a very early age I wanted to be a lawyer – and frequently pictured myself as a brave defender of the truth.

Throughout my childhood years, I was involved in the small farming activities at our little farm. At one stage we had 1,500 fruit trees – mostly peaches but with some plums and apricots as well. We also had strawberries. From my last year at school, right through university, picking and selling fruit was a source of pocket money for me. With the help of one or two of our farmhands I would walk down the streets of Krugersdorp selling peaches from door to door. I soon became very tired of this and then discovered a gold mine – the old-age home in Krugersdorp. I would go there with a load of peaches and sell the whole lot without any trouble at all.

During the period that we lived on our smallholding outside Krugersdorp, my best playmates were the young sons of the black farmhands who worked for my father. We swam in the farm dam and in the stream that ran through the holding. We tried to shoot birds with catapults and played a game called clay stick shooting. My best friend was Charlie, whose father, Jackson, looked after my father's cattle and whose mother, Anna, did our washing. However, in those days such friendships ended at the kitchen door. When my parents called me for dinner, Charlie went his way and I went mine. This seemed to me at that time – and probably also to him – to be the natural course of life.

We young Afrikaner boys felt little or no animosity towards black children – just a strong sense of difference. The same could not be said of our relationship with English-speaking children. We were still strongly anti-British and anti everything that was English. There were two brothers with me at the farm school whose parents were English-speaking. I was twice involved in fist fights with them, after older boys had egged me on. Now that I think back, the only reason we fought was because I was Afrikaans and they were English. It was the Anglo-Boer War all over again.

The positive side of my father's political career was that I was exposed to politics at an early age and grew up among a circle of people that included some leading National Party figures.

One of them was my uncle, Prime Minister Hans Strijdom. He was of medium height, well-built, and had fiery, piercing blue eyes. His sharp features were accentuated by the dark rings beneath his eyes that were caused by serious illness during the last years of his life. He had a dominating presence and was idolized by his Transvaal supporters. Before he was appointed minister in 1948, we used to visit his home in Nylstroom, the constituency that he represented in Parliament and where he also had his attorney's office. Later, we often visited his residence in the exclusive ministerial enclave of Brynterion in Pretoria. When he became prime minister we used to call on him at Libertas, his residence in Pretoria and at Groote Schuur, where he lived in the Cape. Thirty-five years later, Marike and I lived in the same residences. Now Libertas is the home of President Nelson Mandela and has been renamed Mhlambandlhovu. My uncle would never have dreamed that such a development could ever take place or that I would play a major role in bringing it about.

Hans Strijdom also had two children, Estelle, who was my age, and a son who was three years younger than me, and we would play together. On one occasion we all went on a holiday to the Kruger National Park. Mr Blackie Swart, who was then minister of justice, and who later became state president, was also there. The grown-ups used to talk politics around the *braaivleis* (barbecue) fire, while I listened as attentively as possible. Ex-President Swart – who was at least six foot seven inches tall – was a very kind man, who liked children. He would sing us songs and peel avocado pears for us with his pocket knife. One song he sang was an Afrikaans version of 'Daisy, Daisy'. The image we had of him was diametrically different from the image he had in the English-language press and opposition circles as a tough and unrelenting hardliner.

During these game-reserve holidays, my uncle Strijdom would often take us out game-viewing during the hot afternoons when the other adults were taking their naps. He was a restless spirit who could not sleep during the day. He regarded these excursions as educational opportunities and used to share his deep knowledge of nature with us.

We children were more interested in fooling around than in listening to dissertations on the trees of the lowveld. Today, I am sorry that I was not more attentive.

*

The influence of outsiders was, however, small by comparison with the role played by my father. He liked the idea that I would one day follow in his political footsteps. But he also taught me that before one entered politics one should have succeeded in some other profession. This would provide security against the vagaries of political fortune and would also help one to maintain one's political independence. My father exposed me to politics from an early age. He often took me with him to his political and community meetings. As an elder of the Church and as an active member of the National Party and Afrikaans cultural organizations, there were many such meetings. On these occasions he let me stay up late and be part of the grown-ups' company. The result is that I grew up with broader horizons, and was, no doubt, regarded by some as being precocious.

The visit of King George VI and the royal family to South Africa in 1947 provided me with an opportunity to demonstrate my early attachment to Afrikaner republican ideals. My mother was interested in royalty, and was determined to see the King and Queen and Princesses Elizabeth and Margaret when they came to Krugersdorp. She had a pretty hat and a red dress made especially for the occasion and went to town to see the British King. My father, because of his republican convictions, had no desire to do so and decided instead to plant more fruit trees that day. I had a choice and decided to show my republican spirit by staying home with my father and planting trees. Neither of us dreamed as we worked in the orchard that one day I would be invited to have tea with the British King's daughter in Buckingham Palace.

As a thirteen-year-old schoolboy, I actively participated in my father's election campaign when he first stood for the Provincial Council in 1949. I distributed pamphlets on my bike and organized my schoolmates to help me. Later, when I was still at Monument High, I helped to establish a branch of the National Youth League (the youth wing of the National Party) in Krugersdorp. My task was to try to involve older schoolboys in the activities of the League.

We often spoke politics around our dining-room table. My brother Willem, who started university in 1946, was very interested in politics and was a student leader. During my childhood days I was often present when my father, the politician, and my brother, the theological student, exchanged views about the political questions of the day. From time to time there were also heated arguments, in which I participated, which no doubt had a formative influence on me. I was able to listen to different perspectives on the same political questions. Perhaps the most important impression that was made on me during my childhood days was that people are called to serve their communities and that they must make sacrifices for the sake of the cause that they are serving. This later became my norm for community service. And now, as I look back on my own career, I am greatly relieved that my own children do not blame me for the sacrifices that I asked of them and for the long periods of absence and the abnormal family life with which they also had to grow up.

3

My Education

My school career was very unsettled. While I was at primary school I had to change schools five times. I attended the Primrose East Primary School in Germiston – where my father was the principal – for the first two and a half years of my school life. After my father left teaching, I went to a little farm school at Elandsfontein near our smallholding outside Krugersdorp. It was a rudimentary red-brick building with very limited facilities. There was no grass on the rugby field, so I often returned home with bloody knees and elbows. In the mornings I had to get up early and ride my bike about four kilometres to the nearest school bus stop and then repeat the trip on the way home. There were fewer than a hundred pupils in the school and only three or four teachers. Consequently a single teacher had to teach two combined grades at the same time. Nevertheless, I was happy at the farm school.

When I was twelve, I went to boarding school at Monument High School in Krugersdorp, one of the most prestigious Afrikaans high schools in the country. It had imposing buildings and excellent sports fields. The boarding facilities were also quite good – although they were over-crowded. I spent my whole high school career there until I matriculated in 1953.

I had been a sickly child while I was at primary school. I caught almost every childhood illness in the book. I even had scarlet fever, and had to be quarantined for a few weeks while my brother stayed with friends. As a result, I was small and thin. During my first year of high school, Monument High held a carnival with an anti-polio theme as part of a national polio inoculation campaign. One of the main events was a procession through the streets of Krugersdorp, with the administrator of the Transvaal, Dr W. Nichol, on the main float. It was decided that the smallest boy and girl in the school should ride with him. I was chosen as the smallest boy, even though there were other boys shorter than me, because I was so skinny and fitted the polio theme best!

It was perhaps also for this reason that I never did particularly well at sport – which was quite a liability in a sport-mad school like Monument High. Although I played first-team tennis, tennis was at that time not regarded by schoolboys as an important, or even acceptable, sport. Rugby and athletics were the only sports to play and accounted for the popularity of the leading prefects. It was partly because of this that I was never elected as a prefect. Another reason may have been that I was something of a rebel and a loner. I found fulfilment in a few close friendships and did not seek popularity.

I was, however, a politician and a negotiator from an early age. I usually ended up negotiating with the teachers on the postponement of tests or the submission dates for essays and all sorts of such issues where the pupils wanted concessions from their teachers. In our Latin class (we had a wonderful Latin teacher), it was always my task to lead the teacher astray into a lengthy discussion on some or other topic and thus get through our lesson without having to account for homework that we had not done.

I was quite mischievous. We had set study hours in our boarding house, and in our junior years were supposed to do our homework in a common room under the supervision of prefects. One week, two of my friends and I decided to challenge the system. We slipped off every afternoon from Monday to Friday and went to watch movies in town. All went well from Monday until Thursday, but on Friday we were caught. One of the housemasters wrung the truth out of us and gave each of us six strokes with a cane. He overdid it a little and left me with a very badly bruised rear. That weekend I went home and while I was having a bath my father walked into the bathroom and saw what the master had done. He was furious and wanted to lay a complaint with the principal of the school. I begged him not to, because I did not want to be labelled as a tell-tale for the rest of my school career. As an experienced teacher, he knew that I was right and let the matter rest.

Even at school, I was already deeply interested in politics and in Afrikaans cultural activities. I was actively involved in the National Youth League – the youth wing of the National Party – and was forever mobilizing my friends to participate in political activities. I had also been a member of the Voortrekkers – the Afrikaans equivalent of the Boy Scouts – throughout my primary school career. However, when I arrived at Monument High, there was no Voortrekker branch at the school, possibly because there were so many other activities for the pupils. I established a branch, but it never really got off the ground, perhaps because the teachers were not sufficiently committed.

Academically, I did quite well, despite the fact that I was not very diligent. I preferred to take things easy and to enjoy my activities outside the classroom to the full. Right from the start I was in a particularly clever class which eventually achieved the best ever matriculation results in the history of the school. I was always one of the top ten in that class, but from Standard 9, when I was sixteen, I slackened a bit, with the result that I disappointed my teachers somewhat in my final matriculation exams. Despite this, Monument High taught me one lasting lesson in life – to strive for excellence.

Because of the prevailing anti-English attitude among Afrikaans schoolboys, I had neglected English while I was in primary school. However, in Standard 6 at Monument High School, I had an English teacher who introduced me to the world of English literature. I began to read avidly and improved my vocabulary and my English results. However, my spoken English would remain below standard for some years to come.

Musically, I was a total failure. Although I loved music I could never really hold a note. When I was fourteen or so, I participated in an arts competition as a member of our school choir. The day before our participation our music teacher said that somewhere something was wrong in the choir. He gave us a note which we all had to hold while he walked between us and listened to each one of us. When he came to me he grabbed me by the chest and informed me that my singing career was over. I was the problem and without me the choir won the competition.

In looking back, I realize that I never really liked school. From the moment I reached puberty I felt restricted by the rigid rules and discipline of that time. There was too little recognition of the pupil's individuality. I also rebelled against being ordered around by prefects, some of whom I found it difficult to respect. It was thus with a sense of liberation that I finally completed my school career and embraced the freedom and excitement of university.

I went to Potchefstroom University in 1954 to study a combined BA/LLB law course. Potchefstroom was a small country town which revolved around the university – at that time it had only 1,500 students, today it has more than 10,000. It was an idyllic place to study. The Mooi River (the Pretty River in Afrikaans) which ran through the town, had poplars and weeping willows along its banks. The university included a variety of old and modern buildings set in leafy oak-lined avenues, over which the branches met and formed a cool green arcade in the summer heat. There were still water channels beside some of the streets from which householders could take turns to water their gardens.

Potchefstroom had a reputation, even among Afrikaans universities, for conservatism. As its full name – Potchefstroom University for Christian Higher Education – implies, it has a strong religious orientation. Other universities used to make fun of us because dancing was not allowed. But none of this prevented me from having a wonderful time.

I threw myself wholeheartedly into student life. In the traditional rigorous initiation (hazing) activities of the first few weeks, I finally emerged as the spokesman for the first-year male students. In my second year I played a leading role in the organization of the student carnival and established quite an active branch of the National Party's National Youth League, which, among other things, helped the National Party during elections. The following year I served on a number of student organizations and at the end of the year became a member of the Student Council. A year later, I was elected as deputy chairman of the Student Council.

Apart from these activities, I also played an active role in the country-wide Afrikaanse Studentebond (the Afrikaans Student Union), and during my fourth and fifth years served on its National Executive. As with students throughout the world we loved to discuss – and solve – all the problems of the universe. Naturally, we did so from the fairly narrow and isolated perspectives with which we, as Afrikaans students, had grown up. At that time, South Africa was still a monarchy within the British Commonwealth. Our head of state was Queen Elizabeth II. For us this state of affairs was intolerable. The burning issues which we discussed were often dominated by the conflicts of the past – particularly the great ideal of re-establishing a republic. An aspect of this debate in the fifties was how we should resolve the double loyalty that we had to the Afrikaner people on the one hand, and to the white South African nation – which included English-speaking South Africans – on the other. The right wing in the Afrikaans community said at that time, as they still say, that their loyalty to the Afrikaner nation dominated everything else and strove for the establishment of an Afrikaner state. Within the National Party, the more open-minded members postulated that Afrikaners should find a balance between their loyalty to South Africa and their loyalty to the Afrikaans people. Afrikaners would have to realize that, although they were and would remain Afrikaners, their future well-being was inextricably linked to the well-being of all the white non-Afrikaners who lived in the same country. At that time we did not regard non-white South Africans as part of the South African nation. We believed that they should find their own political destiny within their own nations and areas.

Although we were more concerned at that time with relations between the white groups in the country, our policy toward non-white South Africans was increasingly becoming a subject for intense debate.

Many students who loyally supported apartheid were also in favour of programmes to improve the social and economic circumstances of black South Africans. They supported the massive initiative that the government launched soon after it came to power to clear up the slums that had developed around many of South Africa's cities – particularly Johannesburg. Between 1952 and 1972 it built more than 300,000 houses to accommodate people from the shanty towns. Most Afrikaner students were also in favour of the government's far more controversial decision to take over responsibility for black education from the churches. Although Bantu Education (Bantu was an African word which meant people), as it was called, was widely castigated by the government's critics, the fact is that the proportion of the total black population attending school rose from 8.05 per cent in 1950 to 19.8 per cent in 1975. We countered charges that Bantu Education was aimed at producing black pupils with inferior education by pointing to the number of universities and training colleges that we had started to build for blacks during this period.

Many of us within the ASB were excited about the recommendations of a major commission that the newly elected National Party government had appointed in 1950 to report on the future development of the black areas of South Africa. The commission, which became known as the Tomlinson Commission after its chairman, Professor F. R. Tomlinson, produced a 3,755-page report in 1954, which made far-reaching recommendations for the social and economic development of South Africa's black peoples. Among other things, Tomlinson called for the consolidation of the black homelands into more contiguous areas and for the development of fully diversified economies for each of the homelands, with primary, secondary and tertiary sectors. Human development, through an effective education programme, would be a prerequisite for the whole development initiative.

As the director of studies and research of the ASB, I, and a number of other politically motivated students, made a thorough study of the Tomlinson Report. It gave us new hope. Together with many other students I was disappointed when Dr Hendrik Verwoerd, who became prime minister after the death of Hans Strijdom in 1958, refused to accept and implement the report as a whole. For example, he did not wish to allow white capital to be used for the development of the homelands. His theory was that the black peoples would never be economically free if the large multinational companies which dominated the South African market were allowed to get an economic stranglehold on the homelands. The result was that heavily subsidized industries were established in the white areas near the homeland borders and the only investments which took place inside the homelands were those which were financed with grants or soft loans from the government. Verwoerd's approach to the Tomlinson Commission was criticized in resolutions that were adopted at ASB congresses, but few people – and certainly not Dr Verwoerd – ever took any notice of them.

Some of us were also uneasy that National Party policies during most of the fifties made little provision for black constitutional advancement beyond a limited and local role of self-government within their own areas. In terms of the National Party policy of that time, it was accepted that black South Africans would remain under some form of white tutelage indefinitely. Indeed, in his first policy speech after he became prime minister in 1954, my uncle Hans Strijdom had reaffirmed that the view of the National Party is that the white man must remain master of the white areas of South Africa. Yet he added that the National Party was not hostile to blacks and that it believed that separation was in the interest of both blacks and whites.

During the late fifties pressure began to build up within the more enlightened National Party circles to move away from such rigid attitudes. Towards the end of my university career, Professor Wickus du Plessis, who was my professor of Constitutional Law, wrote an article in the Afrikaans Sunday newspaper *Dagbreek* (Dawn) in which he called for the homelands to be led to full independence. He was at that time also the chairman of the Dagbreek Trust, a powerful position in the Afrikaans newspaper world. The National Party had a very strong influence in the Dagbreek Trust. Dr Verwoerd took exception to Professor Du Plessis' article and was shortly afterwards instrumental in having him removed from his position of chairman. Professor Du Plessis called me to his study and told me of his predicament. He asked if I would request from my father, who was also a trustee of the Dagbreek Trust, whether he could try to make peace between him and Dr Verwoerd. It must have been humiliating for him to take a student into his confidence. I promised to speak to my father, and did so. But it was too late – Dr Verwoerd had made up his mind.

Despite his sharp repudiation of Professor Du Plessis, a few months later Dr Verwoerd surprised the country by announcing himself that the homelands would be allowed to develop to full independence. His announcement led to the adoption of legislation in 1959 which for the first time formally recognized the various black peoples as distinctive nations and established the political and constitutional machinery for them to attain self-government, and ultimately full independence. My father later told me that Dr Verwoerd did not even bother to clear this major policy decision with the cabinet. The members of the cabinet were all astounded when they heard his announcement for the first time in Parliament. His grip on the cabinet was, however, so strong that none of them dared to raise the slightest objection.

Together with many young Afrikaners, I welcomed Dr Verwoerd's announcement. He had established the principle that all South Africa's black peoples were entitled to progress to full independence and self-determination within the homelands that they had traditionally occupied. He changed the horizontal differentiation of white supremacy to the vertical differentiation of separate development. He gave us what we imagined would be a moral solution to our complex problems because it would assure the rights of all South Africa's peoples – including our own – to self-determination and full political rights within their own areas. Xhosas from the Transkei and Ciskei, Tswanas from their homeland of Bophuthatswana, Zulus in KwaZulu and all our other black people would be able to exercise their political rights in their own areas, but would still be able to work in the white areas if they chose to do so. The states of southern Africa would form a common market, or a commonwealth, in which we would recognize our economic interdependence while continuing to live as good neighbours.

Dr Verwoerd's vision of a multinational commonwealth was an ideal with which many young Afrikaner leaders, including myself, could identify. The underlying principle of territorial partition to assure self-determination for different peoples living in a common area was widely accepted. It had been the basis for the creation of the nation states that emerged from the Austro-Hungarian Empire after the First

World War, and for modern Pakistan and India after the Second World War. It was difficult for us to conceive that this solution would not also be acceptable to reasonable black South Africans who, in our opinion at that time, did not include the ANC and other revolutionary troublemakers.

As the chairman of the ASB branch at Potchefstroom University I was responsible for inviting interesting speakers to address us. On one occasion this brought me into conflict with the university authorities. We asked the late Chief Albert Luthuli, the president of the ANC and future Nobel Peace Prize winner, to come to speak to us. The ANC was, at that stage, not yet banned, but was already regarded as a dangerous and highly controversial organization because of its links to the Communist Party of South Africa and because it advocated universal franchise. The university refused us permission to make use of the campus for the meeting. I was determined that our students should have the opportunity of hearing all points of view and arranged for the meeting to be held away from the main campus. It was a strange experience for young Afrikaners at that time to converse with black South Africans on an equal basis. Chief Luthuli impressed us as a venerable old man and we respected his position as a Zulu chief. However, his message that all South Africans should have the right to one-man one-vote in an undivided South Africa was at that time utterly alien to us. If that should happen what would become of the right of our people, the Afrikaners, to rule ourselves? Why could the Zulus and the other black nations not seek their political rights within their own homelands? We asked him some very critical questions, and no doubt, he left our meeting despondent about the possibility that Afrikaners would ever accept his message.

My role as a student leader also exposed me to my first international experience. Some years earlier, the late Sir Abe Bailey – a mining magnate – had created a trust that annually sponsored student leaders from all of South Africa's white universities to visit England for six weeks. The purpose was to broaden their minds and, at the same time, to allow Afrikaans and English-speaking student leaders to get to know one another. The sad reality was that there was very little communication between us inside South Africa. The Abe Bailey scholarships were later used to expose South African student leaders from different races to one another, and they still continue to play that role. At the end of my university career I was given an Abe Bailey scholarship. Even though I suspected that the purpose of the invitation was to brainwash us, I grabbed the opportunity with both hands and sailed for England with eleven other student leaders from all the then existing predominantly white South African universities. We had thirteen days at sea followed by six weeks in England and then another thirteen days at sea on the way home.

It was a delightful experience. We participated in discussions at Oxford and Cambridge. We visited the London Stock Exchange and Lloyd's. We went to the Houses of Parliament and to Scotland and the industrial regions of England where we were exposed to the workings of the British economy. It was a wonderful learning opportunity combined with a superb holiday. We saw *My Fair Lady* with Rex Harrison and Julie Andrews. We saw opera and ballet and, of course, we got to know and love the great world city London, which was our main base. The Afrikaners in our group even managed to get on with our fellow English-speaking South African students, many of whom later became friends.

When I met my wife Marike at university she was a B.Comm student who had completed her first year at the University of Pretoria. However, because she had to attend lectures during the evenings, she decided to finish the rest of her degree at Potchefstroom. She came to Potchefstroom at the beginning of my third year in 1956. It was really a case of love at first sight. When she arrived at Potch she already had a boyfriend. He was a friend of mine and sat at the same table as me at my residence – and I had a girlfriend. I decided to change all that. My first real discussion with Marike was to convince her to be my team-mate in a debating competition. It took quite some persuasion, but eventually she said yes. In the process, we discovered a strong mutual attraction.

She soon ended her relationship and I started to take her out. At the end of 1957 she completed her degree and went to work in Pretoria, which meant that during my final year in 1958 we could not see one another so regularly. I did not have a car – very few students did in those days – and we were dependent on lifts to see one another over weekends. On 18 April 1958 we were engaged and on 11 April 1959 – my parents' wedding anniversary – we were married.

Marike was a brilliant student. She was capped as the best female student for the year in which she obtained her degree. From the time that I started dating her, for the first time, I also started giving my studies serious attention. I couldn't allow my girlfriend to outshine me academically! In the end, the new-found diligence that she inspired helped me to achieve my LLB degree *cum laude*.

Potchefstroom University had an enormous influence on my development. Unlike any other university in South Africa, Potchefstroom had the unique right to teach from a specific religious perspective. This right had been established in private legislation that had been adopted by Parliament when the university was founded. The perspective from which Potchefstroom taught was science within the framework of Christianity. It was a viewpoint that permeated the thinking and approach of lecturers and students alike in every subject. For example, as a law student I noticed that there was much greater emphasis on the philosophy of law and on the underlying broad principles than at most other universities. We were taught to think analytically from the perspective of the principles that governed a particular subject. I was taught to base my evaluation of legal questions on clear principles, rather than previous court decisions. The key question was always which legal principles were relevant to the particular case. This approach had an influence on me that went far beyond my attitude to legal problems and my profession. Potchefstroom taught me to distinguish between fundamentals and details; and to strive for solutions within the framework of a value system and morally defensible principles.

4

Law, Community and Politics

I started my law career eager to put my theoretical knowledge of the law into practice. I was very soon brought rudely down to earth. I learned what it means to start at the bottom.

At the time that I graduated from university attorneys were required to serve a two-year apprenticeship as articled clerks with established law firms before they were allowed to practise on their own. Articled clerks were paid a pittance, supposedly because they were still learning their trade. They were required to do a great deal of leg work and office chores, but they nevertheless gained valuable experience. After I completed my degree I did one year of my articles in the Western Transvaal mining town of Klerksdorp, where my main task was the uninspiring business of debt collection. I completed my period as an articled clerk at MacRobert, De Villiers and Hitge, an English-speaking law firm in Pretoria, which I chose because I wanted to improve my spoken English. I was able to broaden my experience beyond debt collection and was finally admitted as an attorney early in 1961.

The early sixties, when I had been doing my articles, and after I started to practise law in Vereeniging, had been momentous and sometimes traumatic years for South Africa. On 20 January 1960, less than three weeks after the beginning of the decade, Dr Verwoerd surprised Parliament by announcing that a referendum would be held on 5 October that year to determine whether South Africa should become a republic. Only two weeks later, on 3 February 1960, Prime Minister Harold Macmillan of the United Kingdom delivered his famous 'Wind of Change' speech to members of the South African Parliament in Cape Town.

Macmillan's message was that the world and Africa were changing rapidly. He said that the most striking of all the impressions that he had formed on his journey through Africa was the strength of the awakening African consciousness. He said that the wind of change was blowing through Africa and, whether we liked it or not, we would all have to take account of this fact in our national policies. Dr Verwoerd replied that South Africa's policies were not out of step with these new realities. He said that it was our policy to provide the black national groups with the fullest rights and opportunities in those areas of the country in which their forefathers had settled. He continued that it was not only the black peoples of Africa who had a right to independence. The whites had the same right.

Ironically, Macmillan made his speech thirty years, less a day, from the day that I made my own 2 February 1990 speech in Parliament in which I announced the steps that led to the democratic transformation of South Africa.

Irrespective of what Dr Verwoerd had said, we could not deny the reality of the wind of change that was soon blasting within our borders. Six weeks after Macmillan's speech, police opened fire on a crowd of several thousand demonstrators in the black township of Sharpeville, killing sixty-nine people and wounding eighty. The demonstrators had been heeding a call by the radical Pan Africanist Congress to protest against the pass laws by handing in their pass books at local police stations. The police, who were probably nervous after the massacre of ten policemen by a black crowd at Cato Manor in Natal two months earlier, opened fire on the crowd. The incident catapulted South Africa on to the headlines of newspapers throughout the world and signalled the intensification of the international condemnation that would, over the years, lead to our growing isolation. A month later Dr Verwoerd survived an assassination attempt when he was shot twice in the head at short range by a white farmer while he was opening South Africa's main agricultural show. In October that year fifty-two per cent of the white South African electorate voted in favour of South Africa becoming a republic.

I had enthusiastically campaigned for the yes vote, and like most young Afrikaners was ecstatic when we won. In March the following year Dr Verwoerd tried to secure South Africa's continued membership of the Commonwealth as a republic. The tide of opinion had, however, turned. The new non-white majority in the Commonwealth – supported by Canada – made it clear that apartheid South Africa would no longer be welcome in the organization. When he realized the futility of the situation Dr Verwoerd withdrew his application for continued membership. Two months later, on 31 May, we finally became a republic. It was the fulfilment of the dreams and efforts of generations of Afrikaners, since their defeat in the Anglo-Boer War. It was also the end of an era. The core problem which South Africa would inevitably have to address was no longer the relationship between Boer and Brit – but between the whites of South Africa and all the other races who inhabited the country.

It was soon clear that the new republic could not expect a tranquil future. In 1962 the ANC – at the prompting of Nelson Mandela – decided to abandon its traditional strategy of non-violence and opted for armed struggle. Mandela left the country clandestinely and travelled extensively in Africa and Europe, drumming up support for armed conflict and undergoing guerrilla training himself. In 1963, after his secret return to South Africa, he was arrested. The following year he went on trial with several other members of the ANC and SACP leadership who had been captured at their hideout in the northern Johannesburg suburb of Rivonia. They were charged with conspiring to overthrow the state and with complicity in over 200 acts of sabotage aimed at facilitating violent revolution and an armed invasion of the country. The Rivonia Trial dominated the headlines for much of 1964 and ended with the sentencing of the main defendants – including Nelson Mandela – to terms of life imprisonment.

My reaction, and that of most of my friends at that time, was one of great relief. We were confident that we had broken the back of a communist-inspired revolutionary conspiracy. Now we could get on with the task of developing the black population and building our commonwealth of southern African states. It never crossed my mind that some twenty-seven years later I would be negotiating with Nelson Mandela and his comrades who had been imprisoned with him – or that thirty years later he would be president of South Africa.

*

When I had finished my articles and an additional year as a professional assistant in Pretoria, another young attorney and I bought a one-man firm in the Transvaal town of Vereeniging, an industrial town on the banks of the Vaal River. Vereeniging (which means unification in Afrikaans) had special significance for Afrikaners. It was there that the treaty which ended the Anglo-Boer War had been signed. One of the town's tourist attractions was a statue by the Afrikaans sculptor, Coert Steynberg, depicting a wounded Boer soldier from whose breast soared a steel figure symbolizing the resurgence of the Afrikaner nation. Vereeniging was one of the main centres of the South African steel industry, which in turn, had attracted other heavy industries to the town. As a result it was badly polluted, especially during the cold highveld winter mornings, when brown smoke lay like a pall above the factory chimneys and the sprawling black townships. One of those townships was Sharpeville, where the police had opened fire on protesters about a year before my arrival. But by the time I started practising in Vereeniging the trauma had subsided and the economy was booming. It was a good place for a young lawyer to set up his practice. And so we began the firm of Theo Rood, Boshoff and De Klerk.

It was a great challenge to build up the firm from its modest beginnings. I practised as a full-time attorney for almost twelve years before I became a member of Parliament. They were formative years during which I gained a great deal of professional experience. After I began to specialize in company and mercantile law, I also learned about the workings of the business world. I derived great satisfaction from building up the practice. By the time I fully retired from the firm in 1978, upon my appointment as a cabinet minister, its name had changed to De Klerk, Vermaak and Partners. It had become a large practice in South African terms and could offer top-quality specialized services to its clients.

After a few years in my new practice we could afford to move out of the flat in which we had been living since our arrival. We built a lovely home on an acre of ground on the banks of the Vaal River in a beautiful neighbourhood. There we started our family. Our sons Jan and Willem were born in 1964 and 1966 and our daughter Susan was born in 1969. After I entered Parliament in 1972 we found that, on the income of a member of Parliament, we could no longer afford the upkeep of our large house. We moved to a more modest home in the same neighbourhood and sold our dream house.

While I was practising as a young attorney in Vereeniging, I had become actively involved in the local structures of the National Party. Every constituency, including Vereeniging, had a number of branches from which a divisional council was composed – which was the most important party structure at the constituency level. I quite soon became the secretary, and then the chairman, of my local divisional council. I thus became the local leader of the National Party, second only to the member of Parliament who represented the constituency.

When I arrived in Vereeniging, and until I became MP for Vereeniging myself, our member of Parliament was Mr Blaar Coetsee. He was a controversial figure who had been a very senior member of the opposition United Party, before crossing the floor with a few other UP members to join the National Party. Politics at that time was a very robust business and he was a political streetfighter *par excellence*. At times it was difficult for me to work with him because our approaches differed so greatly. Nevertheless, we were a good team. He was an expert at street politics while I could mobilize the business and professional community (who did not always like him very much) to support and to help fund our activities.

One of the main concerns of the National Party at that time was to promote the rapid implementation of the homeland policy, a position which I, as an office-bearer in the party, fully supported. The chaos that had accompanied independence in several African countries and the revolutionary threat that we had confronted within South Africa during the early sixties, made me more convinced than ever that we were on the right course. In my perception, our determination to retain the right of white South Africans to rule themselves was not simply a matter of chauvinism. I believed that it was also essential for the maintenance of our physical security and basic freedoms. I was convinced that this was in the interest, not only of white South Africans, but also of moderate and peace-loving black South Africans. At that time our newspapers were full of horror stories brought back by white refugees from the Congo and other newly independent territories, where the hasty transfer of power to former revolutionaries had led in many instances to the collapse of effective government and law and order. I – like most whites – was also deeply concerned about the influence of the South African Communist Party on the ANC. Our fears were not based on McCarthyite hysteria. During the fifties the most prominent vehicle for black nationalist views was the Congress Movement which included the ANC, the White Congress of Democrats and Coloured and Asian Congresses. The role of the Communist Party in the leadership of the Congress Movement was fundamental, pervasive and well documented. The SACP, in turn, was one of the most rigidly pro-Moscow parties in the international communist movement. We were convinced that if the ANC were ever to take over control of South Africa our country would, under the influence of communists within the ANC, quickly become another atheist socialist dictatorship.

We felt, at that time, that we had an alternative that could bring justice to all our people. The realization of Dr Verwoerd's vision of a multinational commonwealth filled us with enthusiasm. The government and the National Party invested a great deal of effort and capital in trying to bring it to reality. We embarked on one of the most far-reaching exercises in social engineering that the world has ever seen.

Capital cities were built in the ten homelands, each with its own Parliament, quite impressive government buildings and bureaucracy. Several well-endowed universities were founded – which were formerly dismissed as tribal colleges, but which are now accepted as fully fledged universities. By 1975 scores of new towns had been established and more than 130,000 new houses had been built in the homelands. Between 1952 and 1972 the number of hospital beds in the homelands increased sevenfold. Decentralized industries were developed and hundreds of millions of rands were pumped into the traditional areas in a vain attempt to stem the flood of people to the supposedly white cities.

Dr Verwoerd was particularly rigorous when it came to the enforcement of social segregation (or what became known as petty apartheid) as opposed to the vision for a commonwealth of southern African states (which became known as grand apartheid). It was as though Dr Verwoerd, who was born in the Netherlands, the country of dikes and threatened inundation, felt that the slightest crack in the apartheid wall would soon become a breach that would ultimately wash away his carefully constructed social design. He accordingly preferred South Africa to face sporting isolation rather than allow visiting cricket and rugby teams to include non-whites in their sides. All this reinforced his image as a man of granite who would make no concession whatsoever to the mounting pressures from the international community. Perhaps this image made it easier for him to persuade his followers to accept the fairly radical implications of grand apartheid, that the homelands would become independent and that, within the context of the multinational commonwealth that he envisioned, blacks and whites would be equal. We persuaded ourselves that these segregation measures were necessary in the short term while we were building the edifice of the commonwealth of South African states. We foresaw a time (when the broad patterns of Dr Verwoerd's vision were generally accepted) when they would no longer be necessary. Then Zulus working in South Africa would have much the same status as Frenchmen working in Germany.

Perhaps the greatest temptation of Dr Verwoerd's vision was that it gave us an idealistic mission. Our idealism was soon transformed into ideology. It lead the National Party to believe that the complex realities of our country could be forced into narrow channels devised by men. Its point of departure was not the world as it was, but the world as we wanted it to be. And if the world and human beings did not conform to our vision, National Party ideologists would use their political power and all the devices of social engineering to force them to do so. If there were inconvenient black or coloured communities located in the wrong areas on the planners' maps, they would have to be moved. The National Party would unscramble the omelette of South African society, and, as we all know, one cannot make an omelette without breaking eggs. So the government forcibly moved more than three million people from the land and homes where many of them had lived and worked, in some cases, for generations. It assured them that it would provide them with equally good accommodation and land in areas that suited the planners of grand apartheid. But, of course, things seldom worked out the way they were planned and the planners forgot that human beings, and not planning statistics, were involved.

I believe that the most important lesson that emerged from our experience in South Africa is that no vision of the future can justify any government to ignore the basic human rights of the human beings involved. No cause is so great that we should allow it to dilute our sense of justice and humanity.

Although my father served as a minister throughout Dr Verwoerd's term as prime minister, I personally had little contact with him. However, on one occasion, as chairman of the National Party's Divisional Executive in Vereeniging, I was a member of a delegation that at the instigation of our MP, Blaar Coetsee, presented a gift to Prime Minister Verwoerd. The gift was a fridge. We saw him at a holiday home on the banks of the Vaal River near Vereeniging, which the Afrikaans publishing company, Perskor, had made available to him. Dr and Mrs Verwoerd received us and invited us in for a cup of tea. Dr Verwoerd was a large man, with short, unruly white hair and small, piercing blue eyes. A British newspaper had once described him as a man who walks well behind his stomach. I remember that he was wearing a suit, but that he didn't have a tie on. While we were drinking tea, I questioned Dr Verwoerd about our policy toward the coloureds – a mixed race Afrikaans-speaking minority who lived primarily in the Cape Province. I asked him where, in the absence of their own separate nationhood, they fitted into the policy of separate development. The essence of his reply was that he also foresaw that the coloureds and the Indians would later have to be brought into some or other common dispensation with the whites. He was of the opinion that it was too early to do so at that stage because, if they did so, the black nations would be less likely to accept independence. His view was that sufficient progress should first be made with regard to the indepen- dence of the various black nations before we could abandon our official view that the coloureds and the Indians should also follow separate constitutional destinies. Although I was pleased to learn of his long-term views, the absence of any principled approach troubled me.

Dr Verwoerd's period as prime minister was cut short on 6 September 1966 when he was stabbed to death at his seat in Parliament by a demented messenger, Dimitri Tsafendas. The messenger – a Greek immigrant – said that he had been ordered to do so by a giant tapeworm. His assassination was an enormous shock to me and most Afrikaners. Marike and I and our son Jan, who was then two years old, were on holiday on the south coast of Natal. Friends of ours, Du Toit van der Merwe and his family, had rented a holiday cottage together with us. Just after lunch we went to take a nap. Du Toit van der Merwe suddenly stormed into our bedroom and said that it had just been announced on the radio that Dr Verwoerd had been stabbed with a knife. We all rushed to the small radio that I had brought with me. It was before the days of FM and the reception was bad. We couldn't hear what was going on. My friend was so overwhelmed with emotion that he suddenly grabbed the radio, and threw it against the wall, shattering it into a thousand pieces. We were suddenly cut off from all communication. We rushed to our neighbour, who was still blissfully unaware of the news, and asked if we could listen to his radio. We finally heard confirmation that Dr Verwoerd was, indeed, dead. I was overcome by disbelief and consternation, on the one hand, and by anguish on the other. I would later have to defend my father in numerous discussions, because his Department of Home Affairs was bitterly criticized for having granted a visa to the assassin to enter the country.

Dr Verwoerd had utterly dominated his cabinet with his intellect and forceful personality. The marginal comments that he had written on government submissions and reports were regarded almost as holy writ and continued to influence policy for years after his death. John Vorster, his tough minister of justice, who had done much to crush the security threat of the early sixties, was chosen by the caucus to replace him.

*

During my years as a young attorney, I was also very active in Afrikaans cultural organizations. At the end of my student career I was approached to become a member of a secret Afrikaans youth organization called Die Ruiterwag (Afrikaans for The Cavaliers). I was to discover that it was the youth organization of the Afrikaner Broederbond – the Afrikaner League of Brothers – of which my father was a member. When I was approached, there were only three or four branches of the Ruiterwag throughout the country. On accepting membership, I became one of a small group that directed the activities of this organization during its first years.

Professor Joon van Rooy, a close relative of my great-grandfather, J. C. van Rooy, was the chairman of the Broederbond during the 1930s. At that time the organization had had a far more aggressively nationalistic agenda than it had when I joined. In 1934 Professor Van Rooy had sent a circular to members in which he had written that the key to South Africa's problems was not whether one party or another would obtain the whip-hand, 'but whether the Afrikaner Broederbond shall govern South Africa'.

Many observers would, no doubt, claim that by 1948 this goal had been achieved, since many of the members of the National Party cabinet were also members of the Broederbond. In my experience the activities of the Broederbond did not directly affect the process of government. By the time that I was admitted to the organization – contrary to the perceptions of the media and outsiders – its main concern was the promotion of the Afrikaans culture, language, traditions and way of life. The Broederbond did not promote the personal interests of its members. There were no strange rituals or unacceptable customs within either the Broederbond or the Ruiterwag, both of which were founded on Christian norms and principles. It was also not directly linked to any particular political party, although, for a long period it was, for all practical purposes, supportive of the National Party. This was the case until the Conservative Party split from the National Party in 1982. Dr Andries Treurnicht, the leader of the Conservative Party, and Dr Carel Boshoff, one of his main supporters, had both been former chairmen of the Broederbond. From that time onward the Broederbond followed a more non-party political approach. During the reform years, since the late 1970s, the Broederbond and the Ruiterwag played a very significant role in stimulating Afrikaans opinion formers to adopt renewal and reform ideas.

They served as a kind of think-tank and played an important role behind the scenes in identifying the need for change and in supporting the transformation process. The chairman of the Broederbond, at that time, Professor De Lange, was deeply involved in initiating the first clandestine contacts with the ANC. The confidentiality that it always maintained – these days it is more transparent – was aimed at creating an environment that would promote uninhibited debate on critical questions affecting the interests of Afrikaners. I served in various capacities in the Ruiterwag and the Broederbond at the local level. But I was never interested in serving in its provincial and national structures and had, on more than one occasion, declined nominations for such posts.

Apart from my membership of the Broederbond and the Ruiterwag – at one stage I belonged to both of them – I also played a leading role in another organization, the Federation of Junior Rapportryers (Junior Dispatch Riders in English). This was a transparent and public youth organization that worked for the Afrikaans language and culture and for Afrikaans interests. From being the chairman of the Vereeniging branch, which a few friends and I had established, I first became a member of the National Executive and then, for two years, I was the national chairman. This position required me to participate in meetings throughout the country and established me as one of a group of emerging young Afrikaner leaders. During my period as chairman, we launched a number of creative initiatives, including a debating competition for high schools, which is still regarded as a prestige event and has helped to develop the analytical and debating skills of many young South Africans.

In the late sixties and early seventies, right-wing elements began to misuse cultural organizations such as the Rapportryers and Junior Rapportryers to undermine Prime Minister John Vorster's first tentative steps in the direction of reform. I chose Vorster's side because I supported his reform measures. A particular Junior Rapportryers Corps – appropriately named the Hendrik Verwoerd Corps – openly confronted Vorster over the question of reform. Its leaders circulated a libellous letter within the organization, which we were able to trace back to them. I took disciplinary action against them and, with the support of the Chief Council, disbanded their corps and stripped all its members of their membership. For a few weeks this story received widespread coverage, particularly in the Afrikaans newspapers, but also in the English press. The Hendrik Verwoerd Corps decided to appeal against my decision and took their case to the Congress of the

Federation of Junior Rapportryers. Their appeal was a direct challenge, not only to me but also to the first awakenings of the reform movement. They believed that if they could gain the support of the majority, they would be able to strike a major blow for their conservative agenda. For me it was a make or break situation. In a debate that swung from the one side to the other, I succeeded in persuading the great majority of the congress to endorse the disciplinary action that I had taken and, by implication, to pass a vote of confidence in favour of the reform initiatives. A year later there was a virtual re-enactment of this incident, because all the right-wing elements had not been removed from the organization during the first confrontation. Once again, reform won.

During the same period, between my twenty-sixth and thirty-sixth years, the Transvaal National Youth League disbanded. A new approach was developed which placed greater emphasis on the mobilization of large numbers of young people to support the National Party cause, and less emphasis on membership, rigid structures and regular formal meetings. Together with a few others, including one or two young National Party members of Parliament, I was given the task of arranging a number of mass youth rallies. This task brought me into the broader mainstream of party politics beyond the local level. I became part of a small team of future politicians.

In 1972 I received an offer out of the blue from Potchefstroom University to take up an appointment as professor of Administrative Law. Until shortly before then, I would not even have considered it, but at the end of 1971 Marike and I went on an overseas tour for the first time together. There were three or four married couples in our group, which consisted mainly of students. We visited most of the countries in Western Europe. Apart from the fact that we greatly enjoyed the experience, the tour had a very marked effect on me. While I had previously been completely happy building up my law practice, after I returned to my office I suddenly felt that the walls of my world had become too small for me. My second exposure to international travel had convinced me that I did not want to remain an attorney for the rest of my life. The drafting of agreements, management of estates, divorces and property transfers were not enough. I could no longer see my future simply as being a successful lawyer, who was already doing reasonably well and who might one day even become rich.

The ideal of community service that had been ingrained in me by my parents, and which I had practised as a student leader and in the

Vereeniging community, had become more compelling. I felt that I wanted to explore new horizons and do things that would make a difference to a large number of people rather than just the short list of my clients. I viewed the offer from Potchefstroom as a heaven-sent opportunity.

Although most of my friends, and myself too, accepted that I would ultimately embark on a political career, I decided to set politics aside for the time being and to grasp the opportunity of teaching law and, at the same time, obtaining a doctorate at Potchefstroom. I was only thirty-six and my wife (who was actually always opposed to the idea of a political career) agreed that we would throw ourselves fully into my new academic life. We would leave the question of whether or not there would be some future call to enter politics in the hands of the Lord. I gave the requisite six months' notice to my partners, put my home on the market and bought a house in Potchefstroom. We were going to move at the end of 1972.

Throughout this period, Blaar Coetsee remained our MP and we continued our somewhat uneasy working relationship. Suddenly, in June 1972, his aggression and irresponsibility caught up with him. He was by now a cabinet minister, but had landed himself in a law suit from which he emerged very badly. This, together, with his wild temperament, finally led Prime Minister John Vorster to fire him from his ministerial post and to withdraw him from the mainstream of politics. But, because of his seniority, he was compensated with an appointment as South Africa's ambassador in Rome. Suddenly, the Vereeniging seat in Parliament was vacant and a candidate had to be nominated.

The general reaction, particularly from the National Party, was that I should stand as a candidate in his place. Once again, Marike and I experienced this development as an indication from above of the direction that our lives should take. We decided to reconsider our decision to move to Potchefstroom. We climbed into our car and drove to a farm in the district of Lydenburg to discuss the situation with Professor Hennie Bingle, the rector of Potchefstroom University, who was then on long leave and whom I knew very well. He helped me by asking me to apply the test of where I thought I could make the greatest contribution. He said that the university would release me from my commitment to them and added that it was more difficult to get politicians of a high standard than to find a replacement for me as law professor. We decided to change our earlier decision.

I became a candidate in the by-election which was held on 28 November 1972. Seven days earlier two other by-elections had been held in the Cape Province, and a week later four – including the Vereeniging by-election – were held in the north. Together they constituted something of a mini-test of the National Party's popularity. During the previous election in 1970 the National Party had lost seats and votes, and there was great interest in whether this trend would continue or not. The National Party was particularly concerned about the effect that the newly established far-right-wing Herstigte Nasionale Party (Re-established National Party) would have on its support. In the event, the National Party passed the test with flying colours. I won the Vereeniging seat with a strong majority against four other candidates, representing the Herstigte Nasionale Party, the opposition United Party, the liberal Progressive Party and another party that had been established just to contest the Vereeniging by-election. My father and mother were present at the election headquarters to hear the result and to help me and my fellow Nationalists to celebrate. My political career had begun.

I felt reasonably well prepared for what lay ahead. My activities in Afrikaans cultural affairs, as well as my early involvement in the party, laid the foundations of my later political career and provided me with invaluable experience and training. My political thinking also developed during this period. It was already clear that the road ahead for South Africa was going to become increasingly difficult and would require bold and creative thought. At that stage, all of us in the National Party still thought that separate development could succeed: that justice to all could be assured, regardless of race or colour, within the concept of separate nation states. The realization also began to grow that we would need a formula to cater for specific groups, such as the coloureds and Indians as well as urban black South Africans, who would not be able to be accommodated within the concept of their own nation states. They did not feel any connection with specific traditional states, but were insisting on full political rights. The reform debate had already begun within the National Party.

5

Parliament

When I entered Parliament at the end of 1972 the National Party, under the leadership of Prime Minister John Vorster, was at the crest of its confidence and power. It appeared at that time that the government had effectively crushed the revolutionary threat. Sanctions and international isolation had not yet become major problems. The economy was booming and we were making progress with the development of the black homelands. The National Party had beaten off the challenge of the right wing that had been posed by the Herstigte Nasionale Party, and had won the five other simultaneous by-elections as well. All of us, including myself, were slipping into a false sense of security.

It was, perhaps, for these reasons that Prime Minister Vorster did not feel under any particular pressure to make any major policy changes. I had already come to know Mr Vorster fairly well before I was elected to Parliament. He and my father were good friends. Our families visited one another's homes and saw each other regularly during holidays in the Kruger National Park. Mr Vorster was also a special friend of my godfather, Mr Peet Pelser, at whose firm of attorneys I had started my articles. I had also met him socially at the Pelsers. After I became a member of Parliament, I naturally got to know him better and even had the privilege, now and then, of playing a round of golf with him.

He was a thick-set man with heavy jowls and intense blue eyes, who was renowned for his deadpan sense of humour and his quick wit. Of course, his enemies did not see him the way we did. Remembering the role that he had played as minister of justice in combating the revolutionary threat, they liked to portray him as a right-wing extremist. Cartoonists in the English-language press invariably depicted him in a fascist uniform and hostile commentators usually referred to the fact that he had been interned during the Second World War for his anti-war activities. But that is not the way I and those who knew him saw him. We recognized that he was a strong leader, but we also knew him as a warm and considerate person.

On a personal level, I got on very well with Mr Vorster. I had great admiration for his debating ability and appreciation for his sharp wit. He was a man's man and relied heavily on his wife with regard to his social responsibilities as prime minister. Mrs Tini Vorster was very active in the mobilization of the women of the National Party. She made an enormous contribution to National Party team spirit through the consideration that she showed to the wives of parliamentarians and the regular social functions that she hosted for members of the caucus at Groote Schuur, the prime minister's official residence in Cape Town. Only when I became state president and Marike played the same exemplary role did I fully realize the importance of the contribution that a first lady could make.

Although he did not deviate from the general principles that had been established by Dr Verwoerd, John Vorster was, nevertheless, a pragmatic politician and a strategist *par excellence*. I believe that he saw the danger signs of growing international isolation beginning to flicker. He realized that Dr Verwoerd had unnecessarily plunged the country into isolation with his rigid attitude and that international pressure would increase.

It was for this reason that he initiated what he called his Outwards Policy, which I enthusiastically supported. Its main theme was that South Africa's future was inextricably linked to Africa and that South Africa's route to the international community ran through its neighbours to the north. This led to diplomatic initiatives in our neighbouring states and the offer of considerable aid to some African countries. These initiatives culminated in 1974 in an historic meeting between John Vorster and President Kenneth Kaunda of Zambia in a railway carriage on the bridge at the Victoria Falls.

Mr Vorster also realized that he would not be able to improve relations with blacks in other African countries if their leaders and representatives were subjected to discriminatory treatment in South Africa. This was particularly the case with the diplomatic staff of the Embassy of Malawi, which was the only African country that maintained full diplomatic ties with Pretoria. He accordingly initiated some tentative and ad hoc steps away from the rigid and inflexible approach of his predecessor. This relaxation of apartheid, which was at first applicable only to black diplomats and VIPs from neighbouring countries, was later extended to black South Africans as well. Thus Malawi – which had broken ranks with the rest of Africa by establishing diplomatic relations with South Africa – probably made a far more important contribution to the initiation of real change in South Africa than all the condemnation and threats that came from the Organization of African Unity combined. However, the accent still fell more on the relaxation of apartheid measures rather than on their abolition. The very first Select Committee of Parliament on which I served introduced exceptions which enabled black South Africans to visit restaurants and hotels. The application of the law in such areas as the Prohibition of Mixed Marriages Act and the Group Areas Act was also relaxed. A limited form of property rights was granted to black people outside the homelands. They still could not acquire full title, but long lease rights for thirty years – and then subsequently for ninety-nine years – were made available to them. In the area of sport there were also attempts at reform, although the government still wished to retain its power to intervene.

The most significant of the steps that were initiated during Mr Vorster's premiership was the appointment of the Wiehahn Commission on labour affairs. The demand of the economy, which had grown rapidly during the sixties, for skilled labour led to the first major step that the National Party took away from apartheid. At that time, although they were not illegal, black trade unions enjoyed neither recognition nor rights. Black workers' employment and advancement opportunities in the white areas were strictly limited by job reservation legislation that demarcated certain trades and employment activities for non-black workers.

During the early seventies this position became increasingly untenable. So many exceptions were made to job reservation provisions that the system became meaningless. There simply were not enough whites to fill all the positions that the expanding economy required. The large mining houses and multinational companies began to exert pressure on the government to reform its outmoded approach to labour matters.

This led in 1977 to the appointment of a Commission of Inquiry into Labour Legislation which was chaired by Nic Wiehahn, a professor at the University of South Africa. The Wiehahn Commission report revolutionized labour relations in South Africa and helped to modernize South Africa's labour practices. The commission found that it was no longer tenable to have racially separate institutions for the regulation of labour relations. Its report led to a whole string of new legislation in which I was deeply involved as one of the National Party's regular spokespersons on labour matters. The new legislation included the establishment of an Industrial Court and a National

Manpower Commission comprising members of all population groups and tasked with the responsibility of advising the minister on labour matters. More importantly, it also dealt with the abolition of job reservation and the official recognition of black trade unions, which soon began to play a vanguard role in agitating for black political rights across the board. Instead of welcoming this major step in the right direction, the ANC and the United Nations rejected the Wiehahn reforms as cunning manoeuvres by the South African government to increase its repression of black workers. According to the anti-apartheid dogma of the time, nothing good could possibly come from the government in Pretoria.

Mr Vorster's willingness to take further steps away from Verwoerdian apartheid was inhibited by his sensitivity to criticism from the right. In 1969 a small number of right-wing members of the National Party – led by Jaap Marais and Albert Hertzog – had broken away to form the HNP (Herstigte Nasionale Party). The split in the party upset him very deeply. I believe that he realized that major changes were necessary, but that he was not prepared to jeopardize party unity by taking them. And so, although his leadership was unquestioned and although he possessed sufficient authority to make the necessary moves, he allowed precious time and opportunities to slip though his fingers. He was more inclined to leave major problems – such as the political accommodation of coloured South Africans – to be resolved by the next generation. Nevertheless, he was a transitional figure between his rigid predecessor, Dr Verwoerd and his reform-minded successor, P. W. Botha. His pragmatism opened the road to the far more important reforms that P. W. Botha tackled right from the beginning of his premiership.

This then was the state of affairs when I went to Parliament for the first time as a young and enthusiastic politician.

The South African Parliament is situated in Cape Town, the legislative capital of South Africa. When the Union of South Africa was created in 1910, the delegates from the four British territories (the old British colonies of the Cape of Good Hope and Natal and the annexed Afrikaner republics of the Transvaal and the Orange Free State) could not agree on which South African city should be the national capital. The compromise that they finally reached was that Pretoria, the capital of the old Transvaal Republic, should be the administrative capital; that the Appeal Court should be situated in

Bloemfontein, the capital of the old Orange Free State Republic; and that Parliament should be situated in Cape Town.

This arrangement meant that generations of parliamentarians and public servants had to undergo an annual migration from Pretoria, and other parts of the country, to the Cape for the parliamentary sessions. The sessions generally began at the end of January, at the height of the dry Cape summer, and ended during the second half of June, with the first winter gales. This migration of some 1,500 kilometres was usually performed by train and included wives, children and pets. Because of the number and variety of the latter, the train to and from Parliament came to be known as the Zoo Train.

During their sojourn in the Cape, most of the parliamentarians and public servants were housed at Acacia Park, a special government village, some 15 kilometres to the north of the city centre. Acacia Park was situated on flat, sandy land which was unprotected from the prevailing south-easterly winds of summer and the north-westerly gales of winter. It had originally been a military base and many of the old barracks buildings had been converted into small units and houses for the session staff. Later, more small houses and flats were constructed.

This was to be our home from home for the first six years during parliamentary sessions. We had a little pre-fabricated house with three bedrooms, which was probably no bigger than two double garages put together. Like most of the other inhabitants, we regarded our sojourns in Acacia Park almost as camping-out experiences. My family and I thoroughly enjoyed our time there. There were plenty of open spaces where the children could run free and a general sense of camaraderie among the residents, whether they were members of Parliament, secretaries, clerks or drivers.

The Parliament buildings themselves are unusual in that they are not situated at the top of a hill, or on some great square or on some broad avenue, as is the case in most other countries. It was almost as though the architects had wanted to conceal the fact we had a functioning parliamentary democracy, limited though it was to white voters. Parliament was built on the site of the gardens that had been planted by the Dutch East India Company in the seventeenth century to provide fresh produce to passing ships. Its entrance looks out across a narrow street onto government offices. The buildings themselves are constructed of red brick with white porticoes and Corinthian columns. According to the Westminster model, the lower chamber – the House of Assembly – was furnished with green carpets and green leather cushions, while the Senate was decorated in red. The House of Assembly was panelled in dark mahogany. The Speaker's throne and the members' benches to its left and right were made of the same wood. The lobby outside the chamber was also carpeted in green, and the walls were decorated with the portraits of stern-faced Speakers with heavy wigs and black robes who had, over the decades, presided over the affairs of the House.

The general atmosphere was one of gravitas. Members of the public, watching the proceedings from the public gallery, dressed and acted with decorum. This was a serious place for serious business and incisive debate. I loved it – and many of my most fulfilling experiences were destined to take place there.

I delivered my maiden speech in the House of Assembly on 14 February 1973 in support of a Bill to establish a new Law Commission, which was aimed at reviewing, rationalizing and improving the South African legal system. I said that such a commission would be in the interest of the community. I added that good legal systems should ensure that there was a balance between the protection of the individual, and his rights on the one hand, and the interests of the community on the other. Law was not only of interest to attorneys, advocates and professors. It was of the greatest interest to every man woman and child, because directly or indirectly it affected every facet of life.

My maiden speech was well received, particularly by Prime Minister Vorster. A number of people, including some of his close friends, let me know that Mr Vorster had a high opinion of me. Later, when he was asked about future leaders of the National Party, he apparently mentioned my name on a number of occasions. In the beginning I was quite unaware of this positive evaluation of me. In retrospect, it is clear that others noticed that he favoured me before I did. This led to some of my colleagues, who were very ambitious, adopting a somewhat negative attitude to me and to my being labelled in the lobby gossip as one of Mr Vorster's blue-eyed boys.

Promotion to the cabinet was the most important personal goal of every ambitious backbencher. Because the National Party had such a large majority, there was vigorous competition among the backbenchers for the relatively few opportunities of being appointed as a deputy minister or minister. There were three places where a young politician could attract attention with a view to promotion: in the caucus, in the caucus study groups that dealt with the various portfolios, and in debates.

The advice that my father and other senior politicians gave me was that one should not speak unnecessarily in the caucus and that, for the first few years, one should be fairly cautious there. I followed that advice and was never sorry that I did so. Some of my other back-bencher colleagues wanted to use the caucus to make an impression and most of them burned their fingers badly.

The study groups and debates were another matter. There was an opportunity for everyone to make a constructive contribution in the study groups where we could participate creatively in the party's internal debates. Indeed, behind closed doors we could influence policy, meet and criticize ministers, and even make suggestions with regard to the amendment of legislation which had already been approved by the cabinet. However, even behind closed doors this could be a risky business. The result is that many backbenchers were over-cautious in the study groups and became yes-men.

I was part of a group of Young Turks who were determined to use the study groups to promote more effective implementation of our policies – and particularly to make a success of the homelands policy. Some of us had long been concerned about the geographic division of the country in terms of which black South Africans had been allocated only 13.7 per cent of the total territory. In addition, the territory of most of the homelands – except Transkei and Ciskei – was fragmented into numerous pieces. Despite arguments that nearly all of the home-lands fell within areas that received adequate rainfall – unlike most of South Africa – and represented the core areas that had historically been settled by black South Africans, some of us, even at that stage, believed that if we wished our policy to work we would have to make more land available. We would also have to consolidate the areas that had already been set aside for the homelands. Our group of Young Turks was critical of the party's proposals for consolidation because we were convinced that they did not go far enough. We suggested quite dramatic adjustments which would result in the expropriation of large pieces of land belonging to white farmers and owners for incorporation into the black territories. Our group proposed that extensive areas of white South Africa should be added to Bophutha-tswana, to give it a contiguous territory that would have stretched from Hammanskraal near Pretoria for several hundred kilometres to the border of the northern Cape Province. This would have entailed the inclusion of a number of white towns and would have constituted a new principle, namely that a considerable number of whites would have to make their future in homelands under homeland governments. Such whites would thus be in the same position as black South Africans who lived and worked in the so-called white areas. We also argued that the government would not have had to buy out all the white land involved, but could adopt a new approach by giving guarantees to whites whose farms and property were included in the homelands.

We mounted a strong campaign to promote this quite dramatic change of policy – but we failed. One wonders how the situation would have unfolded had the National Party made this quantum leap, instead of clutching onto an approach to land consolidation that was bound to result in the rejection of independence by most of the homelands.

My main study groups were justice, labour and home affairs. In the Labour Study Group, I strongly supported the initiatives of the Wiehahn Commission that led to the first major reforms of the apartheid labour system. Ironically, my own father had placed some of the labour legislation involved on the law books when he was minister of labour. I later helped to repeal many of the same laws. I could really come into my own in the Justice Study Group because of my legal training. Also there, during my backbench years, were the beginnings of far-reaching reform. I was, for example, part of the select committee which dealt with the delicate question of admission to hotels and restaurants situated in white group areas, which at that time were not permitted to serve people of colour. This situation was indefensible and became untenable. The result of the activities of that first select committee was the establishment of a network of international hotels and restaurants throughout South Africa in which proprietors had a free hand to serve people of all races on an integrated basis.

In the Home Affairs Study Group, I was deeply involved in an initiative to modernize South Africa's censorship and publication control laws. The legislation that resulted from this initiative succeeded for many years in keeping South Africa reasonably free from the tidal wave of pornography that was already beginning to flood Europe. One of the anomalies of the homelands policy was that the independent states soon dispensed with the strict moral standards that the South African government had always tried to apply. Casinos sprung up in them like mushrooms, many of them within an hour's drive of several of our main cities. Gambling and pornography became major sources of income for the independent homelands – some of which were soon referred to disparagingly as casino states.

The debates in Parliament were the third sphere of parliamentary activities of a young backbencher. We were expected loyally to defend party policy, to tackle the opposition and to come out fighting at every opportunity. Like batsmen in the closing stages of one-day cricket matches, backbenchers were expected to hit as many fours and sixes as possible without throwing their wickets away.

We had very few turns to speak and then it was usually only toward the end of a debate when the terrain had already been thoroughly covered. This made the challenge even greater. I enjoyed this part of politics very much. I relished the cut and thrust of parliamentary debate. The debating style of that time was based more or less on the British model and provided ample opportunity for analytic argument, repartee and for thinking on one's feet. To this day, I still prefer that type of parliamentary debate to delivering prepared speeches from public platforms.

Leading National Party figures in Parliament and the party whips must have liked my debating performance because I was given far more opportunities to participate in debates than many of my back-bench colleagues. The result was that I was quickly catapulted to the attention of the party leadership – all of which improved my chances for promotion. When it came, I felt that it was not a moment too soon. I was beginning to become frustrated by the drudgery demanded of backbenchers and the lack of opportunity to take initiatives.

6

John Vorster's Cabinet

It was widely expected at the end of 1975 that the prime minister would make an announcement after the December holidays on the appointment of a number of deputy ministers. The newspapers speculated that I was a certain candidate for one of the vacancies. Their views were corroborated by two senior members of the government who told my father – who, by then, had already retired from politics – that he should be in Cape Town a week before the opening of Parliament, when they expected my appointment to be announced.

My father naturally passed the message on to me. My proud parents travelled down to Cape Town and booked into a hotel for a week. But the great excitement in the family was suddenly dampened when my father received an indirect message from the prime minister that he was sorry, but a problem had arisen and he would not be able to appoint me as a deputy minister on that occasion. The bitter pill was sweetened by an assurance that my road ahead was open and that I should be patient. The next day, it was announced that Andries Treurnicht and Ferdi Hartzenberg – two prominent right-wing members of the party – had been appointed as deputy ministers.

Dr Andries Treurnicht, a minister of religion, had previously been the editor of *Die Kerkbode* (The Church Messenger), the newspaper of the Dutch Reformed Church, the largest Afrikaans denomination. He subsequently left the ministry and became the editor of a small Pretoria newspaper called *Hoofstad* (Capital City). Under his editorship *Hoofstad*, unlike the rest of the media, was strongly opposed to change and reform. From this platform he very soon became a leading figure in the right-wing camp. In 1971 he was elected as MP for Waterberg (the former constituency of Hans Strijdom) and very quickly became the leader of the pressure group in the parliamentary caucus that opposed and delayed reform in every possible way.

Evidently, the prime minister had been persuaded that the best way to deal with Treurnicht and his right-wing faction would be to bring them into the government, where they could be more closely watched, rather than by leaving them out in the cold and alienating them. It was hard for me to swallow my disappointment. After years of managing my own law firm as a senior partner, I was beginning to find my relative inactivity in the backbenches very frustrating. The most difficult aspect was having to deal with the expectations that had been created by the newspapers. Marike and I had to put on our bravest smiles and hid our disappointment as best we could.

I believe that this episode played a role in John Vorster's decision to appoint me over Treurnicht's head as a minister in 1978. It was unusual for a fairly young and junior politician to be appointed directly to the cabinet as a minister without first having undergone an apprenticeship as a deputy minister. Nevertheless, this is what happened to me. I think that Vorster was already beginning to regret his appointment of Dr Treurnicht, who had not become more loyal to the party as he had hoped. He had instead used his position and prestige as deputy minister to expand his support base within the party and had continued to cause tension between his right-wing faction and the rest of the party.

At the end of January 1978, Mr Vorster's private secretary, Johan Weilbach, called me into the prime minister's office on the eighteenth floor of the Hendrik Verwoerd Building across the street from Parliament. I would later occupy the same office for several years, first as a senior minister and then again for two years as deputy president. At that stage it was the prime minister's office. While I sat in the waiting room I knew that this time I was going to be given an appointment. However, I did not have the slightest idea that I would move straight into the cabinet.

I was called into the office where Mr Vorster and I were served tea. With a twinkle in his eyes he started to talk to me about this and that, and asked me about the health of my father and mother and their circumstances since they had retired. I sat on the edge of my chair desperately anxious for the small talk to end. I wanted to know why I was there. And then suddenly, out of the blue, Mr Vorster asked me if I would like to be minister of posts and telecommunications, and of welfare and pensions as well. I almost fell off my chair. First, because I had been promoted direct to the cabinet and, second, because of the portfolios. They were two portfolios in which I had never been involved during my parliamentary activities. Nevertheless, I understood the reasons for the appointment. In general, they were not regarded as key portfolios and could be safely entrusted to a young and inexperienced minister. I left his office filled with elation. My apprenticeship in Parliament was over. Now I had become part of the first team and I was eager to tackle the task ahead.

Another quite unique aspect of my appointment was that although it was announced together with a number of other ministerial appointments, my admission to the cabinet was delayed until the retirement of the incumbent minister in April of that year. The result was that I had two full months to study the two portfolios – a privilege that new ministers do not generally enjoy because their appointments are usually made with immediate effect. I received enormous assistance from Mr Louis Rive, who was at that time postmaster-general and also from Mr Van Vuuren, the secretary of the Department of Welfare and Pensions.

Mr Louis Rive later became a very close friend. He made it his business to take me – as a young and inexperienced minister – under his wing. I learned a great deal from him about public administration, the economy and state finance. I took over my other portfolio – welfare and pensions – on the eve of the introduction of a new dispensation. Draft legislation had already been approved that would bring about fundamental changes to the whole welfare subsidy system. My first task, after my swearing in as a minister on 1 April 1978, was to introduce the new legislation in Parliament and thus to experience my ministerial baptism with quite controversial legislation. I was in my element.

*

My first cabinet meeting was traumatic. The normal agenda was put aside. On the table was the question of our policy on the former Portuguese colony of Angola. When Angola had become independent in 1975, South Africa had been asked by the United States and several moderate African countries to come to the aid of UNITA and the FLNA, the anti-Communist movements in the country. We had done so, but had had to withdraw our forces when the United States Congress demanded the end to any US involvement in the war. As a result, the Cuban-backed Marxist MPLA government had been able to consolidate its hold over the country. They had begun to make their territory available to guerrillas of the South West African Peoples Organization (SWAPO) to launch attacks against South West Africa/ Namibia, which we ruled in terms of a mandate which we had received from the League of Nations after our forces had conquered the former

German colony during the First World War. While all this was happening, we had accepted a United Nations plan, sponsored by the five Western powers then on the Security Council, for the independence of the territory. Mr P. W. Botha was the minister of defence and was the hawk. On the table was the question of whether we should go into Angola in full force to protect Namibia from further SWAPO attacks and to support the UNITA movement of Dr Jonas Savimbi, or whether we should play a less forceful role with regard to the conflict in Angola.

Mr Vorster was more of a dove on this particular question. There was not much love lost between him and P. W. Botha. After the original presentation and proposal was made by P. W. Botha, Vorster gave each member of the cabinet, in order of their seniority, an opportunity to put his views on the choices before the cabinet. Some of Mr Vorster's confidants spoke against Mr Botha's proposal. However, a large majority of cabinet members supported P. W. Botha's position. As the most junior minister, I had the last turn to speak. By that time it was already clear in which direction the debate was moving and my contribution was of little importance.

Because it was my first meeting, I was uncharacteristically vague and careful not to choose sides. When he realized that the consensus favoured Botha, Prime Minister Vorster accepted his proposal. It was the beginning of a new phase in our involvement in Angolan conflict, which would impact on the lives of millions of South Africans. South Africa's involvement in Angola helped to stop the expansion of Soviet influence in southern Africa – but at the cost of the lives of young South African national servicemen and soldiers, the expenditure of billions of rands and further strains in our international relations. It was a major stimulus for the South African armaments industry and helped to develop the South African Defence Force as a formidable military machine. It also established P. W. Botha as the strong man in the National Party.

My appointment to the cabinet also coincided with the growing debate that had been generated by the so-called information scandal. The scandal had arisen as a result of the exposure by the press of the Department of Information's secret initiatives to improve the government's image overseas and in South Africa. These activities had been directed by the swashbuckling secretary for information, Dr Eschel Rhoodie, with the support of his minister, Dr Connie Mulder, and – as it later transpired – with some knowledge of Prime Minister Vorster himself. Vorster and Mulder were in trouble over the expenditure of secret funds by the Department of Information, and in particular a clandestine investment which had led to the establishment of an English language newspaper in Johannesburg called *The Citizen*. Secret state funds had been utilized to set up an apparently bona fide newspaper evidently with the objective of influencing the South African party-political debate. There could be only one outcome to this scandal: heads would have to roll. The question was: whose? Mr Vorster tried to manage the problem as best he could, but it drained his energy. He began to crack under the strain and his health suffered. In September 1978 he retired as prime minister.

At the end of the cabinet meeting, at which he informed us of his decision to retire, I held back so that I would be the last to leave the room. At that time the cabinet still met in the prime minister's own office in the Union Buildings. I remember that Vorster took off his jacket and hung it up and that he was wearing braces. I told him of my concern and regret over his decision. I was not very keen on any of his potential successors and I was extremely worried about the effect that his retirement would have on the party. He was, however, determined to step down. On a personal level I felt very sorry for him. It was clear that he was bitterly unhappy.

Mr Vorster's resignation as prime minister and leader of the National Party gave rise to a leadership struggle between P. W. Botha, the leader of the National Party in the Cape Province, and Dr Connie Mulder, the party leader in the Transvaal. Connie Mulder had previously been favoured to succeed Vorster, but he had been badly hurt by the information scandal. Although I had strongly supported him when I was younger, as I got to know him better, I had found him to be very opportunistic. At times he courted the right wing. At other times, when it suited him, he projected an open-minded image. I had little enthusiasm for him at the time of the leadership election. I also had little enthusiasm for P. W. Botha. Although I respected his administrative and organizational abilities, I had never liked him. His bombastic style never appealed to me and there was always a cool relationship between us. The third candidate was Pik Botha, the minister of foreign affairs. I had great appreciation for his talents as a public speaker and as a diplomat. He was always a clever and effective politician but I was convinced that he did not possess the qualities – including the emotional stability – to lead the country.

The result was that I did not become involved in the leadership struggle. I did not allow myself to be recruited by any of the candidates and withdrew completely from all the tumult and lobbying behind the scenes. Nobody knew for whom I voted. If it had not been for the fact that I was – and still am – opposed in principle to shirking one's responsibility, I would have abstained. Ultimately I had to make a choice and I voted for Connie Mulder. In retrospect I regretted this and would have preferred to have voted for P. W. Botha, because I have great admiration for the reform initiatives that he subsequently took at the beginning of his leadership.

I was influenced by the north/south rivalry within the National Party, which at that stage was still a major factor. As a born Transvaler, I was accordingly inclined to support Connie Mulder, who, like me, was also a Transvaler from the north, against P. W. Botha, who was the leader of the Cape National Party in the south. Also, at that stage, I still believed Connie Mulder's assurances that his hands were clean as far as the information scandal was concerned. When the time came for us to vote for the new leader in the caucus, P. W. Botha won the first round against Connie Mulder by only six votes. He had 78, Mulder received 72 and Pik Botha had 22. In the second ballot, nearly all Pik Botha's votes went to P. W. Botha – who emerged as the new leader with 98 votes – 24 more than had been polled by Mulder. The National Party had a new leader.

Like John Vorster, Connie Mulder was destroyed by the information scandal. I advised him to retire from politics – at least for a time – because he would not be able to survive the mounting attacks on his integrity that would inevitably flow from his involvement in what, by then, had been labelled Infogate.

Shortly after Mr Vorster's resignation as prime minister, I asked to see him at Groote Schuur, his official residence in Cape Town, which he had not yet vacated. My purpose was to help convince him to make himself available for appointment as state president – which at that time was still a ceremonial post. There were, no doubt, many other influences that affected his decision, but, whatever they may have been, in the end, he decided to make himself available and was soon afterwards inaugurated as state president. His critics speculated that he did so because he thought that, as state president, he would be in a better position to limit the damage that was being done to his reputation by the ongoing information scandal. I did not agree with them and always believed that he acted primarily out of his wish to minimize the harm to the National Party that had been caused by his resignation as leader.

Mr Vorster's period as state president was not a success. He was a politician to the marrow and was not suited to the ceremonial role that the state president at that time had to play. His presidency became more and more controversial with each new revelation regarding his own involvement in the information scandal. All this caused him great unhappiness and contributed to the further collapse of his health. It culminated, in June 1979, in enormous pressure being exerted, not only on him, but also on the National Party government.

P. W. Botha was himself under great pressure to resolve the information scandal. We all realized that something would have to be done. Botha called the cabinet together for an exhaustive preparatory discussion on the crisis. We then asked for an appointment with Mr Vorster and the whole cabinet walked across from Westbrook, Mr Botha's official residence, to Groote Schuur, just a short distance away, where Mr Vorster was still living. Mr Vorster received us in the lounge. He had piles of documents in front of him and was clearly prepared to struggle for his survival. He wanted to convince the cabinet that his hands were clean – and like the advocate that he was, tried to argue his case on all sorts of technical points.

Once again, as with my first cabinet meeting, all the ministers were given an opportunity of expressing their views. I was no longer the most junior minister. One by one, they told Mr Vorster in the most sympathetic manner that it would be better for him to resign. When my turn came I clearly expressed the view, as sympathetically as possible, that for his own sake and for the sake of the country he had no choice but to resign. I said that technical arguments would not win the day, even though they might be correct, because the damage that had already been done was irreparable. I remember that after I had spoken he closed the documents that had up until then lain open before him. Shortly afterwards he ended the conversation by announcing that he would resign.

There was consensus that the situation would have to be managed sensitively and sympathetically. The result was that Mr Chris Heunis – a cabinet colleague and a confidant of P. W. Botha – and I were appointed as intermediaries between Mr Vorster, Mr Botha and the cabinet to draw up a statement on his resignation. We reached agreement with Mr Vorster on the contents of the statement, which was to be released the following day. Mr Vorster telephoned me early the following morning and asked me to come to see him to discuss certain changes to the statement which he had in mind. I did so and after he had fully explained his request, I contacted the prime minister. Mr Botha was dismissive and said that he had gone as far as he was prepared to go in the previous day's decisions and was not prepared to consider further amendments. It was my unpleasant task to convey his refusal to Mr Vorster. He was deeply unhappy, but nothing more could be done.

Vorster's resignation was surrounded by controversy and afterwards led to growing bitterness on his part. My wife and I called on him and his wife once more at their holiday house on the East Cape coast. He received us in a friendly manner but it was clear that he was on the warpath. I got the impression that he wanted to persuade me to become involved in an anti-P. W. Botha strategy. I told him that he had taught me how important loyalty was and, in a friendly manner, rejected his overtures.

After that, I never saw him again and, from his side, there was a growing coldness toward me. When he died in 1983 the Transvaal Congress of the National Party was in session. I was the leader. We immediately adopted a motion of condolence at the congress and I let it be known that I was prepared to break away from the congress to attend his funeral. His son, who has since then died, asked me not to come and said that his father's last wish had been that the National Party government should be represented by Dr L. A. P. A. Munnik, the minister of health, whom he had still regularly seen. For me it was a matter of great sadness. The National Party participated in a memorial service which was held at the Bosman Street Dutch Reformed Church in Pretoria and which was attended by most of the members of the cabinet. Prominent members of the Conservative Party had, by contrast, attended his funeral and had tried to hijack it as a political opportunity.

It was tragic that in his final years Mr Vorster had allowed himself to be misused by his former political enemies in the person of Dr Treurnicht and his followers, who had undermined and attacked him behind his back during the time of his premiership.

My overwhelming sentiment at the end of the Vorster era and following my first participation in the election of a new party leader was one of disgust. I had no appetite for the dark side of politics – the back-stabbing and manoeuvring for position, the rapid changes of loyalty and the intrigues, often inspired by unbridled ambition – which characterized the events of that time. I firmly resolved not to allow myself to become part of this type of politics.

7

Ministerial Career

I greatly enjoyed my ministerial career. I had completed my apprentice-ship. At last I could put my managerial skills to the test. It was exciting to be involved every day in decisions that could make a constructive contribution to addressing South Africa's growing problems.

Full of idealism, I was determined to make a success of the portfolios that had been entrusted to me. I threw myself wholeheart-edly into studying the departments that fell under me. But I quickly became just as involved in the broader multidisciplinary activities of the cabinet and was soon an active member of a number of cabinet committees.

For nearly all of my ministerial career P. W. Botha was the head of the government, first as prime minister until 1984, and then as executive state president until 1989. Botha was born and raised on a farm in the Orange Free State to elderly parents – as what we call in Afrikaans a *laat lammetjie* (a late lamb). It is said that his parents indulged him as a child and that he could have almost anything that he wanted. He had developed an early taste for politics. In fact, in 1936, when he was only twenty, he dropped out of the University of the Orange Free State and became a full-time National Party organizer. During the following years, he established a strong position for himself in the National Party of the Cape Province. He carefully constructed his support base in the province, based on his excellent organizational abilities and unquestioning loyalty: he was loyal to those who were loyal to him and he was ruthless to those who opposed or undermined him. In 1948 he was elected to Parliament as the MP for the town of George in the Southern Cape Province. He represented the constituency for the next thirty-six years, until 1984 when he became state presi-dent. By the end of his career, in the latter part of the eighties he was the last survivor of the generation of MPs who had been elected in 1948. It was in his capacity as minister for defence, from 1966 until 1980, that he really came to the fore. It is said that soon after he became minister, he insisted on inspecting a warehouse at one of the military bases that he visited. When it was unlocked he discovered that it was full of spears – apparently for the armament of black soldiers – in the event of war. By the time he relinquished his post as minister of defence, the SADF had become the most formidable military force in Africa. Botha had also built up the armaments industry to the point where South Africa had become a major exporter of sophisticated arms. It had developed the G5 and G6 artillery systems, which were generally regarded as the best in the world. It had also produced a whole range of excellent armoured vehicles, a sophisticated attack helicopter and its own modified version of the Mirage fighter. As I later revealed in 1993, South Africa had also acquired its own nuclear capability and, at the end of the eighties, was about to test a medium-range missile system which would soon have enabled it to launch its own satellites. When he became prime minister in 1978, Botha's two main power bases were the Cape National Party, of which he became leader in 1966, and the formidable defence sector which he had personally done much to create.

There was a great difference between the managerial styles of Prime Minister Vorster and Prime Minister Botha. In the Vorster government there was far less structure and system. Cabinet minutes were kept in an old A4 notebook by the most junior minister in his own handwriting and only decisions were minuted. There were no actual standing committees and the result was the appointment of countless ad hoc committees. Ministerial submissions to the cabinet, which were intended to lead to decisions, were also disorganized. Although there was a rule that there should be a written memorandum in support of each proposal to the cabinet, there were no detailed instructions on the form and structure of such submissions and oral submissions were widely permitted.

When P. W. Botha became prime minister in September 1978, he introduced sweeping reforms to the management of the cabinet. The cabinet acquired a secretary, who kept proper minutes, which were circulated, together with detailed agendas, for approval at the following cabinet meeting. Instructions were drawn up and enforced for the preparation and submission of cabinet memorandums. Only in the most exceptional circumstances could a matter that had not been previously placed on the agenda, be raised in the cabinet. The cabinet was divided into standing committees for economic affairs, social affairs and constitutional affairs. Matters were referred to these standing committees according to the nature of the subject, which meant that far fewer ad hoc committees were appointed.

Prime Minister Botha established a new Cabinet Room in an elegant wood-panelled office adjacent to his suite at the Union Buildings in Pretoria. In Cape Town, the cabinet met in a large conference room next to the prime minister's office on the eighteenth floor of the Hendrik Verwoerd Building – a modern office tower just across the street from Parliament. The proceedings always started with a prayer by one of the cabinet members on a rotational basis. Coffee or tea were served once or twice during meetings, and each member of the cabinet had a little bowl of sweets, chocolates and peanuts in front of him. The tenser the meeting, the more quickly the sweets and peanuts disappeared. At one stage, P. W. Botha, who was a militant non-smoker, caused a major crisis by banning smoking during cabinet meetings. A No Smoking notice was displayed in the Cabinet Room. This was a hard blow for the ministers, like me, who smoked. Suddenly, the smokers started to withdraw from meetings for short periods on urgent and unexplained business. After two or three such meetings, I asked the prime minister if we could not add to the No Smoking sign the words 'unless absolutely necessary'. He laughed, and smoking was once again permitted in the cabinet – although we reduced it to the absolute minimum.

P. W. Botha sat at the head of the elongated oval cabinet table and presided over proceedings sometimes like a benevolent father and sometimes like a great bird of prey. He was a large, tall man who generally wore three-piece suits. His bald pate, heavy jowls, flashing glasses and wagging forefinger were the delight of cartoonists and satirists. His style did not encourage free and open debate. Ministers who were imprudent enough to embark on courses that did not please him were very quickly, and often quite brutally, cut down to size.

At one meeting chaired by Botha, a senior minister persisted three times in trying to promote his views, despite the obvious and increasing displeasure of the chairman. Predictably enough, P. W. Botha turned all his fury on him. As his cabinet colleagues filed out of the room, one laughingly said to another, 'Poor old chap, when all the signals were Dive! Dive! Dive! he surfaced, surfaced, surfaced!' On another occasion, when a senior minister – one of Botha's most loyal lieutenants – arrived five minutes late for a meeting, P. W. Botha turned on him in rage and said, 'Colleague, if you are not able to arrive at meetings on time, I can find plenty of people to replace you!'

The result was that few ministers were prepared to offer any real opposition to P. W. Botha in the cabinet. Many preferred to discuss proposals with him in private before they brought them to the cabinet to get a sense of whether they would be acceptable to him. This, in turn, often resulted in the prime minister committing himself beforehand to supporting such proposals without first listening to the views and objections of the rest of the cabinet. I was highly critical of this style because it undermined sound decision-making.

In short, P. W. Botha dominated his cabinet. When he visited South Africa in 1983, UN Secretary-General Perez de Cuellar commented that of all the world leaders that he had met, Deng Xiaoping and P. W. Botha had impressed him most in terms of the aura of personal power that they projected. But for me the impression was not so much one of genuine personal power, as of a man who often tended to be a bully. I thoroughly disapproved of this style of leadership in him – or in anyone else.

Another dimension that P. W. Botha introduced into the system of government was the prominent role of the State Security Council. The council became a statutory entity under Prime Minister Vorster, but was seldom convened by him. It was fully activated by Botha and under his leadership began to play an increasingly influential role in all facets of government administration.

After he became prime minister, Botha also made full use of team-building exercises – supposedly to strengthen communication and solidarity within the State Security Council. Sometimes the full cabinet was also involved. We would fly off for a few days to some remote location, often a military base in the bushveld, where we would give in-depth consideration to the major problems confronting the country. These occasions were also supposed to provide the opportunity for a kind of macho bonding between us. Part of the process was taken up with evenings spent eating and drinking around the campfire. Another aspect was the pranks that ministers played on one another. Magnus Malan, who as minister of defence was usually our host on these occasions, was particularly active in this regard. I am told that at one team-building exercise, which I didn't attend, Pik Botha, late at night after a heavy session around the campfire, livened things up by throwing ammunition into the fire. After a while the bullets started to explode and everyone dived for cover. The next morning before breakfast, there was a flurry of activity at the landing strip; medics were rushing this way and that, and soon the rumour spread around the breakfast table that a national serviceman who had been on guard the previous night had been mysteriously wounded by a stray bullet. When a panic-stricken Pik Botha enquired of Magnus Malan whether this was so, Magnus replied that it was, but that it looked as though the serviceman would pull through. Apparently Pik had actually sat down to write his letter of resignation when Magnus burst out laughing and revealed that it had all been a hoax. Other pranks included carefully doctored news reports, supposedly from the SABC, which were played over the radio to unsuspecting ministers concerning disasters in their departments – all elaborately concocted by Magnus Malan and his team.

The net result of P. W. Botha's managerial style and innovations was a significant improvement in the managerial effectiveness of the government and of departments. Botha was a good administrator. However, the intrusive role that the security departments and the State Security Council began to play in government affairs was a source of growing irritation to most ministers, as well as their directors-general (the public service heads of their departments).

I took careful note of the negative aspects of P. W. Botha's managerial style – the tendency to be dictatorial, the inhibition of free and open debate and the inside track afforded to the security departments – and vowed quietly to myself that I would change all this if I ever became president.

*

In each portfolio that I managed there was an opportunity for reform, renewal and progress. During my term as minister of posts and telecommunications, Louis Rive, the postmaster-general, and I were responsible in 1979 for acquiring the latest telecommunications technology for the upgrading of our telephone system. Because of the growing international sanctions, our choices were limited. The technology of many countries, including the United States, had already been denied to us. We were thus reliant on some of our most prominent trading partners of that time: the United Kingdom, the Federal Republic of Germany and France. In the end, we persuaded the government to approve a system which was a quantum leap away from our old mechanical telephone network to the most modern digital telecommunications set-up that was then available to us. We contracted leading companies in Germany and France for this purpose, with the result that we started to install the new system before Germany itself.

This was simply one of many examples of the ineffectiveness of sanctions. For the most part South Africa succeeded in circumventing sanctions, either through import substitution or the adoption of sophisticated sanctions-busting strategies. In many respects the sanctions appeared to achieve the opposite effect of their intention, as is so often the case when governments interfere with economic processes for ideological purposes: the arms embargo led to South Africa establishing its own impressive and highly sophisticated armaments industry, to the point where armaments became a major export; the oil embargo led to South Africa establishing the world's largest and most effective oil from coal industry which provided the base for the expansion of the country's entire chemical sector. It also forced the government to buy vast quantities of oil at pre-oil crisis prices for its strategic reserves. At one stage we had sufficient reserves to be able to survive a total oil boycott for four years. The later sale of these reserves at 1980s and 1990s prices provided the government with a huge and unplanned windfall. Disinvestment by foreign multinational companies, more often than not, enabled white South African managers to buy out the local subsidiaries at bargain prices, and thereby to become very rich. The new owners, no longer restrained by American and European employer codes of conduct, continued to produce exactly the same products, sometimes on a more profitable basis. This is hardly what church groups and pro-disinvestment shareholders in the United States and Europe had had in mind.

Obviously, sanctions also did serious damage to the country. Their general effects were to isolate the South African economy, to make us more inward looking and less competitive and to create serious long-term economic distortions. It is estimated that sanctions cost us about 1.5 per cent in our annual economic growth rate during the eighties and the early nineties. It was a price that the majority of white voters were prepared to pay to fend off the alternative – which they then firmly believed would be the imposition of a Soviet-influenced ANC dictatorship.

On the whole, I believe that sanctions did more to delay the process of transformation than they did to advance it. They further isolated South Africans from the enormous change agent represented by Western cultural and political influences. At a time when our own universities, students, artists and scientists were ripe to become proponents of change within our own society, they were cut off from the very influences that could have encouraged them to play this role. The reality is that isolation, sanctions and unbridled criticism seldom persuade people to change their positions. In our case they created a natural resistance among most white South African individuals and companies and often made them less willing to consider change. The National Party won more than one election by appealing to the resentment that many whites felt against the international community – and particularly the United States – for their role in imposing sanctions against us. Most importantly, sanctions impeded economic growth, which I believe was by far and away the most important change factor in South Africa.

My responsibility for sport and recreation from 1979 to 1980 landed me, almost immediately, at the centre of political controversy caused by the intense debate on how we should respond to our growing isolation in international sport. Dr Verwoerd and Mr Vorster had painted us into all sorts of corners as a result of their insistence on imposing apartheid strictures on sport organizations. Within the National Party caucus the right wing was determined to stop reform and had subjected a former minister of sport and recreation, Dr Piet Koornhof, to intense pressure because of his tentative steps in this regard. I was convinced that simply a moderate reduction of government prescription to sport would not end our isolation and decided that something dramatic had to be done. As a firm believer in the right of civil society to manage its own affairs with minimum government interference, I proposed that we should recognize the full autonomy of sports organizations and sports people to conduct their affairs as they saw fit and to play with whomever they wanted. Sport should be totally depoliticized and the state's role should be limited to assistance and financial support, without any conditions with racial connotations. I managed to persuade the cabinet and the caucus to agree to this proposal. The right wing, led by Daan van der Merwe, was bitterly unhappy, but sensing how deeply white South Africans loved international sport, they decided on this occasion not to be too vocal in their opposition.

The government's new policy of non-interference in sport kept most doors for international competition open and even opened new doors, at least for a period. However, the anti-apartheid groups' pressure on sport did not cease. Despite the new policy, they insisted that until separate development was abandoned in its totality, sport isolation should remain part of the sanctions armoury. Their attitude was seized on with glee by the Conservative Party which claimed that it proved the futility of trying to satisfy international demands for reform. As the sporting net closed more tightly around us, all we could do was to provide financial aid to help sport organizations to continue their struggle and, sometimes, even to arrange rebel tours.

My duties as minister of mineral and energy affairs in the early eighties drew me into the sensitive area of labour reform on the mines. Conservative white unions were staunchly opposed to the government's far-reaching reforms of labour legislation. The practice of reserving skilled jobs in the mining industry for white miners was entrenched in different laws from the legislation that governed industry in general – which had been affected by the Wiehahn reforms. It was my task to abolish it in the mining industry as well. This brought me directly into conflict with the white Mineworkers Union and its secretary, Arrie Paulus. As a result of my confrontation with the Mineworkers Union, white right-wing unions subsequently made a point of actively campaigning against me in my constituency, Vereeniging, whenever there were elections. Despite their efforts, they were never a serious problem and I was regularly re-elected.

The period that I served in the posts and telecommunications and mineral and energy affairs portfolios provided me with invaluable experience and knowledge of the economy, which would later serve me well during my presidency.

My exposure to the management of the economy as cabinet minister during the eighties also convinced me more and more that it would be impossible for us to maintain economic growth, on the one hand, and succeed with the implementation of our homeland policy on the other. I firmly believe that economic growth was a far more powerful agent for change than any of the other factors – including sanctions and international pressure.

The relative stability that the security crack-downs of the early sixties brought to South Africa ironically laid the foundation for the collapse of apartheid. Stability provided the basis for more than a decade of high, sustained economic growth which had far-reaching social, demographic and political consequences for all our people – and especially for black South Africans.

Between 1962 and 1971 the economy grew at an average rate of 6 per cent per annum. During the 1970s growth averaged almost 4 per cent. This resulted in the employment of more and more black South

Africans at higher and higher levels in all sectors of the economy. During the seventies the number of blacks employed in the manufacturing sector increased by 56 per cent. The growing economy also led to an accelerated flow of black South Africans from the rural areas to the urban areas. It further undermined Dr Verwoerd's grand vision that, by 1978, the tide to the white cities would have turned.

Economic growth led to important changes in other spheres as well. After having shown almost no growth during the previous fifty years, the black share of personal income increased from 19.8 per cent to over 37 per cent, between 1970 and 1995. During the same period the white share fell from 71.1 per cent to below 49 per cent. By the end of the eighties black South Africans had begun to move into dominant positions in many sectors of the consumer market. By 1989 they bought more stoves, fridges, televisions, hi-fis, furniture suites, crockery, curtaining and linen than whites. Black South Africans also began to play a dominant role in the country's booming informal sector. By the early nineties there were an estimated 625,000 small businesses in the black informal sector of the economy. According to some reports, the sector had created about 3.5 million jobs, of which almost 500,000 had the potential of being transferred to the formal sector. The black informal sector in South Africa was, by itself, far larger than the total economies of many independent African states.

The reality is that influx control and the pass laws were abolished by the millions of ordinary people who decided, without any political motive, to migrate to the cities in search of a better life. It happened quite peacefully long before the relevant legislation was repealed by Parliament.

I was also minister of home affairs – or the interior, as it was then known – from 1982 until September 1985. In South Africa, unlike many other countries, home affairs did not include responsibility for the police. However, some of its functions were at the very heart of apartheid.

One of the controversial responsibilities of the Department of Home Affairs, in conjunction with the Department of Justice, was the administration of legislation that prohibited mixed marriages and sex across the colour line. Over the years the so-called Mixed Marriages Act and Immorality Act had caused enormous personal suffering to people of different races who had wanted to marry or have sex with one another. It had led to countless sordid incidents, where police had burst into couples' bedrooms. The lives of many people had been ruined as a result of the humiliation of their involvement in prosecutions in terms of the Act. Some had committed suicide. For a number of years the Act had not been rigorously applied, but it was clear by the time that I became minister that its continued existence on the statute books was indefensible. It was my privilege to pilot the Bill that repealed both the prohibition of mixed marriages and sex across the colour line through Parliament on 29 April 1985.

The Department of Home Affairs was also responsible for the administration of the Population Registration Act, which classified all South Africans according to their racial group. In many respects the Act was the cornerstone of apartheid. Racial classification determined where people could live, go to school and work and – before the repeal of the Prohibition of Mixed Marriages Act in 1985 – whom they could marry. Every year there were several hundred applications for racial reclassification – particularly from the coloured community. Many of these cases were tragic and quite often involved decisions that split members of the same family into different racial groups.

More than any other task that I ever had to carry out in government, these cases brought home to me the vast difference between the Verwoerdian theory of separate development and its often devastating impact on the lives of ordinary people. My reaction was to administer the law in the most humane manner possible and to try wherever I could to accommodate the special needs of the human beings involved. These actions could only be palliative and could not detract from my growing acceptance of the indefensibility of such laws.

Another controversial function of the Department of Home Affairs was its responsibility for censorship. I had a special interest in censorship because as an ordinary MP I played a role in drawing up the new legislation that had established new structures and more relaxed standards. Arising from my own convictions I supported the continuation of a reasonably effective system for the prevention of pornography and the portrayal of gratuitous violence. It was also my conviction that we should not be completely out of step with the spirit of the times. The test that I proposed was the standard that would in all likelihood be acceptable to the average reasonable man or woman in the street – and not what would be acceptable to petty minded archconservatives on the one hand or avant garde liberals on the other.

The fact is that by the early eighties the world-views of whites and many Afrikaners were changing rapidly, to a large extent because of the influence of the media and greater exposure to international attitudes. When the National Party came to power in 1948 most of its supporters were blue collar workers and small farmers. Many of the National Party leaders who were elected at that time still had vivid memories of the Anglo-Boer War. Their whole political experience had been moulded by their struggle to resist British cultural domination and to re-establish their own republic.

By the eighties this had changed: two whole generations of Afrikaners had grown up in this period in a rapidly changing world. They were better educated than the voters of 1948 and were far more in touch with international ideas and values than their parents and grandparents had been. They were mostly middle-class white-collar workers and did not share the concerns and agendas of older generations. Like their black countrymen, they were watching the *Cosby Show* on TV and were going to movies starring Danny Glover. The perceptions of black people with which many whites had grown up could not be reconciled with the images that they were receiving through the international media. South Africa's minister for posts and telecommunications during the 1960s, Albert Hertzog, did his best to delay the arrival of a television service in South Africa for as long as he could. (The first TV service did not begin until 1975.) He feared that the little 'devil box' would have a dramatic effect on the attitudes and opinions of young Afrikaners. But there was no way that he – and others who shared his narrow-minded views – could shut South Africans off from information and development.

Of all the portfolios which I held during my ministerial career, national education was certainly the most challenging. During the four years – from 1985 to 1989 – that I held the portfolio it brought me into the midst of the reform stream in one of the most sensitive areas. Education had become a national priority. The government's policy was that each population group should have its own department and its own schools. When I became minister there were no fewer than eleven of these, including the education departments for the various population groups and the Department of National Education itself. It was the task of the Department of National Education to ensure effective co-ordination between all these departments and to establish uniform minimum standards and general policy.

The imperatives of economic growth had also had important implications for education. The white labour and managerial base was nowhere near large enough to meet the demands of a growing economy. The economy required better trained and educated black workers and managers. In 1984, a major policy review, based on the recommendations of the De Lange Commission, set new criteria for education. These included, on the one hand, 'equal opportunities and equal standards for all, irrespective of race, colour, sex or creed', and, on the other, 'full recognition of the cultural diversity of the population and the common values shared by all'.

The existence of separate education departments was not seen at that time by the government as discriminatory, but there was no way in which the unequal per capita expenditure on pupils from different race groups could be justified. In April 1986 I announced a ten-year programme which was aimed primarily at improving the quality of black education and at closing the per capita expenditure gap. We accepted the ideal that all departments should be financed on an equal basis as soon as practicable, in accordance with a financing formula that we had developed. This meant that departments with a very favourable pupil/teacher ratio – such as the white and Indian departments – would have to make painful adjustments. It also meant that, over the years, their share of the overall education budget would become considerably smaller, while that of the black education departments would grow.

We made considerable progress in achieving a fairer division of the available resources and by 1989/90 had substantially reduced the white share of expenditure. We also succeeded in equalizing the salaries and conditions of employment of all teachers with the same qualifications, regardless of race, and had also more than closed the gap in per capita expenditure on university students. In fact, by 1984 per capita expenditure on black university students exceeded expenditure on whites. But we did not succeed in making much visible progress in eliminating the expenditure gap between black and white pupils at the school level.

One of the problems that we encountered in this area was the high population growth rate among black South Africans. Each new school year the total number of pupils at black schools rose by more than 4 per cent. This meant that by 1991 we were having to build new schools and train new teachers for 300,000 additional pupils each year. As a result the additional funds that we succeeded in allocating to black education more often than not had to be used for crisis management rather than for closing the expenditure gap between black and white pupils.

The other problem that we faced was a shortage of funds. We were already spending approximately 20 per cent of the total budget on education – which could hardly be increased without causing shortages in other critical areas. The problem was 20 per cent of what? The economy was stagnant. Instead of a budget that grew with economic growth, we had to deal with a budget that was shrinking in real terms. It was truly a no-win situation. In 1989 I had to concede in Parliament that it would take much longer than ten years to equalize the per capita education expenditure between all our population groups.

We reluctantly had to accept – what the United States Supreme Court had decided in the 1950s – that the concept of separate but equal was unattainable. We also had to acknowledge that, from a political point of view, the central problem was that our whole education system was based on race. While mother tongue education and the concept of culturally rooted education could be defended on educational grounds and had, in fact, been endorsed by a UN-sponsored conference in Addis Ababa in 1961, the racial basis of our education system could not be justified.

Nevertheless, despite all the serious shortcomings in the black educational system, there was significant progress. Between 1982 and 1987 the number of black secondary school pupils increased by more than 80 per cent. Between 1989 and 1993 black university enrolment increased by almost 50 per cent and represented nearly half of all enrolments. Despite the disruption of black education and despite the low pass rates, more than twice as many black scholars passed the school-leaving matric examination in 1992 as whites.

My years as minister of national education convinced me that education was, and would remain, one of South Africa's most pressing challenges. Nothing has changed since then. Not only must the state find sufficient funds to equalize education for all South African children – it must also deal with the effects of the politicization of education by black revolutionaries during the struggle of the eighties. For several years black education was seriously disrupted and standards of discipline were destroyed while radical schoolchildren rampaged through the streets demanding liberation before education.

By the beginning of 1989, I had spent ten years in the cabinet and had dealt at various stages with seven different portfolios. I had gained a great deal of experience and had been involved in several significant reform initiatives. Together with my colleagues, I had worked to improve the daily lives of all South Africans – including blacks, coloureds and Indians. In the process we had made important progress – but also some serious mistakes. Most of these mistakes had their roots in our attempt to govern South Africa on a racial basis. As the years passed I became more and more convinced of the necessity of extricating ourselves from this situation – but in a manner that would not lead to a catastrophe for our own people and for all the other peoples of the country.

8

The Split in the National Party

The first stirrings of reform, that were initiated by Prime Minister John Vorster, created serious tension within the National Party. His tentative steps in the direction of reform had led to the creation of a strong anti-reform pressure group within the National Party, led by Dr Andries Treurnicht. By the time of Vorster's resignation as prime minister, the National Party had become a deeply divided party.

The tensions within the party were reflected in a growing debate in the Afrikaans newspapers which strongly advocated reform and campaigned for a new approach. Already, during 1966, my brother, Dr Willem de Klerk, who was then a professor at the University of Potchefstroom, made a speech that sparked off a major national debate. In his speech he divided the white population, but more specifically the Afrikaners, into three groups: the *verligtes* or enlightened group, who were inclined to over-hasty and ill-considered change; the *verkramptes*, literally the cramped people, who opposed every form of change; and then the positive, balanced group who accepted the necessity of change, but who wanted to promote ordered and goal-oriented change. The speech was seized on by the media and the last category very quickly disappeared from the debate. Only the *verligtes* and the *verkramptes* remained. The *verligtes* were regarded as being good and progressive and the *verkramptes* were seen as being antiquated and unacceptable. The newspapers had a field day hanging the two labels around the necks of leading politicians.

The scene was set for serious clashes between the *verligtes* and the *verkramptes*. The first significant move after Vorster's departure came from the right wing. The shock resignation of Connie Mulder, the leader of the National Party of the Transvaal, following the information scandal, presented Treurnicht and his inner circle with an unexpected opportunity for seizing the Transvaal leadership. There was no one among the senior politicians in the Transvaal who was an obvious successor to Connie Mulder. Fanie Botha, the minister of manpower, although a competent and successful minister, did not inspire confidence as a leader. Hendrik Schoeman, the minister of agriculture, enjoyed widespread popularity, but was not a real politician. I was regarded by the anti-Treurnicht faction as being still too junior.

Treurnicht was a formidable speaker. As a prominent church leader, he had previously commanded great respect, even among those who did not necessarily share his right-wing views. With the support of the right wing and a considerable portion of the centre group, he was elected as the leader of the National Party of the Transvaal. I did not vote for him. Treurnicht's election as leader of the National Party in the Transvaal, following closely on the election of P. W. Botha as the national leader of the party, greatly exacerbated the tensions between the conservative and moderate wings of the party. The two most influential posts in the party were now held by leaders who held strongly opposing views on reform.

P. W. Botha had no time for Treurnicht and, despite the influential post that he now held, did not immediately appoint him to the cabinet. Treurnicht had to wait six humiliating months until Botha finally bowed to pressure and brought him into the cabinet as a full minister. Even then, he gave him one of the least significant portfolios – public works, statistics and tourism. Once Treurnicht had been elected leader of the Transvaal and had taken his place in the cabinet, the battle lines for an ideological and personal showdown between him and P. W. Botha had been drawn. It was just a question of the time and issue.

I disliked Treurnicht. In his earlier years, as chairman of the Afrikaner Broederbond, he had impressed me by the manner in which he had defended Afrikaans cultural interests. However, he forfeited my earlier respect by his behaviour as a politician. Apart from any other considerations, while he was still a deputy minister, Treurnicht had been deeply involved in a government decision to place Afrikaans on an equal footing with English in black high schools in Soweto. He was impervious to the strong objections of the pupils and black educationists, whose opposition was spurred on by the revolutionary movements. The decision was one of the causes of the 1976 Soweto riots, which ultimately resulted in the deaths of more than 500 people, and plunged South Africa into a national and international crisis after thirteen years of relative stability. The Cillié Commission of Inquiry, which investigated the riots, was highly critical of the manner in which the danger signals regarding the Afrikaans language issue had been ignored. I came to know Treurnicht in politics as a narrow and small-minded person who was trapped by his own ambition and who became the prisoner of a handful of reckless right wingers. He and his clique deviously undermined the National Party. Treurnicht, as an outstanding orator, could masterfully manage, on the one hand, to say nothing that was in direct conflict with party policy, while on the other hand, still exacerbate tensions by subtly disassociating himself with positive and reform-oriented aspects of party policy. As a result, it was difficult to find clear grounds on which to discipline him. He was nevertheless systematically challenging P. W. Botha, opposing reform and sowing discord within the National Party.

I was deeply concerned about the impending crisis. I was worried that the party and the cause in which I believed would be seriously damaged if these internal problems were not correctly managed. My dislike for Treurnicht had by that stage developed into distrust. My options were very limited. Although I rejected Treurnicht's *verkrampte* approach and was deeply suspicious of his intentions, I also disliked P. W. Botha's dictatorial style. I felt instinctively that, when an open confrontation came between him and Treurnicht, the crisis would in all likelihood seriously damage the National Party in the Transvaal and the north – where the right wing was strong. While I supported P. W. Botha's reform approach, I was worried that he would allow himself to be too strongly influenced by colleagues like Chris Heunis, Fanie Botha and Pik Botha, who were straining at the leash for a showdown with Treurnicht – regardless of the consequences for the party. Just as the right wing had done, they often caused tension by devising strategies and making statements that were intended to precipitate confrontation. Philosophically, I was positioned in the centre group in the National Party. I supported reform, but wanted to ensure that it was well considered and based on principles. I was a member of the third group that my brother Willem had identified in his *verligte/ verkrampte* speech, but which was of little interest to the media, because we were difficult to label and also because we did not continuously feed it sensational titbits.

At that stage I still saw it as my task to hold the party together; to try to limit the influence of the right wing; and to promote a step-by-step approach to fundamental reform which would enjoy the support of the bulk of our power base. I also wanted to prevent the clashes between the right and left wings from causing irreparable damage to the National Party. The result was that I increasingly began to play the role of a peacemaker and bridge builder – within the cabinet, within the caucus and within the Executive of the National Party of the Transvaal. I had become the party fireman. I increasingly took the lead in our internal debates in formulating compromises and in defusing potential crises. This role held positive and negative implications for me. On the one hand, I was sometimes regarded as a *verkrampte*, because of my unwillingness to identify myself uncritically with the left wing. On the other hand, many of my colleagues began to look up to me as a leader who had the courage to articulate their own centrist views and to accept the risks that accompanied participation in our robust internal arguments. The fact is that the majority felt as I did, but often drew back from the risk of possible confrontations with leaders – and particularly with P. W. Botha.

One of the first public clashes between Treurnicht and P. W. Botha occurred in March 1980. Treurnicht made a statement on sport at a public meeting that, according to P. W. Botha, was in conflict with a recent cabinet decision. Treurnicht's speech contradicted the government's view that there should be no interference by the authorities in the right of sport bodies to manage their own affairs. Treurnicht had said that coloured and white pupils should not participate in the same school rugby competition, known as the Craven Week, but that they should rather hold their own separate competitions. P. W. Botha was furious, and, apparently without first speaking to Treurnicht, issued a strong repudiation of his speech. Treurnicht's supporters were, in turn, angry over the prime minister's public humiliation of their leader. Newspaper headlines proclaimed that the National Party was in crisis and that divisions within the party were boiling. Some of Treurnicht's supporters were already tallying their support and had started to talk about a special Congress of the National Party of the Transvaal with a view to taking over the party – a strategy they finally tried to implement in 1982.

Hendrik Schoeman, the minister of agriculture, and one of the most senior members of the National Party in the Transvaal, and I intervened and tried to restore peace and unity. Treurnicht did not like confrontation. When we went to see him to discuss the crisis he wept like a child. His tears were so intense that one could have wrung out his handkerchief like a wet towel. I reported back to the prime minister, who was in a difficult mood. Nevertheless, as a result of our efforts and those of Mr Alwayn Schlebusch, the minister of justice and the interior, he agreed to meet Treurnicht, together with Hendrik Schoeman and myself. In the end, we managed to achieve an uncomfortable reconciliation and, for a time, the party was once again able to project an image of greater unity. During the crisis, I had tried wherever I could, to smooth the ruffled feathers on both sides. However, at the same time, I supported renewal and unambiguously identified myself with P. W. Botha's reform initiatives.

This incident was the curtain-raiser for the drama that finally led to Treurnicht's split with the National Party, to the founding of the Conservative Party – and consequently to my election to what was probably the second most powerful position in the party, the leadership of the National Party in the Transvaal. During the following two years, until 1982, there were recurrent disputes between the right wing and the rest of the party, particularly with regard to labour reforms. The critical issue that sparked the final confrontation was the question of political rights for the coloureds and the Indians. Already in 1977, the National Party had accepted guidelines for the granting of autonomy to coloured and Indian structures over matters of special concern to their respective groups. In addition, they would, in some or other manner, also be given joint control with whites in decision-making on matters that affected everyone.

In the National Party's newspaper, *Nat Eighties*, the editor, Dr Jan Grobler – a National Party member of Parliament – interpreted these guidelines as implying among other things that there could not be more than one government in one country. Dr Treurnicht registered his objection to this view in a private letter to the editor and said that such a statement required qualification. The existence and contents of this letter became known and gave rise to a debate in the lobbies and in the press. Prime Minister Botha, with whom Dr Treurnicht had made no attempt to discuss his problems or objections, could no longer remain silent. On Monday, 22 February 1982 he called all the available cabinet ministers to attend an extraordinary cabinet meeting. In a long statement, which brought the dispute to a head, he clearly spelled out the policy of the National Party on the coloureds. The two points which precipitated the crisis were Botha's insistence that the concept of consultation and co-responsibility was a healthy form of power-sharing, without violating the principle of self-determination, and his view that a separate sovereign Parliament could not be created for the coloureds, because there could be only one central government authority in the country. For Treurnicht, this was unacceptable because it recognized the principle of power-sharing between coloureds, Indians and whites within the same constitutional system.

Prime Minister Botha made it clear that he expected all his ministers to endorse the statement. The newspapers immediately descended on Dr Treurnicht, but he refused to comment. The next day, at the normal cabinet meeting of 23 February 1982, a special opportunity was created to discuss the statement. Dr Treurnicht – and his chief lieutenant, Dr Ferdi Hartzenberg – did not register their objections or try to put their case. This was typical of Dr Treurnicht who was often reluctant to defend his case unambiguously and forcefully in smaller groups. The parliamentary lobbies were buzzing with rumours. It was clear that Dr Treurnicht and his inner circle were preparing for war and that the first battle would take place at the parliamentary caucus meeting on Wednesday, 24 February 1982. Treurnicht and his inner circle held secret meetings. P. W. Botha also played his cards close to his chest, but it was clear that he was in a fighting mood. I believe that he had by then decided to get rid of Treurnicht, regardless of the consequences. He did not take me into his confidence, possibly because, until then, I had played the role of peacemaker. Nevertheless, I – and everyone else – realized that the moment of truth had arrived.

The caucus meeting was dramatic. Although the question of the party's policy on power-sharing and on the coloureds was not on the agenda, the discussion quickly turned to this topic. Treurnicht was the second speaker and put his case. Although he strongly defended himself, his speech left enough space for some form of reconciliation. But some of his supporters pushed him and their case beyond the point of no return. Their aggressive speeches destroyed Treurnicht's room for manoeuvre and any possibility of reconciliation. In my contribution I created an opening for Dr Treurnicht to acquiesce honourably to the party's policy. He refused to seize the opportunity. After that, a split was unavoidable, particularly after a direct confrontation between Treurnicht and P. W. Botha later in the debate. In an emotionally laden atmosphere the caucus voted on a motion, proposed by Fanie Botha, which expressed full confidence in P. W. Botha and confirmed his right as leader to formulate and interpret policy. A hundred members voted for the motion, twenty-two against and one abstained. Treurnicht and those who had voted against the motion were given eight days to reconsider their position and to accept the caucus decision.

The die was finally cast. The struggle now shifted to the Transvaal. At that stage the National Party was a confederal party which was composed of four provincial parties. Each of the four provincial parties was completely autonomous. If Treurnicht could gain the support of the majority of the National Party of the Transvaal, he and his friends would be able to hijack the party in the Transvaal, together with all its assets and infrastructure. Then we, who did not support him, would have to establish a new party and link up with the National Party in the other three provinces. If Treurnicht could not muster a majority behind him, he would have to leave the National Party and set up a new party. I knew that reconciliation was out of the question. At that stage Fanie Botha, Hendrik Schoeman and I were the deputy-chairmen of the National Party in the Transvaal. Botha and Schoeman decided that I should take the lead in the fight against Treurnicht. Treurnicht thought that his best option would be to try to have a quick decision passed in his favour by the Head Council of the National Party of the Transvaal and convened a meeting, without consulting me or the other two deputy-chairmen. It was clear that he and his advisers wished to seize the initiative.

I felt that we could not allow this. I arranged to meet Treurnicht to register our objection to his one-sided action and to insist that an Executive Council meeting should first be held to decide the procedures for the Head Council meeting. I asked Hendrik Schoeman to accompany me. Treurnicht agreed to our proposal and an Executive Council meeting was convened for Friday, 26 February 1982, the day before the Head Council meeting.

When we walked out of Treurnicht's office we were surrounded by journalists. They believed – and speculated – that Hendrik Schoeman and I had tried once again for old time's sake to make peace. However, for me there was no longer any question of peace. In my mind I had taken a quantum leap and a firm decision for myself. My immediate goal was to save the National Party from the clutches of the right wing. I was fully aware of the challenges that confronted me and knew that my time for leadership had arrived. Suddenly, without any prior planning or canvassing, I realized that even those who might have been regarded as contenders for the leadership of the National Party in the Transvaal were looking to me to save the situation. I was at one and the same time apprehensive but also determined to fill the leadership vacuum in the Transvaal. And I knew that success or failure against Treurnicht at the Head Council meeting would be a make or break test.

*

The Head Council meeting was scheduled for 27 February 1982. At the Executive Council meeting the previous day, we reached agreement on the procedures for the crucial Head Council meeting the following day. Most importantly, an impartial chairman would be elected. He – and not Dr Treurnicht – would run the meeting.

We finalized our strategic planning to the finest detail. Mr Amie Venter and Adriaan Vlok, who were then Transvaal whips, and who later became ministers in my cabinet, played a key role in canvassing support for our position against Treurnicht. I drew up a draft proposal that was aimed at winning the sympathy of the doubters by offering a last chance to Dr Treurnicht and his fellow members of Parliament to reconsider, conform and return to the fold. However, there was a clear proviso that if they did not sign the proposal – which also included a more clearly and better formulated wording of the caucus decision – Treurnicht would be stripped of his leadership; all the others would be immediately relieved of all their posts and would face expulsion from the party. I was going to be the main speaker against Treurnicht, propose the motion and manage and lead the debate. However, we had a surprise plan – to have P. W. Botha present at the meeting in his capacity as national leader of the party. Botha made this offer and I welcomed it regardless of the risk that his increasingly volatile temperament might pose. I was convinced, on balance, that it would serve our cause best and believed that he, as one of the main parties to the dispute, should be heard. The strategy of involving P. W. Botha was known only to a handful of us and was certainly one of the best kept secrets of my political career.

The night before the meeting I slept very little. When I awoke the following morning I knew that that day would inevitably bring a turning point, not only for the National Party, but also for me. Marike and I were staying at a hotel in Pretoria and said a prayer together before we left for the meeting hall. Right from the start a crowd of curious people and journalists had gathered at the Nederduits Hervormde Kerk Synod Hall in Pretoria where the meeting took place. Only people who had the right to attend the meeting were permitted to enter the building. The atmosphere was tense. The headcounts that had been carried out in personal interviews and in telephone calls raised my hopes that we would win. They were, however, not so good that we could be complacent. We won the first test – the election of the chairman – by a vote of 126 to 86. I began to relax a little, but realized that anything could still happen. After the opening of the meeting and the election of the chairman, we detonated the bomb of P. W. Botha's availability. It took the wind right out of the sails of Treurnicht and his supporters. They could hardly object to being addressed by the national leader of the party. P. W. Botha was telephoned and invited to come and the meeting was adjourned until his arrival.

A crowd of inquisitive people had gathered at the glass doors to the entrance hall. With their noses pressed up against the windows, they peered in and tried to see what was going on. This caused Chris Renken, a young MP, to quickly make a poster and display it to the staring crowd. On it was written, 'Please don't feed the fish.'

Shortly after this P. W. Botha arrived outside the hall. The crowd became excited and opened up a path for him. That evening, in the hotel bar, after everything was over, a journalist told me of how one of the right-wing members of the crowd had booed P. W. Botha through a rolled-up newspaper as he had passed by him. P. W. Botha stopped and turned around and, without saying a word, furiously looked the right winger in the eye, for what seemed interminable seconds. The journalist vividly painted the scene of how the right winger had visibly crumbled beneath P. W.'s glare, lowered the rolled-up paper and sheepishly disappeared into the crowd.

The meeting then began in deadly earnest. Treurnicht was the first speaker. Then P. W. Botha spoke. I followed him and proposed my motion after I had fully explained our position. There were several more speeches from the floor. Some of those on my side, as well as some of those on Treurnicht's side, were set pieces that had been prepared as part of our respective strategies. Other members spoke spontaneously. Those who were part of the strategy kept to the positions that the two sides wished to have accepted by the Head Council. Those who spoke from the floor were primarily in favour of reconciliation and made appeals that the inevitable split should be avoided. There was, however, no possibility of this. Treurnicht was not at his best and some of his lieutenants made poor speeches which did his cause more harm than good. Colleagues and the press were very complimentary about my contribution. The final vote showed a large swing in favour of my proposal, by comparison with the voting on the election of the chairman. My proposal was adopted by 172 votes to 36. Treurnicht's reign as leader of the National Party in the Transvaal was over. Within a few days, some of those who had voted against the proposal reconsidered their position and gave notice of their acceptance of the decision. Some talented members of Parliament were among them and I was grateful that we could keep them in the party. Finally, only sixteen members of Parliament, including Treurnicht, walked out of the National Party. After the founding of the Conservative Party a month later, they took up their seats in the opposition benches.

The whole episode was interpreted as a triumph for P. W. Botha and his plans for reform. For me it was the beginning of a new and dynamic chapter in my political career. The following Saturday, at the proposal of Fanie Botha, I was unanimously elected as the leader of the National Party in the Transvaal. The newspapers immediately used my election to proclaim me as the most likely successor to P.W. Botha. A great responsibility was placed on my shoulders. In my acceptance speech I said that I had committed myself to open and unassuming leadership. I did not want to be a leader with fanfares, who was held aloft and applauded. I said that I wanted to be a serving leader – serving not only from public platforms, but also on a personal level. I added that I would like to be the leader of a team that would always be able to speak of 'us'. Throughout my leadership of the Transvaal, and subsequently as the national leader of the National Party from 1989, I tried to remain true to that commitment.

*

My election as the leader of the Transvaal was also the beginning of a long uphill struggle against the Conservative Party that would finally reach its climax in the referendum of 1992. Treurnicht and his inner circle did not have the slightest intention of reconsidering their position. But they made full use of the Head Council decision to sow maximum division in as many National Party constituencies as possible. In the constituencies where they were the sitting MPs, they followed a strategy that forced me and other leading figures to attend meetings of the Divisional Councils involved where the whole dispute was fought over again and again. In Waterberg, Treurnicht's own constituency, there was a dramatic confrontation between us when, shortly after my election as the leader, he and I both attended a meeting of his Divisional Council. When I arrived, I was warned that only two of the more than 150 members of the council supported me. From the unfriendly reception that I received and the jubilant applause that was given to Treurnicht, it was clear that this assessment was not far wrong. An intense debate followed. Once again I came out fighting as I seldom had done in my life. At one stage I accused Treurnicht of misleading the meeting and as proof, held a note in the air that he had written to me in the cabinet. I said that I had a statement from him in his own handwriting that proved that he was misleading the meeting. When I wanted to read it out Treurnicht jumped up and began to shout and whipped up the emotions of his supporters. I was shouted down. However, in the vote that followed twenty-six members of the Divisional Council voted in favour of my position. It was progress.

And so we worked through all of the Conservative Party's constituencies, with a view to gaining control of their assets, their bank accounts, their keys and their minutes. More importantly, however, we had to know who was in favour of us and who was against us, so that we could reorganize our party structures throughout the Transvaal. The fight was on.

The debate between *verlig* and *verkramp* was not limited to politics. It permeated the whole Afrikaner establishment. In Afrikaans cultural societies and even in the Afrikaans churches, the debate raged as fiercely as it had done within the National Party. The establishment of the Conservative Party also caused a split in the Afrikaner Broederbond and led to the establishment by the Conservatives of a rival secret organization called Toekomsgesprek (Future Discussion). There was also a split in the church which led to the formation of the Afrikaanse Protestante Kerk (Afrikaans Protestant Church), which limited its membership to whites and defended racial differentiation on biblical grounds.

In the political sphere, the division between the Conservative Party, on the one side, and the National Party on the other, dominated white politics until the referendum of 17 March 1992. For me and the National Party the split was also a liberation. Treurnicht's departure freed us from his retrogressive influence. Now we could give our full attention within the government and Parliament to reform initiatives which could pull South Africa back from the edge of the chasm on which we were teetering. I was full of determination and worked as never before.

9

The Tricameral Parliament

Visitors to Cape Town during the late seventies and early eighties were often perplexed by a large area of open land to the east of the city centre, on the lower slopes of Devil's Peak, the most eastern of the three mountains which form the backdrop of the city. The open tract was made stranger still by the presence here and there of a few isolated stone churches and ochre-painted mosques, standing amid clumps of green grass, exposed to the south-east winds that howled down from the mountain.

This was District Six. Until its destruction in the 1960s by apartheid planners, it had been a vibrant inner city slum. Its crumbling single-storey dwellings; the colourful washing lines and rubbish bins in seamy alleys, all set against the magnificent profile of Table Mountain, had been a favourite subject for South Africa's fashionable artists. Its dark alleys had been notorious for street gangs and crime, but they had also reverberated to the brassy music of the annual carnivals, for which the coloured people were famous. Now, all that remained were the churches and the mosques, which the government, at the insistence of the religious communities involved, had agreed not to demolish.

The demolition of District Six, perhaps more than any other issue, became the symbol of the coloured people's experience of apartheid.

South Africa's three million coloureds live predominantly in what used to be the Cape Province. They are the descendants of inter-marriage between the original Khoi (Hottentot) and San (Bushman) population of the Cape, white settlers and slaves who were brought from Indonesia and Malaya to the Cape in the seventeenth and eighteenth centuries by the Dutch East Indies Company. In terms of the old apartheid definitions, they included anyone of mixed race. Unlike more homogeneous South African groups such as the Zulus and the Afrikaners, the coloureds did not have a strong sense of common identity. They included two significant sub-groups: the Cape Malays, a proud Muslim community descended from Indonesians and Malays; and the Griquas, the descendants of the Khoi and whites, who had established their own quasi-independent states in the northern and eastern parts of the Cape Province during the nineteenth century.

For years, the National Party did not have a clear view of how the coloureds should fit into the separate development model. Unlike the black national groups, they had no national state in which they had historically ruled themselves and in which they could progress towards independence – and yet according to the National Party's own doctrine, as it had developed over the years, all South Africa's population groups should have maximum autonomy over their own affairs and should also have a say in all decisions on matters of general government that affected them.

Almost 90 per cent of coloureds are Christians and more than 80 per cent speak Afrikaans as their home language. There has always been a close, but ambivalent, relationship between them and the white Cape Afrikaners. Some Afrikaners felt that that the coloureds should be accepted as part of their community – as brown Afrikaners. Others believed that they should develop as a separate community.

During the first decades of National Party rule, the latter view won the debate and the government began to apply the doctrines of apartheid to the coloured community with all the doctrinal vigour and rigour that it could muster. Long-established coloured communities were moved from mixed neighbourhoods to newly designated coloured group areas, often many kilometres from the city centres. The government also began to develop separate constitutional structures for the coloureds to enable them to control their own community affairs to the greatest possible extent. However, these efforts received very little support from the coloured community, some of whose leaders reluctantly agreed to participate only to provide themselves with greater leverage to secure full political rights. As someone who had grown up in the north, I had had hardly any experience of the coloured community as a child and as a young man. Initially, I accordingly supported, almost without question, the prevailing approach of the National Party – that the coloureds should be seen as a separate group; that everything possible should be done to cultivate their own feeling of community identity; and that they should have a form of self-determination within their own institutions. Soon after that I went to Parliament and became increasingly involved in the debate on the constitutional future of the coloureds. Although, as a loyal backbencher, I often strongly defended the official policy of the National Party, my discomfort on this question continued to grow. I remember one evening when a group of young *verligte* academics at Stellenbosch University invited me to address them. They included Willie Esterhuyse, Sampie Terreblanche and Julius Jeppe. The discussion centred on the coloureds and they were sharply critical of the National Party's policy. I strongly defended our policy and think that I probably won the debate by showing that, while they paid lip service to their *verligte* goals, they were in fact themselves extremely paternalistic towards the coloureds and exclusive in their way of thinking about the Afrikaner nation. Although I might have won the debate, I felt very uncomfortable as I drove back that evening from Stellenbosch to Acacia Park.

My discomfort grew and my conscience was further troubled by my interaction as a young MP with prominent coloureds. I recall, in particular, a few discussions that I had with Franklin Sonn, who was appointed as South Africa's ambassador to Washington soon after the inauguration of the Government of National Unity in 1994. We developed a good relationship. I remember that he once told me that just when he was sure how he felt about the state of affairs in South Africa he spoke to an Afrikaner like me, and was confused again. At that stage I was perhaps not so honest with him as he had been with me, because my experience was precisely the same. The more I got to know the coloureds, the more ambivalent I became and the less enthusiasm I had for our official policy. My conviction grew that we would have to think creatively and develop a fair and just dispensation in which the coloureds would come to their full rights as fellow South African citizens. Some sort of separate nationality in their own independent state was simply not possible and continued exclusion from joint decision-making was not morally justifiable.

The other population group which did not fit neatly into the apartheid blueprint was the Indian community. The ancestors of South Africa's 900,000 Indians were brought to Natal from 1860 onwards as indentured labourers to work on the colony's sugar plantations. Most were Tamil and Gujarati-speaking Hindus from the southern part of India, but there was also an influential Muslim minority. The Indian immigrants showed great commercial acumen and resourcefulness and, within a generation or two, most of them had left the sugar fields. Despite legal restrictions and discrimination, many Indians became successful traders and entrepreneurs. Some also practised as doctors and lawyers. The most famous of these was Mahatma Gandhi, whose formative years were spent in South Africa as a young lawyer campaigning for greater rights for members of the Indian community.

Today, almost 85 per cent of the Indian community live in the province of KwaZulu-Natal. Large parts of Durban, the most populous city in the province, and many of the smaller towns – with Indian bazaars, exotic spices, Hindu temples and Mosques – have a distinctly Asian character. The government also tried to force the Indian community to fit into the apartheid mould: it established separate residential and business areas for Indians, often involving the forced removal of traders and families from premises that they had occupied for generations. In accordance with the apartheid doctrine, the government established separate representative institutions for the Indian community to enable them to control their own community affairs – but with even less success than they had encountered with the coloureds. For many years the official policy of the National Party was that Indians should be repatriated to India. Because some prominent Indians were supporters of the ANC and leading members of the Communist Party, there was a certain hostility toward them within the Afrikaans community. Boycotts of Indian merchants were supported by Afrikaans cultural organizations and I, myself, was brought up on the basis that one should never do business with Indians or buy anything from them. But as a young practising attorney, especially after I moved to Vereeniging, I had a few Indian clients and quickly established a good relationship with the local Indian community. It soon became clear to me that they were not getting a square deal. Later, as the minister of home affairs, I had a great deal to do with Indian leaders and institutions. The more I came to know them, the more I realized that, as in the case of the coloureds, government policy was also failing to assure justice to the Indian community, despite their greater prosperity.

I accordingly welcomed the government's decision during the seventies to investigate possibilities for extending greater political rights to the coloured and Indian populations, even though this would be within the framework of separate development. These investigations ultimately led to the appointment of a commission under the chairmanship of the minister of justice and the interior, Mr Alwyn Schlebusch, to develop proposals for a new constitutional system that would make provision for coloured, Indian and white autonomy over the affairs of their respective communities, but a form of joint decision-making on matters of common concern. The Schlebusch Commission proposed the abolition of the all-white Senate and its replacement by a President's Council of sixty whites, coloureds and Indians. It also recommended the creation of a post of vice-president who would be ex officio the chairman of the President's Council. The new council would be appointed and not elected and would advise the government on a range of matters and more importantly make proposals for a new constitution. Mr Schlebusch subsequently became South Africa's first vice-president and, in February 1981 the President's Council commenced its operations. It presented its proposals for reform to the government in May 1982. Although not all these proposals were accepted, they provided the basis for the consideration of a new constitution which would accommodate the whites, coloureds and Indians. Within the cabinet I was closely involved with the drafting of the new constitution and served on a special cabinet committee which dealt with this matter. The committee was chaired by Minister Chris Heunis, who was appointed in 1982 as minister of constitutional development and planning, after he had served for some time as minister of the interior. Behind the scenes our deliberations were sometimes heated. There was also serious tension within the President's Council itself between the chairman, Vice-President Schlebusch and Dr Denis Worral, who served as the chairman of the Council's key Constitutional Committee. This ultimately led to Dr Worral's removal from the council and his appointment as our ambassador in Australia. At the same time, there was occasionally high tension between Mr Schlebusch and Mr Heunis with regard to recommendations of the President's Council that were not accepted.

The new constitution made provision for a single Parliament with three chambers, one each for the whites, coloureds and Indians. These chambers had authority to pass laws governing the 'own affairs' of each community. Matters that affected all three communities, or general affairs, would be discussed directly in a new joint chamber. The combined chambers would be responsible for electing a new executive state president, who would replace the prime minister and the ceremonial state president of the old dispensation. The election formula was so devised, on the basis of voter numbers in the three communities, that it would neither be possible for the Indian and coloured majority parties to outvote the majority party in the white chamber, nor to prevent the white majority from electing its choice as president.

I welcomed the new constitution. We had at last made progress in extending constitutional rights to the coloureds and the Indians in such a manner that they had real power over their own affairs. They would also have a substantial say in matters of common concern through their involvement in general affairs legislation and the participation of the coloured and Indian majority leaders in the cabinet. I was also enthusiastic about the underlying principles of self-determination for whites, coloureds and Indians, with regard to their so-called own affairs – education, welfare, culture and the concept of joint decision-making on matters of common concern. This was a formula that was similar to the multicultural constitutional system in Belgium, and I hoped – rather optimistically as it turned out – it might achieve international acceptability. However, the problem was that the dividing line between the various institutions was still based too much on race and not fully on culture or language, as it was in other multicultural societies. The acceptability of the new constitution was also undoubtedly marred by the baggage of our apartheid history. Whereas the development of cultural self-determination was increasingly acceptable in multicultural societies elsewhere in the world, in South Africa it was regarded as the constitutionalization of apartheid in a different form. These factors eventually sank the concept of Own Affairs. However, within the framework of the political attitudes of the time, the new constitution represented dramatic progress and far-reaching renewal – despite these basic problems.

I was deeply involved in the referendum on the new constitution in my new capacity as leader of the National Party in the Transvaal. The Conservative Party was vehemently opposed to the new constitution and the referendum was the first major battle in the struggle between us. I criss-crossed the country and addressed public meetings almost every evening during the campaign. The two-thirds victory which we achieved in the referendum – with the support of the liberal Progressive Federal Party – was a great boost for further constitutional development and clearly underlined the limitations of the Conservative Party in preventing reform.

The new constitution also received guarded acceptance by authentic coloured leaders, including the Revd Allan Hendrikse, the leader of the anti-apartheid Labour Party. Nevertheless, in the first elections that were held for the coloured and Indian chambers of the new Parliament in July and August 1984, many potential voters did not register and there were voter turn-outs of only 20 per cent in the Indian election and 30 per cent in the coloured poll.

The implementation of the new constitution had important implications for my own political position and image. In 1986 I was appointed as the chairman of the Ministers' Council in the House of

Assembly (the council that dealt with the Own Affairs of the whites). I had the special task of administering, managing and defending the interests of the whites in terms of the 1983 constitution. This, in a sense, made me the prime minister of the white population group. At the same time, as leader of the National Party in the Transvaal since Treurnicht's defection, my main political task was to defend the party against attacks from the right – and all such attacks focused on white rights and interests. Also, my new role inevitably meant that I became the chief advocate for the Own Affairs concept, not only of the whites, but also of the other communities, in our common efforts to protect our autonomy and resources against the General Affairs departments, which had a tendency to try to maintain overall control. This often brought me into confrontation with many of my cabinet colleagues and, at times, also with President Botha.

These roles had a marked effect on my public image. Although I played my full part in the cabinet as the minister of national education and was deeply involved in constitutional reform, I was projected in the media as being overly concerned with white and Own Affairs interests. The result was that I was labelled as a *verkrampte* – an image with which I had to live until I became the leader of the National Party in 1989.

Despite all its flaws, the 'tricameral' constitution was a symbolic beachhead for change and represented a major stride forward in the constitutional development of the country. For the first time South Africans from the three communities gathered together in Parliament to consider matters of common concern. There was genuine political interaction and accountability. White cabinet ministers had to report to the coloured and Indian houses on their activities. They were exposed to criticism and indignation over the injustices of apartheid. They were also taken to task over the remaining elements of discrimination. Sometimes government ministers were shouted down and often they had to listen to moving protestations and views that they had never before experienced or heard so directly. This regular contact, debate and interaction broadened the attitudes of all those involved. It was a learning process for all of us. It not only affected me and my colleagues, but also had a similar effect on the Indian and coloured leaders.

Ironically, in recent discussions, coloured and Indian leaders have told me that their communities had far more political clout under the 'tricameral' constitution then than they now have in the new one-man-one-vote system. Some of them think back with a degree of nostalgia on the powers and autonomy that they had to give up with the adoption of the 1993 and 1996 constitutions. The 'tricameral' constitution helped to bring coloured and Indian South Africans into the mainstream of politics. It also helped to bridge some of the chasms of alienation that had existed between them and whites as a result of apartheid. Coloured and Indian South Africans later became some of the National Party's staunchest supporters and today comprise a major part of the party's constituency. For me, my involvement in the new dispensation was a turning point. As minister of national education I was responsible for the matter that was closest to the hearts of these communities, the education of their children – but I still had to do so within the framework of a policy that was based on racial discrimination. Although it was our policy to equalize expenditure on education for all groups and although I had to transfer funds from white education to the other education departments to achieve this, the fact remained that the whole education system was still based on race. I nevertheless obtained the co-operation of the Indian and coloured education ministers who pragmatically participated in a process that resulted every year in a better allocation for their departments. I made closer acquaintance with many coloured and Indian ministers and MPs and we developed of a bond of mutual respect and acceptance of one another's integrity.

All this powerfully influenced my attitudes and philosophy. I came, more and more, to the conclusion that there could be no solution without the removal of all forms of racial discrimination. I also began to develop a warmth and appreciation for the coloured community, which spoke my language and shared my culture and which had such great developmental needs. This evolution of my attitudes and my deepest emotions laid the foundation for the far-reaching changes that I later initiated, particularly in opening the National Party to members of all population groups and in transforming it into a truly non-racial party. I was already beginning to realize that values were more important than colour and that people who had the same views and who believed in the same things and who shared the same ideals should find a way of working together to maintain those principles.

Few visitors who visit Cape Town now notice the scars on the face of the city that were left by the demolition of District Six. The open green spaces have, over the years, been gradually filled by new buildings, modern townhouses, apartments and a new technical college. All these facilities are open to South Africans of all races. District Six now belongs to us all.

10

The Constitutional Future of Black South Africans

The departure of Andries Treurnicht and the right wing and the constitutional accommodation of the coloureds and Indians – supported by two-thirds of the white electorate – freed the government to turn its attention to the core of its constitutional dilemma. This was the constitutional future of the millions of black South Africans who lived in the so-called white areas and in the black homelands which had refused to accept independence.

By the beginning of the eighties it had become clear that the policy of grand apartheid had encountered two apparently insurmountable obstacles: firstly, the flood of black South Africans to the so-called white cities had not turned by 1978 as the planners had predicted. On the contrary, the demands of the booming economy of the sixties and seventies had turned it into a flood which had washed away for once and all any illusion that whites would ever constitute a majority in the areas of the country that they claimed for themselves; secondly, only four of the ten homelands were prepared to accept independence. KwaZulu, under the leadership of Chief Minister Mangosuthu Buthelezi, in particular, was adamant in refusing to move beyond its self-governing status. Ironically, it was this decision by homeland governments, which were generally derided as being puppets of the South African government, which sounded the death knell for grand apartheid, the very system that had brought them into being. It was clear that the government would have to consider some alternative constitutional framework to accommodate the political aspirations of the great majority of black South Africans who lived either in the non-independent homelands or in the so-called white areas.

In February 1983 P.W. Botha established a Special Cabinet Committee to look into this question and to promote multilateral co-operation between the South African government and the governments of the existing black independent and self-governing states. The committee was chaired by the minister of constitutional development, Mr Chris Heunis, and included myself, the minister of foreign affairs, Mr Pik Botha, the minister of law and order, Mr Louis le Grange, Dr Gerrit Viljoen, the minister of education and training (responsible for the education of black South Africans in the white areas) and the minister of justice, Mr Kobie Coetsee.

The Special Cabinet Committee became the main forum for debate within the government on key constitutional questions. Its activities very quickly became just as important to me as my cabinet portfolio, my chairmanship of the Ministers' Council of the white House of Assembly and my leadership of the National Party in the Transvaal. All the members of the committee were deeply aware that we were at a crossroads. Although we quickly acknowledged the failure of separate development, we continued for some time to include the independence of the homelands as an option – at least for the solution of a part of the problem of extending political rights to black South Africans. However, we accepted from the outset that it was no longer a viable option for the millions of black South Africans who lived outside the homelands.

The key question was how to extend full political rights to everyone on a fair and morally defensible basis without, at the same time, bringing about majority domination and suppression. How could we accommodate the cultural diversity of South Africa – including the various black cultures – but still extend full citizenship to everyone and remove all forms of racial discrimination? In short, how could the whites dismount the proverbial tiger on which history had placed us without being devoured ourselves?

Our search for minority safeguards was perfectly legitimate. However, our legacy of apartheid meant that any proposal that we would make for such safeguards would immediately be construed by our critics as a new form of apartheid.

I developed respect and appreciation for the manner in which Minister Chris Heunis managed the sometimes intense activities of the committee. He was one of the giants of the reform movement and should receive full credit for the great contribution that he made during the P. W. Botha period. He was a large man – tall and thick-set – with an imposing presence. A skilled lawyer, his mind often moved faster than his tongue, which sometimes caused him embarrassment in the media. Nevertheless, I regarded him as a formidable politician with a keen intellect. He too grew to accept me and the contribution that I made. We became a strange team, often at loggerheads, but in the end always able to reach consensus. He tended to attach less importance to the concept of Own Affairs than some other members of the committee and I did. As the chief spokesman for Own Affairs, I was often involved in arguments with him. I did not hesitate to confront Heunis on his tendency, on occasion, to adopt too much of a piecemeal approach to constitutional reform. While I could appreciate his need to deliver tangible and visible results, I insisted on looking at the full picture. As with the case of the coloureds and the Indians, I was looking for a fully principled motivation of reform proposals and a thorough analysis of all the logical consequences of such proposals. Accordingly, I often felt that I had to play the role of devil's advocate – not to slow down reform, but from my perspective, to ensure that what we did was part of a clear vision and that we were aware of where it would lead us.

This, unfortunately, reinforced my image as a conservative. My position was succinctly described by the American journalist, Patti Waldmeir, in her book the *Anatomy of a Miracle*. She wrote that it was my 'relentless pursuit of logic' which caused me to oppose P. W. Botha's piecemeal reforms and which sealed my reputation as a reactionary. She quoted Stoffel van der Merwe, a *verligte* member of P. W. Botha's cabinet, as saying that I inexorably pressured my colleagues into thinking through the full implications of the piecemeal reforms that they were considering. When I spelled out the implications in this manner, 'everybody shrunk from their own proposals'. And then, according to Dr Van der Merwe, I was seen as 'the spoiler'.

The first major fruits of the Special Committee's labours were revealed during President Botha's opening speech to Parliament at the beginning of 1985. In it the government acknowledged the permanence of the large black population in the white areas and the need to accept the political implications of this reality. It also accepted that it could not force the remaining six non-independent black homelands to accept independence and acknowledged that it would have to co-operate more closely with them on matters of common concern. President Botha also offered to release Nelson Mandela, provided he undertook to renounce violence. In his response – which was delivered on his behalf by his daughter Zindzi, to a cheering audience of black support-ers – Mandela rejected the offer out of hand.

At the beginning of August 1985, after the end of the parliamentary session, the cabinet held a special planning meeting at which it considered the latest proposals of the Special Cabinet Committee. The meeting was held at the Military Intelligence College, which was situated in an old converted observatory at the top of a ridge of hills above Pretoria. The cabinet took stock of the escalating internal unrest and increasing international pressure that confronted the country, as well as where we stood with our constitutional reform plans. Chris Heunis also needed approval for a few basic initiatives relating to the constitutional position of black South Africans, to enable him to proceed with his negotiation strategy.

It was finally agreed that President Botha would use his public opening address to the Natal Congress of the National Party on 15 August 1985 as an opportunity to announce a few important new constitutional guidelines. The essence of the new approach was the logical extrapolation of President Botha's statement at the opening of Parliament that year, that the government accepted the permanence of black South Africans in white South Africa. This implied the destruction of a number of the central pillars on which the whole edifice of grand apartheid had been constructed: the government now accepted that the remaining six non-independent black homelands would not necessarily move toward independence; blacks in these territories and in the so-called white areas would become South African citizens; provision would have to be made for their constitutional accommodation, including a voice in decision-making at all levels of government where their interests were involved; and there would have to be negotiations with black South Africans to reach agreement on how they would be accommodated in a new constitutional dispensation, including the possibility of their representation in the President's Council.

Taken together, these new guidelines signalled nothing less than the demise of the whole ideology of grand apartheid. We thought that these new announcements would, if properly presented and marketed, capture worldwide attention and convince the international community that things were really beginning to move in South Africa. We also hoped that the proposed initiative would open the door for negotiations with, at least, non-revolutionary black leaders. I supported the initiative and the marketing strategy. Nevertheless, I felt somewhat uneasy. It was not what would be said that worried me, but what would not be said. I was worried that we were once again acting too much in a piecemeal manner, but decided not to make an issue of my concerns. There would still be ample opportunity to express my preference for a more holistic approach in the Special Cabinet Committee. I was also satisfied that the guidelines would put sufficient emphasis on continued self-determination for the various population groups through the concept of Own Affairs, which was then still one of the cornerstones of our policy.

It was in these circumstances that President Botha asked cabinet members to suggest ideas for the speech that he was due to deliver on 15 August. Chris Heunis drafted extensive suggestions which he sent to the president. So did the Department of Foreign Affairs. In the meantime, the Department of Foreign Affairs had been authorized to brief leading Western governments on the speech and to urge them to respond with a message of encouragement and support. Foreign Minister Pik Botha went on a special mission to Europe, where he met senior representatives of various governments and informed them of the new direction that he expected President Botha to announce.

Unfortunately, the initiative soon became known to the media and gave rise to wild speculation and unachievable expectations. It is still not clear whether these expectations were created by media hype or by overkill on the part of Pik Botha or some of his assistants. The speculation infuriated President Botha, who called us together and told us that he was not going to use the suggestions for the speech in the form and formulation in which they had been submitted to him. He rewrote the speech himself and, in so doing, completely failed to capture the spirit of fundamental reform which had characterized the recommendations that had been submitted to him. There is no truth in allegations that I influenced him behind the backs of my colleagues to tone down the reform proposals that were contained in the drafts.

The speech became known as the Rubicon speech, because of President Botha's reference to the necessity for South Africans to cross the Rubicon to a new constitutional dispensation. However, the Rubicon that Caesar had crossed had become a metaphor for the risks involved in seizing power. The Rubicon that confronted P. W. Botha and white South Africans reflected the even greater risks involved in surrendering power. It was a river that we were not yet fully ready – or willing – to cross.

The speech was probably the greatest communication disaster in South African history – partly as a result of the wild expectations that had been unleashed by Pik Botha's overseas visit and partly because of P. W. Botha's utter failure to communicate his historic message effectively. The crux of his message was completely lost in the eighteen pages of his address. It was tucked away in a single paragraph at the bottom of page twelve of his speech:

> Should any of the black national states therefore prefer not to accept independence, such states or communities will remain part of the South African nation, are South African citizens and should be accommodated within political institutions within the boundaries of South Africa.

The speech attracted enormous national and international attention and was broadcast live on millions of TV sets around the world. According to some reports, President Reagan and Prime Minister Margaret Thatcher were among the viewers who, full of anticipation, watched P. W. Botha's performance. The international audience of millions of viewers were utterly bewildered – and deeply disappointed – by what they saw. Instead of addressing them in terms and in a manner that they would understand, President Botha pitched his speech at the immediate audience of National Party supporters in the Durban City Hall. He spoke in terms that were familiar to them, within the idiom of traditional South African political meetings.

The result was a substantial collapse in international confidence in the ability of the South African government to handle the mounting crises that confronted it on all sides. Coupled with the increasingly alarming TV coverage of the escalating unrest in South Africa's cities, the speech convinced many international observers – friends and critics alike – that South Africa was hurtling headlong toward a cataclysm. Any confidence that they might have had in President Botha's ability to manage the crisis had evaporated overnight.

The irony is that, in its own way, the Rubicon speech contained the core of the historic messages that we had formulated in the weeks preceding the Natal Congress. But, because of the manner in which it was communicated, the significance of the speech was completely lost on P. W. Botha's bemused international audience and on most South Africans as well. In effect, P. W. Botha had announced that the government had decided to abandon the policy of grand apartheid that had been so meticulously designed by Hendrik Verwoerd twenty-five years earlier. He had admitted that blacks and whites shared a common citizenship and that political institutions would have to be devised that would accommodate the justifiable political aspirations of the black majority in the so-called white part of South Africa. But he had done so in such a way that hardly anybody had noticed.

In the speech, President Botha also accepted the need for negotiations with the leaders of the black population to devise such institutions. However, he aggressively dismissed the United Democratic Front and the banned ANC (with whom the government would one day have to negotiate) as 'barbaric Communist agitators and even murderers who perpetrate the most cruel deeds against their fellow South Africans, because they are on the payroll of their masters far from this lovely land of ours'. He also warned his audience that our readiness to negotiate should not be mistaken for weakness and made it clear that his bottom line was the need to protect minorities. He warned that he was not prepared 'to lead white South Africans and other minority groups on a road to abdication and suicide'. For many of those who watched the speech, President Botha's aggressive attitude undermined the credibility of his and the government's simultaneous commitment to genuine negotiations – which would have presupposed a more conciliatory attitude.

The result of the speech was catastrophic. Between the end of June 1985 and September 1985, the rand plummeted from R1.97 to R2.48 to the US dollar. The former governor of the South African Reserve Bank, Dr Gerhard de Kock, estimated that the speech had cost the country several billion rand – perhaps more than a million rand per word.

The speech made an indelible impression on me. It taught me the critical importance of good and effective communication. The probability is that if P. W. Botha had communicated the core elements of his speech in a manner that was more comprehensible and acceptable to his vast international TV audience, the value of the rand would have risen rather than fallen.

Despite the disastrous reception that was given to the speech, it did, indeed, signify that the South African government had, at least, put its toes in the Rubicon. The government had accepted that white and black South Africans shared a common constitutional destiny and that they would have to negotiate with one another about the manner in which this reality would have to be accommodated. The opposite bank of the Rubicon, however, still remained elusively beyond P. W. Botha's reach. Many treacherous currents would still have to be negotiated and the government had yet to take the unavoidable plunge of accepting that its partners in negotiation would have to include the ANC and its radical allies.

At that stage I was still ambivalent on the issue of negotiation with the ANC. I realized that they were a crucial factor which could not be ignored, but it was an indisputable fact that the USSR, with its expansionist policies, exerted enormous influence on the ANC. I was critical of my brother and other prominent South Africans for giving untimely credibility to the ANC through their attendance of overseas conferences with the organization. I anticipated that it would be necessary for the ANC to change its stance on the so-called armed struggle before we could begin to negotiate with them.

The thinking of the Special Cabinet Committee at that time was given further definition in a speech that President Botha made to the Cape Congress of the National Party in September 1985. In his conclusion, Botha said that that he and the National Party were committed to the principle of an undivided South Africa, one citizenship and universal franchise, but within structures of South Africans' own choosing.

His statement was an example of the kind of terminological confusion that bedevilled government thinking on constitutional matters – and against which I fought a rearguard action in the Special Cabinet Committee. What P. W. Botha meant was quite different from what international observers would have thought that he had said. As he subsequently explained, the structures of South Africans' own choosing to which he referred would have to make provision for the multicultural nature of the composition of the population, and would have to ensure that in any dispensation one group would not be able to dominate another. This meant that any future constitutional dispensation would have to be constructed from constitutional units that would be defined on a geographic and group or ethnic basis. Botha even raised the possibility of developing black city states in places such as Soweto, which he said could be recognized as separate entities for constitutional purposes.

In retrospect, it is clear that we would not be able to make any real progress toward a negotiated constitutional settlement before we ourselves had resolved three key issues: firstly, our fear of black domination, coupled with our desire to retain a very high degree of self-determination for ourselves and for others on a group basis; secondly, our reluctance to accept that even in the power-sharing constitution that we ourselves were advocating, the majority would necessarily have a greater voice than the various minorities in the determination of general affairs; and thirdly, our unwillingness to enter into negotiations with the ANC – which, as we very well knew, represented the majority of black South Africans – because of its continuing commitment to violence and its close relationship with the South African Communist Party.

One particular aspect of the debate about full black participation related to the position of the state president. Some members of the Special Cabinet Committee felt that a black president would be a natural consequence of power sharing. Others, including myself, believed that there should rather be a rotational presidency as there was in Switzerland. We also felt that the president should have much less power than our own presidency then wielded. I was then playing in my mind with the concept of a form of collective leadership based on consensus. This debate exploded into public controversy on 6 February 1986, when the foreign minister, Pik Botha, told journalists that, under certain circumstances, he would be prepared to serve under a black president. President Botha publicly repudiated him the next day in Parliament and said that his statement had created a serious problem in respect of the interpretation of government policy. But the president added that he had received a letter of clarification from Pik Botha and that the problem had now been put to rest. I was concerned over Pik Botha's statement, not because I could not accept the prospect of a black president, or had any objection to serving under a black president per se, but because I was worried that Pik's statement might prejudice our ability to opt for a weak rotational presidency or other alternatives. I shared my concerns with President Botha – as well as my fear that our more uninformed supporters might be confused by the whole issue. Chris Heunis, who was with me during my meeting with the president, was worried about the effect that Pik's statement might have on his various constitutional initiatives and because he had trespassed onto his area of responsibility. It is not true, as has been alleged, that we pressurized, and even threatened, President Botha into taking strong action against Pik Botha.

I was at that stage still firmly committed to the concept of Own Affairs, not only because of my position as the chairman of the white Own Affairs Ministers' Council – but also from personal conviction. I had no problem whatsoever in accepting the equality of all South Africans and with sharing power between all South Africans on matters of general concern. I was also in favour of abolishing all forms of racial discrimination. But I believed strongly that in multicultural societies the assurance of group security was the key to inter-group peace. I was convinced that the concept of Own Affairs, offering a high degree of autonomy to the various population groups, was the best way to defuse the tremendous conflict potential in South Africa's complex society. I expressed my support for Own Affairs on a number of occasions, but particularly in the debate that followed the opening of Parliament in February 1986. In my speech I said that recognition of the existence of different groups was not discriminatory. It was a God-given reality. I added that certain fundamental issues were inextricably linked to group security: these included the right of every community to its own neighbourhoods, its own schools, and its own institutions within which it would be able to maintain its own character and promote its own interests. I emphasized that the National Party was committed to the principle of group security, the effective protection of minorities and also the prevention of group domination. I rejected the contention that the protection of group security could be equated with the simplistic concept of apartheid. I believed that what we were asking for ourselves was no more – and no less – than what French Canadians were demanding in Quebec; the Flemish were demanding in Belgium; and that the Catalans and Basques were demanding in Spain. All of these heated arguments relating to what our negotiating position was or was not going to be were, in retrospect, somewhat academic. The reality is that, at that stage, neither we nor the ANC were ready – or prepared – to enter into genuine negotiations. Our position was that we would negotiate with the ANC only if it renounced violence and severed its ties with the South African Communist Party. The ANC was clearly not prepared to consider this. We, in turn, were not prepared to accept their terms for negotiations which at that time amounted to little more than a demand for the unconditional handover of power.

Neither did we make much progress in launching negotiations with credible black leaders inside South Africa. When he opened Parliament on 31 January 1986, President Botha proposed the establishment of a National Statutory Council to provide a forum for negotiations with black South Africans. The council would also serve as the first step to power sharing at the national level between the government and significant black communities. It would comprise members of the South African government, the governments of the six self-governing black homelands, and leaders of black communities and groups outside

Aged six months with my mother.   At the age of three years.

Family photograph, circa 1940. I am seated in front of my father,
Senator Jan de Klerk, who is seated below his brother-in-law Mr J.G.
Strijdom, who later became Prime Minister of South Africa.

With my father, Jan de Klerk.

Aged sixteen.

With friends at Potchefstroom University.

On my engagement to Marike, 18 April 1958.

Our wedding day, 11 April 1959.

A family photo from 1974: Willem, Susan, Marike, me and Jan.

My inauguration as a member of Parliament, Cape Town, February 1973.

My inauguration as minister of post and telecommunication affairs on
3 April 1978 with Prime Minister John Vorster, Senator Jan de Klerk,
State President Dr Nico Diedrichs.

With ex-President P.W. Botha.

With Dr Mangosuthu Buthelezi in 1990.

With President Sam Nujoma at the celebration of Namibian independence,
12 March 1990.

With Revd Allan Hendrickse and Marike at a Labour Party meeting,
December 1990.

Meeting with President
François Mitterrand,
Paris, May 1990.

With President Yeltsin,
the Kremlin, June 1992.

these states. The council, which President Botha would chair, would advise the government on all matters of common concern, including legislation on such matters. But the idea of the National Statutory Council never really got off the ground. Without the presence of the ANC few, if any, internal black leaders of any stature were prepared to enter into talks with the government. Most of them – led by Mangosuthu Buthelezi – insisted on the release of Nelson Mandela before they would even consider participating in constitutional talks with us. This led Chris Heunis to try, unsuccessfully, to exert pressure on President Botha with regard to Nelson Mandela's release from prison. Despite his position as minister of constitutional development and my position as leader of the National Party in the Transvaal, neither Heunis nor I were informed at that stage of the exploratory discussions with Mandela which were being conducted by a few senior officials and Minister Kobie Coetsee.

The black leaders, whom we wished to involve in the National Statutory Council, were also not impressed by the group-based philosophy which permeated National Party thinking and suspected that we merely wanted to tinker with apartheid. With the benefit of hindsight I today believe that we should have given much more attention to the federal option than we did at that time.

Despite all this, the broad proposals developed by the Special Cabinet Committee represented important and essential shifts in the thought processes of the Government and its supporters. In the Special Cabinet Committee we realized that a formal change of policy would be a prerequisite for meaningful negotiation. We consequently developed a more concise formulation of our new policy framework which constituted a 180 degree change in policy for ever away from apartheid, separate development and racial discrimination. The proposed framework accepted the fundamental principles of one united South Africa; one person, one vote; the eradication of all forms of racial discrimination; and the effective protection of minorities against domination. It sought to strike a balance between the ideal of having one nationhood on the one hand, and the reality of our cultural diversity on the other. The new policy framework was accepted by a special Federal Congress of the National Party in Durban in August 1986.

I played a prominent role in the debates at the congress and asked for a powerful mandate to develop a new dispensation that would satisfy two demands: firstly, for co-operation, joint decision-making and power sharing between the peoples of South Africa; and secondly, for the protection of communities, to ensure that they could continue to educate their children as they saw fit and to lead their own community lives without the fear of domination by any other group.

In May 1987, we took the new policy framework to the electorate. We had to do so because the previous election in 1981 had still been fought on a separate development – albeit reform-oriented – platform. In the election campaign I went out of my way to spell out the far-reaching implications of the new policy. I did this to such an extent that some newspapers which had previously characterized me as a conservative or as too neutral evaluated my speeches during the 1987 campaign as the most *verligte* of all the National Party's leading campaigners.

The 1987 election was, indeed, a turning point. In the end, the National Party won with a clear, although reduced, majority. We had our new mandate. I regarded it as a death sentence for apartheid and as the conception of the new South Africa. At that stage I did not expect that it would all happen with me as president.

All this ushered in a significant acceleration of real reform and of the dismantling of the legislative edifice of apartheid. By 1988 more than a hundred apartheid laws had been scrapped. These included most of those with which apartheid had traditionally been associated: segregated hotels and places of entertainment; the pass laws; laws which forbade mixed marriages or sex across the colour line; laws which discriminated against blacks in the workplace; laws which prevented blacks from owning property outside the homelands; laws which prevented the establishment of multiracial political parties; and laws which interfered with mixed sport.

On the positive side, the government had made it possible for black South Africans to establish free and militant trade unions; it had restored South African citizenship to citizens of the independent states who had lost it when their homelands had opted for independence; it had extended a form of authentic political rights to coloureds and Indians and had brought their representatives into the same Parliament as whites; it had established equal local government structures for all South Africa's communities; it had created multiracial provincial administrations; and it had indicated its willingness to enter into negotiations with black South Africans with regard to future constitutional structures for the country on the basis of universally acceptable principles. In short, it had addressed many of the reasons that Nelson Mandela had given in 1985 for rejecting President Botha's offer to release him from prison.

By 1988 the main remaining pillars of apartheid were the continued classification of the population according to race; the lack of full black participation in political decision-making processes; and the maintenance of separate residential areas, schools and hospitals for the different races.

In accordance with the ANC's doctrine that apartheid could not be reformed, little or no recognition was given to these fundamental changes. They refused, either wilfully or because of a deep mistrust, to grasp the opportunities offered by the fundamental shifts in National Party thinking which occurred during the eighties. Instead, the ANC had decided at its National Consultative Conference in Kabwe, Zambia, in June 1985, that the time had come to lead the people in raising the level of struggle to that of a people's war for the seizure of power.

From the middle of the 1980s the accent of the government's activities shifted increasingly from the need for reform to the imperative of counteracting the serious revolutionary threat that had arisen within the country.

11

The Total Onslaught

It was ironically the National Party's first steps in the direction of fundamental constitutional reform – the introduction of the 'tricameral' Parliament at the beginning of the eighties – that precipitated one of South Africa's gravest and most prolonged crises. The National Party's continued efforts during the early eighties to extend black political rights through separate institutions, while the coloureds and the Indians were included in a new constitutional dispensation that went far beyond mere window-dressing, stimulated the government's radical opponents into action. In 1983 they formed a new organization, the United Democratic Front, to coordinate the activities of all those who were opposed to the 'tricameral' constitution. Soon they had united some 700 organizations beneath their broad anti-apartheid umbrella. The organizations included church groups; women's groups; community organizations; student unions, sports organizations, youth groups and trade unions. Each individual organization was free to pursue its own specific agenda, but all supported the mass campaigns launched by UDF leaders such as Archie Gumede, Albertina Sisulu, the wife of jailed ANC veteran Walter Sisulu, and Allan Boesak, a coloured minister of religion from the Cape. The UDF soon broadened its anti-government campaigns to include a wide variety of other grievances – such as the high cost of living, education, the conscription of white South Africans for military service, forced removals, land ownership and even a tour by the New Zealand rugby team.

Within a few months, the UDF campaigns had become the internal front and mobilization vehicle for the banned ANC and its exiled leadership in Lusaka, Zambia. During 1984 and 1985 UDF-instigated unrest spread throughout the country. The trouble was particularly acute in the Eastern Cape, one of the traditional heartlands of the ANC.

A central objective of the unrest was to make South Africa ungovernable. Local government structures and many blacks associated with the government – such as policemen and town councillors –

became prime targets of arson, assaults and assassination. The more responsible UDF leaders, more often than not, lost control over the process that they had started. Many suspected collaborators were hauled before revolutionary kangaroo courts and were sentenced to barbaric punishments. The most horrible of these was the necklace method of execution. Old car tyres were tied around victims' necks with barbed wire. They were then filled with petrol and set alight.

The people who presided over these revolutionary tribunals and who carried out these dreadful sentences were often schoolchildren. Indeed, the uprisings were frequently led and driven by a new generation of radical teenagers. They sometimes turned on their own parents and teachers whom they despised for having acquiesced in apartheid for so long. The objective of their actions was to make their communities ungovernable by establishing no-go areas in black townships which would permanently exclude any government administrative or security presence – or members of any non-revolutionary political organization. The result was that in hundreds of black communities, there was a breakdown of normal services. There were many areas in which the police could not maintain a sufficient presence, except for quick forays in armoured vehicles. Education in thousands of schools was seriously disrupted – or came to a complete halt – in the face of school boycotts and teacher strikes. Principals and teachers who did not agree with the disruption of education were simply expelled from the schools by their radical pupils, who were motivated by their slogan 'Liberation before education'. There was large-scale vandalism of school buildings and facilities.

Street and block committees were formed to take over the running of black communities. They operated under the aegis of larger community organizations called Civics. The Civics tested their strength by organizing widespread consumer boycotts of local white businesses. The contraband purchases of township residents who were caught breaking boycotts were confiscated or destroyed. Boycott breakers were sometimes forced to eat or drink their purchases – even if these included soap and drain cleaning liquid. The Civics also instituted effective boycotts of rent payments for municipal houses and payments for municipal electricity, rubbish and sewage services. Soon, many black municipalities were bankrupt and had to rely on special payments from the government for the continuation of even the most rudimentary services. More than a decade later, the culture of non-payment for basic services continues to plague municipalities throughout South Africa.

An influential component of the UDF was the newly empowered black trade union movement, which instigated strikes in support of the UDF's political objectives. Coupled with the strikes and the campaign to make the townships ungovernable were mass demonstrations, marches and confrontation with the authorities across a broad front.

All this helped to create a vicious circle that was spiralling towards growing anarchy. Together with all my other colleagues in the government, I was extremely concerned about the deepening crisis. I believed that firm action was necessary to prevent anarchy and to create a peaceful climate for negotiation, and I accordingly supported the government's steps to take strong remedial action. I also began to realize that the initiatives that we were planning at that stage to extend political rights to black South Africans were inadequate to defuse the growing crisis. In my mind, the development of a meaningful framework for black political rights became a matter of the greatest urgency.

It has become fashionable to ridicule P. W. Botha's view that there was a total onslaught against South Africa. However, during the mid-1980s fortnight after fortnight the intelligence that we received in briefing after briefing in the State Security Council underlined the very grave situation that confronted us. We were faced not only with a concerted campaign to make South Africa ungovernable as the prelude to a general revolution, we also had to contend with extremely serious external threats. Seldom had such a comprehensive international campaign been mounted against a single country so relentlessly for so long a period, as the campaign that the international anti-apartheid alliance had mobilized against us. The sanctions net was beginning to tighten around South Africa in almost every sphere of its international relations. The Soviet Union and Cuban allies had established threatening positions in some of our neighbouring countries. We were involved in a low intensity war in northern Namibia and southern Angola that had brought the South African Defence Force into direct conflict with Cuban and Russian-led forces. Guerrilla groups, based in neighbouring countries, had begun to launch attacks against South Africa.

In response to this, P. W. Botha and his security advisers developed the concept of a total strategy. The need for such a total strategy arose from military analyses of the fundamental changes that had taken place in the nature of warfare since the end of the Second World War. A new form of revolutionary warfare had evolved in which victory did not come from the clash of two armies on a field of battle. Instead, revolutionary forces sought to overthrow incumbent governments by mobilizing the masses; by making countries ungovernable; by fomenting strikes; by involving churches, trade unions and civil society in their campaigns; by using propaganda to destroy the image and undermine the confidence of governments; by eliminating opposition through the use of terrorism and intimidation; and by continuing to mount guerrilla attacks against its enemy.

The total threat posed by this new kind of unconventional warfare required an equally unconventional response. A government White Paper on defence had already in 1977 identified the need for such a response which would coordinate the state's action in all fields – military, psychological, economic, political, sociological, technological, diplomatic, ideological and cultural.

The vehicle that P. W. Botha chose to implement his government's total strategy and to coordinate all its activities in response to what was viewed as the total onslaught was the State Security Council. The council was established in 1972 during the premiership of John Vorster, but was seldom convened by him. However, P. W. Botha soon elevated the council to a central position in the running of the government. The State Security Council presided over an intrusive bureaucratic system, known as the National Management System, with tentacles reaching into virtually every government department and into every corner of the country. This securocrat system – as it was labelled by the media – constantly interfered in the affairs of other departments across the board. Its influence was quietly resented, not only by the broad public service, but also by cabinet ministers with non-security portfolios.

The prime minister – and subsequently the state president – was the chairman of the State Security Council whose members included the ministers of defence, law and order, justice, foreign affairs, finance, constitutional development and the heads of security and security-related departments. Other senior ministers who were in important leadership positions in the National Party were also co-opted. It was in the latter capacity that, in the early eighties, I also became a member of the State Security Council.

The State Security Council formulated strategies and made recommendations to the cabinet. Theoretically, the council itself had no decision-making powers and was dependent on subsequent cabinet approval to give effect to its proposals. In practice, it became, in many respects, more powerful than the cabinet. Those occasions when P. W.

Botha chose to have Security Council strategies and action plans ratified by the cabinet, often appeared to me to be little more than window-dressing. I disliked being part of a system which I believed was undermining the sound principle of full collective responsibility within the cabinet. However, I could do very little to change this state of affairs and had to be content with playing a watchdog role and, where I could, to exercise a moderating influence. I particularly made it my task to guard against inroads into the policy-making and management authority of the non-security departments and their ministers.

I recall that on one occasion, soon after I became leader of the National Party in the Transvaal, I attended a cabinet team-building and planning exercise at a remote SADF base on the border between Namibia and Angola. One of the main items of discussion was our constitutional options for the solution of the country's problems. At some stage the debate turned to the situation which would arise if all our options for practical constitutional reform failed. The idea was strongly mooted by elements within the security establishment that the government should then consider suspending the existing constitution and should rule by decree. I vehemently opposed this idea and was strongly supported by other senior members of the cabinet, including Chris Heunis and Kobie Coetsee. The idea was never raised again, but from that time I believe I was clearly identified by the security establishment as a dove, and therefore as a person who could not be trusted with their inner secrets. I was someone who was not sympathetic to their cause. The result was that I became somewhat marginalized within the State Security Council – a situation which I frankly preferred.

At one stage, during the State of Emergency, President Botha established special situation rooms at the Union Buildings and in Tuynhuys where all the relevant data concerning the total security situation in the country was displayed. After that, the meetings of the State Security Council regularly took place in the situation rooms, where we would file in and take our seats in strict order of seniority. Every meeting started with a briefing on the latest security developments. All the walls of the situation rooms were covered in movable boards, maps and charts on which the latest security information was graphically displayed. We could see at a glance where the most serious unrest was taking place and where the authorities were making progress in re-establishing order and in restoring basic municipal services.

There were other charts where the latest key economic statistics were displayed and there was even one which indicated the levels of the main dams throughout the country. I regarded these situation rooms with amusement and irritation because they were, in reality, elaborate and expensive white elephants which served little practical purpose.

I regularly experienced a sense of unease in the State Security Council because of my awareness that I was not a full participant in its deliberations and did not have a clear picture of the full scope of its activities. As a minister without any security responsibilities, I was not directly involved in either the formulation or implementation of security strategies. My involvement in the State Security Council was peripheral and I was not in the security loop. I accordingly concentrated my efforts on my ministerial portfolios, the Special Cabinet Committee on Constitutional Development and my leadership of the National Party in the Transvaal. I felt that I could afford to be something of a passenger on the State Security Council because I knew that a few of my colleagues, whose judgement I trusted, went out of their way to ensure the correctness of the decision-making processes in which we were involved. In particular, Mr Kobie Coetsee, since his appointment as minister of justice, was always careful to insist that all the government's actions, especially during the State of Emergency, should be taken in strict compliance with the law. He even established a legal centre to assist government departments with the legal aspects related to the State of Emergency.

Naturally enough, the group comprising the ministers and heads of the security-related departments played the most prominent role in the State Security Council. One of the leading figures in this group was General Magnus Malan. Malan was a protégé of P. W. Botha. He had had a meteoric career in the SADF and during the latter part of the seventies, as the chief of the defence force, had helped Botha to build the force into a formidable machine. In 1980 he had been appointed as minister of defence and served in that capacity until 1991. Throughout the Botha era, Malan had been one of the main planners of South Africa's strategies in southern Africa – including our decision to accept the United Nations' independence plan for South West Africa/Namibia. He had played a key role in devising and executing South Africa's intervention against communist forces in Angola and in managing South African support to anti-government guerrilla forces in neighbouring Mozambique. Other members of the the State Security Council during the eighties included the chiefs of the SADF, Generals Constand

Viljoen, Jannie Geldenhuys and Kat Liebenberg, and the commissioners of the South African police during the same period, Generals Johan Coetzee and Hennie de Witt. The ministers of law and order – responsible for the SAP during the Botha years – were Louis le Grange and Adriaan Vlok, who were responsible for the SAP during the Botha years, also played central roles. Another key figure was the enigmatic Dr Niel Barnard, the head of the National Intelligence Service. Barnard, another protégé of P. W. Botha, had been a lecturer in political science at the University of the Orange Free State. When he was still in his very early thirties Botha had hand-picked him for appointment as head of the National Intelligence Service. Barnard had built the service into an effective organization which had a reputation for professionalism and for playing by the rules. He was quiet, reserved and thoughtful and played a central role in managing and encouraging the first discussions between Nelson Mandela and the government and the government's first contacts with the ANC outside South Africa. Some time after I became state president, I appointed him as the director-general of constitutional development, so that we would be able to make fuller use of his abilities in the negotiating process.

As is the case in many countries, there was keen competition – and often little love lost – between the various components of the security establishment. The difference in culture between the police and the SADF is perhaps best illustrated by a joke that did the rounds during the late eighties. According to the story President Botha had ordered both the SADF and the police to bring him a crocodile by the next day. The Defence Force immediately appointed a planning team, with logistics and special forces support. Within a few hours they had flown a special boat to the Limpopo River by Hercules transport and had parachuted it into the river with a special forces unit. The unit, with reconnaissance support, had quickly located a crocodile, captured it and transported it back to Waterkloof Air Force Base in a specially converted Puma helicopter. The police, on the other hand, had sent a sergeant and a constable to the Pienaars River, just to the north of Pretoria. They had spent the whole day fishing and drinking beer. Just before sunset, the sergeant had ordered the constable to rummage around in the rushes until he found a leguan – a large South African lizard. 'But, Sarge,' complained the constable, 'our orders were to catch a crocodile.' 'Don't worry,' replied the sergeant, 'we'll just slap it around until it admits that it's a crocodile.'

Botha had a special relationship with all the branches of the security forces – although his first and main love was for the SADF. He had appointed personnel from the security forces to key posts within his office: his director-general, Dr Jannie Roux, had been a gifted young general in the Correctional Service, who in turn had appointed a number of his colleagues to key posts in the office. His private secretary, Captain Ters Ehlers, had been a submarine commander.

The other group in the State Security Council was made up of ministers like myself, who were responsible for social, administrative and economic portfolios. We were not informed of the innermost operational secrets of the security forces – and we were not encouraged to ask too many questions about them. I found the air of secrecy which we often encountered irritating and at times childish. We had to content ourselves with the explanation that the interference of the securocrats in the affairs of our departments was necessary to ensure that all branches of government responded in a coordinated manner to the revolutionary threat. The State Security Council also accepted that this threat could not be effectively – or even primarily – countered by military or security action. The 'Total Strategy' required that the main accent should instead fall on the provision of effective government and social services and in promoting inclusive constitutional solutions. With that I fully agreed and it was in this area that I saw my main task. It was a question of 'winning the hearts and the minds of the people'.

During 1985 the climate of general violence and insurrection had reached unprecedented levels and on 20 July the government declared a partial State of Emergency which was lifted in March the following year.

However, after that the situation deteriorated rapidly and critically. Between March and June 1986, 284 black South Africans were killed by revolutionary elements – 172 of them by means of the horrific necklace method of execution. More than 1,400 homes and businesses belonging to black South Africans were either damaged or destroyed. The government had also learned that the revolutionary movements were planning major demonstrations, marches into white suburbs and strikes in the period between 16 and 26 June 1986 to mark the tenth anniversary of the Soweto uprising.

On 12 June 1986, President Botha declared a national State of Emergency throughout the country to counteract these developments and to restore order. I fully supported this decision, because I was convinced that only firm and decisive action could prevent a catastrophe. President Botha made it clear that the objectives of the State of Emergency were to create a situation of relative normality so that every citizen could perform his daily task in peace, business communities could fulfil their role, and the reform programme to which the government had committed itself could continue. I also wholeheartedly associated myself with these objectives.

The State of Emergency gave the state draconian – but not unlimited – powers. The government was required to reveal the names of all detainees to Parliament and to permit private visits to detainees by magistrates not less than once a fortnight. As the emergency continued detainees increasingly used the courts to challenge the government. Nevertheless, the State of Emergency constituted a serious restriction of normal civil rights. Up to 20,000 people were detained and many political meetings and most demonstrations were prohibited. Controversial restrictions were also placed on the ability of the media to report freely on unrest-related incidents. I believed that all these steps were necessary. However, as time went by the urgency of a constitutional solution became more apparent to my colleagues and me. I realized that we could not continue with the State of Emergency indefinitely and that the underlying causes of the unrest had to be addressed. Part of this would have to be acceptance of the reality of the influence and support enjoyed by the ANC and its surrogates.

The State of Emergency nonetheless succeeded in achieving its main objectives. The number of unrest-related incidents declined enormously from more than 2,500 in June 1986 to less than 300 in May 1987. The deaths of black South Africans killed in black-on-black violence declined from 157 to 8 during the same period. Necklace executions dropped from 228 during the first six months of 1986 to 82 during the ten months following the declaration of the State of Emergency. The government was also able to restore normal services and education to most black communities.

In the end, the most important effect of the State of Emergency was to force revolutionaries to adopt more realistic perceptions of the balance of power between them and the government. During the anarchic months before June 1986, many of them believed that the tide of internal unrest was irresistible and that further action would soon lead to the revolutionary destruction of the government. By 1988 these perceptions had changed dramatically. The more realistic leaders of the ANC and the internal uprising realized that there could be no quick or easy victory. They also began to accept that a prolonged struggle between them and the government would be so bitter and destructive that there would be little left for anyone to inherit. This perception was an indispensable pre-condition for the beginning of genuine negotiations.

However, as has been revealed in recent years, the State of Emergency, with its suspension of many normal legal protective measures, also created circumstances and an atmosphere in which serious breaches of human rights could, and did, occur.

The great preponderance of security force action during the conflict took place within the framework of the law. However, conventional action by the security forces could not always counter the unconventional threat posed by new forms of revolutionary warfare. The ANC's revolutionary strategies blurred traditional distinctions between combatants and non-combatants; between legitimate and illegitimate targets; and between acceptable and unacceptable methods.

The normal processes of law seemed incapable of effectively dealing with this situation. Members of the security forces watched, with increasing frustration, while revolutionary movements organized, mobilized and intimidated or killed their opponents, seemingly at will. The security forces were expected to play by the rules while their opponents could, and did, use any methods that they liked. There was a perceived need for unconventional counter-strategies of the kind developed by the British in the successful campaign that they conducted against the communist insurgency in Malaya during the 1950s.

As a result of all these factors, the State Security Council and the cabinet approved, in principle, the utilization of some unconventional methods to combat the revolutionary threat. These methods included information gathering projects, disinformation and assistance to organizations that were opposed to revolutionary movements, and financial and other pressures on countries which harboured revolutionaries and terrorists. Obviously, conventional methods were also used, including military raids against identified military targets, and armed engagements, wherever necessary, against the enemy.

Revelations during the past few years clearly show that at some stage, and in some manner outside the formal meetings of the State Security Council and the cabinet, the scope of these unconventional and covert strategies was expanded to include actions which did lead to gross violations of human rights, including murder and torture. A number of key UDF and ANC activists were assassinated. Many of the detainees who were held without trial during the State of Emergency were tortured or mistreated, despite the provision that magistrates should regularly be permitted to visit them. It also appears that some elements within the Inkatha Freedom Party were helped to wage an undeclared war against the ANC and its allies – a war which the ANC had started.

At the beginning of 1990, after I became president, I learned that in the mid eighties an elaborate front organization, the Civil Co-operation Bureau, was established outside the normal framework of the SADF which was given responsibility and the means for the prosecution of a secret war against the ANC and its allies. A similar clandestine unit, the notorious C10 unit based at a farm outside Pretoria called Vlakplaas, was established within the South African police. The unit was composed of 'Askaris' – ANC members who had come over to the government side – and who were ostensibly combating the revolutionary threat by legal means under the leadership of white police officers. The commanders of the Vlakplaas unit included Dirk Coetsee – who subsequently exposed the real nature of the unit – and Eugene de Kock, who was later found guilty, not only of the murders of numerous people, but also of common law crimes, which had evidently been committed for his personal enrichment and the enrichment of his associates. Allegations were also made about bizarre and horrifying chemical and biological warfare activities and experiments carried out by the SADF.

I still do not know the full truth about all these charges, or who within the security forces authorized these gross violations of human rights. Certainly they were never discussed at any meeting of any body that I ever attended. I am also sure that – like me – the great majority of my cabinet colleagues had no knowledge of such activities until they were exposed in the media; by the Goldstone Commission on Public Violence, which I myself appointed in 1992; by the investigation of the Military Intelligence Division of the SADF which I ordered General Steyn to carry out in November 1992 or by the Truth and Reconciliation Commission. When I became state president and assumed supreme command of the security forces, the ministers of defence and of law and order, the chief of the defence force and the commissioner of the South African police did not inform me of these activities in the course of the general briefings that I was given – despite the fact that some of them continued to operate for some time during my presidency. After the existence of the Civil Co-operation Bureau had been exposed by the media at the end of 1989, General Malan assured me that even he had had no prior knowledge of its existence. Although some of us had heard of the Askaris of the Vlakplaas Unit we had no idea of the real nature of their activities. Minister Vlok, General Johan van der Merwe, the commissioner of the South African police during my presidency, and other senior police generals also assured me that they too had had no knowledge of the murderous activities of the Vlakplaas Unit.

The conclusion that I now, regrettably, have to draw is that somebody must have been lying to us – or at the very least had not provided us with vital information to which we, in the cabinet, and I, as the commander-in-chief, were entitled. It seems clear to me that there must – at least in the initial stages – have been high level authorization for the establishment and funding of the units involved and of the general nature of the operations that they were intended to carry out. It is possible that in the murky world of need to know and plausible denial within which these units operated, those higher up the chain of command were subsequently not fully informed of all their operational activities. It also appears that these units soon acquired a high degree of autonomy and often carried out operations on their own initiative. They became a law unto themselves. They recruited some agents who were criminals. Among their other activities they set up a brothel, on the pretext that it would be useful for the gathering of intelligence. Many of them began to steal for their own account, deal in drugs and to kill at their own whim.

At some further stage, probably about the time that I became president, these murky elements in the undercover structures of the security forces began to formulate their own policy. In particular, they appear to have been strongly opposed to the fundamental change of direction that I initiated. They probably regarded the unbanning of the ANC and the SACP, the release of Nelson Mandela, the opening of negotiations, the termination of secret operations, the dismantling of the National Security Management System and the lifting of the State of Emergency as a surrender to the forces of darkness. My colleagues and I were openly accused of being soft and of being traitors by our political opponents from the right. It is likely that some of the elements involved in illegal security force operations supported this view. Many of their later clandestine operations appear to have been directed against the transformation process that I had initiated. These operations included the instigation of violence between different segments of the population with a view to creating a general climate of conflict in which it might have become impossible to hold elections.

The activities of units such as the Civil Co-operation Bureau and Vlakplaas were deplorable and inexcusable. Apart from the reprehensible methods that they used, the strategic assumptions on which they were based were incorrect. The struggle could not be won by brutal, unconventional operations which were in conflict with common decency and basic morality. There is no evidence that the assassination of opponents had the slightest effect on the final outcome of the struggle – other than causing further personal suffering and bitterness. The activities of these elements during my presidency to undermine the transformation process bordered on treason. It is difficult to understand how such aberrations could have been allowed to develop and continue within the security forces, despite my express orders and the clear steps that I took to ensure conformity with accepted standards. At the very least, these activities appear to have been symptomatic of a serious breakdown in the accepted process of command and accountability. In later chapters I shall spell out the steps that I took to try to uncover and terminate such actions and to work for the ending of violence.

The revolutionary threat of the early eighties was countered, not by illegal clandestine operations, but by the lawful – though draconian – powers that the state assumed during the State of Emergency. The State of Emergency, in turn, could be justified only in so far as it enabled the government to carry out its primary duty of protecting the lives and property of its citizens and because the relative stability that it achieved created a platform for the commencement of comprehensive and inclusive constitutional negotiations.

12

My Election as Leader of the
National Party

The restoration of stability was not, by itself, enough to ensure the commencement of genuine negotiations. As the years passed, it became increasingly evident that P. W. Botha's leadership style had also become a major obstacle. Although I accepted him as our leader and had guarded admiration for the reform steps that he had initiated, I was increasingly irritated by his irascible and egocentric behaviour. Unlike many of my cabinet colleagues, I did not adopt a subservient attitude towards him. As a result, our relationship was cool, but correct.

When P. W. Botha was inaugurated as South Africa's first executive state president in 1984 he adopted an increasingly imperious style, of which I also disapproved. While he had been prime minister, his offices in Cape Town had been in the Hendrik Verwoerd Building across the road from Parliament, where all the other ministers also had their offices. However, when he became president, he moved his office up Parliament Street to Tuynhuys, which had previously been the residence of centuries of colonial governors and, more lately, the office of the last ceremonial state president. A great deal of money was spent refurbishing Tuynhuys. Specially designed and woven carpets were laid in its reception rooms. The double-storey ballroom was decorated with gold baroque mouldings. The government parking lot in front of the building was replaced by an elaborate cobbled square surrounded by high railings and security. The state president's guard, a special unit with plumed caps, was also upgraded. A ceremonial changing of the guard was introduced, with squads of soldiers playing drums, marching up and down the square. While I did not object to the redecoration of Tuynhuys, I was not impressed by the pomp and ceremony with which P. W. Botha sought to embellish the presidency. It was alien to the sober traditions of the National Party with which I had grown up.

All this was symptomatic of P. W. Botha's growing remoteness from his ministers and from National Party parliamentarians. At the same time Botha's inner circle of advisers – most of them officials – began to play a more prominent role in screening the president from his political colleagues and in implementing his strategies. The number of staff in the President's Office grew to over 500. The president's relations with the media deteriorated even further. Correspondents of government-supporting newspapers – like *Die Burger* – found that they no longer had the privileged access that they had traditionally enjoyed with the head of the government. The media were increasingly regarded as the enemy – and the flow of communication between them and the President's Office dried to little more than a trickle.

The degree to which the office of the president had become cut off not only from the media, but from reality, is revealed by an incident that occurred in the latter years of Mr Botha's presidency. Frustrated and perplexed by South Africa's clear inability to change its overseas image, the president's press officer, Mr Jack Viviers, called the head of the government's communication agency to Tuynhuys for a briefing on how he thought the situation could be changed. He said that he had been in the United States when the Americans had succeeded in putting a man on the moon. He had been greatly impressed by how this feat had overnight changed global perceptions of the United States. He felt that South Africa needed to do something that would be equally spectacular, that would capture the imagination of the international community and take their attention away from apartheid. The head of the agency waited in great anticipation to discover what this remarkable achievement would be. Viviers dramatically turned over the top page of the flip chart which he had been using for his briefing and revealed – a picture of a large iceberg. Icebergs, he said, are the answer. He said that we should send tug-boats to the Antarctic to capture icebergs and to tow them to the arid west coast of South Africa. They could provide fresh water to make the desert bloom and to create a paradise in the vast and unpopulated stretches of the western Karoo. This would capture the imagination of the international community to such an extent that they would begin to think of South Africa in different terms.

*

The last few years of President Botha's presidency were marked by a series of unfortunate incidents which were usually caused by P. W. Botha himself. In a book titled *Leierstryd* (Leader Struggle), two leading Afrikaner journalists, Alf Ries and Ebbe Dommisse, described the 'bullying and surly P. W. Botha style' which increasingly caused concern in high government circles. Instead of Tuynhuys (Garden House), the term Kruithuis (Powder House) was heard in political discussions, as President Botha's intemperate clashes with a great number of people became known to a wider circle.

I was one of those who was becoming seriously concerned about President Botha's increasing aggressiveness. I watched with growing alarm how he frittered away opportunities to promote better relations with the leaders of our various population groups and international visitors who came to see him. In particular, instead of drawing closer to the Labour Party (the main party of the coloured community) and its leader, the Revd Allan Hendrickse, who was then also chairman of the coloured Ministers' Council in the 'tricameral' system, P. W. Botha seemed to go out of his way to alienate him.

I recall two incidents, in particular. The first concerned a public protest against the Separate Amenities Act which Allan Hendrickse and other prominent members of his party launched by going for a swim at one of Port Elizabeth's 'white' beaches. We managed to patch up the crisis caused by P. W. Botha's ensuing attack on Hendrickse – but the important relationship between the two leaders was never quite the same again.

The next clash between the two leaders came on 19 August 1987 in the coloured chamber of Parliament. After President Botha had listened to a number of quite aggressive and strongly critical speeches from members of the Labour Party, he lost his temper. He launched a personal and humiliating attack on the Revd Hendrickse and another minister, Mr Chris April. He furiously shouted: 'I don't allow myself to be pushed around. I have never allowed myself to be pushed around – not by the House of Assembly [the white chamber of Parliament], not by this House or the House of Delegates [the Indian chamber of Parliament]. My colleagues know me.' He also said: 'I am heartily sick and tired of being pushed around by threats and destructive criticism. The honourable members have tangled with the wrong person.' A few days later the Revd Hendrickse hit back at a public meeting with a sharp attack on the president. P. W. Botha reacted by informing Hendrickse in a letter that his continued membership of the cabinet had become unacceptable. Hendrickse resigned from the cabinet. This was the end of voluntary co-operation in a multi-party cabinet that many of us felt had held so much promise. The president's inability to maintain a relationship with a key leader of an important minority group threatened the viability of the 'tricameral' constitution – which was one of the centrepieces of our efforts to achieve a constitutional settlement. Many of my cabinet colleagues and I were despondent.

Botha had also begun to alienate leading figures within the National Party – including some of his best friends and supporters. One such person was South Africa's first deputy state president, Mr Alwyn Schlebusch, who in 1978 as the leader of the National Party in the Orange Free State had played a major role in getting P. W. Botha elected as the party leader and prime minister. Another was Minister Chris Heunis. It was, in fact, an incident affecting Chris Heunis, in which I was involved, that destroyed whatever confidence I still had in the president. The background was as follows. Flowing from a report by the President's Council on the Group Areas Act (the law which reserved land for occupation by different race groups), President Botha had laid down guidelines for new legislation which would have relaxed some aspects of the law, while tightening others. The reasoning behind the proposed legislation was that, while it was necessary to make provision for greater flexibility in allowing non-racial occupation of some areas – particularly in city centres – it was also thought necessary to reassure whites that their neighbourhoods would not be threatened.

Chris Heunis was the minister responsible, but had no enthusiasm for the proposed legislation. He warned that it would cause relations with the Labour Party to deteriorate still further and that it might even threaten the continued existence of the 'tricameral' Parliament. He was right. The coloured and Indian chambers quite understandably refused to participate in any way in the legislation and launched a boycott that threatened to bring Parliament to a standstill. Some of the opposition parties in the white chamber also joined the boycott. We were faced with a major crisis. Chris Heunis and I (sometimes together with Deputy Minister Roelf Meyer) held discussions with the Revd Allan Hendrickse over a period of two days, which ultimately resulted in a settlement. We also obtained the support of the Indians for our approach and reached agreement on a joint statement that would be issued by Chris Heunis and Allan Hendrickse. However, we first had to obtain the approval of President Botha. He and his wife were at a flower show in Cape Town that night and it was difficult to track them down. Heunis's personnel nevertheless finally succeeded in getting in touch with him. I was with Chris Heunis in his office when he spoke with Botha by telephone. I listened while he explained the essence of the agreement and obtained Botha's approval for the statement. Botha was not happy, but said that we could go ahead with the announcement. We did so and the crisis was defused.

As leader of the House of Assembly I convened a special caucus meeting to brief National Party members on these developments. President Botha was furious because the caucus had been arranged without his knowledge and refused to attend it. After consultation with my colleagues, I decided to proceed, but to call the gathering 'a special information meeting' and not a meeting of the caucus. The meeting thanked and congratulated Chris Heunis and me for having resolved the crisis.

Our action led to an outburst by President Botha at the following cabinet meeting. He castigated Chris Heunis for not having properly informed him of the agreement with Hendrickse and attacked me and the other provincial leaders of the National Party, who had spoken at the special information meeting of the National Party caucus. Chris Heunis refuted the president's charges and said that he had nothing for which to apologize. For a moment a tense silence descended on the meeting. It seemed that President Botha wanted to let the matter rest. I was very upset because I felt that an injustice had been done to Chris Heunis, which I was not prepared to let pass. I told the president bluntly that Chris Heunis's version was correct, that I had stood beside him when he had received clearance from the president and that it was unfair to accuse Chris Heunis of not having obtained proper clearance for the announcement. Never before in the time that P. W. Botha was prime minister and president had a cabinet minister opposed and challenged him so directly in a cabinet meeting as I did that day. The president suddenly jumped up and, turning on his heel, shouted words to the effect of 'My Lord and My God!' He then stormed out of the Cabinet Room.

As he left there was, for a moment, a shocked silence. After some discussion we then decided to try to defuse the situation. Chris Heunis and I went to speak to President Botha in his office. By that time he had calmed down. Without backing down in any way, we assured him that we were not trying to challenge his authority and convinced him to return to the cabinet meeting. On his return about an hour later, the other ministers also assured him of their loyalty – and so the growing rift between President Botha and the cabinet was papered over.

I was still furious and at the end of the meeting told my friend and colleague Dawie de Villiers that I was going to resign from the cabinet. I felt that I could no longer serve under P. W. Botha and that the time had come to make a stand. His surliness, aggression and poor human relations were doing serious harm to the National Party and to the country. Dawie de Villiers brought in a few other colleagues and they all pleaded with me to reconsider. I finally relented and, for the sake of the National Party, decided not to act overhastily. However, in my mind there were no further doubts: the time to confront P. W. Botha had come. And, as with the split in 1982, I realized that despite the unpleasantness that I foresaw I would once again have to play a leading role. I am by nature a peacemaker. But there comes a time when true peace is no longer attainable and a sham peace does more harm than good. The rest of 1988 was marked by a fairly tense atmosphere within the inner circle of the National Party, but passed without any notable incidents. The December holidays arrived. In January I returned to work with the unspoken presentiment that 1989 would be a difficult year. Little did I realize how dramatic it would in fact be.

*

On Wednesday, 18 January 1989 President P. W. Botha suffered a stroke. Minister Chris Heunis, who was the most senior minister, was appointed as acting president. In the period after his stroke, the only members of the cabinet who had any contact with the president were Chris Heunis and Dr Willie van Niekerk, the minister of health who was also a medical doctor. Dr van Niekerk acted as our link with President Botha's medical team and from time to time informed us of his progress. In the lobbies of Parliament and in the media there was intense speculation on how serious the stroke was and on whether President Botha would be able to continue with his work. In its communication with the media, the State President's Office created the impression that the president was not seriously ill, but had suffered only a slight stroke and was quickly recovering. Medical bulletins were issued from time to time which reinforced this perception. The cabinet and the provincial leaders of the National Party agreed that we should limit speculation about his possible retirement. We decided that the correct and responsible approach would be to await the stabilization of his health. On 24 January President Botha was released from hospital. His office announced that he would convalesce for six weeks before he resumed his duties. Nevertheless, the speculation continued on whether he would ever again be really well enough to run the country.

This was the state of play on 2 February when the National Party's parliamentary caucus gathered for its first meeting of 1989. The following day the acting state president, Mr Chris Heunis, was going to open the parliamentary session. I was the leader of the House of Assembly, and in that capacity played a leading role in planning the National Party's parliamentary activities. I consequently had a close working relationship with the chairman of the caucus, Mr Boet Botma. When I arrived at the Caucus Room, Mr Botma called me to one side. He was clearly upset and informed me that he had just come from Tuynhuys where a letter from President Botha had been handed to him with the instruction that he should present it to the caucus. In the letter P. W. Botha had announced his resignation as leader of the National Party – but not as state president.

I was absolutely astounded. I told Botma that the only course to follow would be to present the letter to the caucus as President Botha had requested and suggested that he should do so right at the beginning of the meeting. When I took my place beside him at the head table in the Caucus Room it was with the knowledge that 2 February 1989 would be a watershed day for the National Party. The meeting was opened with a prayer and after a short welcome by Mr Botma, he read the following letter to the caucus:

Dear friend

Arising from the setback to my health I would appreciate it if you would present this letter to the caucus.

In my opinion the office of state president and the office of leadership of the National Party should now be separated.

I would accordingly appreciate it if the caucus of the National Party would now fill the post of leader so that I can be put in a position to continue only with the office of state president.

The state presidency will then, to a considerable degree, become a unifying force in our country.

I thank all my friends for their trust and friendship in the past.

It is my innermost prayer that you will receive the special grace of God Almighty.

With sincere wishes to you all.

Wishing you prosperity and blessings.

P. W. Botha

The caucus was dumbfounded. I suggested that the party leaders present should withdraw to consider the situation, while the rest of the caucus continued with its normal activities. My proposal was accepted after a short discussion and the provincial leaders and the provincial deputy chairmen left the caucus and gathered in a nearby room. Three divergent views came to the fore. I proposed that we should return to the caucus and proceed immediately with the election of a new party leader. Minister Chris Heunis suggested that we should adjourn the caucus until a later date to create time for consideration, consultation and discussion. Minister Pik Botha said that we, as the leading figures in the National Party, should consider reaching agreement on a successor for P. W. Botha and then recommend to the caucus that our candidate should be unanimously elected.

There was a long and intense debate. I motivated my proposal for an immediate election by drawing attention to two particular considerations. Firstly, I was convinced that a postponement of the election would lead to a drawn out leadership struggle which, as in the past, could damage the party. Secondly, it was clear to me that P. W. Botha's decision to separate the offices of state president and the leader of the National Party would create an extremely delicate situation which could best be managed by a newly elected leader with the necessary authority. When it became clear that the majority of the meeting supported my view, everybody agreed to an immediate election. Our recommendation was accepted by the caucus, although one or two members questioned its wisdom. However, the overwhelming majority wanted to proceed with the election immediately.

The ensuing election was, on a personal level, one of the most dramatic episodes of my career. The party leaders had agreed to some slight amendments to the usual voting procedure. There would be no oral proposals. Members would be able to nominate candidates simply by writing their name on a ballot. Apart from me, there were three other candidates. They were, in order of seniority, Minister Chris Heunis, Minister Pik Botha, and Minister Barend du Plessis. There were no surprises among these nominations. My name and the other three had been regularly mentioned in lobby discussions as possible successors to President Botha.

Minister Chris Heunis, the astute and experienced minister of constitutional affairs, could count on strong support from the Cape MPs. However, he had suffered a serious set-back during the 1987 general election when he had managed to hold his previously safe parliamentary seat by only 39 votes. He was also unfairly held responsible in some circles for the government's failure to make significant progress with constitutional reform in respect of black South Africans. In addition, the media had begun to ridicule his sometimes convoluted manner of expression which they claimed was difficult to decipher.

Pik Botha, the charismatic minister of foreign affairs, was the favourite of a small but dedicated group of *verligte* MPs, most of whom came from the Transvaal. Despite his excellence as a public speaker, his popularity at grass-roots level and his effectiveness in the foreign affairs portfolio, most MPs believed that he was too volatile and unpredictable to be a good leader. Most of the *verligtes* had accordingly rallied around another candidate, Barend du Plessis, the minister of finance. Du Plessis was young, tall and attractive. He had originally been a supporter of Pik Botha, but was eventually persuaded to become a contender for the leadership himself. He was also close to President Botha who, according to reports, hoped that he would win the leadership contest. My supporters were mainly from the centre. The more conservative members of the caucus also tended to support me because they thought that I would be more sympathetic to their concerns than the other three candidates.

The voting began after ballot papers had been hastily prepared. Caucus members were called forward in alphabetical order and, one by one, cast their ballots. It was agreed that the candidate with the least votes would be eliminated until someone attained an overall majority. There were 130 members who were entitled to vote and the winning figure was thus 66 votes.

I had no idea of whether or not I would win. I had not lobbied for votes in the caucus and had never asked my close friends to carry out an informal opinion poll to establish my support. But I knew that I was in a reasonably strong position and was convinced that I would definitely make it to the final round. I was not, however, sure that I would win. The adrenalin pumped through my veins. During the long and drawn out voting, I began to work on two speeches in my mind – the one that I would deliver if I was elected and the other if someone else should win.

In the end there were three rounds of voting. In the first round Minister Pik Botha was eliminated. We were not initially informed how many votes each candidate had received. In the second round Minister Chris Heunis fell out. It was thus Minister Barend du Plessis and myself in the final round. The final result was announced with the number of votes that each of the two candidates had received. I had received 69 votes to the 61 of Mr Du Plessis. I had won by the skin of my teeth!

Later the whole process of the voting was made known and an interesting pattern emerged. I had already received 59 votes in the first round – only seven fewer than I needed for an absolute majority. Barend du Plessis had received 30 votes, Chris Heunis 25 and Pik Botha 16. In the second round I gained five more votes. With 64 votes I was just two short of an absolute majority. Barend du Plessis had then received 40 and Chris Heunis 26. And in the third round I received only five of Chris Heunis's 26 votes, while Barend du Plessis picked up an impressive 21.

This voting pattern carried with it an interesting message. My interpretation of it was that there was an urgent desire among many members of the caucus to move quickly ahead with reform. The unexpectedly strong showing of Du Plessis resulted from his image as a *verligte*, as opposed to my more centrist image. It also indicated a taste for renewal within the party itself. The Young Turks had become tired of what they regarded as the exaggerated deference that was paid to seniority and experience.

In my acceptance speech, just after the announcement that I had been elected, I strongly emphasized the need for reform. I said that we had reached a point where we would have to take bold initiatives. I committed myself to freeing the party from the corners into which we had been painted – or had painted ourselves. When I said that we would need to take a carefully considered quantum leap to achieve this, someone in the caucus responded by shouting, 'Leap F.W.! Leap!'

As far as President Botha's unilateral separation of the state presidency and the party leadership was concerned, I said that we would try to reach a sensible agreement with the state president, as soon as he was better. Obviously, there were clear risks involved.

After the election, the other three candidates expressed their full support for me and promised me their loyalty – promises which, in essence, they were to keep during the difficult days which were to follow in 1989.

The media was caught completely off guard. Only the *Nasionale Pers* newspapers had received a tip-off (not from the caucus) and were immediately on the scene. And even they did not know exactly what was going on – only that something dramatic was happening. The news spread like a bush fire.

Marike had been shopping in town that morning. Not expecting anything, she had gone to the shops in a normal day dress. I wanted to share these dramatic developments with her. Win or lose, she was the first person that I wanted to see after the election. I got a message through to my office that they should stop her when she returned to the office and keep her there until I could join her. My office also did not know what was going on. Later some of my key personnel said that they realized that it must have been something momentous.

When I walked into my office followed by a few journalists and *Die Burger*'s photographer, the intense emotions that I had experienced throughout the morning overwhelmed me. I greeted Marike with an emotional, 'Hello, Ma,' walked into my office and closed the door behind us. Deeply moved, I told her what had happened. We both realized that we were once again at a new threshold. Without the slightest warning, and within the space of a few hours, I had been placed before the greatest challenge of my life.

13

President Botha's Departure from Politics

The crucial issue immediately after my election as the leader of the National Party was the question of who would call the tune – the state president, divorced from his political power base, or the leader of the party commanding a majority in Parliament? Botha had, in fact, been toying with the idea of splitting the two offices at least since 26 February 1986 when he had suggested that the Special Cabinet Committee should consider its merits. It appears that Botha had two main motivations for 'splitting the offices': firstly, he wished to reduce his own work load, particularly in the wake of his illness, and secondly, he had an idea that by relinquishing his office in the National Party, he would somehow be able to rise above party politics and would thus be more acceptable to South Africans of all political persuasions in his efforts to promote constitutional change. The fact that he evidently thought that he could detach himself from his main power base in this manner is an indication of the degree to which he had already become alienated from the National Party's broad leadership, and also of the detrimental effect that his stroke had evidently had on his usually canny party political judgement.

The National Party, with its large majority in Parliament, had a strong tradition that its leader was the final interpreter of policy. It had grown accustomed to the idea that the leader had to have all the power necessary to implement the party's policy. Suddenly a situation had arisen in which the state president had all the constitutional power, but was no longer linked to, or bound by, the majority party with the political power. What would happen if the state president refused to carry out the policy instructions of the National Party, as articulated by myself as the new leader of the party? There was an enormous potential for confrontation built into the separation of the two offices. Already at my first press conference on the afternoon of my election, I dealt with the matter, by trying to defuse speculation. I said, among other things, that a special relationship would naturally have to develop between the state president as executive head of the government on the one side, and me as the leader of the National Party on the other. I added that we had worked well together in the past and I had no doubt that we would successfully manage our new relationship in the future.

This approach did not succeed for long in containing the inevitable rumours and speculation, which were further fuelled by P. W. Botha's reaction to my election and to me as a person. On the contrary, his behaviour exacerbated the tensions within the party. We were increasingly confronted with an untenable situation. From my side I did not initially do much to develop an understanding with President Botha, because he was still too ill. I did pay a courtesy call on him, after he let me wait for a few days. It was clear to me from our discussion that he was still a very sick man and I felt that we should not place him under any form of pressure at that stage. But from the very beginning, in all sorts of ways, I felt that he adopted a dismissive attitude towards me. He never congratulated me in public on my election as leader and in numerous statements went out of his way to ignore my position. A good example was a press release that he issued on 2 March 1989 after he had held discussions with Acting State President Chris Heunis, with me, with Pik Botha and with Barend du Plessis – the four people who had been candidates for the leadership of the party. In his statement, which announced that he would resume his duties early in April, he referred to the four of us by name, mentioning our portfolios without mentioning the fact that he had also spoken to me as the leader of the National Party.

The next day he gave an exclusive interview to Alf Ries of *Die Burger* in which he continued his strategy of subtly undermining my authority as the new party leader. In the interview he said that the leader of the National Party was coincidentally also a member of his cabinet and that relationship was healthy because the relationship of a minister to the state president was determined by mutual trust and respect for one another. He added that the same principle held true for the relationship with other leaders who sat in the cabinet.

As P. W. Botha very well knew, the actual relationship between him and ministers in his cabinet was one in which his dominance was unquestioned. He was clearly not prepared to give any recognition to my special position as the leader of the party but wished, instead, to place me on the same level as other ministers and 'leaders who sit in the cabinet'.

He was also asked how he foresaw the separation of the two posts would work in practice, especially in view of the fact that I, as the National Party leader, would be the main interpreter of National Party policy but would not have the constitutional power to carry it out. Botha replied that he would 'take note' of the National Party's congresses and would proceed from the position that he had a power base among all good South Africans.

These statements, as well as others that were made in the same interview, caused astonishment and concern in National Party circles. Botha evidently wanted to minimize my influence as the new leader of the party. More seriously, he did not seem to be prepared to give an unequivocal commitment to carry out the policy of the majority party in Parliament.

The interview further exacerbated the tensions within the party. For those who could read between the lines, warning lights began to flash. I reacted cautiously to Botha's controversial interview with Ries, but gave a clear indication that I would bring the uncertainty to an end. If necessary, I said, I would call the Federal Council of the National Party together to discuss the whole matter.

Critical articles appeared in the newspapers expressing the untenable nature of the situation. One cartoon, in particular, succinctly summed up the situation. P. W. Botha was depicted at the window of Tuynhuys outside of which a large crowd had gathered. An aide informed him that the people had come to say goodbye. Botha's response was, Where are they going?

The situation developed rapidly after P. W. Botha announced that he would resume his official duties as early as 15 March. On 9 March I convened a caucus meeting at which a large majority expressed their dissatisfaction with President Botha's attitude. They wanted the assurance that I, as the leader of the party, would be granted the necessary authority to interpret and implement party policy and that President Botha would stop undermining my position. They also wanted assurances that the separation of the offices would be only temporary and that, after the coming election, the leader of the party would once again be the president. After the meeting, the provincial leaders and I went to see President Botha and informed him of the party's views. The discussion did not go well and ended inconclusively. Sentiment within the party began to boil over after I reported back to the caucus and informed them that we had failed to make any progress with the president.

On Friday, 10 March I convened a meeting of the Federal Council of the National Party to discuss the growing crisis. A minority, led by Minister Chris Heunis, favoured a conciliatory approach and suggested continued negotiations with the president. The majority was, however, convinced that the time for diplomacy had passed. I tabled a carefully worded proposal that it was 'in the best interest of the country and of the party that the leader of the National Party as the majority party in the House of Assembly, should also hold the office of state president'. The proposal recommended that this principle should be pursued in consultation with the cabinet and the state president, with due consideration for the position of the present state president. My proposal was adopted by 22 votes to 7 and was later unanimously endorsed by the caucus. Even this statement was mild by comparison with the wishes of a significant element in the caucus who actually wanted to demand P. W. Botha's resignation.

After this there was no question of my maintaining good relations with P. W. Botha. Nevertheless, I knew I had to deal with the former leader of the party with kid gloves. He had no intention of making it easy for me to do so. I decided to manage the matter in such a way that we would continue to protect him – also against himself – to the greatest possible extent until the general election. We agreed, amongst the cabinet ministers, that we would avoid actions and debates in cabinet meetings which might cause him stress. The strategy was that we would sort out such matters between ministers in the cabinet committees, so that we could come to the cabinet with consensus proposals. After this, the president and the cabinet observed a kind of truce, but the cold war undercurrents continued. The opposition and the newspapers had a field day while we wrestled through this painful period. The impasse began to take its toll on the party and became a major threat to our prospects in the coming election.

The timing of the election became a major point of contention between the party and President Botha. For a long time Botha insisted that it was his prerogative to determine the election date. He wanted it to be held only in early 1990 – the latest possible moment to which it could be constitutionally delayed – because of his view that a new delimitation of constituencies would first have to be completed. The crisis was averted when, after lengthy discussions, he grudgingly agreed that the election should be held as early as possible – at the beginning of September – and that the voting could take place on the basis of the old delimitation. We could now console ourselves with the knowledge that the unnatural situation that had been created by the separation of the offices would continue only until September. On 3 May it was officially announced that the election would take place on 6 September. I could, at last, begin to focus my attention on winning the election.

As a part of our election strategy we decided to convene a Federal Congress of the National Party on 29 June, to launch the election campaign. At the same time, in a genuine effort to bridge the growing rift between Botha and the party, we planned to hold a banquet on the eve of the congress to bid a proper farewell to the president and Mrs Botha. The proposed banquet was discussed with President Botha who indicated that it would suit him. Special invitation cards were printed and sent out. However, President Botha suddenly lost his temper because he had not received prompt written confirmation of the invitation and informed us that he would no longer attend the banquet. It later emerged from a letter that he wrote to me on 2 June that the real reason for his decision was not the manner in which the invitation had been handled, but the decisions that the Federal Council had taken concerning his position and his feeling that he was being ignored in the formulation of policy.

Once again, we had a crisis. Ministers Kobie Coetsee, Dawie de Villiers, Barend du Plessis and I went urgently to his holiday home in the Wilderness to convince him to change his mind. He was, however, implacable and we had no choice but to accept the situation. I, nevertheless, proposed a warm motion of thanks and appreciation to P. W. Botha and his wife at the Federal Congress. Despite the shadow that this had cast over the proceedings, the congress was a great success. I was the uncontested leader of the party. The wonderful support that I received inspired me and filled me with confidence for the coming election.

Another factor that contributed to the increasing surliness of P. W. Botha was the extensive contacts that I began to develop with political leaders in Europe and to a lesser degree in Africa. Just before the Federal Congress I visited Europe where I held talks with Prime Minister Margaret Thatcher, Chancellor Helmut Kohl, Prime Minister Cavaco Silva of Portugal and Prime Minister Andreotti of Italy. I also went to Switzerland and held talks with three of their ministers. Later, in July, I visited President Chissano of Mozambique in Maputo. Pik Botha played the key role in the initiation and arrangement of these visits.

The success of my foreign visits received wide and favourable publicity in South Africa – something that apparently irritated President Botha. From the point of view of the National Party and of South Africa the contacts that I made were of great importance. I felt that it was essential that we should waste no time in convincing the key leaders of the world that the National Party and I planned to initiate dramatic changes in South Africa. All those I spoke with – and particularly Margaret Thatcher and Helmut Kohl – encouraged me to adopt far-reaching reforms and had assured me of their full support should I decide to do so. These visits laid the foundation for the improvement in our international relations which occurred soon after I became president.

Pik Botha and I agreed that, at the end of July 1989, we would stop the international visits and concentrate all our attention on the election campaign. Pik Botha would inform Dr Kaunda, and a few other African leaders who had indicated that they wanted to meet me, that we would make arrangements for such meetings after the election.

From then on it was just the election. I criss-crossed the country to address public meetings, to generate enthusiasm among voters and to motivate National Party workers. On 8 August 1989 I was in Natal, where I was due to address a public meeting that evening. In the afternoon I received a telephone call from Pik Botha in which he asked me to reconsider my decision to meet Kaunda only after the election. He wanted to send two emissaries to Kaunda to brief him fully on developments in South West Africa/Namibia and efforts to end the wars in Angola and Mozambique. There was at that time a serious risk that the United Nations might take decisions which could jeopardize these efforts. The so-called frontline states in southern Africa (the anti-South African states bordering South Africa) were amongst the main players and Kaunda would be able to exercise a restraining influence on them. Pik Botha anticipated that Kaunda would once again express the wish to meet me as quickly as possible and that a positive reply could make an important contribution to ensuring his co-operation. In the light of my heavy programme I reluctantly agreed and told Pik that the only date on which I could fit in such a visit would be Monday, 28 August. The two emissaries went with the message to President Kaunda in Zambia on 9 August. The following day they reported to Pik Botha that they had obtained Dr Kaunda's co-operation and that he was keen to meet me. It was agreed that the meeting would take place on 28 August and that neither side would, for the time being, make any public announcement about the meeting.

Pik Botha instructed Neil van Heerden, the director-general of foreign affairs, to inform President Botha during the course of the day about our planned meeting with Kaunda. However, he expected no problems, since he believed that the question of a visit to Dr Kaunda had already previously been approved by the state president in principle and was a fait accompli. His office was subsequently informed by Reuters that Dr Kaunda had announced that the meeting would take place on 28 August. According to Pik Botha, he immediately decided to speak to the state president about the visit, before he heard about it from the media. He telephoned President Botha and reminded him of his concern that the UN was about to adopt anti-South African resolutions and that there was a possibility that President Kaunda could help to avert this, if a meeting could be arranged between him and myself. He did not mention the specific date of 28 August during the conversation, but was under the impression that President Botha had given his approval in principle. He later recalled P. W. Botha saying that he should arrange the visits to Africa as he saw fit.

That same evening of 10 August the crisis broke. P. W. Botha called Pik Botha from a meeting to speak to him by telephone. The president was deeply upset because he had heard that President Kaunda had announced that he would be meeting me on 28 August. Pik Botha reminded the president that he had informed him of the visit a few hours earlier – but the president refused to accept that he had done so. Once again, President Botha had failed to remember his telephonic approval of actions by his ministers – just as he had done with Chris Heunis less than a year before.

In the middle of that night I received a telephone call from Pik Botha. He told me that, according to General Magnus Malan, the minister of defence, the president was very upset about the Kaunda announcement. Angered by his perception that the cabinet was ignoring and by-passing him, he threatened to issue a critical statement on the visit. Magnus Malan also phoned me within a few minutes with the same message. The president had clearly decided to throw down the gauntlet.

Early the following morning Pik Botha received another telephone call from President Botha. The president was still angry and once again threatened to issue a statement repudiating me, Pik Botha and other ministers. Pik Botha pleaded to see President Botha, to clear up the misunderstanding. President Botha replied that there was no misunderstanding, that this time we had gone too far, and that he was going to issue a statement. When Pik Botha told him that he had witnesses who heard how he had informed President Botha by telephone of the Kaunda visit, the president became very angry and ended the conversation.

From my side, I felt that I could not remain on the sidelines, even though I was not directly involved in the dispute between the two Bothas. I asked the cabinet members whom I could track down in Pretoria to come to see me and briefed them on the latest developments. I also tried to persuade President Botha to receive a delegation to discuss the problem in a more calm and relaxed atmosphere. He refused. The die was cast and his statement was issued. It was cryptic and went as follows:

> I have no knowledge, in terms of the rules that deal with the foreign travels of ministers, of the discussion of 28 August announced by Dr Kaunda.

It was a direct contradiction of Pik Botha's statement which had clearly stated that the meeting had been arranged after consultation with President Botha.

The final crisis had come. I asked Pik Botha to join me and the other cabinet ministers who were already in Pretoria. We decided that he would once again make an attempt to speak to President Botha. Pik phoned him from my office, but the president refused flatly to receive him or anyone else. According to Pik Botha he was once again aggressive and repeated that various ministers and the cabinet were ignoring him.

I realized that a full-scale confrontation had become almost unavoidable. Nevertheless, I issued a statement in which I tried to keep the door open to prevent a complete break. I said that all the available cabinet ministers had met to consider the president's statement and that there had possibly been a misunderstanding over the information given by Minister R. F. Botha. I added that attempts by ministers to have an urgent meeting with the state president to clarify the matter had until then been unsuccessful and that, in the light of this, I was calling an emergency meeting of all National Party ministers as soon as possible to consider the matter.

P. W. Botha's reaction was to call a special cabinet meeting in Cape Town for Monday morning, 14 August. On Saturday, 12 August, all the ministers of the cabinet, of the Ministers' Council of the white House of Assembly and deputy ministers gathered at my ministerial residence in Brooklyn, Pretoria. I emphasized that this was not a cabinet meeting, but a meeting of the broad leadership of the National Party. After I informed them fully and clinically of all the relevant facts and all the efforts that had been made to try to prevent the crisis, we held a general discussion. There was unanimous support for Pik Botha and me which reassured me I would be able to count on the support of the whole cabinet during the coming confrontation. I did not ask my colleagues to reject P. W. Botha or to force him from the presidency. We were convinced that we were still dealing with a man who was seriously incapacitated by the after-effects of a major stroke. Our first prize would be to achieve a settlement that would save him to the greatest possible degree from humiliation.

We were also determined to send out an unambiguous message on where the National Party stood at that delicate stage shortly before the election. The softest option was to convince President Botha to take sick leave until after the general election and the election of a new president. He would then be able to hand over the seal of office – the symbol of the state president's power – to his successor in as dignified a manner as possible. We felt that it was not only in the party's best interest that he should go on sick leave, but that it was also in his own interest as well as in the interest of the country. The hard option, which we wished to avoid, would be to demand his resignation. At no stage did we consider causing a constitutional crisis by all resigning from the cabinet and leaving him alone in office. Only if he rejected both the soft and hard options would we give attention to more risky alternatives. While we were meeting at my ministerial residence on 12 August, a crowd of local and foreign journalists and TV teams began to gather. After we had finished, a number of senior ministers and I walked out of the house and I read out a statement in which I said that we had discussed all the implications of the recent developments in depth and that we were completely unanimous on how the situation should be handled, in discussion with the president. I added that the National Party in no way underestimated the seriousness of the situation and would act in the best interest of South Africa and its voters. I appealed to voters and asked them not to allow themselves to be side-tracked by these developments so far as the election was concerned.

On Sunday we all went down to Cape Town. There was a beehive of activity. Outsiders with good intentions tried to broker a compromise. Among them was Mr Boet Troskie, a good friend of the state president and Dr Niel Barnard, the head of the National Intelligence

Service. As a result, a number of senior ministers and I met the president at his residence, Westbrooke, on Sunday evening. There we tried to lay the basis for a settlement in exploratory discussions. He used the opportunity to give us a long lecture. He was reasonably calm, but it was clear to us that he was not in the mood for a settlement. After reporting back to most of the members of the cabinet in my ministerial conference room, we departed with the realization that, unless there was a change of attitude on the part of President Botha, the time for a showdown had come.

*

When I went to bed that night I was determined to bring the whole distasteful matter to a head the following morning. I would go out of my way to limit the humiliation of P. W. Botha, but I realized that I would have to be very firm. A wishy-washy outcome to the cabinet discussions would do the National Party irreparable damage and seriously hurt it in the election, only three weeks away on 6 September. I was very tense, but again experienced the same certainty on the course that I would have to take as I had when I took the lead in the confrontation against Andries Treurnicht and his followers.

The historic meeting was held the next morning in the Cabinet Room at the State President's Office at Tuynhuys. After President Botha had opened the meeting, I led the discussion from the side of the members of the cabinet. Firstly, I gave a short briefing on the background to the proposed meeting with Kaunda and the meeting of the ministers the previous Saturday. I then presented our proposal that President Botha should take sick leave and that an acting state president should be appointed. After that, each minister, in order of seniority, had the opportunity of putting his views. They all supported my proposal and quite a number used the opportunity to show warmth to P. W. Botha, to praise him for the great and good things that he had done and to thank him for the role that he had played in their lives and careers.

I could not help thinking back to the meeting eleven years earlier when, one by one, the members of the cabinet had urged John Vorster to resign as state president. I also recalled how little sympathy P. W. Botha had shown to his predecessor when Vorster had asked him to soften some aspects of the statement on his retirement.

Only once did President Botha interrupt anyone. That was when Minister Eli Louw said that the P. W. Botha that he had known before the stroke was not the same man that he had come to know after the stroke. President Botha accused him angrily of having said a terrible thing. He asked him why he had raised his illness, which had nothing to do with the matter that they were discussing.

After all the ministers had expressed their support for my proposal and made their contributions, there was a short adjournment, following which the president addressed us at great length. He cleared his chest of all his grievances since his resignation as leader of the party. At times he was quite aggressive. In the process he bitterly attacked me and the other provincial leaders.

As I listened to him, two emotions in particular were aroused in me. There was sorrow for a man who, in his serious illness, had become isolated because of his irascible and cantankerous nature. But it was also clear to me that he had fallen prey to the suspicion and petty-mindedness which, according to experts, were typical symptoms of some stroke victims. My other emotion was a firm certainty that we had acted correctly and that it was in the best interests of the party and of the country that he should vacate the office of state president. He was no longer fit to rule.

President Botha rejected our proposal. He was adamant that he was healthy and dismissed our suggestion that he should go to rest at his holiday home in the Wilderness as an invitation to be party to a lie. In retrospect there was a little black humour when he referred to his health:

> I am healthy. I am healthy. Is every one of you in a position to produce a medical certificate that you are healthy? Let me know how many of you are sitting here with pills in your pocket?

Ultimately, he came up with what he called an offer. He said that he was prepared to resign on the basis that his resignation would take effect at midnight of that same day, 14 August, and that he would have the opportunity of fully spelling out all his reasons for resigning on television. His statement posed the clear threat that he intended to politicize his resignation. My reaction was to accept his offer and to reserve our right to challenge him on any issue that he might raise during his TV broadcast.

He and I then had an unpleasant discussion in front of the whole cabinet. He was indignant that we had dared to insinuate that he was too ill to hold office. We then adjourned for a while before reconvening. Suddenly, it was as though a change had come over P. W. Botha.

One by one he shook our hands in a benevolent spirit. It was one of the few times that he ever called me F.W. and not Mr De Klerk. I left the Cabinet Room with sorrow but also with a sense of great relief. I went directly to the airport to fly to Johannesburg to attend a reception at the Rand Afrikaans University. On our arrival there, the media were clamouring for a statement. But in the light of the agreement that Mr Botha would first announce his resignation on television and give his reasons, we kept them at a distance. Just after that Pik Botha and I went to the South African Broadcasting Company where we watched P. W. Botha's television interview. It was an aggressive and muddled performance but contained nothing new. Pik Botha and I – in a subsequent interview – did not shy away from responding very frankly to P. W. Botha's charges. Among these was his argument that we had played into the hands of the ANC with the proposed visit to Kaunda. We refuted this. P. W. Botha's aggressive and rambling television interview ultimately did little or no damage to the National Party, but was widely interpreted as clear proof that he was no longer in a fit condition to continue in office.

The media supported and welcomed the firm stance that we had taken and was damning toward P. W. Botha. Damage was limited to a minimum and we could go ahead full steam with our election campaign.

The following morning, in accordance with the constitution, I was appointed by the cabinet as the acting president and was shortly afterwards sworn in by the chief justice. It was four years to the day after P. W. Botha had delivered his Rubicon speech.

From then until 6 September I was caught up in a whirlwind of activity. I addressed fifteen public National Party meetings throughout South Africa within the space of eighteen days. In between I had to take control of the reins of the country, while still managing my ministerial portfolios. I recall these few weeks as being amongst the most hectic of my life. However, I was young and brimming with energy.

We fought the election on a straightforward reform platform. The National Party – under my guidance – had distilled our reform programme into six key goals: we were asking for a clear mandate to normalize the political process; to remove racial discrimination; to negotiate a new constitutional dispensation; to promote economic effectiveness; to maintain law and order; and to remove mistrust by building bridges between our divided communities.

Late on the evening of 6 September, many ministers, members of Parliament and close friends joined me in watching the election results coming in on a giant screen in a large conference room at the Union Buildings. The atmosphere was tense. How would the voters react to our request for a mandate for fundamental reform? And to what extent had our public clash with P. W. Botha damaged us? As the results flowed in, the statistical experts started to identify trends. Shortly after midnight, it was clear that we would win. One of the last results was from my old constituency, Vereeniging. My previous comfortable majority had been slashed and our candidate succeeded in holding the seat only by the skin of his teeth. In the end we won the election comfortably, although with a reduced majority. Nevertheless, it was large and strong enough to provide a clear mandate for the continuation of reform and the creation of a new dispensation. I was determined to carry out this mandate with everything at my disposal. It was the last South African election to be held on a racial basis. It was also the twenty-third anniversary of Dr Verwoerd's death.

14

The First Months of My Presidency

I was formally elected as state president on 14 September 1989 by an electoral college comprising eighty-eight members appointed by the majority parties in the three chambers of Parliament. Because the National Party was the majority party in the white House of Assembly and because the House of Assembly, in turn, appointed fifty members to the college, my election was a foregone conclusion. However, it was a positive sign that I was elected unopposed and that the other parties in the electoral college had decided not to make the symbolic gesture of nominating another candidate. I felt that even the opposition parties wanted to give me a chance to meet the expectations that I had raised.

The inauguration ceremony on 20 September 1989 was marked by simplicity, the minimum ostentation and solemnity. The swearing-in before the chief justice took place in the Dutch Reformed student church of the University of Pretoria. Not only did it have far more seats than any of the other churches in Pretoria, but it also had a simple and appropriate beauty.

Before Chief Justice Corbett administered the oath of office, my own pastor, Dr P. W. Bingle of the Gereformeerde Kerk in Cape Town, delivered the sermon. It was a stirring message which called on me to answer for the decisions that I would take as president in the Council Chamber of God. The administration of the oath was an emotional moment. For me, it was far more than just a formality. I experienced it as though I was indeed standing before God and quietly promised that I would try to carry out the responsibility that He had entrusted to me with the biblical principles of justice, peace and charity as my guidelines. The organ music in the church was majestic and the choir of Potchefstroom University – my old alma mater – sang beautifully. It was a lovely and fitting ceremony.

From the church we went through crowded streets to the Union Buildings. The jacaranda trees, for which Pretoria is renowned, were beginning to show their first flush of mauve blossoms. Members of the security forces saluted as we drove by and the public of all races looked on inquisitively, waved and gave us a friendly reception. Fortunately, we could wind down the windows of our armoured Mercedes-Benz a little way and Marike and I could wave back.

At the Union Buildings a stage had been erected on the same spot where President Mandela would be inaugurated with far more pomp and circumstance a little more than four and a half years later. There was just the minimum ceremony – the military bands, canon salutes and the fly-past of the South African air force.

First, we were entertained, together with a large number of VIPs, friends and family by the then administrator of the Transvaal in his stately official residence, Overvaal, which would later be my official residence as deputy president. During the evening it was a family occasion – the De Klerks and Coetzers from my side and the Willemses and Heyns's from my wife's side. We entertained them at Libertas, the stately fifty-year-old official residence of former prime ministers and later President Botha.

Libertas had been designed in the Cape Georgian style with a flat roof, white-washed walls and large wooden sash windows. It was built at the top of the same ridge as the Union Buildings, a couple of kilometres further to the east. Its reception rooms commanded a beautiful view across the northern suburbs of Pretoria toward the ramparts of the Magaliesberg mountains. Its cool interior was decorated with paintings by some of South Africa's foremost artists. It was full of reminders of Afrikaner history. In the dining room there was a large tapestry of the Great Trek and in the entrance hall there was a bronze statuette of a Boer soldier. It was the residence that my uncle, Hans Strijdom, had occupied when he had been prime minister, and which I had visited as a teenager. It would be our northern home for the next five years.

When I was elected as leader of the National Party on 2 February 1989 I was determined to introduce a new spirit into the South African political scene. In my very first public speech, shortly after my election, I said that our goal was a new South Africa: a totally changed South Africa which would rid itself of the antagonisms of the past and would be free from domination and suppression, in whatever form. Our goal was a South Africa in which all reasonable people would unite behind mutually acceptable goals and against radicalism, regardless of its origin.

The National Party used the essence of this message as our

platform for our 1989 election campaign and as the basis on which we had asked the electorate to give us a mandate for fundamental reform. As state president I had now received the mandate for which I had asked. In my inauguration speech, I made a commitment to all South Africans that the promises that the National Party had made during the election campaign would provide the basis for my period of office. I said that the mandate of 6 September had placed us irrevocably on the road to a new South Africa. I added that there was only one way to peace and justice for all: it was the way of reconciliation; of searching together for mutually acceptable solutions; of talking together about what the new South Africa must look like; and of constitutional negotiations which would lead to lasting understandings. It would also require a balanced economic plan to ensure growth and to break the back of inflation. It would require us all to accept the need for sacrifices and adjustments. I committed myself to searching for peace and justice and invited all South Africans to join me in this search. My government's specific goals would include the elimination of mistrust; the initiation of negotiations to develop a new constitutional dispensation; economic growth and prosperity; and a firm stand against unrest, terrorism and violence.

My inaugural speech was well received – not only by those present, but also by the media. Now I was state president in my own right: no longer acting as a result of a crisis in the National Party, but duly elected in terms of the constitution of that time. I was deeply aware of the responsibility that went with the position. I had no illusions about the enormity of the task that awaited me and my team, but I was full of the confidence that accompanies the conviction that one is on the right road.

*

I had already announced my new cabinet two days before my inauguration on 20 September 1989. There were some novel aspects in the composition of the cabinet; firstly, Rina Venter was appointed as minister of health and population development. She was the first woman ever to serve in a South African cabinet; secondly, I appointed Dr Wim de Villiers, one of the most respected industrialists in South Africa, as the minister of administration and privatization. I would later bring Mr Derek Keys and Mr Louis Shill into the cabinet from the private sector to make up for the lack of expertise which existed within the National Party in the area of the economy and finance and to utilize the knowledge and experience of truly top managers available in government.

During the following months until the December holidays, I also began to dismantle the powerful structures that the securocrats had developed under P. W. Botha.

I was determined to normalize the role of the security forces. I knew that they would have to play the key role in maintaining the framework of stability that would be essential for our constitutional initiatives. In the new political environment which we were about to enter, they would have to maintain an impartial stance towards the political role of the ANC and other revolutionary organizations. I realized how difficult it would be for them to change their attitudes, virtually overnight, to organizations that they had over decades come to regard, in all respects, as their mortal enemies. But I knew that it had to be done. I believed that I could count on the support of the top echelons of the officer corps, but I was aware that many security force members – particularly in the part-time forces – supported the Conservative Party.

Soon after my inauguration I gave instructions for the investigation of all secret covert operations of the security forces with a view to determining whether their continuation could be justified in the light of my commitment to reform, transparency and cabinet rule. By March 1990, we had succeeded in phasing out a number of such operations and had substantially reduced funding on secret projects. At that stage I was under the impression that I had taken adequate steps to establish proper control over secret projects. Years later I would discover just how much was still being hidden from me.

On 28 November 1989, I announced that the National Security Management System – which had played a central role in counteracting the revolutionary threat of the mid eighties – would be dismantled and replaced by more conventional and civilian-oriented coordinating mechanisms. This was important, not only for the normalization of the role of the security forces, but also for the re-establishment of the authority of the non-security departments after years of securocrat intervention in their activities.

On 10 January 1990, I addressed some 800 senior police officers at the South African Police College and told them that it was their duty to be absolutely impartial; that they would no longer be required to promote or oppose any particular political cause; that they should refrain from any political involvement; and that they should restrict their activities to combating crime and protecting the lives and property of all South Africans. On 2 March 1990, I repeated the same exercise with senior officers of the South African Defence Force at Voortrekkerhoogte, the main SADF base outside Pretoria. On both occasions the atmosphere was slightly tense. I could sense that a substantial percentage of the officers present were sceptical or apprehensive.

Soon after my speech to the senior police officers – which I had told them was confidential – a verbatim text of what I had said appeared in the press. It was clear that one of the police officers had made a recording of my speech and had leaked it to the newspapers. Because it was a blatant breach of the confidentiality that I had requested I was annoyed, but the leak did serve a very useful purpose. It provided proof that I was saying the same things in confidential meetings that I was saying in public. It consequently helped to confirm the credibility of my commitment to making the political playing fields even. The leak was one of the first symptoms of the dissatisfaction of a part of the security forces with the reforms and the approach that I had adopted. This was a factor which I would have to watch very carefully throughout the whole transformation. It was essential for me to retain the support of the broad leadership of the security forces.

The disaffection of some elements of the security forces was not based only on their opposition to my reform policies. They also opposed my moves to put an end to the special influence in decision-making that my predecessor had given to the South African Defence Force, in particular. There was, undoubtedly, resistance to my initiatives in this area. Nevertheless, I was determined to press ahead with them.

By the end of 1989 I had re-established the principle of cabinet rule. In my team there was no place for inner circles and no by-passing the cabinet. All important decisions were taken by the cabinet, which was given full access to all the facts that could influence its decisions. We established a new style of fully participatory decision-making in which ministers were free to speak their minds on any topic under discussion. At the same time, I greatly reduced the size of the State President's Office from more than 500 people at its peak to fewer than 90 people – including domestic staff – later in my presidency. I did not think that it was necessary to keep parallel teams of expert advisers within my office. My ministers and their teams would be my primary advisers. I also quietly phased out the state president's guard and adopted a generally lower profile for the ceremonial functions of the office.

During the same period, the cabinet began to work methodically, but with a sense of urgency, on our broad reform strategy. Apart from our normal governmental activities, such as the preparation of the budget and legislation, there was also special focus on a number of general aspects of government which required attention. These included our need to improve our international relations; to rationalize state administration and to promote economic growth.

I realized at the outset of my presidency that one of the greatest challenges that we would face during the coming years would be to improve the parlous state of our economy. We had to wrestle with the aftermath of isolation and the political uncertainties that had been unleashed by the process of transformation. Our isolation had caused major distortions in our economy. For example, we were committed to the completion of the Mossgas project, an uneconomic twelve billion rand strategic investment to reduce our dependence on foreign oil imports by producing petroleum from a small gas field that we had developed off the southern coast of the Cape Province. We still had to contend with capital outflows caused by the repayment of US $1 billion per annum on our outstanding loans. Our industries had grown sluggish after years of protection from foreign competition. To add to our woes, our opponents frequently used the economy as a political battleground by trying to delay the lifting of sanctions and by launching politically motivated strikes and stay-aways.

We needed rapid economic growth, above all, to enable us to address one of our central problems, the widespread poverty of millions of black South Africans, particularly in the rural areas. We realized that, whatever constitutional system we might ultimately negotiate, the long-term stability of South Africa would depend on our ability to bring tangible improvements to the day to day lives of all our people and to work towards closing the gap between rich and poor in the country.

Although apartheid was undoubtedly responsible for many of the distortions in the economy and in wealth distribution, it was certainly not the only, or even the major, cause of poverty. The fact is that we had to grapple with many of the same developmental problems – such as high population growth rates and lack of urbanization – that were at the root of poverty throughout the lower and middle income group of countries. The irony is that between 1960 and 1994 – under National Party rule – there was a fairly substantial redistribution of income in favour of black South Africans. During this period, the black share of per capita income increased from less than 20 per cent in 1960 to almost 40 per cent in 1994, while that of whites declined from 72.5 per cent to under 50 per cent (coloureds and Asians accounted for the remainder). According to a study of the South African economy that was undertaken by the International Monetary Fund in 1992, the trend toward more equal distribution of income was slowed down during the eighties by the reduction in economic growth which accompanied international financial sanctions and increased domestic uncertainty.

Contrary to the general perception, the average income of whites declined in real terms from the early seventies, while that of blacks – particularly urbanized and unionized blacks – increased. At the same time, there was a substantial transfer of wealth from whites to blacks through social programmes for black South Africans that were funded overwhelmingly by white tax payers. In 1975 whites paid 77 per cent of taxes and received 56 per cent of the social benefits provided by the government. By 1987 their share of taxes had declined marginally to 72 per cent, but their share of social benefits had fallen to (a still disproportionate) 35 per cent. The IMF found that at 32 per cent of its 'income, the tax burden of the white sector of South Africa is very high by the standards of other middle income countries and at least comparable to that prevailing, on average, in the industrial countries'. It also found that the comparative tax burden of whites (the difference between their tax contribution and the social benefits that they received) was exceptionally high – accounting for 23 per cent of their incomes. The main conclusion that the IMF study drew from all of this was that 'poverty in South Africa is so severe that redistribution policies, which alone will not be able to counter it, must be supported by policies designed to place the economy on a higher growth path. Only then could the economy be expected to generate the resources necessary to satisfy the needs of the least privileged sectors of society on a sustained basis.' I wholeheartedly agreed.

We also had to break out of our international isolation, and in particular improve our relations with our immediate neighbours in southern Africa and in the continent as a whole. For decades we had lived in a state of quasi-hostility with the so-called frontline states, which had consistently given the ANC moral and material support. I realized that this would have to change if we wished South Africa to play its proper role in our region and throughout Africa.

It was for this reason that my first visits as state president were to countries in Africa. On 2 December 1989 I visited President Felix Houphouet-Boigny of the Ivory Coast. He was a true gentleman and one of the few African leaders who had consistently supported dialogue with South Africa during the years of our international isolation. He was also renowned as one of the elder statesmen of Africa and as a leader who had brought peace and a measure of prosperity to his people. He met me at Yamoussoukro airport and received me with a guard of honour and a troupe of Ivorian traditional dancers. We stood together at the back of his open car and drove past enormous crowds of cheering and dancing people. On more than one occasion I had to hold up the eighty-four-year-old president to prevent him from falling over. Despite his age we had a very fruitful meeting during which he once again assured me that the rest of Africa regarded the whites of South Africa as fellow Africans and urged me to work for a solution to our problems which would enable South Africa to resume its proper place in the continent.

On 15 December I visited President Joachim Chissano in Maputo, the capital of Mozambique – which is less than 500 kilometres to the east of Pretoria. He was trying to lead the recovery of his country from the parlous circumstances in which it found itself – including its unhappy distinction of being one of the poorest countries in the world. Our meeting convinced me that he also dearly wished to establish full relations with South Africa and was hoping that I would initiate the constitutional reforms in South Africa which would make this possible.

My warm and spontaneous receptions in the Ivory Coast and Mozambique confirmed my view that the key to the re-establishment of our relations with our neighbours in Africa was the development of our own constitutional relationship with black South Africans. It was yet another reason to embark upon the course of dramatic transformation that we had already begun to plan.

*

Two days before my meeting with Chissano I had had my first meeting with Nelson Mandela – the man with whom I was destined to work for the following four years to make the transformation of South Africa a reality. Under the cover of darkness on the evening of 13 December 1989, he was smuggled into the basement garage of Tuynhuys. He was ushered into my office where I was accompanied by Ministers Gerrit Viljoen and Kobie Coetsee, General Willemse, the commissioner of prisons, Dr Niel Barnard, the head of the National Intelligence Service and his deputy, Mike Louw. After the usual greetings and pleasantries, the others withdrew and left Mr Mandela and me to hold private talks.

'So this', I thought to myself, 'is Nelson Mandela.' This was the man who, during his twenty-seven years of imprisonment, had become a global icon of the struggle against apartheid. Like a grain of sand trapped in an oyster, Mandela had been a continuous and growing source of irritation to previous governments. Over the years layer after layer of myth – created by our own fears and the adulation of his supporters – had accreted around him. Now, after twenty-seven years, he and the political realities that he represented had emerged into the full glare of global and national attention. Part of the process that had created the myth was that, because of our security laws, hardly a photograph had been published of him since his imprisonment. Newspapers and magazines had had to employ artists to construct images of his probable appearance. Now Nelson Mandela, the man, stood before me.

He was taller than I had anticipated, slightly stooped by his seventy-one years. The first impressions that he conveyed were of dignity, courtesy and self-confidence. He also had the ability to radiate unusual warmth and charm – when he so chose. He was every inch a Tembu patriarch and bore the mantle of authority with the ease of those who are not troubled by self-doubt. His heritage, his training as a future adviser to the paramount chief of the Tembu, his volatile political career, the hard lessons of self-control and fortitude that he had learned in prison had all prepared him for this moment of history. As – no doubt – my own political heritage, my family, my political training, my climb to the leadership of the National Party had prepared me.

During most of the meeting, each of us cautiously sized up the other. Mandela raised the issue of the National Party's commitment to group rights and said that he thought that this was a mistake and that it looked as though we were trying to reintroduce apartheid by the back door. I reminded him that in March the year before he had sent President Botha a memorandum in which he had said that two broad issues would have to be addressed during negotiations: the ANC's demand for majority rule in a unitary state and the insistence of whites on structural guarantees that majority rule would not mean domination of the white minority by blacks. I told him that our support for group rights was simply a mechanism to provide such guarantees. I allowed him to do most of the talking and took his measure while he spoke. I think that we both reached more or less the same conclusions: that it would be possible for us to do business with each other. We parted on a friendly note and with the assurance that we would meet again fairly soon for another meeting – and next time we would also discuss his release.

15

2 February 1990

I began to lay the foundation for the announcements that I would make on 2 February 1990 even before I became president. On 12 September 1989, just a few days before my inauguration, I announced a new policy to permit protest marches which had until then been forbidden under the State of Emergency regulations. Some of my security advisers were strongly opposed to the decision. At that time they were haunted by the spectre of the mass demonstrations that were taking place in Eastern Europe and had led to the overthrow of Communist governments in country after country. There were, however, a number of factors which to my mind necessitated a change of policy: Archbishop Desmond Tutu – the Nobel Peace Prize winner and Anglican archbishop of Cape Town – had announced his intention of leading a protest march through the streets of Cape Town, which would include businessmen from multinational companies and the white mayor of Cape Town. We had also received messages from foreign governments – including one from the British ambassador, Sir Robin Renwick – that they would appreciate it if the march could be permitted. We were faced with the fact that it would be impossible to avoid the gathering of thousands of people committed to the march. The choice, therefore, was between breaking up an illegal march with all of the attendant risks of violence and negative publicity, or of allowing the march to continue, subject to conditions that could help to avoid violence and ensure good order. These were important considerations, but none of them was conclusive. The most important factor, which tipped the scale, was my strong conviction that the prohibition of peaceful protests and demonstrations could not continue. Such an approach would be irreconcilable with the democratic transformation process that I was determined to launch and the principles of a state based on the rule of law, which I wanted to establish.

The decision to allow the march was a seminal moment and sent a strong message to all concerned regarding our intentions. Archbishop

Tutu – who disappointingly refused my invitation to discuss the march beforehand – now claims that it was the march which precipitated the whole transformation process and that we simply bowed to the pressure that had been brought to bear on us. That is simply not true. We decided to allow protest marches and rallies because they were essential for the democratization process that we envisaged. We were greatly helped by the efforts of the Revd Johan Heyns, the moderator of the Dutch Reformed Church who played a useful role in persuading all the parties involved to act in a responsible manner. We permitted the march on condition that the organizers agreed to follow set routes and to co-operate with the police to ensure that the demonstrations were peaceful and orderly. In announcing our decision I said that in the light of the government's clear commitment to negotiate change, it was not necessary for any person to give vent to his political aspirations through disorderly protest and rioting. I appealed to those involved rather to encourage their leaders to come to the negotiation table. I said that the door to a new South Africa was open – it was not necessary to batter it down.

This change of policy was widely welcomed. We were given recognition for restoring what was regarded throughout the world as a basic democratic right.

During those first few months we also continued the systematic release of high profile prisoners that had tentatively begun the previous year with the release of Govan Mbeki. It was crucially important to set orderly precedents to prepare the way for the inevitable release of Nelson Mandela himself. On 10 October 1989 we announced the release of the last prisoners, apart from Mandela, who had been convicted during the Rivonia trial in 1964, including the legendary ANC leader, Walter Sisulu. In making the announcement I said that such releases were intended to promote peaceful solutions to the problems of the country and added that Mr Nelson Mandela had been fully apprised of our proposed action. Discussions had been held with him and he had confirmed yet again that his own release was not then on the agenda. The releases clearly signalled that important policy changes regarding the government's attitude to the ANC were imminent.

The first few months of my presidency coincided with the disintegration of Communism in Eastern Europe which reached its historic climax with the fall of the Berlin Wall in November 1989. Within the scope of a few months, one of our main strategic concerns for decades

– the Soviet Union's role in southern Africa and its strong influence on the ANC and the SACP – had all but disappeared. A window had suddenly opened which created an opportunity for a much more adventurous approach than had previously been conceivable.

The cabinet needed to take stock of this situation. Although we had started to create a climate for negotiations, our actions were still piecemeal. We needed a comprehensive negotiation strategy. I initiated a process of deep analysis which culminated in a *bosberaad* (a bush conference) between 3 and 5 December. In the course of the following months and years we frequently went off to some isolated area to plan our strategy and to consider our next moves.

The December *bosberaad*, like many others that were to follow, was held at the D'Nyala game reserve in the north-western Transvaal, quite close to the Botswana border. D'Nyala included a secluded camp set in the flat, sandy bushveld. All around the camp, the bush stretched away for scores of kilometres into the shimmering blue haze of the summer heat. Within the camp there were a number of comfortable double-storey thatched cottages interspersed between the trees. The focal point was a *boma*, a large circular area where guests came together to drink their sundowners and enjoy a *braaivleis* (barbecue) together. Beside the *boma* was a well-equipped conference centre and office area. It was an ideal setting for discussion, analysis and brain-storming. We began by asking ourselves how we could promote negotiations for a new constitutional dispensation. We agreed on the importance of seizing the initiative and of occupying the moral high ground. We tossed proposals around and weighed the implications of each option. We also considered the enormous risks involved in reform and discussed fall-back positions should things go wrong. As chairman, I concentrated on focusing discussion on the principles of the policy for which we had now received a mandate. The final test would be whether our strategies and actions could establish a new dispensation which would ensure justice for all South Africans within the frame-work of universally accepted democratic values.

From all of this, we began to develop a clearer picture of how we wanted to make concrete our core vision of a united South Africa where everybody would have equal rights and opportunities and within which our many minorities would not be threatened or suppressed. It was hard work – but we also had some fun. The informal drinks and dinners in the *boma* were often interrupted by our chief prankster, Magnus Malan, and the theatrical Pik Botha. Roelf Meyer had us in stitches with impromptu performances involving preposterous mimicry, in the course of which ministers were dragged up from the audience to perform as well.

At the end of our December *bosberaad* the whole cabinet (even its most conservative members) were ready for the quantum leap I had promised them when I became leader in February 1989. They accepted the full logical consequences of power-sharing – provided there would be reasonable protection for minority rights – and agreed that the ANC would have to be part of the process. This would require a strategy to bring the ANC to the negotiating table. We reached consensus on the need for an approach that would surprise our opponents and give us the early initiative. We would have to ensure that we would, throughout, stay in control of the process, and maintain good government and law and order.

On this note we all went on holiday. It had been an exhausting year and I was really tired. I had a holiday home in the coastal resort of Hermanus, about 120 kilometres east of Cape Town. It is set on a rocky bay, between the ocean and a range of mountains, covered in proteas and fynbos, the heather-like natural vegetation of the Cape. Despite the limitations that were now placed on my movements by the security requirements of the presidency, I loved the few opportunities that I had to break away to the coast. It was wonderful to be able to relax with my family and friends; to get in as many rounds of golf as possible; to soak in our Jacuzzi; to go for long walks on the beach; and to put my barbecuing skills to the test.

But there was to be less rest for me during that holiday than usual. I now had the responsibility of giving practical effect to our strategic framework for constitutional transformation. I spent much of my three weeks' holiday deep in thought and reflection. Throughout my life I have found that, when I have been faced with major decisions, it has been necessary to allow myself sufficient time to think. It has often happened that after days of thought and juggling loose ideas, I suddenly wake up one morning with a clear idea of what I must do – almost as though my subconscious has all the while been sorting out my ideas and arranging them into a logical whole.

This was the case with my speech of 2 February 1990. The key decision that I had to take for myself was to make a paradigm shift. My natural instinct was to adopt a step-by-step approach, and I had to overcome that. I did so because I realized that we would have little chance of success in the coming negotiations if we did not grasp the initiative right at the beginning and convince the important players that we were not negotiating under pressure, but from the strength of our convictions. We had to convince them that our acceptance of a unified South Africa with universal franchise was not simply a negotiating ploy and that we were not trying to cling to elements of apartheid under a different guise. Only if we could succeed in so doing would we be able to launch an orderly step-by-step process of meaningful negotiation.

It was with this certainty that, together with a few key ministers, I began to put together the package that I announced on 2 February 1990. It was a powerful package that went far further than even the most optimistic expectations in both *verligte* and anti-government circles. Apart from the release of Nelson Mandela it also included the unbanning of the ANC, the SACP, the PAC and a number of lesser organizations; the release of a further category of ANC prisoners and the lifting of the State of Emergency regulations affecting the media and education.

We decided that the Separate Amenities Act would have to be repealed and that there would have to be a moratorium on the death penalty. I intended to underline our commitment to establishing an internationally acceptable culture of human rights by instructing the South African Law Commission to produce a report on a charter of human rights with a view to a future constitution.

This package was presented to the cabinet in its entirety on 31 January 1990, only two days before I was due to deliver the speech. Secrecy was now the key to success. Cabinet ministers promised not to tell even their wives. I did the same – not because I did not trust Marike, but to honour the firm agreement that we had reached in cabinet.

These decisions set the framework for my speech of 2 February. It was now up to me to package them. I cut myself off and started to write. I passed my first draft formulations on particular matters to the responsible ministers to obtain their comments and suggestions. When I had received these, I completed the first full draft during the morning of 1 February. I called together a few key ministers and worked through the speech with them. With the benefit of our discussion and their contributions I returned to my desk. I began the speech from the start again. I weighed every word, and where necessary, reformulated and added passages. And as I completed each page my secretary Pets van Niekerk typed it and gave it to Chris Renken (an adviser in my office who had previously been a journalist and a member of Parliament) for translation into English.

At about 6 p.m. on the evening of 1 February I was more or less satisfied. I rushed back home because I had to propose the toast at the sixtieth birthday of a very close family friend, Dr Fana Malherbe. Back at my office the work continued at a frenetic pace. The speech had to be finally prepared in Afrikaans and English, then checked and reproduced for distribution to the media a few hours later. This process took place in the office of my director-general, Dr Jannie Roux. On a mantelpiece in his office there were small brass busts of South Africa's first six prime ministers. While he, Casper Venter, my press secretary, and one or two others worked through the speech, they politely turned the faces of the busts to the wall. They were pretty sure that Hendrik Verwoerd, in particular, was turning in his grave. I returned to the office late that evening to check the final copies for myself and – even at that late stage – to make a few changes. It was nearly midnight when, tired but satisfied, I climbed into my car and returned to Groote Schuur to grab a few hours' sleep before the opening of Parliament the next day. My faithful office staff worked right through the night to have everything ready for the closed press briefing at 6 a.m. and the opening ceremony the following morning.

We had prepared a comprehensive media strategy to ensure that the speech received maximum favourable publicity. We avoided some of the fatal errors that President Botha had made with the planning and delivery of the Rubicon speech. In particular, we had been very careful not to raise expectations higher than they already were, and to try to ensure that the speech was not leaked before delivery. We succeeded in achieving a complete surprise.

The scene was set for a massive marketing exercise. An unprecedented number of foreign and local journalists and TV crews had descended on Cape Town at the end of January. After the release of Walter Sisulu and the other high profile ANC leaders in October 1989, Nelson Mandela's release from prison had become the biggest news story in the world. Ted Koppel had decided to broadcast his *ABC Nightline* programme from South Africa for a whole week. Leading foreign correspondents and the news anchormen of several of the European and American TV networks were in town. There was white-hot anticipation that I would announce Mandela's release during my speech at the opening of Parliament and that he would probably walk out of prison a few hours later. The day before the opening of Parliament we had to douse wild and inaccurate rumours that I had met Mr Mandela that morning at Tuynhuys. In short, the eyes of the world were more intensely focused on South Africa on 2 February 1989 than at any time before in our history.

The contents of the speech were first broken to the media at a special briefing at 6 a.m. on 2 February by Gerrit Viljoen, the minister of constitutional development, Kobie Coetsee, the minister of justice, and Stoffel van der Merwe, the minister of information. We wanted to make sure that journalists would have a good opportunity to study the speech and to be authoritatively briefed on its implications before they rushed off to file their first copy. The journalists, who had been locked in a special briefing room at Tuynhuys until after I had delivered the speech, were thunderstruck. Allister Sparks, a veteran critic of the National Party government, gasped to David Ottaway of the *Washington Post*: 'My God, he's done it all!'

We had succeeded in catching the media, the political opposition and the world completely by surprise. Although most observers had anticipated that I would announce the release of Nelson Mandela, no one had dreamed that I would do so much – that with one stroke I would remove all the reasonable obstacles to genuine constitutional negotiations.

I awoke on the morning of 2 February with a sense of destiny. I knew that my speech would usher in a new era. I felt like an athlete in the starting blocks waiting for the crack of the starter's pistol. I was also tense. Despite our careful planning I still could not be sure of the success of our initiative. The test would be the reaction of the media, the leaders whom we wanted to involve in negotiations, the international community and the public.

I still had not yet fully informed my wife about what I was going to say. We left Groote Schuur with an escort of motorcycles and arrived at Parliament a few minutes later. On the stairs outside the main entrance Marike and I received the national salute from the guard of honour. While we were standing there I said to Marike, 'After today South Africa will never again be the same.' There was a sense of excitement in the great hall of Parliament, where members from the three chambers had gathered to attend the opening of Parliament. The public gallery was packed and the proceedings were televised throughout the country. Hundreds of thousands – perhaps millions – of South

Africans were watching the opening of Parliament on TV after their interest had been stimulated by the intense media speculation of the preceding days.

According to tradition, the Speaker, Mr Louis le Grange, opened the session with a prayer. My speech was ready for me on the podium. We had made sure that half would be in English and half in Afrikaans – but I decided to deliver the announcements which I knew would have the greatest local and foreign impact in English. I strode to the podium, put on my spectacles and began to speak – perhaps more slowly and more deliberately than usual because I was deeply conscious of the importance of the moment.

The most important announcements in the speech were included in the last few pages. When I made them, there was clear support and excitement from the ranks of the National Party, the Democratic Party and the members of the coloured and Indian chambers. The only dissenting interjections came from the horrified ranks of the Conservative Party.

I cannot pass a judgement of my own on how I delivered the speech. All I know is that I experienced a sense of great calmness and certainty. I believed that I was doing the right thing at the right time.

When we left the chamber and my wife joined me once again I asked her: 'Can you live with all that?' She was beaming and replied, 'Naturally, your arguments and explanations were so logical and fitted so well with one another that nobody would even be able to force the tip of a knife point between them.'

The reaction everywhere else was even better than I had hoped for. The surprise element that we had built into our strategy had worked. We had achieved our objective of convincing our friends and foes alike that the National Party had made a paradigm shift. On that day and the days that followed, the media trumpeted their overwhelmingly positive reaction. Newspaper headlines told the whole story:

'South Africa and the World Rejoice'; 'South Africa breaks through political sound barrier'; 'A new dimension of hope'; 'No more reason for violence'; 'Politics open to all'; 'New steps may open doors'; 'New era for South Africa: Tributes pour in from around the world'; 'World welcomes F.W.'s major step forward'; 'Bush wants to review sanctions'; 'Pope may visit'.

Foreign reaction was equally positive. Apart from the overwhelmingly favourable media coverage, I also received messages of congratulation and encouragement from a number of world leaders including President George Bush, Prime Minister Margaret Thatcher, President François Mitterrand, President Mario Soares, President Kenneth Kaunda, Dr Xavier Perez de Cuellar, the secretary-general of the United Nations and many other leaders.

The only negative reaction was from the Conservative Party. The headlines in its newspaper, *Die Patriot*, was 'Talks with ANC are treason', and 'F.W. and company are naïve about Communists says Dr Treurnicht'. An irate Dr Treurnicht immediately called for a new election.

The one matter that aroused the greatest expectations, and that I had deliberately played down in my speech, was the release of Nelson Mandela. I had no illusions why the world media had focused their attention on Cape Town: they had not done so to hear me speak but to witness the release of Nelson Mandela. For us it was crucially important that the fundamental decisions that we had taken should be judged on their own and not be overshadowed by an announcement on Mandela's release. I linked my reference to his release to our commitment to negotiations and to our negotiation goals. I said that Mr Nelson Mandela could play an important part in negotiations, and that we had taken note that he had declared himself to be willing to make a constructive contribution to the peaceful political process in South Africa and that we wanted to bring this matter to finality without delay. I announced that the government would soon take a decision on the date of his release.

The timing of Mandela's release was of crucial importance from a communication point of view. For example, had we announced beforehand that the release would take place on 11 February, most of the international media would have jetted into South Africa on the 9th or 10th and my own speech would have been given only a fraction of the coverage that it had in fact received. What this meant was that for a whole week we were able to keep the media ball in our court. The international media was camped on our doorstep and, for the moment, we were the only show in town. We used our opportunity well. Each year after the opening of Parliament, the government had traditionally provided a week of briefings to the media on its programme for the coming session. On this occasion we were able to make specially good use of the briefing week, as cabinet minister after cabinet minister reinforced and expanded upon the message that I had communicated in my opening speech. My concern was not simply to generate positive publicity, but to get the point across that things really were changing in South Africa – that we were actually involved in a paradigm shift.

The week reached its climax on Saturday afternoon, when I called an international press conference to announce Mr Mandela's release. Even then, we might have wasted this unprecedented communication opportunity. Until late that morning some of my key advisers had been urging me to play down the communication of Mandela's release. They wanted me to make the announcement by way of a simple press statement – because they felt that we should not draw unnecessary attention to our action. Fortunately, the wiser council of my own communication team prevailed. In the event, my press conference was carried by TV networks around the world and was seen by hundreds of millions of people. (One of the more notable exceptions was SABC TV which decided to cover the end of a local cricket match rather than take a live feed from the press conference.) I was able to reinforce the central messages of my speech at the opening of Parliament. Within the scope of eight days, we had succeeded in dramatically changing global perceptions of South Africa.

I deliberately postponed my second meeting with Nelson Mandela until after I had delivered my speech of 2 February 1990. On the evening of 9 February he was once again brought to a meeting with me at Tuynhuys. We had prepared our plans for his release, but I knew that it would be necessary to consult him about the logistical details. We wanted to release him, at short notice, two days later in Johannesburg. We were worried about the risk of an uncontrollable gathering to greet him after his release and felt that we could avoid this if we kept the time and place secret until just before it was due to take place. His reaction to these arrangements was clearly negative. To my surprise, he wanted his release to be delayed for at least a week so that he, his family and his organization could make the necessary preparations. He also told me that he wanted to be released in the Cape – as he put it, he wanted to be able to walk through the gates of the Victor Verster prison as a free man. After some quick consultations with my colleagues we agreed to a compromise: he could be released from Victor Verster, but it was impossible for us to change the date of his release. He was initially adamant about postponing his release for at least a week. In the end he reluctantly accepted the compromise.

During our meeting we discussed two other issues: the ending of the State of Emergency and the position of people who were serving sentences for politically motivated crimes as well as others who had also committed such crimes but who were then overseas.

I stressed the importance of creating conditions that would make it possible for me to lift the State of Emergency without jeopardizing the maintenance of law and order. I said that although the position of those who had committed politically motivated crimes should be dealt with in negotiations, exploratory talks could in the meantime begin. Just before we parted, one of our photographers took the first pictures of Mandela – standing beside me – that had been taken for decades. Through some administrative glitch they were not released to the media until the following night. The late arrival of these first photographs of Mandela created a major crisis in our Sunday newspapers, which had already put their last editions to bed. One of them quickly brought out a special edition which had these first images of the new South Africa splashed across its front page.

During these first two meetings, Mandela and I established a reasonable rapport with one another. We accepted one another's integrity – but in the full knowledge that we were opponents with divergent goals. We realized that we both bore the ultimate responsibility for ensuring that there would be a negotiated settlement and we were both committed to carrying out this responsibility. This tacit understanding would carry us through the first years of tentative negotiations, through the agreements that we reached at Groote Schuur and Pretoria and finally to the first multiparty negotiations at Codesa (the Convention for a Democratic South Africa) in December 1991.

*

The whole world watched and waited on Sunday 11 February as Nelson Mandela, after twenty-seven years in prison, took his first steps as a free man. Much later that day, at the Grand Parade in Cape Town, the disorder that we had feared occurred. Tens of thousands of people had gathered in front of Cape Town's Victorian City Hall to hear Mandela speak. After hours of delay the crowd became restless and there was some looting and violence. Finally Mandela appeared at the front entrance of the City Hall and addressed the masses. His message, which had evidently been drafted by hardline ideologues within the ANC alliance, brought us little comfort or reason to share in the general rejoicing. For once, Mandela failed completely to rise to the occasion. Instead of calling for peace and reconciliation, he recommitted the ANC to the armed struggle – saying that 'the factors which necessitated the armed struggle still exist today. We have no option but to continue.' Instead of allaying widespread fears regarding the ANC's links with international Communism, he stressed his solidarity with the South African Communist Party and singled out its secretary-general, Joe Slovo, for special recognition. Instead of calling for a common effort to rebuild the economy and create a better life for all, he called on 'the international community to continue the campaign to isolate the apartheid regime. To lift sanctions now would be to run the risk of aborting the process towards the complete eradication of apartheid.'

I realized once again that the road ahead would be extremely difficult. As Marike and I watched Mandela on TV, walking hand-in-hand with his wife Winnie through the gates of the Victor Verster prison, I was struck by an inescapable truth: an irreversible process had begun – and nobody could predict precisely how it would end.

My speech of 2 February 1990 had opened the way for South Africa to remove one of the main causes for our long confrontation with the international community – the whole question of apartheid. Our other major dispute with the international community, over the decades, had centred on our continued rule of the mandated territory of South West Africa/Namibia. It was also about to be finally resolved with the independence of the territory on 21 March 1990.

In 1978, after years of international litigation, South Africa and the Western powers then on the Security Council agreed to a process for the independence of the territory. However, it was only towards the end of the 1980s – after Cuban forces had withdrawn from the neighbouring territory of Angola – that the independence plan was finally implemented. The internationally supervised elections were held in the second week of November 1989, soon after I became president. On 13 November, when the results were announced, I immediately issued a statement in which I congratulated SWAPO (the South West African People's Organization) on their victory and pledged our willingness to co-operate with the future independent Namibia.

On 20 March 1990, I flew to Windhoek, the capital of Namibia, to participate in the independence celebrations. When I arrived at Windhoek Airport I was astounded to see the number, variety and size of the presidential aircraft on the apron. I was happy to note that our Falcon 50 aircraft was one of the smallest there. That night the outgoing South African administrator-general, Louis Pienaar, hosted an international banquet for the guests to the independence celebrations at his official residence. One of the main guests of honour was to have been Sam Nujoma, the leader of SWAPO, who was about to be inaugurated as the first president of Namibia. However, he arrived after the dinner had been served and only a few minutes before the guests were due to depart to the main stadium for the independence celebrations. Nujoma's escort to the stadium was completely disorganized, so I offered him assistance from my own entourage's traffic escort, which we had brought with us from South Africa, to ensure that he would reach the stadium in time. The result was that we ourselves became hopelessly stuck in the traffic. Surrounded by security men, we had to climb out of our cars and force our way on foot through the friendly crowds for the last kilometre to the stadium.

The situation at the stadium was quite chaotic. Fortunately, Marike and I were able to find our way to our seats on the special stand beside those of the president and Mrs Nujoma. However, Pik Botha, who had dedicated much of his life to the solution of the South West Africa/Namibia problem, had to sit on the stairs of the main pavilion. While we were waiting in our seats for the ceremony to begin, Yasser Arafat suddenly embraced me from behind and kissed me on my cheek. An alert photographer captured the moment on film and the following day the photo was splashed over the front pages of several newspapers. I was embarrassed, because he was at that time still a very controversial figure, not only in South Africa but also in countries of the free world which supported Israel.

It was my task to carry out the formal handing over of power to the new Namibian president. My speech was short and in English, because Namibia had decided to make English their official language. This was despite the fact that Afrikaans was the general lingua franca in the country, even more so than it was in South Africa itself. I decided to be a little mischievous and added a few sentences in Afrikaans. The result was one of the loudest rounds of applause of the whole evening. The fact is that a large part of the crowd had not understood a word of any of the speeches in English.

When the South African flag was ceremonially lowered for the last time after seventy-five years of South African rule, and our national anthem was played, I and all the South Africans present were deeply moved. During this period many Afrikaners had made South West Africa their home and the ties between the countries had become extremely strong. South African soldiers had died defending the territory from SWAPO incursions across the northern border. Had it all been worthwhile? My view was that it had been. For more than two decades, we had successfully held the expansion of Soviet influence in our region at bay. We had secured the withdrawal of Cuban forces from neighbouring Angola and had ensured that the rights of all of the parties in the territory had been properly protected in the independence constitution. We also left the territory with one of the best infrastructures in Africa – with extensive and efficiently functioning road, rail and telecommunication systems.

And so it was with a sense of sadness that I presided over the final moments of South African rule in the territory. But I also felt a sense of great relief that one of the major stumbling blocks to our rejoining the international community had now been removed. With a degree of trepidation, and yet of excited anticipation, I thought of what lay ahead for us in South Africa and wondered precisely where all this would end.

The change that my announcements of 2 February and the independence of Namibia had brought about in international reactions to South Africa was immediately evident from the reception that I received from the many heads of state and government who had gathered in Windhoek to participate in the independence celebrations. During my short visit to Windhoek, I managed to hold talks with many of them, including President Hosni Mubarak of Egypt, who was then the chairman of the Organization of African Unity, and the presidents of Angola, Nigeria, Mali, the Cape Verde Islands, as well as President Kaunda of Zambia. I also had the opportunity of holding talks with the secretary-general of the United Nations, Dr Xavier Perez de Cuellar and with the foreign ministers of Germany and the Soviet Union, Dr Hans-Dieter Genscher and Mr Eduard Shevardnadze. All of the leaders with whom I spoke were anxious to learn more about our plans for the transformation of South Africa. They were supportive of our initiative and showed a warmth and understanding that gave me encouragement.

16

Starting to Talk

From the outset of my presidency – and particularly after my announcements of 2 February 1990 – the promotion of constitutional negotiations became the main focus of my administration. I knew from the start that the negotiations would be difficult and that their outcome was unpredictable.

An image that I sometimes used was that of a canoeist who must pass through dangerous rapids to reach his destination. At the end of 1989 the river of history was in full flood. It was sweeping us all along in its course. Those of us who found ourselves in leadership positions had not created the flood. Our task was to understand the river, to appreciate its forces, its currents and its eddies. Our challenge was to navigate a course through the rapids, to avoid the whirlpools, to watch for submerged rocks, to ensure that our craft did not capsize, and to pilot our charges to the safety of broad and tranquil waters.

With my speech of 2 February 1990 and the release of Nelson Mandela on 11 February 1990, there could be no doubt that we had entered the white water. Our immediate task was to try to steer a course towards the channel of negotiations.

The negotiation process could be divided into three distinct phases. The first phase was the tentative negotiations which had already taken place with Nelson Mandela and the ANC behind the scenes before I became president and during the first months of my presidency. The most notable of these was a series of talks in the United Kingdom between senior members of the ANC and leading Afrikaner intellectuals – including my brother Willem. I was kept informed of the meetings – and took note of the impressions of the ANC and its intentions that had been gained during the discussions. However, together with most members of the government I was very wary of such exercises. I felt that when the time came, the government and no one else from our side should determine the timing and direction of the process. We were worried that well-intentioned efforts by businessmen and academics would serve only to muddy the waters and complicate the government's task. We were also in possession of secret SACP documentation which clearly indicated that the ANC/SACP alliance believed that it should use all means (including talks) to advance the process of 'breaking the cohesion and unity of the ruling class' and to 'isolate and weaken its most racist and politically reactionary sector'. They added that this area of the politico-military struggle had already served to 'weaken the cohesion of the enemy and needed to be pursued with even more vigour'.

Far more significant for me and for other members of the government – even though I was not informed of them at the time – were the discussions that had taken place between Nelson Mandela and members of the government (particularly Minister Kobie Coetsee, the minister of justice and of correctional services) since the mid-eighties. The government had first sent out feelers to Mandela during the late seventies and had offered to release him conditionally on a number of occasions. At some time during 1985 Mandela reached the same conclusion that many leaders in the government had also by that time reached – that neither side could win a military victory and that sooner or later there would have to be negotiations. In his book, *Long Walk to Freedom*, Mandela wrote that it was clear to him that a military victory was a distant if not impossible dream: 'It simply did not make sense for both sides to lose thousands if not millions of lives in a conflict that was unnecessary.' He assumed that we must have known this as well and concluded that 'it was time to talk'.

The discussions with Nelson Mandela, in which he participated without initially consulting the ANC leadership in Lusaka, led to a lengthy dialogue with the government. The talks were exploratory and were aimed at finding out whether circumstances could be created which might open the way to negotiations without either the ANC or the government losing face. Ultimately, the initiative led in 1989 to the first meeting between Mr Mandela and President Botha. I did not attend that meeting, but Kobie Coetsee cleared it with me beforehand in my capacity as the leader of the National Party. On 12 September 1989, just a few days before my inauguration, a successful exploratory meeting took place in Switzerland between senior officials of the National Intelligence Service and an ANC delegation led by Thabo Mbeki and Jacob Zuma. It was the first official and direct contact between the South African government and the ANC. The meeting had taken place without my direct knowledge, in terms of a vaguely worded decision of the State Security Council. When National Intelligence reported back to me on the meeting, I was surprised, but not displeased. I made it clear that no such initiatives should again be taken without full and proper authorization.

Parallel with these first exploratory contacts with Nelson Mandela and the ANC, there were also negotiations with the non-revolutionary black, coloured and Indian leaders that had been conducted across a wide front by Dr Viljoen's predecessor, Chris Heunis. Although there was no possibility of these talks leading to comprehensive constitutional solutions, they helped to establish useful relationships with moderate non-white parties and leaders.

The second phase of the process was aimed at preparing the way for structured negotiations. This involved making the political playing field level and the removal of obstacles in the way of structured negotiations. This phase began on 2 February 1990, but ultimately took much longer than I had hoped or anticipated. As matters turned out, we were not able to launch an inclusive negotiating forum until the Convention for a Democratic South Africa (Codesa) was established in December 1991. Codesa would introduce the third phase of structured and representative negotiations, which culminated in December 1993 with the adoption of the transitional constitution.

To assist me with the negotiations, the Department of Constitutional Development had been transformed into a mechanism that could initiate, direct and support constitutional negotiations. I appointed Dr Gerrit Viljoen as the minister of constitutional development and national education. Dr Viljoen, with spectacles, a shock of white hair, a generous moustache and an old grey cardigan, whatever the weather, looked exactly what he was – an eminent university professor. He was then already in the cabinet following a period as the administrator-general of South West Africa/Namibia. Before that he had been the rector of the Rand Afrikaans University. As an academic and a classicist, Dr Viljoen was one of South Africa's stars. He was counted as one of the cleverest of the clever in South Africa and commanded respect from friends and foes alike – if, indeed, he had any foes.

As his deputy minister I appointed Roelf Meyer, who would later succeed him and conduct the negotiations until the adoption of the interim constitution in 1993 and the final constitution in 1996. Roelf Meyer was one of the rising young stars in the National Party. He was lean, youthfully good looking, personable and politically ambitious. The revamped Department of Constitutional Development under Dr Viljoen and Mr Roelf Meyer would not only have the task of stimulating, directing, conducting and supporting negotiations. It would also develop the government's policy into more detailed concepts so that we would be able to put well-considered proposals and fall-back positions on the table when the real negotiations began.

Our broad negotiating team included all the ministers whose portfolios would be primarily involved in the negotiating process. Dr Stoffel van der Merwe – a former diplomat and political scientist – was part of the team because, as minister of education and development aid, he was responsible for black education in the white areas and for relations with the six self-governing black states. Minister Pik Botha, the mercurial minister of foreign affairs, was also a key role-player. Apart from his international role, he was responsible for our relations with the four independent black states – Transkei, Ciskei, Bophuthatswana and Venda. Their independence was recognized only by Pretoria and they would have to be persuaded to accept re-incorporation into South Africa and to join the negotiating process. Minister Hernus Kriel, as the minister in charge of planning and provincial affairs, would also have an important role to play. The three security ministers, Mr Kobie Coetsee, the minister of justice, General Magnus Malan, the minister of defence, and Mr Adriaan Vlok, the minister of law and order (responsible for the South African police), were also an integral part of the negotiation team. They were responsible for matters such as the release of prisoners who had committed crimes with political objectives, the return of exiles, the ending of the State of Emergency and the ANC's suspension of the armed struggle – which were all at the top of the original agenda in our bilateral discussions with the ANC.

By the beginning of 1990, Dr Viljoen could report that a great deal of ground work had already been done. Certain principles, guidelines and negotiating strategies had already been cleared by the *bosberaad* that we had held early in December 1989. We were ready to start work as soon as Nelson Mandela was released. The ANC, however, was not. Our package of 2 February caught them completely off guard and they had to play for time while they rushed to get their negotiation team and strategy into place.

From the outset I was determined that the negotiations should be as inclusive as possible. We could not afford the kind of two-sided approach that the ANC would have preferred – with the 'forces of liberation' ranged on one side of the table under their leadership and the government on the other. There were other important parties and organizations that would have to be drawn into the process because of their interests and their proven support bases. These included the leaders of the six self-governing states (most notably Dr Mangosuthu Buthelezi, the chief minister of KwaZulu), the leaders of the majority parties in the Houses of Assembly (the coloured chamber) and Delegates (the Indian chamber); opposition parties in Parliament; the leaders of the independent states (Transkei, Ciskei, Venda and Bophuthatswana), traditional leaders of the various black peoples and leading figures from all population groups in the sphere of local government. Apart from all this, we also had to keep channels open for dialogue with other important pillars of the community, such as the churches, the private sector and relevant professional organizations.

I had to maintain a difficult and delicate balance between the essentially well-disposed and peaceful parties and organizations which operated within the system, and the militant organizations that operated outside the system – of which the ANC was the most important. Three tendencies very soon became apparent which would have to be dealt with and managed right through the whole negotiating process.

Firstly, smaller parties developed all sorts of techniques to try to exercise more influence on decisions than their numbers really justified. In the process, there were quite a few that pursued a double agenda and sometimes tried to play the ANC off against the government.

Secondly, the government and I tried to form a bloc of parties and organizations that believed in the same principles. The ANC's reaction to this was to accentuate the question of race whenever it suited them, regardless of the principles involved. Enormous pressure was exerted on black leaders, who were in principle strongly anti-ANC, to become part of an anti-government negotiating bloc.

Thirdly, the ANC made use of mass demonstrations and marches and tried to create a climate in which negotiations would continually have to take place under a cloud of threatening unrest and crisis. They also did not hesitate to use intimidation, particularly against black South Africans, to ensure support for their mass action campaigns. Neither did they tolerate any opposition in the areas that they controlled. Although the ANC leadership, from time to time, pretended to disapprove of such methods, a great deal of evidence came to my attention that regular mass demonstrations were an integral part of the ANC's strategy. Time and again, they would use mass action and the threat of riots and public disorder to try to force us and other anti-ANC parties to make concessions during the negotiating process.

Three good examples of these tendencies deserve attention. After long preparation, the government arranged an exploratory meeting for 5 April 1990 with the six chief ministers of the self-governing states and the leaders of the majority parties in the 'tricameral' Parliament. Among other things, we were going to discuss the structuring of the constitutional negotiating process and related matters. Mandela and the ANC were determined to prevent this. Enormous pressure was brought to bear on the leaders whom we had invited and suddenly four of the six chief ministers discovered reasons for not attending the meeting. Mr Allan Hendrickse, the leader of the majority party in the coloured House of Representatives, let the cat out of the bag. He attended the meeting, but informed the conference that he had received a telephone call from Mr Mandela in which he and the Labour Party were asked not to attend the meeting as a gesture of solidarity with the four leaders who had decided to boycott it!

We nevertheless went ahead with the meeting and the leaders who had stayed away from the first meeting later began to join what was to become a conference of political leaders who served in South African government bodies. Together with the April meeting, four such conferences were held during 1990 and succeeded in making useful proposals for the structured negotiating process that would later ensue.

A second example relates to the churches in South Africa. Early in 1990 I decided to involve the churches in an attempt to help to deal with the climate of violence in South Africa. The greatest single threat to the whole process was still the high level of violence that prevailed throughout the country. If we could not succeed in stopping it, we would not be able to end the State of Emergency and achieve success with negotiations. We went to a great deal of trouble to assure the churches that they would not be politicized. Our efforts were aimed at all the churches – including those which during the apartheid years had espoused freedom theology and supported the ANC, and even its armed struggle. In interaction with the ANC, this latter group of churches very quickly let us know that they would have nothing to do with any action or conference that had been initiated by the government. Their unspoken message was that, although they recognized that the churches had a special role in combating violence, the ANC would have to be part of the organization of any such effort. I persevered and eventually an important conference took place on 20 July 1990, which was attended by almost 200 church leaders, church associations and missionary groups, but which did not include the important pro-liberation-movement churches.

In the meantime there were negotiations behind the scenes, in which I was personally involved, with those churches that had not wanted to participate. We agreed that the conference in July would serve as a preliminary and exploratory meeting which would be followed by a fully representative conference of Christian churches.

The third example of the ANC's spoiling tactics relates directly to the bilateral discussions between them and us. The whole country – and indeed, the whole world – were waiting anxiously for the commencement of formal negotiations between the two main role-players: Mandela and me, the ANC and the government. There was really no doubt in anyone's mind about one fact: the government had the power and the authority and the ANC the numbers. A settlement between us was thus essential. If this could not be achieved there would be no peace and a new dispensation could not be established.

There was a great deal of effort behind the scenes during February and the first days of March 1990 to structure such a meeting. We formed a bilateral steering committee and on 16 March I was able to announce that a meeting between the government and the ANC had been scheduled for 11 April 1990. Its purpose would be to discuss the obstacles in the way of negotiations.

On 30 March 1990 Nelson Mandela telephoned me and informed me that the ANC had unilaterally decided to cancel the meeting. The reason that he gave was an incident that had occurred at Sebokeng near Johannesburg four days earlier. Eight black protesters had been killed when the police had opened fire on 50,000 demonstrators, who were protesting against local councils and rents. The demonstrators had not obtained permission for the protest and the police claimed that they had been attacked and had been forced to open fire in self-defence.

The ANC bitterly attacked the government and the police for their handling of the incident. They called for the immediate lifting of the State of Emergency and for the withdrawal of security forces from the black townships. They announced that they would no longer be attending the scheduled talks with the government.

In my response, I expressed my astonishment at the ANC's decision. I said that it was difficult to understand why an organization which claimed to be interested in peace, refused to talk about that very issue. They had wanted to discuss their perceptions of the obstacles in the way of negotiations, and so did we. I added that a continuing commitment to violence and peaceful negotiations were mutually exclusive. I said that the ANC could not send armed men into the country in the dark; order mobs to rampage through the streets; use intimidation and at the same time negotiate peacefully. I identified this dichotomy as lying at the root of the ANC's hesitancy to align themselves fully with the negotiating process.

I also announced that Mr Mandela and I would meet to discuss the problem. As he and I would often have to do throughout the long negotiating process, we had to resolve this first deadlock ourselves. It did not happen without difficulty. These regular discussions were always riddled with his wild accusations against the police; requests from me for some or other form of hard evidence, long arguments on what was reasonable under the circumstances and so on. Nevertheless, the two of us succeeded in saving the first bilateral talks and in defusing the crisis. It would not be the last time that we would do so.

The first historic meeting took place between 2 and 4 May 1990 at Groote Schuur, the former residence of South Africa's prime ministers. Groote Schuur – which means the large granary – was originally built in 1657 as a barn at the foot of Devil's Peak. Over the centuries it was transformed into an elegant residence, particularly at the end of the last century by Cecil John Rhodes, the fabulously wealthy mining magnate and former prime minister of the Cape Colony. The white-gabled Cape Dutch residence is set in beautiful gardens beneath the towering grandeur of Devil's Peak. Once again, there was overwhelming media interest in the meeting. Scores of journalists waited patiently for a couple of hours in the garden for the delegations to arrive. Fortunately, it was a brilliant late autumn day, so the wait was not too unpleasant. At last the delegations began to sweep up to the entrance of the building, ferried in BMWs and Mercedes-Benzs and surrounded by security men. Before entering the residence, we gathered on the stairs above the garden for a photo session and short introductory remarks by Mandela and me. The media were rewarded for their long wait with photographs of us clasping hands and of our delegations behind us. Both he and I were careful in our remarks not to anticipate the outcome of the talks. I nevertheless clearly identified the question of violence as a central issue and said that from our side there was serious concern about the escalating spiral of violence and intimidation. I added that it was absolutely essential that negotiations for a democratic solution should be conducted in peaceful circumstances.

We entered Groote Schuur and took our places at opposite sides of a long table – Mandela and me in the middle with our delegations on both sides of us. We were eleven on each side. On my side were the key members of our negotiation team. On the ANC side, apart from Nelson Mandela, there were Walter Sisulu, Joe Slovo, Alfred Nzo, Thabo Mbeki, Ahmed Kathrada, Joe Modise, Ruth Mompati, Archie Gumede, Revd Beyers Naudé and Cheryl Carolus. Some of them were, at that stage, not well-known names to us and I wondered exactly how they had been chosen. During the three-day long talks it became clear to me that most of them were there for political correctness. They contributed little or nothing to the discussions. There were only three main speakers on the ANC side – Nelson Mandela, Thabo Mbeki and Joe Slovo. Alfred Nzo also participated to a lesser extent in his capacity as secretary-general of the ANC, but his contributions were on the whole insignificant. Ruth Mompati and Cheryl Carolus provided gender representivity. Archie Gumede had been included to give recognition to the UDF. Beyers Naudé, the veteran anti-apartheid clergyman, was there because he was an Afrikaner. Several members of this original delegation played only marginal roles and were soon replaced in key negotiations by the real brains trust of the ANC – people like Mac Maharaj, Dullah Omar, Valli Moosa, Matthews Phosa, Jacob Zuma and later Kader Asmal.

The first day of the negotiations was exploratory and was spent in getting to know one another. My first impressions of Nelson Mandela were confirmed during this extended meeting. He was a good listener and argued his case well, as one would expect from a trained lawyer. His tendency to admonish us with long monologues full of recriminations was not apparent during these early meetings, but only came to the fore as he grew in self-confidence. I found Thabo Mbeki to be positively disposed to negotiations. But he played a more passive role than I had expected. Beyers Naudé was an enigma to me. Although he was part of their team, he neither spoke nor acted like a real ANC supporter. On one occasion, in an aside to me during a break in the talks, he referred to the ANC as 'they'.

On the second day we discussed a whole list of specific matters in an attempt to define our mutual differences and to lay the foundations for compromises and solutions. At this stage the focus was on the levelling of the playing fields with a view to negotiations; stopping political violence; and dealing with the problem of ANC members who had been convicted for politically motivated crimes. Constitutional issues were not discussed at all. Good progress was made and our advisers were instructed to prepare draft resolutions which we discussed on the last day. The result was the production of what became known as the Groote Schuur Minute. Both sides felt that they had achieved enough. We had made good progress with the agenda and concluded that we would be able to get along with one another in the future. For us, the heart of the Groote Schuur Minute lay in its first and penultimate paragraphs:

> The government and the ANC agree on a common commitment towards the resolution of the existing climate of violence and intimidation from whatever quarter, as well as a commitment to stability and to a peaceful process of negotiations.
>
> Efficient channels of communication will be established between the government and the ANC in order to curb violence and intimidation from whatever quarter effectively.

It was the clearest commitment to the ending of the armed struggle that we could get from the ANC at that stage. They were extremely sensitive about not being seen by their more radical supporters to be making too many concessions too soon – particularly with regard to the armed struggle. The rest of the document dealt with the problems of the so-called political prisoners; exiles; the lifting of the State of Emergency as soon as possible; and the amendment of security legislation to establish a more normal and free political climate. The working group, which was set up to deal with these matters, subsequently experienced serious difficulties in reaching agreement on issues such as amnesty, the ending of the ANC's underground activities and the stockpiling of arms.

Late on the evening of 4 May, Mandela and I, together with most of our delegations, went to the large auditorium of the Hendrik Verwoerd Building opposite Parliament to address the press. Once again, the whole world seemed to be there. Cameras flashed, Mandela and I shook hands and the message was sent to the world that the first step to a negotiated settlement had been successfully taken. It would, however, take far longer than I had hoped to complete the second step.

The success of our first formal talks with the ANC facilitated my task in pursuing another of the main goals that I had announced in my speech of 2 February 1990 – the challenge of re-establishing normal relations with the international community. I needed to do so for a number of reasons.

We urgently needed to gain access to foreign investment and to resume full economic relations with the rest of the world. Our economy had been stagnating for almost a decade and the lack of growth had already become a source of social unrest. We knew that it would be much easier for us to negotiate an acceptable constitutional solution if all the parties felt that their material circumstances were improving and would continue to improve. We needed to break free from the overprotection, restraints and distortions that decades of sanctions had created in our economy and to break into fiercely competitive global markets.

It was also essential for me to be able to show my own supporters, as soon as possible, that the course that we had adopted was producing dividends. Visible progress in eliminating the restrictions that had been imposed on South African citizens and companies would help in this regard. In particular, the removal of sanctions, a dramatic rise in our exports and our early return to international sporting competition would help to illustrate the benefits of rejoining the international community.

Finally, I wished to ensure that key international leaders would lend their support to a balanced process of negotiations in which the reasonable concerns of all South Africans – its minorities as well as its majority – would receive adequate attention. It was important to break down the stereotypes that many people overseas had developed of white South Africans and the National Party – and to persuade them that we were no longer the problem but an indispensable part of the solution.

My main efforts to break out of the grip of isolation during 1990 were focused on Europe and the United States. I made an extended tour of Europe between 9 and 26 May, accompanied by Pik Botha and Marike. We visited France, Greece, Portugal, Belgium, the United Kingdom, Germany, Switzerland, Spain and Italy.

We held talks in Paris with President François Mitterrand, Prime Minister Michel Roccard and Jacques Chirac – who was then mayor of Paris. My meeting with President Mitterrand was, at first, rather cold and formal. I felt that I had not really reached him. As I was leaving his office, I mentioned that, at Marike's insistence, we had broken away from our formal programme for an hour to visit the

Rodin Museum. I said that we had thoroughly enjoyed the experience. Suddenly, President Mitterrand stopped in his tracks, took me by the arm and guided me back into his office. He showed me a model of a giant new library project and told me how he had changed the president's office from the manner in which General De Gaulle had furnished it. It was as though a different facet of his personality had opened up when he had heard that this Afrikaner, with his apartheid history, had a warm interest in French art and culture. My meeting with him and with President Mario Soares in Lisbon were of special importance because they showed that it was not only the conservative governments of Europe that supported our constitutional initiative, but moderate Socialists as well.

Prime Minister Margaret Thatcher, as always, received me in the most cordial manner. Once she had decided that she could trust me and that I would do what I said I was going to do, she did everything that she could to support me. She went to considerable trouble – and often endured bitter criticism – to promote understanding and support for what we were doing, in her interaction with the president of the United States, the leaders of the European Union and the heads of government of the Commonwealth countries. After she retired from politics, I invited her to visit South Africa and presented her with our highest order, the Order of Good Hope, which, I believe, she had richly earned. This was not least because of the courageous manner in which she had endured vicious personal attacks from Commonwealth prime ministers because of her insistence, at successive Commonwealth heads of government meetings, in maintaining a balanced approach to the complex problems of southern Africa. I think that the award pleased her.

We spent a weekend together at the lovely Mala-Mala game reserve in the Eastern Transvaal, together with the then British ambassador, Sir Robin Renwick, and his wife. Lady Thatcher succeeded in spotting not only the big five (leopard, rhinoceros, elephant, buffalo and lion), but also the very rare wild dogs and King Cheetahs. The last animal on her list was a lion. On the final afternoon of her visit she said, in her usual forthright manner: 'Mr Game Warden, I came to Africa to see a lion. Please show me one.' Just as the sun was setting, we came across two lions – a beautiful male and female – involved in their drawn-out mating process. Lady Renwick asked if we had noticed the love in the lioness's eyes.

Chancellor Kohl of Germany made a positive impression on me.

He was always very straightforward and blunt, both in the questions that he asked about our plans for constitutional transformation and in his support for what we were doing. As the leader of one of our most important trading and investment partners, I took his views very seriously.

Prime Minister Gonzales of Spain provided me with a useful insight into the thought processes of revolutionary organizations, which greatly helped me throughout the negotiations. With his own background and experience of resistance, he warned me that I should prepare myself for a great deal of mass action and protest during the negotiations with the ANC. I should also expect that they would say one thing at the negotiating table one day, and something completely contradictory the next day in public. His explanation was that resistance organizations felt that this was the only countermeasure they could use to keep the playing fields even when confronted with the power of the state.

When I returned to South Africa on 26 May I could report that we could once again look the international community squarely in the eye. We could do so because what we were doing in South Africa was based on a moral principle that could hold its own anywhere in the world. I also reported that I had found understanding for our need to find a formula which would ensure a fully democratic system of government for all South Africans and would also protect all the various components of our society. I emphasized that I had not ventured overseas with a begging list to get sanction A, B or C lifted. I had simply requested the international community to re-evaluate South Africa's position in the light of the changed circumstances in our country. The visit had been an unqualified success. After forty years of confrontation and growing isolation South Africa had, at last, taken its first steps toward rejoining the international community.

17

The Pretoria Minute and the Birth of the New National Party

The months following the Groote Schuur conference were marked by intense interaction between representatives of the government and the ANC at the working group level. This resulted in the second important meeting between us in Pretoria on 6 August 1990. Just before the meeting took place, the ANC came with a surprise move: they unilaterally announced that they had suspended the armed struggle. I was delighted. It was the first real breakthrough and the realization of the first goal that I had set after my speech of 2 February 1990. The ANC's strategy of announcing their decision unilaterally and not making it look as though it was the result of the meeting of 6 August was clever and was aimed at seizing the moral high ground. I gained respect for their strategic planners. We had done much the same thing when, two months earlier, we had unilaterally decided to lift the State of Emergency.

On 7 June 1990, in keeping with the commitment that I had given in my speech of 2 February 1990, I announced in Parliament that the emergency would be lifted throughout the country, except in Natal, where the level of violence was still unacceptably high. The continuation of the State of Emergency was a major obstacle to the launching of negotiations and to the fulfilment of my promises to restore the role of the courts and to uphold basic human rights. I also announced the release of forty-eight ANC prisoners who had been convicted of politically related crimes and the granting of temporary indemnity for exiles, despite the fact that the ANC was still busy considering our latest proposals in this regard. These initiatives also prepared the way for the success of the meeting of 6 August 1990. At the same time I applied unrelenting pressure on the ANC to suspend the armed struggle and accused them of vacillating about violence. I said that the time had come for it to state unequivocally where it stood, and by its actions and statements give proof of its adherence to the principles of the Groote Schuur Minute. I asked how the ANC's continuing support for the armed struggle could possibly be reconciled with all the positive developments of the preceding months.

The meeting of 6 August took place at the Presidency in Pretoria, which was at that time being used as a government guest house and conference centre. It was a stately old residence that had been designed by Sir Herbert Baker, one of the most notable British imperial architects. It had been the residence of South Africa's governors-general while we had still been part of the British Commonwealth and later of South Africa's non-executive state presidents. This time there were seven members on each delegation. It was much more a nuts and bolts meeting on the ending of the ANC's armed struggle, violence and the creation of a climate for negotiations. We agreed on target dates for the implementation of our agreement and for the removal of what the ANC regarded as obstacles in the path of negotiations. These included the release of prisoners, amnesty for crimes committed with political objectives, the continued revision of security legislation with a view to the normalization of the political process, etc. The Pretoria Minute concluded on a very optimistic note and proclaimed that exploratory talks would soon be held to open the way to full constitutional negotiations.

But the 'soon' did not materialize. It would take a full sixteen months before Codesa (the Convention for a Democratic South Africa), the first structured multiparty negotiations, would begin.

The ink of the Pretoria Minute had hardly dried before the right wing launched a campaign depicting it and the Groote Schuur Minute as the selling out of the white man and as surrender under pressure to the ANC. The ANC's clear acceptance of the suspension of armed action with immediate effect was immediately dismissed by right-wing propagandists as a meaningless ceasefire. Their undertaking that no further armed action and related activities of the ANC and its military wing Umkhonto We Sizwe would take place was ignored by the same critics. As I explained to audiences at the time, the ANC had changed its position on key questions such as the armed struggle and the government had succeeded within a period of only eleven months in establishing its credibility at home and overseas. This had strengthened our negotiating hand and our ability to take firm steps against violence, intimidation and terrorism.

The Pretoria Minute was the start of a very difficult phase in our talks with the ANC. It very quickly became clear that the ANC had a very limited ability to ensure that its supporters and cadres honoured the undertakings that it had given. News, reports and evaluated intelligence continued to stream in, implicating the ANC in violence, crime and intimidation. On more than one occasion in my regular meetings and telephone discussions with Mandela, I confronted him on these charges. Cabinet ministers did the same in negotiations on the implementation of the Pretoria Minute. Typically, Mandela and the ANC reacted in two different ways: they either pleaded for understanding for their problem in communicating effectively with their people in the underground movement; secondly, they followed the maxim that attack is better than defence and maintained a continuous barrage of criticism and propaganda against the police and the Defence Force. Mandela very quickly began to say that I was not in control of the security forces and that the government and I had a secret agenda to strengthen our stranglehold on the ANC and to confuse and weaken its supporting organizations.

Despite these difficulties, the Pretoria Minute was a major milestone on the road to a negotiated solution. It also greatly strengthened my hand in achieving my next major foreign policy goal – acceptance by the United States. Despite the success of my European trip, I realized that Europe alone was not enough. It was essential that we should also make a breakthrough to the United States – the world's leading super power. The United States would also be a more difficult nut to crack. Although President George Bush wished to support the process of responsible reform in South Africa, Congress had adopted very hostile and deeply entrenched positions against South Africa, which were embodied in the CAAA – the Comprehensive Anti-Apartheid Act. The CAAA had imposed a wide spectrum of sanctions on South Africa and had laid down stringent conditions with which South Africa would have to comply before they could be removed. Despite my announcements of 2 February 1990, there had been concerted opposition to my visiting Washington before we had fully complied with all of these conditions. Nevertheless, thanks to the skilful diplomacy of Pik Botha and the basically sympathetic approach of the White House, an announcement was made on 7 September that I would be visiting Washington for talks with President Bush on 24 September.

The South African Airways 747, the *Hantam*, was the first SAA plane to land in the United States for more than four years, because of the airline sanctions that the United States had imposed against us. I was the first South African head of government to pay an official visit to the United States since Field Marshal Jan Smuts forty-five years earlier. Our reception in Washington caught me off guard. For so many years I, like so many other South Africans, had grown used to switching on all my defence systems each time I travelled abroad. Whenever I arrived in Europe or North America I had to prepare myself for the inevitable criticism from the media and anti-apartheid groups and for the cold shoulder that was usually presented to us by politicians and government officials. It was accordingly a wonderful moment for me when I was received with full military honours at Andrews Airforce Base and when I saw our flag flying from lampposts along the street outside the White House. Our party was accommodated at Blair House, the elegant official guest house in Pennsylvania Avenue which was used for the accommodation of visiting heads of state.

Our first official engagement was the laying of a wreath at the tomb of the unknown soldier at Arlington National Cemetery. An honour guard lined both sides of the shrine. We walked up to the tomb between servicemen holding the flags of the fifty American states. When the military band played the 'Star Spangled Banner' and our own national anthem, '*Die Stem*' (the Voice of South Africa), as I was about to lay our wreath, I found it difficult to hold back my tears. After so many years in the wilderness, I felt as though we had once again rejoined the mainstream of humanity. A hectic programme had been arranged for my visit which included public appearances, media interviews and meetings with politicians, the private sector, the World Bank and the International Monetary Fund. Wherever I went, Americans supported our initiatives and were anxious for news about developments in South Africa.

My talks with President Bush went well. He showed great sympathy and understanding for the problems that we faced and support for the initiative that I had launched. Most importantly, he used the key word 'irreversible' in describing the transformation process in South Africa. His response would have an extremely important influence on the attitudes of the International Monetary Fund and the World Bank toward South Africa. President Bush acknowledged that a new reality existed in South Africa. He assured us of American support and encouragement and confirmed that the goalposts set for meeting US demands for the lifting of sanctions would not be shifted. He also acknowledged that South Africa had already met most of those demands. On 2 October, less than a week after our departure,

President Bush reported to the American Congress that the process of reform in South Africa was irreversible, dramatic and remarkable and that the further application of stringent sanctions was fast becoming irrelevant. During the visit, Marike and I struck up a warm personal relationship with President Bush and his wife Barbara, which has continued ever since then.

We achieved all our objectives with the visit and on my return to South Africa I was able to strike a very optimistic note about the future of our relations with the United States.

The following month Marike and I paid an official visit to the Netherlands. It had special significance for us and for most Afrikaners with Dutch ancestors. Relations between our two peoples had grown particularly bitter during the apartheid years. It was all the more gratifying to be able to restore our old ties. During my visit I held constructive talks with the Dutch prime minister, Dr Ruud Lubbers, and addressed the standing committees on foreign affairs of the two houses of the Dutch Parliament – who greeted my message with a standing ovation. Wherever we went in the Netherlands we spoke to our hosts in Afrikaans, which is still close enough to Dutch for us to be able to understand one another. Some words that sounded the same had developed different meanings – as we discovered when Mrs Lubbers teased Marike about an item in her CV. Marike had written that, among her hobbies, she likes to *stap* – or hike. However, in Dutch, *stappen* means to go on a pub crawl. We became friends with the Lubbers and were also warmly received by Queen Beatrix and her husband, Prince Claus.

While we had been strengthening relations with old friends overseas, and with former revolutionary parties inside South Africa, I had, in my capacity as leader of the National Party, also been giving attention to the party's role in the era of multiracial politics that the country was about to enter. I was naturally only too aware of one central fact: successful negotiations would culminate in a new constitution and in elections in which all South Africans would for the first time be able to participate. Our first great test would be to negotiate the best possible constitution. The second would be to ensure that that first election would result in a reasonable distribution of power between the various parties.

National Party strategists had, for some time, been making a clinical analysis of the party-political scene. Detailed opinion polls, which had been commissioned by the South African Communication

Service since mid 1986, revealed that the ANC would win more than 60 per cent of the votes in an open election. The same polls consistently showed that National Party support was in the region of 19–23 per cent – but that a considerable portion of this support came from coloured, Indian and black voters. The fact that the National Party was still a white party devoted to the protection of white interests obviously limited our potential growth to the relatively small percentage of the total votes represented by white voters – even if we could succeed in winning all the white votes. The only other party with any prospect of doing reasonably well was the Inkatha Freedom Party of Dr Mangosuthu Buthelezi. Apart from this, there were other smaller homeland parties, but they were in general badly organized and had little hope of any appreciable success. Something had to be done.

I decided that, as a first step, the National Party would have to transform itself. My motivation was not only the practical mathematical realities of politics. A racially based party, as the National Party then was, would simply not be in step with the new South Africa. If racial discrimination and differentiation were removed from the statute book, then the National Party would have to remove them from its own constitution so that it could become a political home for everyone who supported its policy and principles. If we wished to present an effective counterbalance to the ANC, with its Communist allies and socialist tendencies, we would have to find a way of allowing moderate South Africans to join hands in a new non-racial political movement. All these ideas ripened in my mind – just as my thoughts had done prior to my speech of 2 February 1990.

Toward the end of August 1990, I told the Provincial Congress of the National Party of Natal that our party would have to be transformed into a non-racial party and open its membership to all South Africans. By the end of 1990 all the Provincial Congresses had accepted the changes to the constitution and the National Party became a truly non-racial party. It was a great moment. The party of apartheid and separate development had become a party which could also offer a political home to those who had been disadvantaged by apartheid.

I have long wrestled with the question of whether we should not have changed the name of the National Party when we transformed the party. Today, with the advantage of hindsight, I think that we made a mistake by not doing so. At that time I thought that the National Party's break with its apartheid past was clear enough for everyone to see and believe. A change of name would probably have made it more difficult for our political opponents to keep on hanging the albatross of apartheid around our necks, even though we ourselves had ended and abolished apartheid.

As 1990 drew to a close, there was much for which I could be thankful. We had successfully launched the transformation process. The ANC had suspended its armed struggle and was involved in negotiations with us. We had made remarkable progress in breaking free from the stranglehold of international isolation, and we had transformed the National Party, the former party of apartheid, into a multiracial party. On the negative side, progress with the negotiating process was not as rapid as I had hoped it would be. The main obstacle was the violence that continued to plague the country and cause distrust and recriminations between the ANC and the government.

18

Violence and Operation Vula

The most serious problem that we experienced during my presidency was the insidious and pervasive violence that afflicted the country, and particularly the province of Natal – which is now known as KwaZulu-Natal. During the four and a half years of my term of office, it led to the deaths of over 14,000 people – the great majority of them black South Africans. It soured my relationship with Nelson Mandela and on a number of occasions almost destroyed our efforts to achieve a negotiated constitutional settlement.

My colleagues in the government and I were fully aware that when we took the lid off the South African pressure cooker on 2 February 1990 the pent-up political forces in the country were bound to boil over into increased violence. We anticipated that there would be vigorous competition for support and for territory between rival political groupings. We were also wary of the possibility of right-wing reactionary violence. It was for this reason that, in my speech of 2 February 1990, I stressed the importance of maintaining firm control over violence. I said that violence from any source would be fought with all our might and warned that peaceful protest could not become the springboard for lawlessness, violence and intimidation. I was determined to limit any increase in political violence to the absolute minimum.

Another dimension of the problem of violence was the increasingly bitter dispute over who was responsible for instigating it. Almost from the inception of my presidency there were persistent rumours and reports that hit squads, constituting a shadowy third force operating within the security forces, were responsible for the instigation of violence. These reports were given further impetus toward the end of 1989 by the confession of two former policemen, Dirk Coetzee and Almond Nofamela, concerning the murder of a political activist, Griffiths Mxenge, in Durban in 1981. I initially resisted calls for the appointment of a commission of inquiry to investigate these allegations because of my general approach that the state should make use of the existing judicial processes to deal with such matters. My first response to these allegations was accordingly to refer them to the relevant authorities for proper investigation and attention. In a statement on 7 December 1989 I said that I had instructed the minister of justice to investigate allegations of politically inspired assassinations. I said that he and the minister of law and order should use all the means at their disposal to apprehend the guilty and bring them to trial.

My concern over third-force allegations deepened during the summer holidays early in January 1990 while I was vacationing at Botha House, a presidential residence on the south coast of Natal. I realized that there was a serious problem when General Magnus Malan, the minister of defence, informed me that he wanted to fly down to Durban to discuss a very sensitive matter with me. After he arrived at Botha House, Malan told me that he had just discovered the nature of the operations of a secret SADF front organization, called the Civil Cooperation Bureau (CCB). He said that he had learned that the CCB, which had been established within the framework of the underground structures of the South African Defence Force in the mid-eighties, had been using totally unacceptable methods and strategies against the ANC and other revolutionary organizations. General Malan appeared to be as shocked as I was and assured me that he had taken immediate steps to investigate and disband the organization. Although I had been given a supposedly full briefing on the activities of the SADF soon after I had become president, I had not been informed of the existence of the CCB. I realized that despite all the assurances that I had been given about the bona fides of the SADF's covert operations, something was seriously amiss. After I returned to my office in Pretoria I consulted some of my colleagues on the steps that I should take in the light of media speculation and General Malan's revelations. I concluded that the plethora of allegations, accusations and rumours regarding the involvement of elements of the security forces in violence could no longer be dealt with adequately by the normal legal processes. Accordingly, towards the end of January 1990, I appointed a highly respected judge, Louis Harms, as chairman of a one-man commission to investigate alleged incidents of murder and other unlawful acts committed in South Africa and in the homelands in order to achieve or promote constitutional or political aims in South Africa.

Whatever the role of elements within the security forces may or may not have been in the instigation of violence, I was convinced that by far the greatest part of the conflict in the country was the result of the struggle between the ANC and the IFP in the province of Natal. During 1989, the year in which I became president, 91 per cent of the 1,403 people who died in political violence throughout the country were killed in Natal, overwhelmingly as a result of the conflict between the two organizations.

Natal, which is about the same size as Austria, was the smallest province in the old Republic of South Africa, but was the second most populous. It stretches along the east coast of the country between Mozambique and Swaziland in the north, to the Transkei, the home of the Xhosa people, in the south. The province drops from the ramparts of the Drakensberg mountains in the west, through the lush, rolling hills of the Natal midlands to the sugar fields and holiday beaches of the subtropical coast. It is the landscape, filled with thousands of green hills and deep valleys, that was made famous in Alan Paton's novel, *Cry, the Beloved Country*.

By far the largest part of the population is made up of Zulus, the proud descendants of fierce warriors. At the beginning of the nineteenth century their military conquests, inspired by their great founder-king, Shaka, had reverberated throughout much of south-eastern Africa. Later, they fought against the Afrikaner Voortrekkers led by Andries Pretorius in 1838, and after them, against the British. Under their king, Cetshwayo, they bravely resisted the expansion of the British Empire and in 1879 inflicted an unprecedented defeat on a modern British army, at the battle of Isandlhwana. Ultimately, they were forced to submit to the British. Their kingdom, north of the Tugela River, was incorporated into the British Empire as part of the Colony of Natal to the south. Later, after the establishment of the Union of South Africa, a patchwork of blocks of Zulu territory throughout Natal – and comprising about 37 per cent of the total area of the province – was included in what was later called the homeland of KwaZulu. By the 1980s the homeland had, according to the policy of separate development, attained self-governing status. It administered a budget that was larger than those of several African countries and enjoyed a high degree of autonomy, including responsibility for finance, justice, home affairs (including its own police force), agriculture and forestry, public works, health and welfare. The homeland was ruled by Chief Minister Mangosuthu Buthelezi, the leader of the Inkatha movement, which was strongly supported by the *amakosi*, the chiefs and sub-chiefs of the Zulu nation. In the Zulu tradition, the 'inkatha' was a ring tightly woven from straws taken from the thatched huts of each of the *amakosi*. It was thus a powerful symbol of the unity of all the Zulu clans, dispersed through the rolling hills and deep valleys of KwaZulu. Initially, Buthelezi had founded Inkatha with the blessing of the ANC, as a fifth column within the homeland system. However, he and the ANC soon quarrelled over its commitment to the armed struggle and to socialist policies.

During my presidency, I would have many meetings with Chief Minister Mangosuthu Buthelezi. He was, in many respects, a jumble of contradictions and a difficult man to get along with. Normally, he would be charming and courteous, radiating sophistication, moderation and adherence to democratic values. He could also be tenaciously obstinate and frustratingly sullen. As president, I often experienced difficulty in persuading him to discuss his differences of opinion openly with me. Whenever we met, he would start by providing me with a copy of a prepared statement on the subject at hand, which he would then rapidly read out in full. Sometimes his opening statements were very long. If I rejected some of his points in my reaction and argued about the positions that he had adopted, he would shut up like a clam. I later learned that, in Zulu tradition, it is an important rule of protocol that one always defers to a president or to a king and never challenges him openly in face-to-face discussions.

As I came to understand the Zulu traditionalist side of Buthelezi, our discussions became more constructive. This facet of Buthelezi was well illustrated by an anecdote that a colleague once told me about the wedding of King Goodwill Zwelithini to his fifth wife, which he had attended at a stadium at the Zulu capital of Ulundi. The king and his bride had first gone through a Western Christian ceremony. The royal bride arrived in a late model Rolls-Royce, dressed in a magnficent white gown. The king and his hereditary prime minister, Mangosuthu Buthelezi, and the other leading guests were immaculately dressed in cravats and elegant grey morning suits. After the Western ceremony, the bridal party withdrew to change into their traditional attire. They then returned to the stadium for a traditional Zulu ceremony, which involved a parade of Zulu maidens, led by the new queen and a magnificent dancing competition between the family of the king and the family of the bride. Chief Minister Buthelezi participated enthusiastically in the dance on the side of the king's family. Only the ostrich-plume head dress of the king was higher than his, and only the king danced with greater vigour. Later, the chief minister took the lead in the singing of ancient Zulu battle hymns extolling the valour and exploits of the great Zulu warriors of old.

Chief Minister Buthelezi took great pride in his position as the hereditary prime minister of the Zulu king, the young, amiable and pliable Goodwill Zwelithini. Although a fiercely committed Zulu nationalist, Buthelezi was also in many ways a moderate. While resolutely opposing apartheid, he was committed to non-violence and to using his power-base as the chief minister of KwaZulu to achieve his objectives. He made a major contribution to the demise of grand apartheid by refusing adamantly to accept independence for KwaZulu and by insisting on the release of Nelson Mandela and the unbanning of the ANC before he would enter into constitutional negotiations with the government. He staunchly favoured free-market principles and opposed sanctions, which he quite correctly believed were primarily harming black South Africans. While he himself presided over a de facto one-party Zulu state from the traditional capital of Ulundi, he favoured a liberal and strongly federal constitution with maximum devolution of power for a future South Africa.

I received regular briefings on the violence in Natal. Its origins were complex and difficult to unravel. Certainly, a central element was the attempt of the ANC and its UDF surrogates to move into areas that had previously been the undisputed domain of the Inkatha Freedom Party. In many respects, the conflict was between the older, traditional and rural Zulus who tended to support the IFP, and the younger, better educated and unionized city-dwellers – who, of course, were also Zulus, who generally supported the ANC. Other aspects included the depressed socio-economic conditions in which most of the province's inhabitants lived. Tensions were exacerbated by high levels of unemployment and crime and the migration of millions of people from the rural areas to the squatter camps that mushroomed around the cities. Added to this, was a long-established culture of deadly feuding between different Zulu clans, which had often led to the deaths of scores of people.

The ANC blamed the IFP for initiating the violence. The IFP hotly denied this, and claimed that the ANC had embarked on a systematic campaign aimed at taking over IFP communities and assassinating IFP leaders. Certainly, both sides had ample evidence to support their versions of the truth. The ANC could cite the blatant attacks against its communities by IFP warlords. The IFP could point to the behaviour of Harry Gwala, one of the leaders of the SACP/ANC alliance in the province, who was a self-proclaimed Stalinist. In April 1991, he had reportedly told a rally, 'Make no mistake, we will kill the [IFP] warlords.' On another occasion, he told ANC students that they should learn how to handle firearms and that they should negotiate through the barrel of an AK-47. Another hot-headed ANC leader, Peter Mokaba, had congratulated ANC supporters in the Richmond area for having evicted IFP members and made it chillingly clear what was meant by the establishment of no-go areas: 'If Inkatha comes to Richmond let them enter the township. But they will never return.'

The most accurate assessment of the situation was probably the finding of Judge Richard Goldstone, the chairman of the commission of inquiry that I appointed in 1991 to investigate public violence and intimidation. In its second interim report, the commission wrote that it had

> no doubt at all that both African National Congress and Inkatha Freedom Party members and supporters have been guilty of many incidents that have resulted in the deaths of and injuries to large numbers of people. Both organizations have been over hasty in accusing the other of being the cause of such conduct. Each has been tardy, especially at the level of top leadership, in taking adequate and effective steps to stop the violence by imposing discipline and accountability among its membership.

Initially the top leadership of the ANC and the IFP were aware of their responsibility to meet and to try to end the violence. Two weeks after his release, Nelson Mandela visited Natal and implored a large crowd of his supporters in Durban to 'take their guns, their knives and their *pangas* [machetes] and throw them into the sea'. He called on them to 'close down the death factories and to end this war now'. This was not the message that his followers wanted to hear. Instead of heeding his call, some of them angrily cut the picture of his face from their T-shirts. The radical ANC/SACP leadership of the province thwarted Mandela's plans for an early meeting with Buthelezi to try to find some way of achieving peace. I realized that if the two leaders could not come together to resolve their differences, the chances of their followers doing so were bleak indeed. For this reason I consistently urged them both to meet and to take resolute action to bring the violence between their organizations to an end. I ascribe their failure to do so primarily to the high-handed approach which Mandela and the ANC adopted toward Buthelezi at that stage.

However, by the first months of 1990 Natal was no longer the only part of the country that was racked by widespread conflict. Following my speech of 2 February 1990, and the unbanning of the ANC and the SACP there was a dramatic increase of violence throughout South Africa. During 1989 there had been 124 deaths caused by political violence outside Natal. By the end of 1990 this figure had soared to 1,888. Part of the escalation could be ascribed to the spreading of the IFP-ANC conflict to the Witwatersrand region of the Transvaal. Here, the conflict was primarily between migrant supporters of the IFP, living in crowded and squalid all-male hostels and the surrounding communities – most of whom supported the ANC alliance and who often condescendingly regarded the hostel-dwellers as country bumpkins.

Another factor was the ANC's efforts to consolidate its support and to eliminate political opponents. Unrest, protest marches and strikes in the wake of the unbanning of the ANC led to further deaths. One such case was the incident that occurred on 26 March 1990 in the township of Sebokeng, which had led to the ANC's initial cancellation of the bilateral talks that had been scheduled between it and the government on 11 April 1990.

This was the first of many clashes that we would have with the ANC during my presidency over the question of violence. Despite the ANC's subsequent decision to meet the government at Groote Schuur on 24 May 1990 – and the success achieved at that meeting – the high level of conflict throughout the country continued to cause immense tensions between the negotiating parties. Virtually every incident led to bitter allegations from the ANC that the security forces had either instigated or been involved in the violence, or that they had been negligent in preventing or investigating it. It was the ANC's custom to play down the role of its own supporters and cadres in violence. Sometimes it defended their actions and sometimes it denied that the elements involved were under its effective control. The fact remains – and was repeatedly confirmed by the findings of the Goldstone Commission – that the ANC itself and its followers were deeply involved in the instigation and perpetration of violence.

The ANC's continuous vilification of the security forces – together with their vitriolic accusations that I, myself, was either personally involved in security force violence, or had lost control of the security forces – caused deep disaffection and tension between Nelson Mandela and me. I still do not know whether his increasingly strident attacks on me were motivated by a genuine belief that I was, somehow or other involved in violence, or was not doing enough to combat violence – or whether they were aimed at breaking down the positive image that I then had among many black South Africans. Perhaps both factors played a role. Mandela regularly telephoned me at all hours of the day and the night with new accusations and allegations. I repeatedly asked him to provide us with evidence to support his allegations and the names of witnesses to help us to establish the truth relating to particular incidents. I always immediately instructed the police to investigate all such allegations. I recall one occasion when I called him back after I had obtained more information from the police on allegations that he had made to me. The explanation that I gave him – that was based on the information that had been given to me – did not satisfy him and he launched another tirade against me. For once, I lost my temper and curtly interrupted him with the words: 'Mr Mandela, I did not telephone you to be insulted. Goodbye!' And I slammed the telephone down in his ear. After that, he was, for a while, more careful with his accusations and with the tone that he adopted with me. In the meantime, the violence continued.

On 2 April 1990 and again on 7 June 1990, when I lifted the State of Emergency throughout the country, except in Natal, I announced further measures to strengthen the ability of the security forces to maintain peace and to improve security in Natal.

It was not only Mandela and the ANC who felt that they had reason to complain about the escalating violence and who harboured suspicions about the motives and actions of others. They, themselves, were vulnerable because of their continued involvement in violence. In July 1990 the security forces uncovered a major ANC plot, code-named Operation Vula, which was entirely at odds with the organization's undertakings in the Groote Schuur Minute and its professed commitment to a peaceful and negotiated constitutional settlement. In terms of the plot, the ANC had infiltrated key operatives into South Africa – including Mac Maharaj and Siphiwe Nyanda in 1988 and Ronnie Kasrils in 1990 – to organize an underground network to prepare for revolution. (They would later become, respectively, the minister of transport, the chief of the South African National Defence Force and the deputy minister of defence!) Maharaj and eight of his co-conspirators were caught and charged with attempting to overthrow the government by violence.

For a moment the whole negotiation process was in jeopardy. The securocrats felt that their worst suspicions regarding the real intentions of the ANC/SACP alliance had been proved. I asked Mandela to come to see me urgently and confronted him with some of the evidence that the security forces had acquired. During our meeting on 26 July, he seemed to be genuinely surprised by these revelations. In his book *Long Walk to Freedom* he says that, after his meeting with me, he questioned Joe Slovo of the SACP about the operation. Slovo shrugged off the incident with an explanation that the documents that I had shown Mandela were taken out of context and that the whole operation was moribund.

I again discussed Operation Vula with Mr Mandela on 1 August 1990. I told him bluntly that recent developments had caused an imminent breach of trust between the government and the ANC. I referred to statements and actions by prominent ANC and SACP members, which I said were irreconcilable with the spirit and letter of the Groote Schuur Minute. I warned him that this situation seriously jeopardized the continuation of discussions and the creation of a climate conducive to negotiations. The talks could continue fruitfully only if trust were re-established and all those involved kept to the letter and spirit of the Groote Schuur Minute. In the light of Mandela's assurances, I agreed to proceed with the next round of talks which culminated in the signing of the Pretoria Minute.

It was subsequently revealed that 'Vula' had been authorized by ANC President Oliver Tambo himself in the mid eighties. After 2 February 1990, the ANC had decided to keep 'Vula' in place as an 'insurance policy', should constitutional negotiations not succeed. It is ironic that Mandela originally knew nothing of this. He would later frequently accuse me of having known about everything that happened in the security forces and of having a double agenda. Despite his assertion that 'Vula' was moribund, a year later in July 1991, he, himself, publicly praised members of the ANC/SACP who were still involved in the operation. He lauded them for having continued their activities and avoided arrest during the intervening period and boasted about the achievements of the operation which he said had included the bringing of personnel and weapons into the country. He claimed that it was common knowledge between the government and ourselves that the majority of this personnel and the bulk of this material did not fall into the hands of the security forces despite the arrests. Mandela went on, somewhat disingenuously, to deny that Operation

Vula constituted a double agenda on the part of the ANC. On the contrary, he said, it strengthened negotiations rather than undermined them.

But still the violence continued. On 22 July 1990 – at about the same time as the 'Vula' revelations – a further twenty-four people were killed in clashes between IFP and ANC supporters in Sebokeng. At the beginning of September 1990 there was another series of horrifying incidents, including further violence in Sebokeng and the random killing of commuters on trains and at Jeppe Station in Johannesburg. The next day Mandela came to see me and complained bitterly about the inability of the police to prevent the attacks and to find the culprits.

I expressed the shock of the government and the country at the senseless, cruel and repulsive killings and announced yet further steps to combat violence. These included strong measures against the illegal possession of arms and the appointment of special units headed by an attorney-general or a deputy attorney-general to investigate political violence and to recommend what action should be taken by the minister of justice. In addition, I said that I was thinking of the appointment of an independent, highly respected person to investigate allegations of abuse of power by governmental institutions, organizations and individuals. These ideas came to fruition the following year (1991) when I appointed the Commission of Inquiry Regarding the Prevention of Public Violence and Intimidation, which came to be known as the Goldstone Commission after its chairman, Judge Richard Goldstone.

Despite all these actions Mandela repeatedly charged the government with doing nothing to counteract the atrocities. The ongoing violence continued to erode our relationship. Most of our meetings – and particularly our meeting of 11 September 1990 – were dominated by the issue, especially the conflict in Natal, and by ANC complaints about the behaviour of the security forces and the role of the KwaZulu government.

In fact, I reject without qualification that my government was ever behind the violence. Although it is now indisputable that some elements of the security forces were involved in secretly instigating and perpetrating violence, their actions were in direct violation of my explicit instructions and of everything that my government and I had been trying to achieve since my inauguration. In cabinet and in all my interactions with the responsible ministers and generals I continuously exerted pressure to ensure that the security forces would act within the law. In cases where there was sufficient evidence, we acted firmly against suspected transgressors, and where possible they were prosecuted. In the end, the actions of such elements within the security forces were directed as much against the government and its reform policies as they were against the ANC and its allies. The question that Mandela should have asked himself was why the government and I should instigate – or connive at – violence which seriously jeopardized the initiative into which we had sunk all our moral and political capital?

We, from our side, regarded many of Mandela's representations as the height of hypocrisy – given the ANC's own deep involvement in violence in Natal and throughout the country – as well as its apparent unwillingness to rein in members and supporters who were clearly involved in violence. If Mandela was so concerned about violence why would he not agree to meet with Chief Minister Buthelezi to try to resolve the issue?

In the meantime the Harms Commission had been continuing with its investigation into so-called hit squad activities in the security forces. Judge Harms presented his report to me on 13 November 1990. He found that, on the evidence before him, Coetzee and Nofamela had been lying about death squad activities in the South African police. At the same time, he made a scathing attack on the CCB. He reported that the organization had arrogated to itself the right to try, sentence and punish people without the persons knowing of the allegations against them or having the opportunity of defending themselves. There was evidence to link the CCB with bombings and attempted murders. Although he could find no evidence that the CCB had actually been responsible for the deaths of activists, Judge Harms found that their actions before and during the commission created the suspicion that they were involved in more crimes of violence than the evidence showed. Part of the problem that Harms experienced was that the CCB had destroyed or removed all its files and had disobeyed instructions from the chief of the defence force and the minister of defence to provide the commission with the documentation that it required to complete its investigation.

It was subsequently revealed by the Goldstone Commission and others that Coetzee and Nofamela had, in fact, been telling the truth. The police had, indeed, been running a death squad from a farm outside Pretoria, known as Vlakplaas which, if anything, was even more horrifying than the initial revelations had suggested. There were also allegations that the police team that was appointed to assist Judge Harms in the investigation of Coetzee and Nofamela's claims was itself involved in a massive cover-up and grossly misled the commission.

However, I knew nothing of this at the time. All that I had to go on was the findings of the Harms Commission and an earlier report by the attorney-general of the Orange Free State, Mr Tim McNally, that Coetzee and Nofamela had not been telling the truth. Naturally, steps had already been taken to disband the CCB, but I was told that there was still not enough hard evidence on which to base the prosecutions which I had hoped for.

In retrospect, it is clear that the truth was not established by the Harms Commission and that we failed at that stage to get to the root of the totally unacceptable covert activities in which some elements of the security forces were involved.

19

Peace Initiatives and Commissions

The continuing violence made it more important than ever to press on with the negotiating process. The basis for progress was laid by the ANC's suspension of its armed struggle and the adoption of the Pretoria Minute on 8 August 1990. In terms of paragraph three of the Pretoria Minute, it was agreed that a working group would be established to resolve all outstanding questions arising from the ANC's decision to suspend the armed struggle and to report back by 15 September 1990.

In fact, the working group did not finally report back until 12 February 1991, at a meeting between the government and the ANC which was held at D. F. Malan Airport in Cape Town (now known as Cape Town International Airport). The agreement reached between the two sides at that meeting became known as the D. F. Malan Accord. The ANC agreed that there would be an immediate halt to attacks by means of armaments, firearms, explosive or incendiary devices; infiltration of men and material; the creation of underground structures; statements inciting violence; threats of armed actions; and (military) training inside South Africa. It was further agreed that all political parties should participate in the democratic process peacefully and without resort to the use of force; that although people had a right to express their views through peaceful demonstrations, it was urgent and imperative that violence and intimidation from whatever quarter accompanying mass action should be eliminated; that no political party should have a private army; and that control should be exercised over ANC cadres and arms caches that were already in the country.

I was happy with the terms of the agreement – which I felt could make a major contribution to the restoration of peace and stability – but was apprehensive about the ANC's role in its implementation. Unfortunately, it soon became evident that my apprehension was well founded. The ANC was either unwilling or unable to abide by the terms of the D. F. Malan Accord and dismally failed to carry out its undertakings.

And so the situation continued to deteriorate through the end of 1990 and the first few months of 1991 with accusations and counter-accusations as to who was responsible for the violence. In his book *Long Walk to Freedom* Mandela says that by this time he was becoming more convinced than ever that the government was behind much of the violence and that violence was impeding the negotiations. He added that my supposed failure to respond had put our relationship in jeopardy.

At the beginning of April 1991 Nelson Mandela expounded his views about the government's complicity in violence to a meeting of the ANC's National Executive Committee. On 5 April, following their meeting, the ANC wrote the government an open letter in which it threatened to suspend constitutional negotiations if the government did not meet seven demands by 9 May 1991. Their demands included the dismissal of the ministers of law and order and defence, Mr Adriaan Vlok and General Magnus Malan; the outlawing of traditional weapons (the spears and clubs carried by IFP supporters at ceremonial functions); the dismantling of counter-insurgency units; the appointment of an independent commission of inquiry to investigate the security forces; and the phasing out of IFP hostels in the urban areas.

I, of course, rejected these demands. In an effort to break the cycle of violence, I called for a tripartite meeting between Mandela, Buthelezi and myself and suggested the appointment of a standing commission to investigate all forms of violence originating from whatever source. The ANC alliance rejected both proposals. I also announced that I would convene a conference on violence and intimidation to cut to the root of the causes of conflict. The government invited all parties and interested groups – including the churches and business – to attend the meeting. The ANC, Cosatu (Congress of South African Trade Unions), the PAC and AZAPO (a small black consciousness organization) refused to attend – despite their professed interest in ending violence. Mr Mandela dismissed the initiative as pointless since the government knew exactly what it had to do to end the violence. Evidently, he was still operating under the delusion, cherished by so many revolutionaries, that possession of the levers of government enabled those in power to achieve whatever goals they wanted. His words would return to haunt him. After he became president in 1994 he found it equally difficult to put an end to the violence in KwaZulu-Natal.

Our conference on violence and intimidation went ahead without the ANC and its allies. It was held on 24 and 25 May 1991 at a conference centre in the eastern suburbs of Pretoria. The conference was attended by some 200 delegates representing a wide range of political parties and organizations; trade unions, community organizations and churches – including some of the anti-government churches that had boycotted the church conference the previous year. In my opening speech I noted that some of the parties who were able to make an important contribution were not present. I said that it was ironic that the absentees included those, in particular, who were forever accusing the government of not doing enough to stop violence and intimidation. However, when the government took steps to combat the violence, they protested and withheld their co-operation.

I asked the conference to make suggestions on what further steps the government could take to combat violence. The conference brought together widely divergent groups. Among those who addressed it were Archbishop Tutu, King Goodwill Zwelithini – who made a fiery nationalistic speech; Eugene Terre'Blanche, the leader of the far-right-wing AWB (Afrikaanse Weerstandsbeweging, or Afrikaans Resistance Movement) who gave a theatrical performance from the far-right Afrikaner perspective; and Oscar Dhlomo, then a leading member of the IFP. The conference ended by making some sensible proposals, including the drafting of codes of conduct for the security forces and for political organizations. It set up a facilitating committee comprising prominent business and church leaders – including the secretary-general of the South African Council of Churches, Dr Frank Chikane; the moderator of the Dutch Reformed Church, Dr Johan Heyns; Archbishop Desmond Tutu; and Mr Bobby Godsell of the Chamber of Mines. Two of the committee's members, Dr Louw Alberts and Mr John Hall, played particularly active roles in maintaining the momentum of the peace initiative and in working to involve parties that had boycotted the conference. In June 1991 they succeeded in transforming the facilitating committee into a preparatory committee for the National Peace Initiative which included three nominees each from the government, the ANC and the IFP. Their task was to prepare the way for the signing of a National Peace Accord, three months later in September.

Just when it appeared that things were going well with the peace initiative, I was struck by another bombshell. In July 1991 disclosures began to appear in the media that the government had for some time been providing clandestine assistance to the Inkatha Freedom Party. The allegations were soon labelled Inkathagate by the media.

The ANC wrung every possible ounce of political advantage from the situation. Nelson Mandela claimed that the transformation of Natal and many parts of the Reef into killing fields had to be laid squarely at the door of the government (as though the ANC itself was not deeply and primarily involved in the violence). He demanded once again the dismissal of Ministers Adriaan Vlok and Magnus Malan; the appointment of an independent judicial commission of inquiry to investigate the security forces; and the visible disbanding of the special counter-insurgency units of the South African police and the SADF. He again accused me of seeking to promote my cause over the corpses of his supporters.

My first reaction to the crisis was to try to establish the facts. It transpired that the government had, indeed, been providing wide-ranging assistance to Inkatha for a number of years and that elements of this programme had continued into my presidency. During the unrest of the eighties, the security establishment had identified Inkatha as an important ally in its struggle against the ANC and its internal surrogates, especially in Natal. Although there were at that time significant differences between the government and Inkatha, there was widespread respect for Inkatha's refusal to support the ANC's armed struggle or sanctions. At the very least, it was felt that Inkatha should be helped to resist the encroachments of the ANC and its internal front organizations. Quite considerable sums of money were given to help Inkatha establish its own trade union movement in opposition to the pro-ANC unions. Funds and assistance were also made available to help Inkatha improve its political organization and to hold large rallies, some opposing international sanctions. Some 200 members of the KwaZulu police were given special training by the South African Defence Force to enable them to protect leaders of the KwaZulu government from ANC attacks.

These clandestine projects had their origins in the period of conflict before my initiatives of 2 February 1990. Although most cabinet ministers – including myself – were at the time unaware of most such projects, we would probably not have objected to them had they come to our attention. For example, when it was discussed in the cabinet, we regarded the decision to train KwaZulu police to protect KwaZulu government leaders as quite logical, given the circumstances which prevailed in Natal at that time. The issue involved, as we understood it, was the provision of VIP protection to members of a legitimate government structure and definitely not the creation of an anti-ANC strike force. It was later revealed that some of the trainees were subsequently involved in murderous offensives against the ANC and its followers. In 1995 this led to the dramatic prosecution, under the ANC-led government, of General Malan and other senior SADF officers in an attempt to establish a nexus between the training decision and the subsequent murderous activities of some of the trainees.

Although I could understand the justification for these projects during our period of conflict, it was totally unacceptable that some of them had continued after my initiatives of 2 February 1990 – and despite the instructions that I had given that such projects should be terminated. When I took them to task for this the security forces explained that it took time to close down such projects, some of which involved complex contractual obligations. The possibility can not be discounted that, like the ANC with Operation Vula, some elements in our security forces were reluctant to dismantle their clandestine capabilities or to abandon people that they had come to regard as their allies.

I realized that I would have to take drastic action. The retirement of three cabinet ministers late in July created the opportunity for me to announce a major cabinet shuffle. In particular, I realized that I would no longer be able to keep Magnus Malan and Adriaan Vlok in their high-profile security portfolios. The attacks on Malan over the CCB affair, the manner in which the CCB had defied the Harms investigation and the latest Inkathagate revelations made his removal from the defence portfolio unavoidable. Despite Judge Harms (incorrectly) finding that Coetzee and Nofamela had been lying about the existence of a police hit squad, pressure had also been mounting inexorably on Minister Adriaan Vlok, particularly over the often unfair criticism of the police's lack of success in stopping the violence. Vlok had been an exceptionally conscientious minister of law and order, who had gone out of his way to identify himself with the bobby on the beat. He was renowned for accompanying policemen on their operations, often wearing their blue-grey fatigues in the process. If anything, there was criticism that he identified too closely with the force and did not keep the subtle degree of distance from his department that ministers are wise to maintain. Although I had decided to move them from their security portfolios, I specifically did not link my decision to the package of actions which I was to announce two days later in response to the Inkathagate crisis, because I wished to avoid any impression that I was surrendering to the ANC's demands. Both ministers had solemnly and repeatedly assured me that they had had no personal knowledge of, or involvement in, the totally unacceptable criminal activities – such as murder, assassination, torture and the instigation of violence – of which elements within the security forces were being accused. Their denials had been corroborated by senior generals in the SADF and the SAP. Both had been loyal colleagues and strong supporters of the reform process. I accordingly decided to keep them in the cabinet, but to move them to less controversial portfolios. I appointed Malan as minister of water affairs and forestry and Vlok as the minister of correctional services – responsible for the country's prison system. However, toward the end of my presidency, Vlok informed me and other members of the cabinet that he intended to apply for amnesty for ordering the bombing in 1988 of a number of buildings used by the government's opponents, including the head-quarters of the South African Council of Churches and Cosatu, the Congress of South African Trade Unions. He later revealed that the bombings, which were not intended to injure anyone, were carried out on the instructions of former President P.W. Botha.

The cabinet shuffle gave me the chance of replacing them with less controversial ministers who were not regarded as hawks and who, I hoped, would be able to lead their respective departments through the transformation process which lay ahead. I appointed Roelf Meyer, the deputy minister of constitutional development, as the minister of defence and Hernus Kriel, the minister of planning, as minister of law and order. My cabinet shuffle helped to clear the decks for my response to the Inkathagate onslaught.

On 30 July 1991 I convened a press conference in the large banqueting hall of the old Presidency in Pretoria, to deal with the Inkathagate crisis. The huge room was packed with local and foreign media and with diplomatic observers. It was one of the most difficult press conferences that I have ever had to face.

I started by sketching the circumstances of conflict and sanctions that had prevailed in South Africa during the mid-eighties. According to the ANC's own view, we had been in a state of war. The ANC had been committed to the violent overthrow of the state and had suspended its armed struggle only in August 1990. It had persisted with Operation Vula, and its option for violent revolution, until well after the Groote Schuur conference, despite its professed commitment to peaceful solutions.

I explained that the government had to defend the country against these threats, and, like other countries, had made use of secret projects. However, the whole political landscape had changed after 2 February 1990. I recounted how, in keeping with our new approach, I had taken action to normalize the role of the security forces and had ordered a review of secret projects. As a result, numerous secret projects had, by the second half of 1990, been terminated, including assistance to Inkatha's trade union movement, UWUSA, and many of our projects to circumvent international sanctions.

I committed the government to levelling the political playing field and gave the assurance that all projects favouring political parties or organizations had accordingly been terminated. In future, secret projects would be limited to a minimum and would have to comply with norms and principles that were generally acceptable in democratic countries. I announced that I would appoint a small advisory committee – the Kahn Committee – from the private sector to advise me on the necessity of existing secret projects and on the adequacy of control mechanisms.

I emphasized that it had always been the norm that secret projects should be conducted within the law. Any evidence that the security forces were involved in the instigation, promotion or commission of violence would be referred to the Commission on the Prevention of Public Violence and Intimidation for thorough investigation – which would soon be appointed. I promised that relentless action would be taken against any members of the security services who incited or assisted members of Inkatha or any other movement to perpetrate violent actions.

By the end of the press conference I was exhausted. I had tried to place the government's record on secret projects in perspective and had announced remedial action that I hoped would prevent any recurrence of the problems that we had encountered. However, the media were sceptical. I could not escape the fact that our credibility had been seriously damaged.

I was angry and frustrated by the tardy and ineffective implementation of my repeated instructions to eliminate all questionable activities. I also began to suspect that some elements in the security forces might be dragging their feet or wilfully undermining my initiatives. I was determined to ensure, once and for all, that any remaining unacceptable secret projects should be brought to an end as soon as possible.

The instrument that I established to achieve this purpose was the Advisory Committee on Special Secret Projects, otherwise known as the Kahn Committee after its chairman, Professor Ellison Kahn, the retired dean of the Faculties of Law and Commerce (and former vice-chancellor) of the University of the Witwatersrand. The other members of the committee were Professor S. A. S. Strauss SC, professor of Law at the University of South Africa; Mr J. O. McMillan, former editor of the anti-government *Natal Mercury*; and Mr J. A. Crafford, a respected chartered accountant. The committee's task would be to ensure that no secret projects benefited or harmed any political party or organization, and to advise me on whether ongoing secret projects were in the broader national interest – for example, the promotion of peace and the combating of violence, intimidation, sanctions and isolation. The committee would also advise me on the adequacy of existing controls over secret projects.

In the course of its deliberations the committee recommended that a number of secret projects should be terminated. To ensure that these recommendations were carried out I appointed a Ministers' Committee on Secret Projects which was originally chaired by Barend du Plessis, the minister of finance, and after him by Kobie Coetsee, the minister of justice. Its other members were Ministers Gerrit Viljoen, Derek Keys and Amie Venter. The Ministers' Committee required departments to report, not only on their compliance with the recommendations of the Kahn Committee, but also on any special secret projects that had been completed before the commencement of the activities of the Kahn Committee and which, for this reason, had not been submitted to the Kahn Committee; or that had commenced after the termination of the Kahn Committee's activities; or any existing secret line-function activities that should, in the opinion of the departments concerned, be brought to the attention of the Ministers' Committee.

The Ministers' Committee also recommended that individual ministers should accept full accountability for compliance with the recommendations of the Kahn Committee and once again brought to their attention new guidelines relating to secret projects that the cabinet had approved on 29 June 1990. Among other things, these guidelines required that ministers and officials should accept full accountability for the secret projects in which they were involved; that the responsible minister should give written approval for the principle, purpose and objectives, methods and funds involved in each secret project; that the principle of plausible denial should wherever possible be avoided; that no indemnity from criminal prosecution could be granted to anyone;

and that the auditing of expenditure should occur in terms of the Auditor-General's Act.

On 19 December 1991, the Kahn Committee reported that all the ongoing secret projects complied with these requirements. Wherever the committee had recommended the termination of a project, the government had accepted the recommendation. The committee also reported that it was satisfied that departments such as the National Intelligence Service, the South African Defence Force and the South African police had to continue, of necessity, with certain legitimate line-function covert activities.

At my press conference of 30 July 1991, I also announced the establishment of the commission of inquiry regarding the prevention of public violence and intimidation, to get to the bottom of all the accusations and counter-accusations regarding who was responsible for the violence that was racking the country and undermining the negotiations. Earlier in the year, Parliament adopted legislation – the Prevention of Public Violence and Intimidation Act of 1991 – to enable me to appoint a standing commission to investigate violence. The composition of the commission was the subject of consultation with other parties and led finally to the appointment of Judge Richard Goldstone as the chairman of the commission, which subsequently became widely known as the Goldstone Commission. Richard Goldstone was a small, dapper man with receding black hair and a lively, intelligent expression. Although he was widely respected, he also had his detractors. Some of his colleagues criticized him for being overambitious. Rumours that he even aspired one day to being appointed to the post of secretary-general of the United Nations – then held by Boutros Boutros Ghali – had led some of his, no doubt, mischievous colleagues to refer to him behind his back as Richard Richard Goldstone. Nevertheless, he had a well-deserved reputation of being a fearless, tenacious and liberal judge. I liked him and developed a healthy respect for his fairness and thoroughness.

During the rest of my presidency he played an invaluable role in relentlessly investigating violence and tracking down perpetrators. As a result of his work, we were slowly able to escape from the miasma of unfounded allegations, accusations, disinformation and propaganda which had previously shrouded the question of violence. Slowly, piece by piece, the Goldstone Commission began to make some sense of the masses of data that he and his team of investigators collected. He criticized any party or organization – whether the security forces, the ANC or the IFP – that he believed was responsible for violence and made useful recommendations regarding remedial action. I did everything I could to support him in the execution of his difficult task. For me, it was of the greatest importance to have a reliable and neutral organization to whom I could refer the increasing avalanche of accusations and allegations from political parties and from the media regarding the origins of violence.

I thought that by appointing the Kahn Committee, supported by the Ministers' Committee on Secret Projects, and the Goldstone Commission I would, at last, be able to stanch our haemorrhaging credibility by putting an end, once and for all, to allegations regarding the involvement of the security forces in wrongdoing. Events were later to prove that I was over-optimistic.

A week or two after I announced my Inkathagate package, I received a sharp reminder that the threat of violence did not come only from the conflict between the ANC and the IFP, or from faceless elements within the security forces. The far right, which for months had been rumbling with discontent, was about to show its teeth. Despite his attendance of the Conference on Violence and Intimidation a few weeks earlier, Eugene Terre'Blanche brazenly used violence and intimidation to try to stop me from addressing a National Party meeting in his 'stronghold' in the western Transvaal town of Ventersdorp. I was scheduled to address a meeting of the National Party in Ventersdorp on 9 August 1991. Terre'Blanche warned me to stay away and threatened to disrupt the meeting if I went ahead. Naturally, as leader of the National Party, I could not accept the right of any party to stop me from addressing my supporters anywhere I liked. Even more importantly, if I, as president, were to bow to his threat, it would be tantamount to admitting that the government could no longer maintain law and order. I was certainly not prepared to do that and decided to go ahead with the meeting.

As the date of the meeting drew nearer, the tension rose. The National Party had made arrangements for the proceedings to begin during the afternoon. Because of this, most of our supporters arrived at the venue early and were not troubled by the AWB. Marike and I were due to arrive only during the evening. On the morning of the meeting the police informed me that it looked as though the AWB protest would be more serious that they had expected. By midday they were even more concerned and sent in strong reinforcements.

At sunset Marike and I left Potchefstroom by car for Ventersdorp, about 70 kilometres away. For security reasons, my motorcade was longer than usual. As we approached Ventersdorp my advisers told me that it would be unsafe to proceed by car. A police helicopter picked us up beside the road and flew us to Ventersdorp. However, before we could descend to our designated landing spot at the hospital, the helicopter had to circle the town once again because the police spotted an AWB sniper on one of the rooftops. We finally landed at the hospital where we boarded one of the police's armoured personnel carriers which took us to the venue. We had to walk the last few yards to the hall, surrounded by a phalanx of police.

The situation was extremely tense. The Commando Hall, where we held the meeting, was protected by some 2,000 policemen and was surrounded by razor wire, police vehicles and police dogs. An equal number of AWB members, armed with pistols and hunting rifles, arrived at the hall just before the meeting was due to begin. They were determined to break through the police barricade and disrupt the meeting. The AWB members were egged on by one of their leaders, Piet Rudolph, the secretary-general of the AWB, to take on the police and to charge the razor wire. After their initial attempt was repulsed with tear-gas, members of the AWB reportedly opened fire on two minibuses. The police returned their fire, killing one of the AWB men and wounding another, who subsequently died in hospital. A third AWB supporter was killed when one of the minibuses, which had been attacked, careered through the crowd. Altogether, forty-eight people, including six policemen, were injured in the fracas.

At the end of the meeting, which took place without incident inside the hall, Marike and I visited a few of the injured in hospital, before being whisked away in the helicopter. I was deeply concerned about the deaths and the injuries. However, to have backed down before Terre'Blanche's threats would have been tantamount to admitting that free and fair elections would be impossible.

As far as I could recall, it was the first time that the police had shot and killed right-wing whites in this type of confrontation. The incident starkly underlined the need to to make progress with our efforts to counteract political violence. Fortunately the Preparatory Committee for the National Peace Initiative – which had emerged from the National Conference on Violence and Intimidation – had been making encouraging progress. In an unusual show of common purpose, the ANC, IFP and ANC members of the committee had reached agreement on the text of a draft National Peace Accord and had set 14 September 1991 as the date for the signing of the accord.

Three days before the accord was due to be signed, on 11 September 1991, I had a very confrontational meeting with Mr Mandela. We were deeply concerned over the ANC's clear failure to abide by the terms of the D. F. Malan Accord. If they were not willing to do so, what value would the Peace Accord have? During our meeting I told Mandela that I had not attacked him publicly for his blatant disregard of his undertakings in terms of the D. F. Malan Accord. Unlike him, I had refrained from scoring political points by publicly accusing him personally of being a killer, or of being responsible for the suffering of the people. I told him that his public attacks on me had become more outrageous by the day. I took him to task for accusing me overseas of wanting to make progress over the dead bodies of black people, to which he defiantly replied that he had also made such accusations in South Africa!

I then sharply accused Mandela of having breached every single provision of the D. F. Malan Accord. In terms of Operation Vula, it had infiltrated men and arms into the country and had continued to establish extensive underground structures manned by Umkhonto We Sizwe (MK) cadres. It had been involved in numerous armed attacks, particularly against the IFP in Natal. It had continued to make regular statements and threats, particularly those by people like Chris Hani, the head of Umkhonto We Sizwe (MK) that were bound to incite violence. I confronted him with recent statements by Hani in which he had said that MK was establishing regional command centres and structures throughout the country. In Nelspruit, Hani had said that 'the ANC was going to get what we want, all the weapons are here'. In Uitenhage he had boasted that 'if told, MK would go back to the bush, irrespective of what the NEC (National Executive Council) of the ANC is saying. We will get the mandate from the people and not from the executive of the ANC.'

Mandela's first response was to try to evade the issue. He questioned the information that the ANC had been shooting and killing people and had been organizing and training people underground. As I had done on many occasions when he had charged the security forces with wrongdoing, he asked where the evidence was. He said that if the law had been broken we should charge those responsible in court. I assured him that we had evidence, including the statements of people like Chris Hani – such as those which I had already quoted – and the details of weapons that had been seized in ANC-controlled squatter camps. However, the problem would not be solved simply by proceeding with prosecutions as Mandela had suggested. The ANC had to honour its agreements and bring the violent activities of its followers to an end. I threatened to scuttle the Peace Conference that was scheduled on 14 September 1991 if they did not do so. The meeting ended on a more conciliatory note, with a commitment from Mr Mandela to discuss my serious complaints with his senior advisers.

As things turned out, we received yet more firm assurances from the ANC that it would carry out its commitments under the D. F. Malan Accord. We accordingly decided to proceed with the Peace Accord, which was signed on 14 September 1991 by twenty-nine signatories, including the government, the ANC, the IFP and the trade unions. The accord made provision for codes of conduct for political organizations and the police, a National Peace Secretariat and a network of local and regional Peace Committees. One of its most important achievements was to endorse the establishment of the proposed commission of inquiry to investigate and prevent public violence, which I had announced at my Inkathagate press conference on 30 July 1990. However, the ANC would prove to be as lax in carrying out its commitments under the Peace Accord as it had been in honouring the D. F. Malan Accord.

20

Codesa I

The ANC and the government had divergent views on how the constitutional negotiations should take place. The ANC demanded that the National Party government should hand over power to a non-elected interim multiparty government. They maintained that such a multiparty government should rule the country while elections were held for a constitutional assembly which would write a new constitution. Elections would then be held in terms of the new constitution for a fully representative Parliament and government. The National Party and most of the other parties utterly rejected the idea that there would be a constitutional hiatus during a period of rule by a non-elected interim government. We were also adamantly opposed to the idea that the elected constitutional assembly would be given a blank cheque to impose whatever constitution it liked on the country. The National Party and other important parties such as the Inkatha Freedom Party of Chief Minister Mangosuthu Buthelezi insisted that a multiparty constitutional convention should draw up a new constitution, in terms of which the first democratic elections for a new Parliament would be held.

In January 1991, the ANC agreed to the convening of a multiparty conference, not to draw up a new constitution, but to decide on the next stages of the transformation process. The ANC continued to insist, however, that before this could happen, all the remaining obstacles to negotiations should first be removed. It was thus not until the end of November that year that twenty parties and political entities, deemed to have a proven basis for support, gathered at the Holiday Inn near Johannesburg International Airport to reach agreement on the rules for the first multiparty conference. It was decided that the conference would be known as the Convention for a Democratic South Africa (Codesa) and that decisions would be reached through a vaguely defined concept of 'sufficient consensus'. It was generally accepted that this would, in practice, mean that at least the major parties – the National Party, the ANC and the IFP – would have to agree before a proposal could be adopted by the Codesa. The IFP later marginalized itself by its obstructionist approach and its strategy of boycotting the proceedings. The PAC insisted that the convention should be held outside South Africa and objected to the two chairmen that had been proposed, Judges Ismael Mahomed and Piet Schabort. When it was overruled by the other parties, including the ANC and the National Party, it withdrew from the process. The Convention for a Democratic South Africa – which came to be known as Codesa I – was convened in a climate of crisis. Despite all Nelson Mandela's solemn undertakings before the signing of the Peace Accord, the ANC had still done hardly anything to honour its commitments under the the D. F. Malan Accord. Once again, on the eve of an important multiparty conference, the cabinet had to decide how to deal with the ANC's failure to carry out its commitments.

The issues involved included the demobilization of Umkhonto We Sizwe, the need to place arms caches under proper control and the question of amnesty. In the run-up to Codesa, I had insisted that these matters should be resolved to our satisfaction. On a number of occasions Minister Kobie Coetsee, and those who assisted him, reported back that the ANC was using delaying tactics. During the last few days before 20 December, the day on which the Codesa was due to begin, I met virtually on a daily basis with the ministers and the senior officials who were most closely involved in the negotiations – who were known as the Policy Group – to plan our strategy for the convention. The last meeting of the Policy Group before Codesa began at 5 p.m. on the evening of Thursday, 19 December.

At that meeting we learned that a deadlock had been reached in the working group that was dealing with the implementation of the D. F. Malan Accord and the ending of the ANC's armed struggle. The last-minute breakthrough, which the ANC had promised and for which we had all been hoping and waiting, had not occurred. Minister Coetsee and his team placed the blame squarely on the shoulders of the ANC. Once again I was faced with a stark choice: should I proceed or should I precipitate a crisis that would scuttle the launching of Codesa? I gave Kobie Coetsee instructions to contact the ANC in a final attempt to find a solution and to inform them that I was seriously considering not going ahead with Codesa. He reported back that the ANC had once again promised to make rapid progress in the immediate future on the outstanding issues relating to their compliance with the D. F. Malan Accord, and had committed itself to rectifying the matter. A long discussion ensued within the Policy Group during which we considered the pros and cons of all the alternatives. In the end, we reached consensus that the cancellation of Codesa at that stage would be catastrophic. I was extremely irritated, because I had been placed in a catch-22 situation. There was also consensus that we could not simply sweep the problem under the carpet. The softest option was to continue with the launching of Codesa, but to adopt a very strong position during the conference on the ANC's delaying tactics and failure to implement its undertakings.

I instructed Minister Kobie Coetsee to convey a message to Mr Mandela that we would continue with Codesa, but that he should know that we would make a number of sharply critical comments about the ANC's breaches of the D. F. Malan Accord. He left the meeting and reported back a little later that the message had been conveyed to Thabo Mbeki, who had promised to pass it on to Mr Mandela. He also reported that there was understanding for my concern over the delays and the fact that I would consequently have to take a strong line. It was within this context that I finalized the drafting of the speech that I would deliver at Codesa the next day on 20 December. On the whole it was a very positive speech. However, I was sharply critical of the ANC's delaying tactics.

Codesa began on the morning of 20 December at the World Trade Centre at Kempton Park, which would subsequently become the main centre for the negotiations. The World Trade Centre is a cavernous exhibition centre, immediately adjacent to Johannesburg International Airport. It is a large squat building comprising two floors. Most of the building is taken up by an enormous exhibition hall surrounded on three sides by first-floor balconies leading to the suites of the various delegations and large entertainment areas and conference rooms. The twenty delegations (the nineteen parties that had emerged from the Holiday Inn preparatory conference and the South African government) were seated in a large U-form around a stage set against the rear wall of the hall. Behind the stage, where the co-chairmen and the secretariat of the conference sat, there was an enormous modernistic black-and-white mural which depicted, not altogether successfully, the racial harmony which we all hoped would emerge from the convention. Diplomatic representatives, international observers and the small army of local and international journalists, photographers and TV crews, watched the proceedings from the first-floor balcony surrounding the hall.

The twenty delegations, with almost 300 delegates, were seated in alphabetical order in the hall itself. They included five parties from the 'tricameral' Parliament (the National Party and the Democratic Party from the House of Assembly; the Labour Party from the (coloured) House of Representatives; and the National People's Party and Solidarity from the (Indian) House of Delegates); delegations from the six self-governing homelands (including the IFP government of KwaZulu) and the four independent states; and four delegations from outside the 'tricameral' Parliament, including the ANC and its allies the South African Communist Party, the Natal Indian Congress and the Transvaal Indian Congress. In addition, there was a separate delegation from the South African government – of which I was the leader – because it was accepted that, as one of the main custodians of the process, the government's role would, of necessity, not be quite the same as that of the National Party. The parties that had decided not to participate in Codesa included three right-wing parties, the Conservative Party, the Afrikaner Weerstandsbeweging (AWB) and the Herstigte Nasionale Party and three small radical black parties, the Pan Africanist Congress (PAC); Azanian People's Organization (AZAPO) and the Black Consciousness Movement (BCM).

As the delegates gathered for the opening session, there was a hum of excitement and expectation in the cavernous hall. It was almost like a carnival. The proceedings were presided over by the two chairmen – Judge Schabort, who was identified, more or less, with the old order, and Judge Mohamed who was a voluble advocate of the new. The great spectrum of faith within South Africa was reflected in the prayers, incantations and mantras during the religious opening, in which virtually every denomination and recognized religion participated. We had, at last, arrived at the threshold of structured negotiations.

The arrangements for Codesa I had been planned to the finest detail. The main participants had already reached broad agreement on what would be included in a Declaration of Intent which would be signed by all the parties. Understandings had also been reached regarding Codesa's infrastructure and the working procedures that it would follow. There was even agreement on the order in which the leaders of delegations would deliver their introductory speeches. In terms of this agreement I, as state president, would speak last.

The convention started with opening speeches by all the delegation leaders. The general tone was positive, constructive and optimistic. Still, most speakers found a way of staking out the key negotiating positions that their respective parties would adopt. As agreed, my turn came right at the end. Before I dealt with the ANC's delaying tactics, I made a surprise announcement. In what the media later described as a breathtaking policy switch I announced that the government would be prepared to consider a compromise to bridge the fundamental difference between the ANC's position that the new constitution should be drawn up by an elected constitutional assembly, and ours that it should be written by a multiparty constitutional convention. I proposed a two-phase process of constitution writing: a new interim constitution would be drafted by the Codesa process, in terms of which the first fully representative Parliament would be elected, which would in turn draft and adopt the final constitution. This proposal was, in fact, much closer to our own opening position than that of the ANC and laid the basis for the historic compromise that would ultimately open the way to a constitutional solution. The negotiating parties would reach agreement on an interim constitution which would be adopted by the 'tricameral' Parliament, with its National Party majority. A new fully representative Parliament would be elected under the new constitution, which would also act as a constitutional assembly. It would write and adopt a final constitution that would have to comply with pre-agreed immutable constitutional principles. Before the final constitution could come into effect a new Constitutional Court would have to certify that it complied with the constitutional principles. During this period the country would be ruled by an elected transitional multiparty government under the interim constitution. My proposal meant that the core demands of both sides would be essentially satisfied.

The initiative had caught the ANC and all the other parties completely by surprise. After this, I dealt with the ANC's delaying tactics. I said that the ANC had still not ended its armed struggle. It had not complied with important undertakings in the Pretoria Minute and the D. F. Malan Accord and was applying delaying tactics. I explained that before we had signed the Peace Accord on 14 September, I had considered making this problem, which included the identification of illegal arms caches, a condition for the signing of the Peace Accord. However, in the light of renewed promises from the ANC to honour its undertakings without further delay, I had decided not to do so. I also accused the ANC of breaking these renewed promises and placed a question mark over its participation in Codesa while it still had a private army. I concluded with the observation that an organization which was still committed to armed struggle could not be completely trusted when it, at the same time, committed itself to peacefully negotiated solutions. I accordingly demanded that the ANC (and the PAC) should make a clear choice between peace through negotiation or a power struggle through violence. On a more constructive note, I summed up the real challenge that confronted Codesa as being the need to achieve a win/win outcome and to reconcile the many conflicting claims of the diverse interests within the country in a reasonable manner. I dealt in some detail with the differing needs and conflicting demands of the privileged and the less privileged; of the employed and the unemployed; and of the majority and the cultural minorities. I made a plea that we should all learn to proclaim not only the truths that suited our own causes, but also to recognize and understand the truths that did not suit us.

According to the newspapers my speech was received with loud applause – but not from Mr Mandela and Mr Cyril Ramaphosa, the ANC's chief negotiator, who sat stiffly silent while I spoke. Mandela was coldly furious about my sharp attack on the ANC and its failure to honour its agreements and insisted on a second turn to speak. His speech, labelled a tirade by the press, was one of the most vicious personal attacks on a political opponent that most of those present at Codesa had ever heard. He accused me of being the head of an illegitimate, discredited minority regime and of being incapable of upholding moral standards.

As he piled insult on insult, I found it difficult to control my fury. My first reaction, while he accused me of dishonesty and of having manipulated the procedure by insisting on speaking last, was to walk to the microphone and rip off the ANC's mask in the strongest possible verbal counter-attack. Never before had I been subjected to such an unjustified attack on my integrity – and this, despite the fact that he had been warned that I would sharply criticize the ANC's non-compliance with the D. F. Malan Accord. I found it extremely difficult to suppress my temper and my deep sense of indignation. Fortunately, Mandela spoke long enough to give me time to regain control of myself. When he returned to his seat, I was calmer. I realized that all the reform initiatives for which my team and I had worked so hard would be in jeopardy if I gave in to my natural political instincts and responded to Mandela in his own abusive terms. National interest demanded that I should transcend my own ego. In a very brief reply I accordingly refrained from launching a personal attack on Mandela, even though I had good reason to do so.

I said that unless the problem of Umkhonto We Sizwe was resolved, 'we will have a party with a pen in one hand while claiming the right to have arms in the other'. It was the only party at the convention with its own armed wing and secret arms caches. I said that I did not believe in playing the man, but rather the ball. For that reason, I had not attacked Mr Mandela as a person, although he had frequently made hurtful remarks about me both locally and abroad. I insisted that the armed struggle was a stumbling block to progress towards the ideals that Codesa represented. The problem had to be resolved, despite the fact that bilateral negotiations between the government and the ANC had not thus far produced acceptable results. I denied the charge that I had acted in bad faith by going public on a matter under discussion with the ANC leadership. I informed Codesa that I had warned the ANC that if there was not sufficient progress, I would have to raise this question at Codesa.

On that dramatic note the convention adjourned until the following day. At a press conference shortly afterwards Mandela had already begun, once again, to adopt a reconciliatory tone. He played down his attack on me as something which he believed had to be said, but was now over and done with. The following morning he and Ramaphosa made a special point of walking across the hall to shake my hand. At the end of the second day's proceedings when we adjourned for the Christmas recess, he did so once again. I accepted Mandela's gestures as gracefully as I could, but felt that there was no longer any possibility of our ever again having a close relationship. The fact remained that Mandela's vicious and unwarranted attack created a rift between us that never again fully healed. Nevertheless, we would both frequently have to rise above our personal antipathy to resolve deadlocks and keep the negotiations on course during the tumultuous months and years that lay ahead.

There was widespread speculation in the press concerning the reasons for Mandela's outburst. Some said that although the ANC had been warned that I would criticize them, they had not expected such a sharp attack. Others wrote that the presence of international observers and the world media spurred Mandela to attack me. Others suggested that he might have been irritated over the fact that I had once again seized the reform initiative with my surprise announcement of the possibility of an interim government and an early election. In retrospect, the least generous interpretation that one can place on Mandela's behaviour is that he wilfully set out to humiliate me as part of a calculated political strategy to denigrate his main political opponent. The kindest explanation that I can accept, is that he either did not receive my message on the eve of Codesa, or that he had genuinely misunderstood my position and misinterpreted my motives.

Before Codesa adjourned eighteen of the twenty delegations solemnly signed the Declaration of Intent that had been agreed upon during the preparatory negotiations. It contained a commitment to all the basic elements of a democratic state: South Africa would be a united, democratic, non-racial, non-sexist state; the constitution would be sovereign; we would have a multiparty democracy with universal franchise and regular elections; there would be a division of powers between the executive, the legislature and the judiciary; the diversity of the languages, religions and cultures of the people of South Africa would be respected; and universally accepted rights would be protected and entrenched in a Charter of Human Rights. The two delegations which did not sign the declaration were those of Bophuthatswana – because it implied the re-incorporation of the independent states into South Africa – and of KwaZulu because, in the view of the IFP, the reference to an undivided South Africa precluded the establishment of a genuine federation.

For me – despite Mandela's vicious attack – Codesa I had been a great success. I believed that the constitutional compromise that I had announced in my speech had once again given us the initiative and that we were well positioned to achieve our basic goals. We had at last embarked on the constitutional negotiations which would create a new South Africa.

21

Governing the Country
and the Referendum

While all of this negotiation was going on, we still had to govern the country. Next to the crisis of violence and the constitutional process, the economy and the effective provision of basic services to all our people was our most urgent priority. In my 2 February 1990 speech, I sketched my plans for economic reform. I said that a new South Africa would have to be bolstered by a sound and growing economy, with particular emphasis on the creation of employment. To achieve this the government would have to make fundamental structural changes to its economy, just as its major trading partners had done a decade or so earlier. In particular we would gradually have to reduce inflation to the levels of our principal trading partners; we would have to encourage personal initiative and savings; all our economic decisions would have to be subjected to stringent financial measures and discipline; we needed to reform our tax system; and we had to encourage exports as a key element in promoting economic growth.

Right from the beginning of my presidency we tried to give a higher priority to the economy than my predecessors had done. To assist me with this task, I appointed Dr Wim de Villiers, a former executive chairman of General Mining, one of South Africa's leading mining houses, as minister of administration and privatization. I believed that the National Party was short of talent and experience in the economic and financial fields and that we needed to break the mould that only politicians could be appointed to ministerial posts. In March 1990, I strengthened Wim de Villiers' role in the overall management of the economy by giving him responsibility for economic coordination. Before his untimely death at the end of 1991, Dr De Villiers made an important contribution to the government's privatization strategy and to the rationalization of the public service. At the beginning of 1992 I appointed another leading businessman, Mr Derek Keys, the chief executive of Gencor, one of South Africa's largest conglomerates, to the cabinet, first as minister of trade and industry and of economic coordination.

In May 1992, Barend du Plessis, the minister of finance and my main opponent for the leadership of the party in February 1989, resigned because of the heavy toll that his duties had taken on his health. He was one of a number of members of my original cabinet who left politics during the first years of my presidency. At the end of 1991, the cabinet lost Dr Stoffel van der Merwe who had been a prominent member of our negotiating team. During 1992 the crippling workload of the minister of constitutional development, Dr Gerrit Viljoen, began to affect his health. I first lightened his load by appointing him as minister of state and by shifting Roelf Meyer to the constitutional development portfolio. However, Dr Viljoen's health continued to deteriorate and at the end of November 1992 he retired completely from politics. His retirement was a heavy blow to me. I had come to rely on him as one of my key advisers and his contribution to the negotiating process had been exceptionally valuable.

Derek Keys succeeded Barend du Plessis as minister of finance in May 1992. During the following four years he played a leading role in ensuring the success of the transition to the new dispensation. He had the remarkable ability to express complex economic concepts in simple and comprehensible terms. He also had the advantage of having virtually no political profile at all. This made it much easier for him to communicate with the ANC's economic experts in the newly established National Economic Forum (NEF), which brought together government, business and labour to discuss the country's economic problems and challenges. The NEF became a kind of economic Codesa in which ANC and Cosatu members were able to gain firsthand experience of the enormous economic and financial problems that confronted the country. With irresistible logic, Keys was able to spell out the difficult options which confronted South Africa and to steer the ANC in the direction of fiscal discipline and acceptance of the stark economic realities of the globalized economy. The basic requirements of the South African economy were so clear that Keys sometimes referred to himself as the 'minister of the obvious'. The six guiding principles which he believed were essential for economic restructuring and recovery were: the generation of sufficient investment in labour to improve skills and promote employment; macro-economic stability with regard to prices, interest rates and the exchange rate; fiscal discipline; trade liberalization with a view to strengthening the competitive position of South African producers in both domestic and foreign markets; the promotion of effective competition; and the strengthening of market forces.

Derek Keys was the right man in the right job at the right time. I gave him all the support I could. However, we faced a very difficult challenge. Our economy had grown at an average rate of only 1.4 per cent during the 1980s. At the beginning of my presidency the effects of the world economic recession on South Africa were further aggravated by one of the worst droughts of the century and the plummeting prices of gold and many of our other exports.

The economic recession cut deeply and led to a 4.5 per cent drop in employment and a serious decline in government revenues.

Nevertheless, despite the adverse conditions, we were able to make headway in dealing with many of our economic problems. We reduced interest rates and the growth in government consumption expenditure and cut inflation from 16 per cent to less than 10 per cent. At one stage, I suggested to Derek Keys that we should consider a dramatic initiative to restore national and international faith in our economy. I had in mind a kind of economic 2 February 1990 speech, announcing a bold package of economic reforms and initiatives including the immediate abolition of the financial rand and a dramatic relaxation of exchange control. Derek Keys was interested in the proposal and promised to give it careful consideration, together with his advisers. He later reported back to me that, great though the temptation was, he and his advisers were of the opinion that the situation in South Africa was still too uncertain and the risks were too great. I accepted his advice but have often wondered what the results would have been if I had followed my instincts which were telling me to take an economic quantum leap.

Our main reason for wanting economic growth was, of course, to provide the resources to address the pressing socio-economic needs of millions of South Africans who lived in conditions of unacceptable poverty. It was – and remains – critically important that constitutional transformation should be accompanied by tangible improvements in the standard of living of most South Africans.

It was for this reason that I placed special emphasis on the improved provision of social services. When I became president, government spending on housing, health, education, welfare and social security amounted to 38.3 per cent of the national budget. By my last year as president it had increased to 44 per cent. This increased expenditure reflected our concerted effort to improve the quality of life of all South Africans. It enabled us to equalize state old-age pensions for South Africans of all races by 1 September 1993; to continue our efforts to close the gap in per capita expenditure in education and to redirect resources from first world medical services to primary health care aimed at improving the general health of the third world segment of our population. Sadly, the delivery of improved services to people on the ground was often disrupted by our opponents for political purposes.

Throughout this period, while we were negotiating with the ANC and other parties and while we continued to grapple with the problems of day-to-day government, I still had to be able to take my power base in the National Party with me. The Conservative Party, under the leadership of Andries Treurnicht, was taking full advantage of the fears and uncertainties that had been generated among a segment of the white population by our reform initiatives. Every effort that we launched to promote negotiations and every agreement that we reached were dismissed in Conservative Party propaganda as concessions and deviations under pressure from the election promises that we had made during the 1989 election campaign. The on-going political violence and the ANC's inability to control its followers were energetically and often deftly exploited by the right wing to sow fear, suspicion and doubt in the minds of white voters. And the unfavourable economic circumstances were tailor-made for exploitation by an opposition party.

This onslaught from the right increasingly began to take its toll. At the end of 1991 the National Party suffered a painful defeat in a by-election in Virginia, a gold-mining community in the Orange Free State. In 1989 we had held the constituency with a narrow majority. In the 1991 by-election the Conservative Party had won with a majority of more than 2,000. It was a large swing and, according to the experts, indicated that the Conservative Party would be able to win a general election among white voters.

I was deeply concerned. As a democrat I have always believed that a government should have a valid mandate from the voters for the implementation of important policies. The mandate that I had received in 1989 from the white electorate was visibly slipping away from me and the National Party. Our credibility was being seriously eroded. I realized that something would have to be done to tip the scales back in the National Party's favour. The conviction grew in me that I would have to advance the date of the referendum – which I had in any case promised to white voters – and make it the final test of white support for my reforms. However, I decided to wait for the result of another by-election which was due to be held in February 1992 in my old university town of Potchefstroom. For the moment, I kept my ideas about an early referendum to myself. I nevertheless cautiously tested the water at a *bosberaad*, which I held together with the cabinet and other leading members of the National Party at D'Nyala on 5 and 6 December 1991.

The main objective of the *bosberaad* was to prepare for the first session of Codesa I. It was there that we laid the foundation for my surprise announcement regarding our acceptance of an interim government and an interim parliament. Because we had intended that this initiative should also accelerate negotiations, leading to an early election, the question arose of when a referendum should be held. No definite conclusion was reached. However, I said that a referendum might well be held before the end of 1992, followed by the adoption of an interim constitution early in 1993 and an election before the end of October 1993. As it happened, the interim constitution was adopted only in December 1993 and the election took place only at the end of April 1994.

The by-election in Potchefstroom was caused by the death of the Speaker, Mr Louis le Grange. Potchefstroom had, for decades, been a safe National Party seat. I decided that the National Party should throw everything it had into the by-election – which was due to be held on 19 February 1992 – to reverse the swing away from us to the Conservative Party. From their side, the Conservative Party did the same. The media emphasized the importance of the Potchefstroom by-election as a major test of white support for the National Party's reform initiatives. The result of all this was that the Conservative Party fought a tough, dirty and emotionally laden campaign. The National Party mobilized a major effort in support of its candidate. Minister after minister from the National Party addressed house meetings and even canvassed from door to door. In my own support for the campaign I went out of my way to give a clinical analysis of the National Party's goals and policy framework regarding new constitutional developments. I did not shy away in any manner from the logical consequences of one-man, one-vote in a united South Africa. This led the *Financial Times* to comment, after the result of the by-election, that the National Party campaign had been blunt about political realities and short on promises. There was no attempt to put on a *verkrampte* face to reassure Nat waverers.

On the evening of the Potchefstroom by-election, most of the members of the cabinet and I were guests of the board of directors of Sanlam, one of South Africa's giant insurance companies. This function was an annual event arising from the close ties that existed at that time between the National Party and Sanlam. Sanlam, together with the Volkskas Bank and a few other institutions, meant for the Afrikaner in the economic sphere what the National Party meant for the Afrikaner in the political sphere. Late that evening before we all went home, I excused myself and went to telephone the National Party's key people in Potchefstroom. Some of the veteran organizers had predicted that we were going to lose and that the Conservative Party would win with a large majority. I called aside my colleague, Dawie de Villiers, who was one of my confidants, and told him that if their prediction was right, I would call a referendum.

When I received the result of the by-election, it was like a punch on the chin for the National Party and for me. Our majority of almost 2,000 in 1989 was reversed and the Conservative Party won with a majority of 2,140 votes. The by-election result was widely interpreted as a no to the National Party's constitutional reform proposals and sent shock waves through the whole country which also reverberated overseas. The *Nasionale Pers* newspapers commented that the implication of the result was that I could not be sure of a majority if a referendum on a new constitution were to be held among white voters at that stage. Election pundits also interpreted the result as proof that a countrywide election among whites would lead to a Conservative Party victory. The Conservative Party immediately demanded an election.

At 9 a.m. on 20 February, there was a meeting of the Executive Committee of the Federal Council of the National Party. The members of the executive thought that it was just an ordinary scheduled meeting. However, I had long planned that it should take place on the morning after the Potchefstroom by-election. I informed the executive that I had decided to call a referendum in the face of the devastating result in Potchefstroom. There was a shocked silence. Some members argued against my decision, but I was convinced in my view that the National Party and I could not continue with the negotiations if we did not get a democratic endorsement of our policies, which had undergone a fair amount of adaptation since the general election of 1989. In addition, the National Party was in essence a new party as a result of its transformation into a true non-racial party. If we wished to win respect in the negotiating process we would have to have an endorsement in our favour from the white voters so that our mandate could not be questioned.

The normal weekly National Party caucus meeting took place at 10 a.m. that morning. When I told the caucus that I was immediately going to call a referendum, there was shock and consternation. It was clear to me that if I had put my decision to the vote the majority of the caucus would have opposed what they then regarded as an over-hasty and risky decision. However, under the caucus rules and the conventions governing the powers of the party leader, I was not required to put the matter to a vote. I decided to bite the bullet and to resign as leader of the National Party if the referendum did not produce a positive result.

I announced the referendum at a press conference immediately after the caucus meeting. I rejected the idea of an election on a constituency basis because it would not give the same weight to every vote and because, in an election, all sorts of matters such as unemployment, the state of the economy and such things often play a decisive role. I was determined to focus attention on one matter and one matter alone: the necessity for constitutional reform based on the National Party's commitment to a united South Africa; the abolition of racial discrimination; universal franchise; and a constitution which would extend fair democratic protection to minorities. On Monday, 24 February I announced that the referendum for the voters of the House of Assembly (the white voters) would take place on Tuesday, 17 March 1992. The question to which they would have to answer yes or no was:

> Do you support the continuation of the reform process that the state president started on 2 February 1990 and which is aimed at a new constitution through negotiations?

In my statement I said that the referendum was being held only among whites because it was only they who were divided on the necessity of constitutional transformation on which I had embarked. I explained that we had reached a stage in the multiparty negotiations where it would soon be necessary for me to commit the government to binding agreements. In reiterating my commitment to a new constitutional system that would bring violence to an end and ensure stability, progress and justice for all, I asked the white electorate to give me a strong mandate. I promised to abide by the verdict of the referendum. Everybody accepted that this meant that I would resign and call a general election if we were defeated.

During the following weeks I campaigned vigorously for a Yes vote throughout the country. I addressed meeting after meeting during which I reassured voters that we would ensure that their basic interests would be reasonably protected in the negotiations which lay ahead. I stressed that we had already reached consensus in the negotiations on a number of key aspects relating to the future constitution – including a multiparty democracy; a bicameral Parliament; a Charter of Fundamental Rights; the division of powers between the branches of government; an independent judiciary; proportional representation; a strong basis for regional government; the maintenance of language and cultural rights; and community-based education for those who wanted it.

While making it clear that consensus still had to be reached on a number of minimum requirements, I committed myself and the government not to accept any agreements that did not offer reasonable provision for the prevention of domination and the effective protection of minorities; the protection of property; career security for the public service; a market-oriented economy with free enterprise and fiscal responsibility; constitutionally protected devolution of power to regional and local governments; and a form of power-sharing.

Later, and especially since the 1994 election, there would be heated debates and vicious recriminations on whether the National Party and I delivered on the undertakings that we gave during the referendum. I sincerely believe that we did – as I will explain in the conclusion to this book.

We ran a good campaign and managed to generate enthusiasm for reform which surpassed our expectations. As I did my walkabouts and addressed public meetings I was overwhelmed by the warmth of the reception that I was given. I received a strong impression that the great majority of white South Africans had accepted the need for change and wanted to see rapid progress with our reform initiatives.

We were helped by positive media coverage, as well as by the business sector and the small opposition Democratic Party, which threw their weight fully behind the Yes vote and mounted their own campaigns in support of our common effort. Only the Conservative Party, the Afrikaner Weerstandsbeweging (AWB) and the tiny Herstigte Nasionale Party campaigned for the No vote. They claimed that the referendum was the white voters' last chance to stop what they called the 'National Party/ANC alliance from imposing a black government on the country'. Their campaign was essentially racist, while ours was clearly aimed at a non-racial South Africa in which there would be no form of racial discrimination.

The voting took place on 17 March 1992 and the results were finally available the next day – which was also my fifty-sixth birthday. I could not have asked for a better present. Sixty-nine per cent of the white voters had voted Yes. There had been a Yes vote majority in all the voting regions – except for Pietersburg in the Northern Transvaal, where we had nevertheless received 43 per cent of the vote. Despite the initial misgivings and dire predictions of some of my colleagues in the National Party, my calculated gamble had paid off handsomely. We had received the unambiguous mandate that we needed to continue with the negotiation process.

Although the ANC had publicly objected to the idea of a whites-only referendum and were apprehensive about the outcome, they had sensibly done nothing to impede our campaign. They realized that a loss for the Yes vote would throw South Africa into turmoil. After the result was made known, Nelson Mandela said that it was a great source of relief for the whole country and that it had endorsed the position of the majority of black South Africans whose voices could not be heard.

I made a short victory speech to a group of well-wishers and the media from the back steps of Tuynhuys, the seat of centuries of colonial governors and white heads of state. I said that it did not happen often that a nation was given the opportunity of rising above itself, but that was exactly what the white electorate had done. I added that that day, in a certain sense, was the birth of the new South Africa. In retrospect, it was not – but it did show that the infant was alive and kicking in the womb.

I was jubilant. I felt that the result freed my hands to concentrate on the job at hand – the successful conclusion of the negotiating process.

22

Codesa II and Mass Action

Codesa I established five working groups to prepare the way for a second plenary conference – Codesa II – which was scheduled to be held on 15 May 1992. Working Group 1 dealt with the creation of a climate in which all parties could compete freely. It also considered the role which the international community might play in the transition process. Working Group 2 dealt with constitutional principles – including the key question of whether South Africa should be a unitary, federal or confederal state. Working Group 3 was given the task of considering arrangements for the transition from the old system to a new constitution. In particular, it had to make proposals to ensure that in the run-up to national elections the political playing fields would be even. Working Group 4 dealt with the future constitutional position and probable re-incorporation of the independent homelands – Transkei, Ciskei, Venda and Bophuthatswana. The task of Working Group 5 was to work out a plan for the speedy implementation of the agreements reached by the other working groups. Because they took longer to complete their deliberations than had been anticipated, Working Group 5 had very little work to do.

During the first four months of 1992 the working groups made substantial progress. All of them – except Working Group 2 – succeeded in reaching agreement on the questions that had been referred to them. Although Working Group 2 could not agree on some key issues, it nevertheless reached consensus on a broad constitutional framework, much of which was subsequently incorporated into the transitional constitution of 1993. This framework included: a Transitional National Assembly, elected on a proportional basis with half the members elected from national lists and half from regional lists; a Parliament comprising a National Assembly and a Senate which would be bound by constitutional principles agreed by Codesa; a multiparty transitional government; and a final constitution which would be written and adopted by the National Assembly, acting as a Constitutional Assembly.

The critical issues on which consensus could not be achieved were the mechanisms for the adoption of the final constitution. The National Party originally insisted on a 75 per cent majority, while the ANC wanted a two-thirds majority. The ANC also refused to accept the National Party view that the Senate, which would represent minorities, should have the same powers as the National Assembly in defending the constitution and guarding over regional rights.

The National Party's insistence on a high majority for the acceptance of the final constitution was misinterpreted – particularly by the ANC and its allies – as an attempt to entrench a disproportionate minority role in a future constitutional dispensation. This was not the case. The principle was accepted throughout the world that constitutions – because of their fundamental importance – should be adopted or amended only by special majorities. For example, in the United States any amendment of the constitution requires a two-thirds majority in Congress and the approval of three quarters of the states. In the Federal Republic of Germany, some of the basic democratic provisions of the constitution – the so-called Eternity Clauses – cannot be amended at all.

However, Mandela and the ANC insisted that the National Party and the minorities that it represented should, as he put it, simply submit their fate to the will of a simple majority. They regarded our proposals to build in checks and balances into the system or to accommodate justifiable minority concerns as efforts to cling to some form of minority veto. Their position was clear and uncompromising: any party that secured more than 50 per cent of the vote would have the right to impose its wishes on the rest of society.

A distinction should be made between our position on the majorities required to adopt the new constitution on the one hand, and our proposal with regard to power-sharing on the other. An essential element of our mandate in the election of 1989 and the referendum of 1992 was the concept of power-sharing. This was the National Party's answer to the ANC's simplistic concept of majority rule in a complex and divided society. We wanted to prevent too much power from being concentrated in the hands of any single party or institution. It was, and remains, a fallacy that our approach to power-sharing related only to multiparty participation in the cabinet or other executive bodies. We advocated a power-sharing package which included concepts such as the separation of powers; the devolution of power to regional and local governments; increased majorities for very important decisions and the limitation of the powers of the president. I went out of my way at all times to explain that while power-sharing at the cabinet and executive level was an important aspect of our power-sharing vision, it was certainly not the only goal.

As far as the multiparty participation at the cabinet and executive level was concerned we chose to adopt a very ambitious initial negotiating position, namely a model broadly similar to the practical arrangement in Switzerland. Our position was that a winner-takes-all constitution, where a party with 51 per cent of the vote would have 100 per cent of the power, would be the worst possible model for a country like South Africa with its complexities.

Instead, we proposed a system in which all the most important parties emerging from an election would compose the government. We suggested that a small Executive Council consisting of the three, four or five most important parties, should determine policy on the basis of consensus. The cabinet would be appointed by such an Executive Council on the basis of consensus and negotiations. The chairman of the Executive Council, who would be appointed on a rotational basis for a period of six months or a year, would be the president of the country during his term as chairman.

We did not see this as an attempt to cling to power, or to co-opt others into our government, but as a means of ensuring that the complex nature of our society would, at least during the extended period of transition, be accommodated in our governmental institutions. Neither was it out of step with constitutional theory relating to the maintenance of democracy in divided societies. In the view of the respected British political scientist, Vernon Bogdanor, 'Some kind of power-sharing has been a feature of governments in all societies that have successfully overcome their internal divisions; I am not aware of any divided society that has been able to achieve stability without power-sharing.'

Nonetheless, our specific proposal was never part of our bottom line. I realized that the whole question of power-sharing at the executive level was a very sensitive issue in the negotiating process. I accordingly urged our researchers and negotiators to work on alternatives and fall-back positions.

By 13 May, the government and the ANC had still failed to resolve a number of deadlocked questions – including our demands for power-sharing and increased majorities. Once again, a crisis loomed on the eve of an important constitutional conference. The opening of the plenary session on 15 May 1992 was delayed until twelve, then until 2 p.m. and finally until 4 p.m. while the National Party and ANC delegations wrestled unsuccessfully in Working Group 2 with the outstanding issues. The ANC delegation was led by Cyril Ramaphosa, its chief negotiator. Ramaphosa had previously been the secretary-general of the National Union of Mineworkers – where he had gained extensive experience in tough negotiations with the Chamber of Mines, which represented South Africa's large mining companies. Ramaphosa's large, round head was framed by a beard and receding hair of about the same length. His relaxed manner and convivial expression were contradicted by coldly calculating eyes, which seemed to be searching continuously for the softest spot in the defences of his opponents. His silver tongue and honeyed phrases lulled potential victims while his arguments relentlessly tightened around them.

The National Party team in Working Group 2 was led by Deputy Minister Dr Tertius Delport, a former professor of law who had a conservative reputation. At the working group meeting on the morning of 15 May Ramaphosa, in his mellifluous tones, appeared to make a concession which could break the deadlock: the ANC would agree that the final constitution would be approved by a 70 per cent majority, and the Bill of Rights by 75 per cent. Then came the sting: Ramaphosa insisted that should the National Assembly fail after six months to pass the final constitution by the required majority, it could then be adopted by a 50 per cent majority in a national referendum. Delport immediately saw the trap. Ramaphosa's deadlock-breaking proposal meant that the ANC could simply delay the constitutional process for six months and then submit whatever constitution it liked to a referendum, which it would in all likelihood win. Delport frequently had to break away to consult me and other members of our delegation. I instructed him to hold firm. He did – and the ANC never forgave him for his dogged refusal to bow to their bullying tactics.

Later that evening Ramaphosa announced that the ANC was withdrawing from Working Group 2. He blamed Delport's unwillingness to drive the working group towards an agreement for the breakdown. In fact, as Ramaphosa later revealed to the media, it was he, himself, who had engineered the collapse of Codesa II. He said that he wanted to show the people of South Africa that they were dealing with an enemy that will not give in easily.

At 10 p.m. that night Mandela and I met over a cup of coffee to discuss the deadlock. Both he and I were determined to keep the negotiating process on course and to accentuate the many positive achievements of the Codesa working groups. We decided that the outstanding matters should be referred back to the Codesa Management Committee for further consideration and discussion. The next morning both he and I made conciliatory closing statements to the conference and to the press. I said that although we had started off on the wrong foot, we had managed, jointly, thanks to the wisdom and the commitment of the leaders of all the delegations, to make sure that we transformed crisis into success and progress.

Our efforts to put a positive gloss on Codesa II could not conceal for long that very serious strains had developed which would soon usher in one of the most critical periods of the whole transformation process.

The fact is that by May 1992 the constitutional negotiations at Codesa no longer suited the ANC and its allies. Many elements within the ANC alliance were frustrated by the long, drawn-out process and were worried that the ANC negotiators had made too many concessions in the talks that had preceded Codesa II. Important factions of the alliance – particularly the powerful Congress of South African Trade Unions (Cosatu) – were worried that they had been marginalized during the negotiations. In fact, Cosatu had wanted to be represented by its own delegation at Codesa, but its application had been rejected. Other radicals within the alliance – and particularly leading members of the South African Communist Party – were also wary of the Codesa talks. The negotiated, step-by-step transfer of power to a new constitutional dispensation did not accord with their revolutionary doctrines and inclinations. They still favoured the revolutionary expulsion of the government and the seizure of power by the people. They believed that they could achieve this goal by bringing enough people into the streets; by crippling the economy with national strikes; by widespread civil disobedience and by occupying government buildings and facilities. All this, together, became known as the Leipzig option after the mass demonstrations that had taken place in Leipzig a few years earlier and which had led to the collapse of the East German government.

In March 1992, Cosatu had tried to by-pass Codesa by launching its own campaign for the establishment of an interim government by June, followed by elections for a Constituent Assembly before the end of the year and the adoption of a new constitution during 1993. They had also announced a programme of mass action in support of these demands which would include mass rallies and protests. Following the failure of Codesa II the centre of gravity in the ANC/SACP/Cosatu alliance shifted to Cosatu and the radicals. Early in June, the alliance announced its intention of launching a four-phase programme of rolling mass action which was intended to culminate in the ousting of the South African government and its replacement by an interim government. The first phase, which would begin on 16 June (Soweto Day), would include sit-ins, rallies and the occupation of government buildings; the second phase would include more nationwide campaigns; the third phase would centre on a three-day general strike and the fourth phase – called operation Exitgate – was supposed to force the government from power.

The ANC's support for this programme was in direct contravention to the letter and spirit of all the agreements that we had painstakingly reached since the Groote Schuur Minute at the beginning of May 1990. On 15 June I said that protest actions of the envisaged extent and nature did not accord with the spirit of honest negotiation to which the ANC and its alliance partners had committed themselves at Codesa. They were also at variance with the spirit of the Peace Accord. I rejected the argument that the deadlocks at the time justified mass action which would be extremely harmful to the country as a whole. The planned actions of the ANC and its allies were untimely, uncalled for and, given the present climate of violence, irresponsible. I called for continued negotiations.

Two nights later, on 17 June 1992, the climate of violence exploded into the slaughter of some forty-eight people at the little township of Boipatong, about 50 kilometres south of Johannesburg. As it transpired later, IFP migrant workers from the nearby Kwa-Madala hostel, seeking revenge for earlier ANC attacks on IFP members, had crept into the township under cover of darkness and indiscriminately slaughtered anyone – including women, children and babies that they had come across.

The next day I immediately issued a statement in which I expressed my shock and revulsion at the mindless killings. I said that we would not rest until we had found the perpetrators of this shocking act and had brought them to justice. I appealed to all South Africans to reject violence and any actions which might further exacerbate the situation. I also appealed once again to all leaders to ensure discipline and restraint amongst their followers.

The ANC immediately seized on the Boipatong incident to elevate its campaign of mass action against the government to a new fever pitch. In a statement issued following the massacre, the ANC placed the blame squarely on my shoulders. It insinuated that the massacre was part of a dark plan that I had concocted to counter mass action. It also implicated the police in the massacre, repeating unsubstantiated 'eye-witness' reports that the murderers had been ferried in police vehicles.

Because of the genuine revulsion that I felt over the massacre, I decided to show my own personal concern for the victims and their families by visiting Boipatong myself. I also thought that such a visit might help to defuse the volatile situation that had been created by the senseless murders. The visit was scheduled for Saturday 20 June – but news of the arrangements unfortunately leaked to the media on Friday evening. After consulting with my security advisers, I decided to go ahead despite the possibility that the ANC would have time to organize a demonstration in the town.

Accompanied by Hernus Kriel, the minister of law and order, I flew by helicopter from Pretoria to a police depot near Boipatong and then joined a motorcade to travel to the township a few kilometres away. It was a typical highveld winter's day, with dry grass and eggshell blue skies. Above us another police helicopter circled, watching developments on the ground in Boipatong. The police officer in charge of the visit assured us that the situation seemed safe enough – although a group with placards and banners had gathered on one side of the township to protest against my visit. Our motorcade consisted of my armoured Mercedes, a security car behind me, and several Nyala police armoured vehicles. Behind us there was also an ancient bus carrying the media. We drove through the dirt streets of Boipatong, past small matchbox brick houses and turned right down another road at the back of the community. As we proceeded I noticed through the bullet-proof windows of the Mercedes that the crowd was becoming thicker and more hostile.

We stopped at a point where I had planned to leave the car and speak to members of the community. But, no sooner had the door been opened for me, than my security people pushed me back into the car and shouted to the driver to leave the area. It was clear that the crowd was just too large and hostile for safety. Some of them were shouting 'Kill the Boers! Kill the Boers!' We made our way back through the township toward the main road. Some of the roads had been blocked off with barricades and on a few occasions we had to career over the sidewalks, scattering rubbish bins and sending chickens flying, in our efforts to avoid them. Finally, we were out of Boipatong and sped off past shouting crowds back to the police depot. My private secretary, Noël Basson, who was in the security car behind us with two police generals, later told me that while we were weaving our way through the township, one of the generals had grunted to the other in Afrikaans: 'Now he can see what his f—— new South Africa looks like!'

In the skirmishes that followed my visit, two or three more people were killed in clashes with the police. We were lucky that there were not more casualties. My press secretary, Casper Venter, was almost isolated in the mob from the press bus. He and a colleague had to run for their lives before being hauled aboard the bus by journalists. Just as they closed the bus door, a bullet zinged into the bus a few centimetres above their heads.

Ramaphosa and Mandela, after having attacked me for being insensitive to the deaths of black South Africans, now attacked me for having tried to show my condolences to the families of victims.

Apart from my visit to the township, I immediately requested the Goldstone Commission to investigate the incident and suggested that international experts should be involved in his team. I also reiterated that we would not rest until those responsible for the massacre had been brought to justice. Early the next month the Goldstone Commission reported that no evidence had been submitted to the commission which justified in any way allegations of direct complicity in, or planning of, the current violence by the state president, any member of the cabinet or any highly placed officer of the South African police. The international police expert, Dr Waddington of the United Kingdom, who assisted the commission with its investigation, could also find no evidence that the police had been involved in any way in the incident. He was, however, extremely critical of their policing methods and general levels of competence.

We also kept our promise to bring the perpetrators of the massacre to justice. Some two years later, in June 1994, the six leaders of the attack on Boipatong were each sentenced to eighteen years' imprisonment and nineteen others received sentences of between ten and fifteen years. Despite all this, in his book *Long Walk to Freedom* Nelson Mandela writes the following of the Boipatong incident: 'The police did nothing to stop the criminals and nothing to find them: no arrests were made, no investigations began. Mr De Klerk said nothing.' Some years later, Archbishop Desmond Tutu, in his capacity as chairperson of the Truth and Reconciliation Commission, would also unfairly accuse me, in effect, of having done nothing about the Boipatong massacre.

On 20 June, after having compared the behaviour of the National Party with the Nazis in Germany, Mandela issued a statement announcing that the ANC had decided to withdraw from the Codesa negotiations. He presented us with a list of new demands with which we would have to comply before the ANC would resume negotiations.

We were at a crossroads. Not for a moment did I consider acceding to the ANC's demands, some of which were outrageous. I decided to stand very firm and to pursue the negotiation route by other channels. On 2 July 1992, I made a TV and radio broadcast to the nation on the critical situation that had arisen in the country. I said that I had kept my promise of abolishing apartheid and of initiating negotiations for a new constitution which would assure full political rights for all South Africans. We had already succeeded in reaching agreement on many aspects of the new constitution. We would also be able to find solutions for the obstacles that we had encountered at Codesa II. However, the ANC and its allies had planned to sabotage negotiations and to precipitate a crisis, even before Codesa II began.

It was clear that the ANC and its allies, particularly Cosatu and the SACP, wished to impose their views on the rest of society by confrontation and unacceptable mass action. The government would not tolerate this. I promised that law and order would be maintained and insisted that any change of government would have to take place in a negotiated and constitutional manner. I repeated that the government remained ready and willing to resume negotiations which would culminate in a democratically elected government.

On the same day, I responded to Mandela's demands by sending him a memorandum, in which I insisted that we should resolve our differences through negotiations. I also pointed to his own alliance's deep involvement in violence and its failure to carry out its commitments in previous agreements. The root of the violence lay in the conflict between his party and the IFP and I accordingly suggested that he, Chief Minister Mangosuthu Buthelezi and I should meet as soon as possible to try to defuse the violence.

Mandela replied to me in a long and rambling letter on 9 July 1992. It was clear from the letter that most of the constitutional aspects that he believed were obstacles to a negotiated settlement rested on a wilful misunderstanding or distortion of our own positions. There was no reason why we could not address these misunderstandings and resolve our remaining differences through genuine negotiations – except, of course, that the ANC and its allies had at that stage decided that, for the time being, they did not want to pursue a negotiated settlement. They wanted to stage a show of strength through mass action and intimidation with a view to imposing their own agenda on the rest of the country.

The alliance's campaign of rolling mass action began in deadly earnest at the beginning of August. Its programme made provision for the following:

> *Monday, 3 August and Tuesday, 4 August:* a complete
> withdrawal of labour with local rallies, marches, pickets and
> other actions.
> *Wednesday, 5 August:* city and town demonstrations, occupations
> and marches.
> *Thursday, 6 August and Friday, 7 August:* actions by workers
> and others, determined at a local level.
> *Saturday, 8 August:* local, regional and national assessment
> meetings and report-backs.
> *Sunday, 9 August:* combining a celebration of Women's Day with
> religious activities and prayers for peace and democracy.

There were differing views regarding the effectiveness of the campaign. Cosatu claimed the general strike on 3 and 4 August had been about 90 per cent effective, with more than 4 million workers staying away. The South African Chamber of Business questioned these figures and estimated that fewer than 2.5 million workers had participated in the strike. In the opinion of a labour expert the mining, agricultural and public sectors of the economy, which together accounted for 55 per cent of the gross domestic product, had hardly been affected at all.

The mass action campaign reached its climax on 5 August with a massive march of an estimated 60,000 demonstrators in Pretoria. For hour after hour, singing and chanting black protesters marched through the streets of central Pretoria, shouting slogans calling for the removal of the government. Many were carrying brightly painted banners and placards, most were toyi-toying, and some entertained their fellow marchers with displays of break dancing. Finally, they gathered for a mass meeting on the large lawns far below the terraced gardens of the Union Buildings. It was another clear blue winter's day. The director-general of my office, Dr Jannie Roux, strolled onto the portico outside his office, overlooking the gardens and the city beyond. Standing between the massive sandstone pillars, he could see the crowd on the pale yellow lawn far below. He took a bet with one of his colleagues that there could not be more than 10,000 or 20,000 people. He could just hear the megaphones and the occasional roar of the crowd from far below, but could not make out what was being said. Later, wc found out that one of the speakers was Cyril Ramaphosa. He was shouting that today they had taken over Pretoria – but the next time they came they would take over De Klerk's office.

That morning we proceeded as usual with our weekly cabinet meeting. As I left the Union Buildings that afternoon, I spoke to a few journalists on the steps outside my office: Yes, I had taken note of the mass action and was concerned about its effect on the climate of violence, but we in government had to continue with the task of running the country. As far as I was concerned it was business as usual.

The march in Pretoria had been fairly good-natured and had not resulted in any significant violence. However, I knew that it was only a question of time before the increasingly aggressive campaign would sooner or later spark off conflict somewhere in the country. The spark came during the first week of September at Bisho, the little capital of Ciskei, one of the four independent black states.

Having failed to dislodge the government in Pretoria, the radicals in the ANC alliance had persuaded the ANC leadership during the last week of August 1992 to accept a strategy to dislodge the far less formidable governments of Ciskei, Bophuthatswana and KwaZulu. Ciskei, which had prevented the ANC from participating in free political activity in its territory, seemed to be the easiest target. On 3 September I received another demand from Mandela, this time insisting that I should depose Ciskei's military leader, Brigadier Oupa Gqozo and establish an interim administration in the territory which would permit free political activity. I, naturally, could not agree. I did not have the constitutional authority to overthrow the leader of a state which, in terms of South African law, was independent. In the following days I sent Mr Mandela a number of letters and messages in which I warned him of the dangerous situation that was developing in the Ciskei area because of his alliance's plans to march on Bisho, the Ciskei capital, and occupy government buildings and installations there. I pleaded with him to exercise restraint and to ensure that the situation did not get out of hand. I instructed our foreign minister, Pik

Botha, to remain in contact with all the parties involved – and particularly with Brigadier Gqozo – and to do everything in his power to defuse the situation.

All to no avail. On 7 September, with the inevitability of an unfolding Greek tragedy, the alliance's latest attempt to carry out the Leipzig option played itself out on the outskirts of Bisho. That day we had convened a conference on federalism in Pretoria – to discuss what was clearly one of the key issues in the stalled constitutional negotiations. We had invited the ANC to attend, but characteristically they had refused. We nevertheless went ahead with the conference which was held at the Old Presidency. During the course of the day I received regular updates on the critical situation in Bisho. Behind the scenes, Pik Botha and I continued to work feverishly to avoid the looming catastrophe. We exercised strong pressure on the ANC and Brigadier Gqozo to show restraint and to draw back before it was too late.

Not only did the ANC leadership utterly fail to heed our pleas, but they had actively endorsed the action. A number of ANC leaders, including Cyril Ramophosa, were in the vanguard of the 70,000 demonstrators who marched the three or four kilometres from King William's Town, in the Eastern Cape Province, across the undesignated Ciskei border to the outskirts of Bisho. The demonstrators had received permission from a Ciskeian magistrate the previous night to hold a legal demonstration in Ciskei, provided that they came no nearer to Bisho than its independence stadium just outside the town. However, one of the alliance's radical leaders, Ronnie Kasrils of the SACP, had previously reconnoitred the terrain and had found a gap in the stadium perimeter through which he believed he would be able to lead marchers onwards to their objective of occupying the Ciskeian capital buildings. At a critical moment he and several hundred of his followers broke away from the main march and ran across the stadium toward the breach. As they did so, nervous soldiers of the Ciskeian Defence Force opened fire with rifles, machine guns and hand grenades. Twenty-eight demonstrators were killed and some 200 were injured.

The Goldstone Commission immediately began an investigation of the incident. In his findings, Goldstone was sharply critical, not only of the Ciskeian troops – whose behaviour he found to be indefensible – but also of the organizers of the march. They had failed to inform the local Peace Committee, established in terms of the National Peace Accord, that they intended to deviate from the conditions laid down for the march, and had recklessly led their own followers into a desperately dangerous situation. Among his recommendations was a plea to the leaders of all organizations which used forms of mass public demonstration to do so only as a peaceful means to popularize political policies. He recommended that they should immediately and publicly abandon any political action calculated to result in conflict and violence.

The Bisho incident was a turning point in the transformation process. It allowed the ANC leadership to assess the folly and the extreme peril of pursuing the Leipzig option. The potential for conflict in pursuing such tactics – particularly a similar proposed march on the KwaZulu capital of Ulundi – was apparent to all rational people. The centre of gravity in the ANC alliance consequently shifted back to the moderates, where it would remain for the rest of the transformation process. Once again, the ANC had concluded that the time had come to talk.

23

The Record of Understanding

On 21 August 1992, during the darkest days of mass action, talks resumed between the ANC and the government – despite the ANC's public position that it had broken off constitutional negotiations with the government. They did so via a back channel that was established between Roelf Meyer from our side and Cyril Ramaphosa from the side of the ANC. The dualism involved in the ANC's approach – of publicly protesting and boycotting, while continuing to talk with us behind the scenes – reminded me of the insight that Prime Minister Gonzales of Spain had given me about the complications of negotiating with revolutionaries. Despite all the ANC's rhetoric, I was quietly confident that, before too long, we would get the negotiations going once again.

The Bisho massacre, I believe, brought the ANC to a point of greater realism. Nelson Mandela was made to understand that the radicals in the ANC were playing with fire. The back channel had, in the meantime, prepared the way for a resumption of talks. Shortly after Bisho, I invited Mandela to meet me to see whether there was not some way in which we could return to the path of negotiations. He accepted my invitation. In an obvious effort to save face, he said that since it appeared that the government was now willing to accept the ANC's demands for an interim government and a constitutional assembly, the organization had decided to reduce its original fourteen conditions for the resumption of negotiations to three core demands: the banning of the carrying of dangerous weapons on public occasions, including so-called cultural weapons; the fencing of hostels; and the immediate release of what the ANC termed political prisoners.

I guardedly welcomed his response. The fact was that he was climbing down and I could afford to be magnanimous. In the final analysis, rolling mass action had not turned out to be nearly as successful and potent as the ANC had hoped. Instead of declaring victory, I decided to work for a win/win situation. The road to negotiations was once again open and we agreed to hold a major bilateral meeting on 26 September.

I regarded Mandela's claim that we had now accepted the ANC's demand for an interim government and a constitutional assembly as absolute nonsense. As he was very well aware I had accepted the concept – although not the ANC's version of it – in my speech at Codesa I. The questions relating to a transitional government and a Parliament acting as a constitutional assembly had also been largely resolved in the Working Group 2 talks that had preceded Codesa II. Simultaneously I believed that the other three core issues posed by Mandela, although sensitive, could be resolved through negotiation.

I had already decided to take an initiative on cultural weapons and hostels, irrespective of what the ANC said or did, because they had regularly featured in incidents of violence. The Goldstone Commission and a United Nations mission led by former US secretary of state, Cyrus Vance, that had visited South Africa in July 1992, had also already recommended action on these two questions. They were nevertheless much more sensitive than they seemed to be at first glance. Cultural weapons, the *assegais* and *knobkerries* (short stabbing spears and wooden clubs), of the Zulus played a central role in their cultural traditions. For example, it was not possible for a traditionalist Zulu to be properly married if he was not allowed to carry his cultural weapons at the ceremony. Many state functions presided over by the king also required Zulus to carry such weapons. I knew that any total ban on the weapons would alienate the IFP and traditional Zulus for ever. But I felt that we would be able to negotiate some reasonable provision whereby a judge or a magistrate could grant permission for the carrying of cultural weapons at bona fide Zulu functions.

The question of the fencing of hostels was also problematic. Doing so would inevitably be regarded by the IFP as provocative and as a serious breach of the rights of their supporters in many of the hostels. The hostels provided accommodation in the cities for migrant workers, who left their families in the homelands and returned home only for short periods each year. In recent years some hostels had served as bases for the IFP in the bitter urban war between them and the ANC and its allies. Only a small proportion – some twenty-four – of the hostels spread throughout the country had really been associated with violence. Fencing off all the hostels would not only have been unnecessary – it would also have involved enormous expense and logistical problems. Nevertheless, in the light of the recommendations of the Goldstone Commission and the United Nations, I accepted that something meaningful would have to be done in this regard. However, I believed that the fencing could be limited to those hostels that had been associated with violence and that it could be carried out success-fully, if we acted sensitively and in close consultation with those involved.

The ANC's third demand, for the unconditional release of its followers that it regarded as political prisoners, was much more difficult for me to accept. When we had started the negotiations we had made arrangements for senior ANC members – most of whom were liable to arrest under then existing legislation – to return to South Africa to participate in the negotiations. We did so by granting them temporary immunity from prosecution. We knew that we would also have to establish mechanisms for the release of imprisoned ANC supporters who had been convicted of politically motivated crimes. We addressed this problem by adopting the Indemnity Act of 1990. The act extended indemnity to prisoners, those awaiting trial and exiles who wished to return to South Africa who, in the process of conflict and the pursuance of a cause, may have committed some or other offence. When considering what actions constituted political offences the government followed the internationally acceptable Norgard prin-ciples which had been devised to deal with similar problems and which had been applied in neighbouring Namibia. The Norgard definition excluded the gratuitous murder of civilians and other crimes with a high degree of premeditation and violence. I felt comfortable with the Norgard principles because I believed that violent crimes, such as cold-blooded murder and assassination, should under no circumstances be allowed to go unpunished, irrespective of who had committed them.

By the middle of September, the government had already extended indemnity to several thousand ANC members, and had released all those prisoners who could comply with the Norgard principles. Hank Cohen, the US assistant secretary of state for African affairs, had told us that we had actually gone beyond what they had regarded as political prisoners. Jacob Zuma, a leading member of the ANC, had signed a document during talks with Minister Kobie Coetsee in which he had confirmed that the government had fulfilled all its obligations as far as the release of ANC prisoners was concerned. However, Zuma was severely criticized by many of his colleagues for having done so. The ANC raised the ante and began to insist on the release of all its imprisoned followers, including those who had committed heinous crimes against civilians. Among these was Robert McBride, who had been convicted of the murder of several people in a bomb attack on a crowded beach-front bar in Durban, called Magoo's Bar. They also included many ANC members who had been sentenced for necklace murders.

I was strongly opposed to releasing this category of prisoner and had the full support of the minister of justice, Kobie Coetsee. Moreover, I simply did not have the powers under the constitution to deal with such serious cases. Neither did I have powers to intervene where people either had not been charged or were on trial. To enable me to comply with the ANC's demands, we would at the very least have to pilot new indemnity legislation through Parliament. But I did not want us to do so and planned to stay as near as possible to the Norgard principles.

On 22 September 1992 I had a meeting with Mr Virendra Dayal and Hisham Ommayad of the United Nations Secretariat, who visited South Africa to follow up on Cyrus Vance's mission in July. I briefed them on the current situation and the government's position on the ANC's demands. I told them that that regardless of whether or not we could reach an agreement with the ANC, we would still unilaterally try to resolve the issue of hostels, dangerous weapons and the release of prisoners.

In the run-up to our summit with the ANC of 26 September, I was also acutely aware of the importance of maintaining clear channels of communication with Chief Minister Mangosuthu Buthelezi and the IFP. I realized that the ANC had tailored its demands on questions such as the carrying of traditional weapons and the fencing of hostels, in the hope that they would be able to drive a wedge between the government and the IFP. Simultaneously, I had to deal with Goldstone's recommendations as well as those of Vance. I decided to try to win Buthelezi's support.

On 17 September I held a two-hour-long meeting with Chief Minister Buthelezi and a senior delegation. Our discussion focused on the violence in KwaZulu-Natal and on the deadlock in multiparty negotiations. I specifically discussed the demands that the ANC had made, including dangerous weapons, the Goldstone Commission's recommendations on hostels and the dispute over the release of political prisoners. As was often the case during our formal meetings, Buthelezi was noncommittal. At the end of our meeting we described our discussions as constructive and agreed to hold further meetings. However, it was clear to me that he had not liked what we had told him and that we could expect problems on the road ahead.

By 24 September, in preparation for the summit, our negotiators had reached broad agreement on a basis for consensus, except in respect of the release of the ANC's political prisoners. In the days preceding the planned summit up until the morning of the meeting itself, there were a number of exchanges between Mandela and me regarding the release of the political prisoners. During the course of these exchanges, Mandela threatened that if I did not release McBride and two other high profile prisoners who had been convicted of terrorist crimes (one of them a necklace murder), the meeting would be cancelled. I was not particularly impressed by his threat, having become used to his bluster and bullying tactics during my many preceding exchanges with him. I nevertheless immediately consulted senior members of the cabinet and of our negotiating team. My own instinct was to turn Mandela down flat and risk a further delay in the resumption of negotiations. However, in the course of my consultations with my colleagues, it became clear that they were in favour of a far-reaching compromise. Some believed that the release of the prisoners was not too high a price to pay for the resumption of negotiations. In retrospect, it is possible that others within the security establishment might have had their own reasons for favouring the widest possible definition of political crimes.

Mandela's threats were subsequently portrayed by Cyril Rama-phosa and Mac Maharaj as a major turning point in the negotiations, the point at which Mandela 'had held the line against this chap, De Klerk', and had established a 'psychological ascendancy' over me. It was nothing of the sort. It was ironically pressure from my own side – and not from the ANC – that, in the end, persuaded me with the greatest reluctance to change my position on the Norgard principles. However, Kobie Coetsee, who had not been fully involved in the negotiations on this matter, was bitterly upset when he learned of the decision. He had wanted to use this issue as a bargaining chip to force the ANC to accept the principle of a blanket amnesty. He came to see me and offered to resign over the issue. I told him that it had also been a difficult decision for me to swallow. I assured him that he was a valued member of our team and that he had an important role to play. He agreed to remain in the cabinet.

Once again, on 26 September 1991, we all gathered at the World Trade Centre in Kempton Park to open the next chapter in the negotiation saga. I held a quick planning session with my delegation before the meeting started. As far as political prisoners were concerned,

I grudgingly agreed that we could consent to new legislation which would make it possible to indemnify even the most serious crimes. We would insist, however, that the legislation should apply to all those who had been involved in politically motivated crimes, and not only ANC cadres. As far as the hostels and dangerous weapons were concerned, our strategy would be focused on the fine print in order to ensure that our undertakings would be limited to what was practicable. We also had to propose formulations which could be acceptable to the IFP, if they were prepared to be reasonable.

In our opening addresses, both Mandela and I emphasized the importance of the conference for the future of South Africa. He pledged that his delegation would do everything in its power to ensure that the summit succeeded. 'There is no alternative for South Africa,' he said. Nevertheless, the meeting did not go well. There was a great deal of haggling about detail and Mandela was playing politics. At times, the discussions became unnecessarily acrimonious. Despite the somewhat disappointing performance of some of my ministers, I was, in the end, relatively satisfied that we succeeded in achieving our main goals.

At one stage Mandela and I met on our own for a short while to discuss our wish to include wording that would limit the ANC's ability to embark on divisive and dangerous mass action campaigns. Mandela had serious reservations about preventing his followers from participating in what he regarded as legitimate political activities. We ultimately agreed to a formulation with which both sides could live: the government acknowledged the right of parties to participate in peaceful mass action. The ANC reaffirmed its commitment to conducting mass action in a peaceful manner and agreed to re-examine its mass action programme.

Despite Mandela's remark in his opening statement that the ANC had not come to the summit to claim victories, that is exactly what they subsequently did. Senior members of their delegation gleefully related to journalists how Mandela had twice threatened me and forced me to back down. This was absolute nonsense. The truth is that we did not accede to anything that we had not previously decided to accept, while the ANC had had to climb down on the long list of demands that they had issued on 20 June 1992. The ANC had reduced its original fourteen demands to three. We had already agreed to implement the recommendations of the Goldstone Commission with regard to the fencing of hostels and the carrying of dangerous weapons – but even here, we had been able to include provisions in the agreement which we hoped would be more acceptable to the IFP. I had, indeed, agreed to the release of prisoners that I did not want to release – but here, ironically, I had done so more at the behest of some of my own colleagues than because of the ultimatum of Mr Mandela.

At the conclusion of the summit, Nelson Mandela and I were able to sign an agreement which became known as the Record of Understanding. As matters turned out, the Record of Understanding would be almost universally misunderstood.

The ANC's three demands, which generated all the political pyrotechnics, were in reality peripheral to the crux of the Record of Understanding – which was the extensive provisions it contained for a new constitutional framework. However, this facet of the Record of Understanding attracted little media attention, precisely because it was not controversial. Most of the constitutional principles included in the Record of Understanding had been drawn up in the negotiations that had preceded Codesa II – but which, until then, had never been ratified by any of the parties. They included provision for an interim constitution with a Bill of Rights, a democratically elected Constitutional Assembly, which would at the same time act as an interim Parliament;' and for a transitional Government of National Unity. Most importantly, the final constitution would have to be adopted by a special majority and it would be bound by agreed constitutional principles.

In other words, it contained all the key bottom-line provisions for which we had been working since Codesa I and from which the ANC had distanced itself by withdrawing from the negotiations. The Record of Understanding did not bring the ANC one single new constitutional concession and validated the tentative agreements reached in the previous negotiations. There would be an elected Constitution Writing Assembly and interim government – but they would be very different from the institutions that the ANC had originally had in mind and in support of which they had launched their rolling mass action. The Constitutional Assembly would be bound by immutable constitutional principles and the interim government would not be an appointed body which would rule the country in a constitutional vacuum for six months, but a properly elected government, operating in terms of an interim constitution which would be legislated by our own Parliament. For our part, we would get constitutional continuity; an interim constitution with a justiciable Bill of Rights; fairly strong regional government; a multiparty Government of National Unity and the assurance that the final constitution would have to comply with pre-agreed constitutional principles. At last we had the ANC's signature on this crucial deal. Most importantly, negotiations were back on track. As I said in my closing remarks to the conference, the obstacles which had arisen had been sufficiently cleared to once again put two of the major role players – there are also other important role players – back on the road of communication and negotiation. The channels of communication were open again.

Unfortunately, the other important role players, particularly Chief Minister Buthelezi and the IFP were incensed by what they quite incorrectly regarded as a bilateral deal between the ANC and the government to decide the future of South Africa between ourselves. In addition to the meeting that I had held with Buthelezi two weeks earlier, I had instructed our negotiating team to brief Buthelezi's senior advisers fully on the background of our meeting with the ANC of 26 September. It appears that either my message did not get through to Buthelezi, or he misunderstood my intentions. Buthelezi angrily announced that the IFP would withdraw from the negotiations and that it and the KwaZulu authorities would not be bound by the agreement. A few weeks later Buthelezi led a march of several thousand Zulus, all armed with *assegais* and *knobkerries*, through the centre of Johannesburg. They presented a petition to the police in which they protested against the decisions in the Record of Understanding to ban the carrying of cultural weapons and to fence the hostels. However, their real purpose was to show that these decisions were unenforceable. They proved their point. How would a few hundred policemen be able to disarm thousands of Zulus without risking a pitched battle and unacceptable loss of life?

The next month, Buthelezi joined President Lucas Mangope of Bophuthatswana, Brigadier Oupa Gqozo of Ciskei, the Conservative Party, the Afrikaner Freedom Foundation and the Afrikaner Volksunie in forming the Concerned South Africans Group (Cosag). This unlikely bunch of bedfellows called for the abolition of Codesa and its replacement by a more representative negotiating forum. They also demanded that the armed wing of the ANC, Umkhonto We Sizwe, should be fully disbanded before negotiations could proceed.

Thus, no sooner had we succeeded in getting the ANC back on board the negotiation train, than other important parties jumped off. We once again set about the laborious task of getting everyone back on board again.

On 1 October 1992, I issued a statement in which I tried to place the Record of Understanding in its correct perspective. I pointed out that the bilateral talks with the ANC were an essential step toward the resumption of inclusive multiparty negotiations. They were not intended to exclude any party. The Record of Understanding did not prevent any other party from adopting whatever positions it liked in future multiparty negotiations. They were not a fait accompli. In any case, all the agreements relating to future constitutional developments were in line with agreements on which broad consensus had already been achieved at Codesa by most of South Africa's major parties – including those which now rejected the Record of Understanding.

One of the first results of the Record of Understanding, during the following days and weeks, was the release of a large number of prisoners who had been convicted of terrible crimes. Because we could not limit indemnity only to ANC prisoners we were obliged to extend it to anyone who could reasonably claim that his crime had been committed with a political motive before 8 October 1990. This meant that we also had to release Barend Strydom, a member of a lunatic fringe right-wing organization called the Wit Wolwe (White Wolves) who had been convicted of the callous murders of several innocent blacks during a shooting spree in the centre of Pretoria. During a short session at the end of the year, Parliament adopted the Further Indemnity Act, in terms of which a panel of judges was established to consider indemnity applications and to determine whether the applicants had committed crimes with a political motive. The legislation was widely misinterpreted as an attempt by the government to create a mechanism to enable members of the security forces to obtain indemnity through the back door without having to reveal the nature and extent of their actions. While it was true that the security forces could make use of the legislation, it was also available to the ANC and all the other parties to the conflict. In fact, members of the ANC were by far the main beneficiaries of the Further Indemnity Act.

Never before in my political career did I have such little appetite for a task as I had for the adoption of legislation which allowed those who had committed heinous murders to get off scot free. At times I still reproach myself for having acceded to pressures from both within our own ranks and from outside, although I realize that we had no rational alternative to the course that we finally took.

The negotiation train was once again on the tracks, albeit without its Cosag passengers, and it was gathering speed. This new momentum was soon illustrated by an initiative from an unlikely source. In the

October 1992 edition of the *African Communist*, Joe Slovo floated the idea of including a sunset clause in the negotiation package to make provision for an extended transitional period. He reasoned that the government had not been defeated in battle and could hardly be expected to accept a process that did not address its core interests, such as guarantees for civil service pensions and jobs and a five-year period of a multiparty Government of National Unity. This opened the door for negotiations on issues on which little progress had been made since Codesa II. The fact that the proposal came from a Communist with impeccable revolutionary credentials made it easier for the ANC to sell the compromise to its radical followers. The pension and job guarantees would help us to retain the support of white civil servants and members of the security forces for a negotiated constitutional settlement. Although the acceptance of a Government of National Unity was a major concession by the ANC, the sunset clause provision to limit it to five years did not meet our requirements for long-term power-sharing. In the end, we accepted it, however, as a point of departure for future negotiations on the inclusion of some form of power-sharing at the executive level in the final constitution. This issue would later be the cause of my and the National Party's withdrawal from the Government of National Unity in 1996.

On 26 November 1992 I was able to announce a timetable for the completion of the constitutional process. We would try to launch a new, inclusive, multilateral negotiating forum before the end of March 1993. We hoped that agreement could be reached on a transitional constitution before the end of May, with a view to it being enacted before the end of September. The first elections under the transitional constitution would then be held not later than March/April 1994.

24

The Steyn Investigation

By November 1992, it seemed as though our programme for the transformation of South Africa was well under way. We had reached agreement with the ANC on most of the principles for a sound constitutional blueprint and we had announced a timetable for further negotiations leading to elections no later than April 1994. Although important parties, like the IFP, were still boycotting the process we had not given up hope that they and other important parties might be prepared to rejoin a new negotiating forum early the next year. From my side, I continued to pressure my team to try to bring the IFP back on board.

Then, out of the blue, on 16 November 1992, the Goldstone Commission issued a dramatic statement in which it revealed that it had made a surprise raid on an office building in a Pretoria suburb, which had turned out to be the headquarters of the Directorate of Covert Collection (DCC), an ultra secret branch of the Military Intelligence Division of the South African Defence Force. During the raid the commission had seized files that pointed to unacceptable activities in the area of the commission's investigations.

Among other things, it had discovered that Ferdi Barnard – who had previously been employed by the disbanded Civil Co-operation Bureau – had been re-employed by the DCC, apparently to conduct propaganda activities against Umkhonto We Sizwe, the military wing of the ANC. In his statement, Goldstone also said that his commission required extra resources and needed to expand the scope of its investigation.

Since its inception, I had made full use of the Goldstone Commission to investigate incidents of violence and to deal with the plethora of charges and insinuations regarding responsibility for violence. Goldstone and I had developed a good working relationship. I gave him the support that the commission needed to carry out its task and was frequently in communication with him. He sometimes came to see me at Libertas and submitted his reports to me as state president, after which I released them to the media. There was an informal arrangement that Judge Goldstone also briefed Nelson Mandela on his activities and investigations and I had no problem with this. In my view, the more we could do to promote the credibility of the commission and to facilitate its work, the better.

For more than a year, the ANC and radical newspapers, like the *Vrye Weekblad* and the *Weekly Mail*, had been making allegations that a sinister third force within the security forces was responsible for much of the violence that had been plaguing the country. Such accusations had become a refrain of Nelson Mandela in our meetings – although, when pressed, neither he nor the ANC had been able to provide me with any usable evidence to substantiate his general charges.

The Goldstone Commission had investigated these allegations, but had stated in its second interim report that it had received no evidence which would suggest that 'there is a third force . . . i.e. a sinister and secret organization orchestrating political violence on a wide front'. It had also found that there was no basis to many other allegations by radical newspapers and the ANC of government or security force complicity in violence.

It was only in March 1994, a few weeks before the elections of 27 April 1994, that a subsequent report of the Goldstone Commission revealed that elements in the South African police had, in fact, been involved in murders and had used a farm called Vlakplaas as a base for their activities. This was the first definitive indication from the commission that elements of the security forces had, indeed, been involved in what had been described as a silent war against the leaders and activities of the ANC and its allies.

Until the Goldstone Commission's revelations of March 1994, its findings had seemed to confirm the repeated assurances that I had received from the security establishment that they were not involved in any kind of third force activity. However, I had not relied only on the Goldstone Commission in trying to get to the bottom of the allegations regarding a so-called third force. I had also repeatedly exerted pressure on members of the security establishment in my own efforts to establish the truth. In her book *Anatomy of a Miracle*, the American journalist, Patti Waldmeir, quotes an unnamed member of my cabinet on my attempts to establish the truth regarding the so-called third force. 'Every time we would discuss it, they (the security establishment) would try to convince us that there was no third force.' The cabinet minister said that he had been present several times when I had challenged the security establishment on this question, and that I had really got into them. 'But,' continued the cabinet minister, 'they always had very convincing answers. I think it was a question of trusting the people who advised him.'

At the time of Goldstone's statement of 16 November 1992 I was, of course, still unaware of the later revelations. I was, nevertheless, shocked and dismayed by Goldstone's statement in November 1992. It indicated that elements in the South African Defence Force might be contravening the direct undertaking that I had given after the Inkathagate imbroglio that the security forces would no longer involve themselves in actions in favour of, or against, political parties. I also did not like the sensational manner in which Goldstone had publicized preliminary and untested findings. As the chairman of a judicial commission of inquiry, he was supposed to submit his reports to the state president after all the evidence had been properly tested and weighed – and not make precipitate and sensational statements to the media. However, in this case he had done so and I had to deal with the situation in such a manner that it would not impact negatively on the legitimate intelligence gathering activities of the SADF.

The cabinet considered Goldstone's statement at its next meeting, on 18 November 1992. It was clear to me that we would have to intervene – more directly than ever before – to get to the bottom of allegations regarding the clandestine activities of the South African Defence Force. Even though Judge Goldstone would continue with his investigation, more was needed. I decided to appoint a trusted member of the SADF to carry out an in-depth investigation into all the intelligence activities of the SADF. I chose Lieutenant-General Pierre Steyn, the chief of defence force staff. General Steyn was a widely respected air force officer with an impeccable record. I believed that he would have a reasonable chance of obtaining the essential co-operation of key elements within the SADF and would also be in the best position to make proposals for the restructuring of the intelligence services of the SADF.

I instructed him to provide me with a complete and comprehensive analysis of all of the SADF's intelligence activities and to report to me as soon as possible on the advisability of restructuring these functions. To facilitate his task, I placed him in direct immediate command of all the intelligence functions of the SADF. I also ordered him, in conjunction with a senior police general, to ascertain whether any activities had taken place which might be in contravention of the law or of government policy. I stressed in my announcement of these decisions that General Steyn's activities would take place in support of, and in conjunction with, the investigation which was then being carried out by the Goldstone Commission.

Two days later Judge Goldstone came to see me at the Union Buildings to discuss the manner in which he had publicized his findings and his request for further resources. I told him that we would have to find some way of ensuring that his investigations did not harm the bona fide activities of the security forces. We also discussed the manner in which the commission would, in future, liaise with General Steyn to ensure that it received any information that might be relevant to its mandate and offered to make additional resources available as and when required. Judge Goldstone agreed that his commission already had sufficient powers to carry out its mandate.

On 26 November 1992 I held a meeting at the Union Buildings with General Steyn, the late General Kat Liebenberg, the head of the South African Defence Force, Mr Eugene Louw, the minister of defence and Kobie Coetsee, the minister of justice, to discuss General Steyn's investigation.

The minister, Gene Louw, had only recently been appointed to the portfolio and had almost certainly not been brought into the loop of the inner workings of the SADF. (I now wonder whether any ministers appointed from the ranks of the politicians ever were.) The key player was General Liebenberg. He was tall, gaunt and bald. He wore heavy-rimmed spectacles and, with a generous military moustache, he was every inch a tough, professional soldier. He had won his spurs in the long war against SWAPO on Namibia's northern border. His whole career had been devoted to fighting the encroaching forces of communism and its ANC, SACP and SWAPO surrogates. I could sense that he was unhappy with the brief and the wide-ranging powers that I had given General Steyn – which had no doubt wrought havoc with the traditional SADF lines of command and authority.

I said that the appointment of General Steyn was not a sham. It would involve a thorough review of military intelligence. At the same time, we did not want to throw out the baby with the bath water. I said that I wanted a proper division of responsibility between the intelligence activities of the South African Defence Force, National Intelligence and the South African police. I wanted military intelligence to get rid of any function that did not belong with it, so that I would be able to state categorically that it was no longer involved in any unacceptable activities. We had to take firm action against those who had been guilty of any form of misconduct. I needed an absolute assurance that the South African Defence Force's activities had been fully cleaned up. I stressed that these things had to happen – and they had to happen quickly. I had given General Steyn a hands-on instruction with direct authority over all the relevant commanders.

I could see from General Liebenberg's body language that he was unhappy with what I had said. I asked him if he had a problem. He raised a number of procedural difficulties and said that all this was part of a plot to discredit the SADF. I replied that we were wrestling with the image of a defence force that could apparently evade the scrutiny of the auditor-general; that had been accused of sinking the Harms Commission and of frustrating the government's attempts to obtain information. And yet nothing had happened. Hardly anyone had been disciplined. I added that whatever we did, we should be very careful not to damage the morale of the South African Defence Force. I insisted, however, that the South African Defence Force should for once and all get its house in order.

I received the first indication of how serious the problems in military intelligence were on 10 December. General Steyn came to see me at my office in the Union Buildings to give me a preliminary report on his investigations. He told me that, with the help of the directorate of counter-intelligence, he had started to uncover what appeared to be a veritable rat's nest of unauthorized and illegal activity within military intelligence. What concerned me was his visible nervousness. He seemed to be worried that his investigations were leading him into areas where his own personal safety might be at risk. I urged him to press ahead with his investigation as quickly as possible and offered him any support that he might require. I also instructed the National Intelligence Service – long-time rivals of military intelligence – to provide General Steyn with any assistance that might be relevant to his investigation.

A short while later, on 18 December 1992, General Steyn flew from Pretoria to the air force base at the De Hoop nature reserve in the southern Cape. I flew in by helicopter from a nearby holiday home, where I had arrived a few days earlier. What he had to tell me was deeply shocking. We flew to Cape Town within an hour where General Steyn gave an oral report on his initial findings to a meeting that I had hurriedly convened in the Cabinet Room in Cape Town. Most of the members of the cabinet had already dispersed for the Christmas holidays and I had to call them back to Cape Town for the meeting. Those present included Ministers Pik Botha, Kobie Coetsee, Dawie de Villiers, Hernus Kriel, Eugene Louw and Dave Steward, who had been appointed as the new director-general of my office the previous month. General Steyn based his oral briefing, inter alia, on a report that had been prepared for him by the chief director of counter-intelligence. No written report was submitted to me, as was later alleged inside and outside Parliament. The following quote, taken from documents that were handed to the Truth and Reconciliation Commission much later, sums up the essence of General Steyn's provisional findings:

> some members, contract employees and collaborators of certain components of the South African Defence Force had been involved in, and in certain instances were still involved in, illegal and unauthorized activities which could be prejudicial to the security, interests and well-being of the state.

According to the same document

> some members of the senior command structure were largely caught up in the momentum of activities from the past, which were currently receiving negative publicity, while others were possibly promoting their own agenda against the interests of the state.

We listened, dumbfounded, while General Steyn unravelled a complex web of unauthorized, illegal and criminal activities within some units of the Defence Force. He alleged that some units had been illegally stockpiling weapons in South Africa and abroad; that they had been providing arms and assistance to elements within the IFP; that they were involved in the instigation and perpetration of violence; and that they were involved in activities to discredit the ANC and to sabotage the negotiation process. One particularly shocking allegation was that elements of the Defence Force had been involved in carrying out a chemical attack on Frelimo soldiers in neighbouring Mozambique. Time and again, he indicated that these activities had been unauthorized or self-initiated. The picture painted by General Steyn was of a defence force in which a number of units were no longer under effective control and were actively pursuing their own political and criminal agendas. The report which the chief director of counter-intelligence had submitted to General Steyn divided the culprits into three categories: those in command positions who could not rid themselves of what it called the albatrosses of the past (their involvement in former anti-ANC activities); those in command positions who could be discredited by the activities of their subordinates; and those who were following their own agendas against the interests of the state. General Steyn told us that he believed all this to be true, even though his information was generally based on unconfirmed reports which would not stand up in a court of law.

In my relationship with the security forces, I sometimes felt like a man who had been given two fully grown watchdogs – say, a Rottweiler and a bull terrier. Their previous owner had doted on them. He had given then the tastiest morsels from his table and had allowed them to run free and chase cats all over the neighbourhood. I had put a stop to all that. As a result, they did not particularly like me – although they had an ingrained sense of obedience. When I took them for walks in the neighbourhood, I put them on leashes and stopped them from chasing cats. I could determine the general direction in which they would move, but they would walk at their own pace, sometimes wanting to go back, sometimes straining to chase a passing cat, sometimes walking happily in my direction. I could guide them, but I knew that if I pulled too hard, I might choke them – or they might slip their collars and cause pandemonium in the neighbourhood.

The reality was that the SADF and the SAP, like military and police forces throughout the world, had their own strong and distinctive cultures. Part of that culture was the acceptance of ultimate civilian control – but part of it was also a certain disdain for civilian politicians. The SADF was a very effective military machine. It was also one of the first institutions within the state to acknowledge the need for a political solution to South Africa's problems. Its command structure generally supported the negotiation process and played a positive role in the democratic transformation of South Africa. However, I sensed that although the SADF accepted that the politicians might be in ultimate control, they lacked the discipline, consistency and strategic insight of the security forces. The security forces also probably believed that civilian politicians were naïve about the true nature and intentions of the ANC/SACP alliance and that, under these circumstances, it would be irresponsible to dismantle all their covert anti-ANC capabilities – just as the initiators of Operation Vula within the ANC had decided to maintain their covert anti-government capabilities as an insurance policy in the event of the failure of negotiations. And as the initiators of Operation Vula had launched and run their initiative without apparently informing Nelson Mandela, the initiators of the security forces covert projects against the ANC probably decided that the less the civilian political leadership knew of such activities, the easier it would be for them to pursue the negotiation path without being contaminated by the realities of the continuing underground struggle.

I was now faced with one of the most critical decisions of my presidency: how should I deal with this situation? It was clear that, if General Steyn's allegations were true, the top structure of the South African Defence Force was either no longer in full control of several key units or was itself condoning or involved in actions that were illegal and in direct contravention of the policy and express instructions of the government. It was either a question of gross incompetence, gross insubordination or active subversion of the state. Under normal circumstances, the obvious course would be to carry out a thorough purge of all those involved in wrongdoing and in the line of command which had allowed such wrongdoing to occur. I seriously considered the option of dismissing General Liebenberg and a few other generals in the top structures of command.

However, these were not normal circumstances. The South African Defence Force represented the government's ultimate power base and was the final guarantor of the constitutional process that we had initiated. We did not at that time know whether the whole process could be completed peacefully. Anything might happen between then and the elections in April 1994. The ANC might once again unleash mass action. Its radical faction might once again gain the upper hand and revive Operation Vula and the armed struggle. KwaZulu might try to secede. There might be a right-wing uprising. Under these circumstances it would have been the height of folly to dismantle the command structure of the South African Defence Force and cripple the force's morale, without clear and indisputable evidence.

In the briefing, General Steyn stressed the point that the greatest part of the information that was presented to us was based on untested allegations which would have to be confirmed or refuted by further intelligence and investigation before a proper evaluation would be possible. I could hardly turn the whole of the SADF upside down on the strength of untested information.

Yet it was equally important that I should take firm, immediate and decisive action. My first decision was to confront the top leadership of the SADF with General Steyn's allegations. I immediately summoned the minister of defence, Mr Eugene Louw, the chief of the SADF, General Kat Liebenberg, the chief of the army, General Georg Meiring and the chief of military intelligence, Lieutenant-General Joffel van der Westhuizen to my office in Tuynhuys.

General Liebenberg was clearly nervous. He was a chain-smoker, and immediately lit up a cigarette. I summed up the allegations that General Steyn had made and asked him to comment on them. He said that he was surprised and shocked and had no knowledge of such illegal activities. He agreed that we would have to take immediate steps to cut to the root of the malpractices within the defence force. I instructed him to identify any officers or employees of the defence force who might be guilty of the abuses listed in General Steyn's allegations and to report back to me within the hour as to what steps should be taken against them. I insisted on firm action. Simultaneously, the activities of units involved in Steyn's report should be immediately suspended. I also asked for the names of officers whose services would no longer be required because of the envisaged restructuring of military intelligence activities. He agreed to do so immediately and, in conjunction with General Steyn, he and the other generals present drew up a list of those who had been implicated in the preliminary report and of those whose services would no longer be required. They also recommended what steps should be taken against the relevant officers. After they had reported back to me, I told them that I would announce the decisions that had been taken.

The following day I held a press conference and issued a statement. I said that the information provided by General Steyn indicated that a limited number of members, contract members and collaborators of the South African Defence Force had been involved, and in some cases were still involved, in illegal and/or unauthorized activities and malpractices.

I emphasized that immediate steps were being taken to bring an end to these activities. Firstly, a further sixteen members, including two generals and four brigadiers, had been placed on compulsory retirement. Also, as part of the reorganization of the SADF, seven members had been placed on compulsory leave, pending the conclusion of further investigations. I announced that General Steyn would continue with his investigation; quick and firm disciplinary action would, where necessary, be taken; General Steyn would continue to co-operate with the Goldstone Commission; and, where prima facie evidence was available, cases would be referred to the South African police and the attorneys-general for possible criminal prosecution.

Under the circumstances, I believe that this was the best and most effective action that I could take. It was a judgement call and as president I had to decide what to do. I still think that I took the right decision. I had to achieve two goals. On the one hand I had to bring the security forces to heel: I had to stop any possibility of the continuation of the illegal and totally unacceptable activities alleged by General Steyn. On the other hand, I had to ensure that the overall effectiveness of the SADF would not be seriously damaged. In retrospect, I believe that both of these goals were achieved. It is true that some of the officers against whom action had been taken later sued the government – and won. But the majority did not.

However, the truth or otherwise of the allegations contained in General Steyn's preliminary oral report was never fully established. Although General Steyn succeeded in puncturing the steel-belted culture of the SADF and in exposing some of its inner secrets, the self-sealing properties of the culture were soon activated. All the efforts that I set in train to establish the truth were effectively neutralized. Neither General Steyn's further investigations, nor the parallel investigation of the Goldstone Commission, nor the investigations of the attorney-general or of the South African police succeeded in getting to the bottom of the matter. Only much later, as a result of the disclosures of applicants for amnesty, was corroborating evidence produced to support the allegations that General Steyn had made. General Steyn was ostracized by his former colleagues and was ejected from the inner circle of the SADF culture.

25

The Multiparty Negotiating Forum, Atom Bombs and Assassination

During the last weeks of 1992 and the first weeks of 1993, we spent much of our time in bilateral discussions with other parties, trying to coax and cajole those who had withdrawn as a result of the Record of Understanding to join the next round of multiparty discussions.

I had a good round of meetings with the homeland leaders at which we discussed their participation in new negotiations and the implications of the re-incorporation of their territories into South Africa. Throughout my presidency, the self-governing territories and the independent states caused the government endless difficulties and frustrations. The best administered states were KwaZulu, Bophuthatswana and QwaQwa, a small Sotho homeland bordering Lesotho. The rest were at differing stages of financial and administrative disintegration – despite our genuine efforts over the decades to train and support competent public servants and administrators. Most of them had bloated, overpaid and ineffective civil services. For example, Transkei, with no discernible foreign relations outside South Africa, had a department of foreign affairs with over 400 employees. I was once told that it had also appointed almost as many chief magistrates as there were in the whole of South Africa. In most of the homelands, corruption was rife and control over expenditure was extremely lax. The irony is that these states – which were monotonously labelled as puppets of Pretoria – were remarkably autonomous. Our powers of intervention were very limited. We tried consistently through intergovernmental meetings to impose controls and standards – but it was a difficult and unrewarding struggle. I insisted that the responsible ministers should increase pressure on the homeland governments to ensure better administration. At times we temporarily withheld transfer payments in our efforts to force them to put their houses in order – only to be subsequently blamed for the ensuing breakdowns in services. I remember on one occasion in 1993, the chief minister of Lebowa (the homeland of the North Sotho people in the northern Transvaal), Mr Nelson Ramodike, coming to see us at the Union Buildings and blandly asking for an additional R300 million to tide his administration over until the end of the financial year. Derek Keys, our finance minister, almost exploded, 'Three hundred million rand, Mr Chief Minister, is exactly what I do not have!'

As the prospect of their re-incorporation into South Africa drew closer, the governments of most of these states gravitated towards the ANC camp. Nelson Mandela wooed them like long-lost friends, despite the ANC's rejection of the system that they represented – and despite the fact that two of the homelands which joined them (Transkei and Venda) were military dictatorships. In the end, the ANC happily took them under its wing and accepted them as part of its negotiating group at the World Trade Centre. However, they proved to be empty shells and probably brought the ANC no more than a few thousand votes between them. Those who remained outside the ANC camp included President Mangope of Bophuthatswana, Brigadier Gqozo of Ciskei, Chief Minister Mangosuthu Buthelezi of KwaZulu and Chief Minister T. K. Mopeli of QwaQwa. Also, as their demise approached, many of the homeland governments and public services accelerated their efforts to strip the remaining resources from their states by granting themselves across-the-board promotions and handsome pensions. The rest of South Africa would have to pay a heavy bill for these depredations after the 1994 elections.

Since the Record of Understanding, our main challenge had been to persuade Chief Minister Mangosuthu Buthelezi to return to the negotiating process. It was always difficult to predict what he was going to do next. On 1 December 1992 he published a draft constitution for KwaZulu-Natal which, if implemented, would have come close to a unilateral declaration of independence. Among its provisions was a stipulation that no federal armed forces would be allowed to be stationed in KwaZulu-Natal and no federal law would be able to override any state law and no federal taxes could be levied in the state without the express permission of the state. Buthelezi said that he planned to hold a referendum on the draft constitution. Implicit in this was that, if it was approved by the people of KwaZulu-Natal it would become the supreme law of the state regardless of what might or might not happen in negotiations at the central level.

The next day, I expressed my concern about the impression of unilateral action which had now been created by the KwaZulu government's latest initiative. I said that it had the potential of bringing the KwaZulu government into direct confrontation with the government, with other parties in South Africa and in Natal and with the international community. In the end, Buthelezi backed down and did not proceed with the referendum.

On 10 December 1992, I had a meeting with Buthelezi and the other homeland leaders who had joined COSAG – President Mangope and Brigadier Gqozo. I had to endure, once again, emotional attacks on the Record of Understanding and frantic accusations that I had capitulated to the ANC and to the SACP – many of them from the diminutive Ciskeian dictator. Nevertheless, the meeting was not altogether fruitless. Negotiations with Chief Minister Buthelezi were usually a difficult, lengthy and frustrating process. He was seldom prepared to move beyond the positions adopted in his customary opening speech. This led to a frustrating rigidity in his approach and created the impression that he had decided what the outcome of discussions would be before we even began to talk. Sometimes in the ensuing talks I thought that I had made some headway with him. Just as often, a few days later he would issue a statement or make a speech that radically differed from what I thought we had agreed. However, on this occasion, reading between his attacks on the Record of Understanding and his deep suspicions of our relationship with the ANC, I discerned a willingness to return to some or other multiparty negotiating forum. This arose, I think, from his growing concern that he and the IFP were being marginalized – and led him to propose the convening of what he called a multiparty conference of review. It was an ingenious idea, but without viability under the prevailing circumstances. It did, however, keep the door open for further talks.

Another party still out in the cold was the Pan Africanist Congress (PAC). The PAC had broken away from the ANC in 1958 because of non-black communist influence in the organization. It supported black nationalism and radical African socialism. It had refused to join Codesa, because it favoured an immediate and virtually unconditional transfer of power to the black majority. It was an irritation to the ANC, because it consistently articulated views which the alliance's own radical factions tended to support. Although the PAC – together with the ANC – had been recognized by the United Nations as a national liberation movement of South Africa, it had never enjoyed more than 2 to 3 per cent support inside the country. It was, however, playing a very negative and destructive role. It had not yet suspended its armed struggle – which was being waged by its armed wing, the Azanian People's Liberation Army (APLA) and its radical statements and slogan of 'one settler, one bullet' were generating anger and anxiety among whites.

After preliminary talks in Nigeria earlier in the year, our negotiators had succeeded, in October 1992, in holding bilateral talks with the PAC in Gaborone, the capital of neighbouring Botswana (the PAC had refused to meet the government in South Africa itself). The talks had gone well and seemed to open the way for the PAC's participation in a newly structured negotiating forum. However, all this suffered a serious setback early in December 1992 when an APLA spokesman said that his organization had declared war on white South Africans. The number of attacks on whites – and particularly on farmers in the Eastern Cape – increased. The government immediately broke off its talks with the PAC and made it clear that there could be no further progress until it agreed to abandon its armed struggle.

In its report of 15 March 1993 into APLA's role in violence, the Goldstone Commission found that APLA attacks had resulted in the deaths of sixteen whites – most of them civilians. The attacks had included the random shooting of whites at a golf club in King William's Town and at restaurants in Queenstown and Cape Town. The commission had also found that APLA was using the Transkei homeland as a base for its attacks, with the full knowledge and support of the government of General Bantu Holomisa. Holomisa immediately reacted by attacking the commission as a kangaroo court and by refusing to co-operate with it in its further investigations. He also warned that the South African government would have to station men in every white home in Transkei to protect them from 'possible revenge by the people'.

Obviously, I could not tolerate this situation. On 1 April 1993, members of the government and I held a meeting with a Transkei delegation led by General Holomisa at Tuynhuys in Cape Town. Holomisa arrived for the talks late and alone. The rest of his delegation had apparently lost their way and were able to join us only towards the end of the meeting. Holomisa was a small, compact man. He had done well in the tough South African army staff courses that he had attended while he had been an officer in the Transkeian army. He was a keen rugby player and later played in the parliamentary team together with National Party MPs. However, he always struck me as being equivocal and opportunistic. To start with, he had seemed to be a strong supporter of Transkeian independence. Later, he gravitated toward the ANC and became part of their group in the negotiations. And as the Goldstone Commission had revealed in March 1993, he apparently also maintained close ties with the PAC and APLA.

At the start of our meeting, I told him that I would hold his government responsible for any harm which might be done to South African citizens or property in Transkei. Throughout the meeting Holomisa looked quite uncomfortable and operating no doubt on the premise that the best form of defence is attack, criticized Pik Botha for some or other matter related to our bilateral relations. Pik Botha retorted with a blistering counter-attack which left Holomisa sullen and subdued. I also took him to task for his unwarranted attack on the Goldstone Commission and insisted that he should co-operate with it in its further investigations of APLA. He was clearly reluctant to do so and offered instead to set up his own inquiry. This was completely unacceptable and the meeting ended inconclusively. To reinforce my message to Holomisa regarding our concern over his assistance to APLA, and to tighten security, we set up road blocks on all of the routes leading into and out of Transkei. The SADF was also placed in a state of readiness so that it would be able to move into Transkei, should circumstances deteriorate.

Despite our difficulties with Transkei and the PAC, multiparty negotiations commenced once again at the World Trade Centre in March 1993. This time they were even more inclusive. Not only did we succeed in persuading the IFP to rejoin the fold, but the Conservative Party, the Afrikaner Volksunie (the Afrikaner People's Union), the PAC (even though it had not yet unequivocally suspended its armed struggle) and three delegations representing traditional leaders also participated – making twenty-six delegations in all. However, we dropped the Codesa label, which since the collapse of Codesa II had too many negative connotations for too many of the participants, in favour of Multiparty Negotiating Forum.

Just after the middle of March 1993 I announced that I would be taking the unusual step of addressing a joint session of Parliament on 24 March. My announcement caused wild speculation among the local and foreign media. There were no obvious reasons to hold such a session at that time. Speculation ranged from some major breakthrough in the negotiating process to a new initiative to crack down on violence. None of their guesses came close to the mark.

When I stood up in Parliament on 24 March, I announced that after I had become president, South Africa had become the first country ever to dismantle a nuclear weapons capability. I revealed, for the first time, what the international community had long suspected, that South Africa had, at one stage, developed a limited nuclear deterrent capability. The decision to do so was taken in 1974, against the background of the Soviet expansionist threat in southern Africa, the deployment of Cuban forces in Angola from 1975 onwards and the knowledge that because of our international isolation, we would not be able to rely on outside assistance in the event of an attack.

The programmes included the construction of seven fairly simple nuclear fission devices (in the end only six were completed) similar to the bombs that had destroyed Hiroshima. The weapons were considered the minimum for testing purposes and for the maintenance of a credible deterrent capability. However, they were never tested – despite persistent reports of a mysterious event over the South Atlantic towards the end of the 1970s. We had developed our nuclear capability by ourselves, at great cost, without the co-operation of any other country. Our own unique uranium enrichment process contributed to the project.

When I became president in 1989 I was already aware of the programme because as a former minister of mineral and energy affairs, responsible for South Africa's Atomic Energy Corporation, I was one of the few members of the government who had to be involved in the project. I had no enthusiasm for this massive spending programme, but it had already reached a point of no return when I became involved. Our nuclear programme was never discussed in the cabinet or the State Security Council and was managed on a strictly need to know basis. It crossed my mind during that period that there were, no doubt, other top-secret matters that were dealt with in the same manner. After I moved to my next portfolio I lost touch with the programme, but again picked up the threads when I became president.

By the time that I became state president, the global and regional strategic situation had changed dramatically. On 22 December 1988 we had signed an agreement with Cuba and Angola which provided for the independence of Namibia and the withdrawal of 50,000 Cuban troops from Angola. The Cold War had come to an end with the collapse of Communism in the former Soviet Union and Eastern

Europe. Also, I expected that the reform policies which I intended to introduce would help to end confrontation with our neighbours in southern Africa and with the international community.

Under these circumstances, the retention of a nuclear capability no longer made any sense – if it ever had in the first place – and had become an obstacle to the development of our international relations. I accordingly decided to dismantle our capability. I did so with the support of those ministers who knew about the programme, as well as that of the late Wynand de Villiers, the head of the Atomic Energy Corporation and who, like me, had inherited the programme from his predecessors. Towards the end of 1989, I gave instructions for the decommissioning of our pilot enrichment plant at Pelindaba and for the destruction and dismantling of the nuclear devices. I appointed the highly respected scientist and former principal of the University of the Orange Free State, Dr Wynand Mouton, to monitor the process and to report directly to me. I had to make sure that everything was accounted for properly. On 10 July 1991, South Africa acceded to the Nuclear Non-Proliferation Treaty (NPT) and opened all our nuclear facilities to regular inspection by the International Atomic Energy Agency.

Our announcement was widely welcomed and further helped to strengthen our international credibility. South Africa is still the only country that has ever renounced and dismantled its full nuclear weapons capability. I have no doubt that it was the right decision. In 1997 I attended an international symposium on the declaration of a nuclear-free zone in north-east Asia in Hiroshima. After visiting the Hiroshima Peace Park I was able to fully understand for the first time something of the true horror of nuclear weapons. Although our own programme had enabled us to supply nuclear fuel to our nuclear power station at Koeberg and to our research reactor at Pelindaba, it had constituted yet another major expense which we would never have undertaken had it not been for our growing isolation and sense of confrontation with the international community. Ultimately, it was yet another cost of apartheid and of sanctions. Although our decision was widely welcomed within South Africa and abroad, I suspect that it was resented in some circles in the military establishment which were already disaffected and alarmed by the direction in which I was beginning to lead the country.

*

We all felt that we could take a well-earned break over the Easter long weekend. Everything seemed to be going quite well. The multiparty negotiations were under way once again and were more representative than ever before. I had a family engagement in Steynsburg, a village in the Karoo (the vast semi-desert in the interior of the Cape Province). Steynsburg and other neighbouring towns such as Burgersdorp and Bethulie had long associations with my family and my ancestors on my father's side. On Saturday, 10 April, we had a family reunion of the Van Rooy family. I was involved because my grandmother had been a Van Rooy. As we were all happily preparing to sit down to lunch, my security team brought a local police officer to me with a message that I had to telephone my director-general, Dave Steward, urgently. When I got through to him, he had shattering news. Chris Hani, the former commander of Umkhonto We Sizwe and the secretary-general of the Communist Party, had just been assassinated. He was getting out of his car in the driveway of his home in Boksburg, to the east of Johannesburg, when a white man, who had been parked across the road, walked up to him and shot him several times. Fortunately, one of Hani's neighbours, an Afrikaans woman, memorized the licence number of the killer's car – which enabled the police to arrest him within fifteen minutes. He turned out to be a Polish immigrant, Janusz Waluz, who had planned the assassination with an English-speaking Conservative Party member of Parliament, Clive Derby-Lewis.

I realized that Hani's assassination had the potential of igniting a major crisis. He was one of the ANC/SACP alliance's most popular heroes. I immediately arranged for a statement to be issued in which I expressed my shock and conveyed my deep condolences to Mr Hani's widow and family. I said that 'although he and I' were at opposite poles of the political debate, we were both prepared to resolve the problems of our country through the process of peaceful negotiations. He can no longer do so, but we who remained must rededicate ourselves to peaceful negotiations and to the creation of a society in which brutal acts such as this 'will no longer occur'. I called on all leaders to show maximum restraint in the face of this act and to exercise the strongest possible discipline over their followers.

As soon as I could, I telephoned Nelson Mandela and discussed the situation with him. I urged him to do whatever he could to calm down his followers and reassure them that we would bring the culprits to justice. From where I was in the middle of the Karoo it would have been difficult for me to get to a TV studio to make an appeal to all South Africans to exercise maximum restraint. I also sensed, however, that this was Mandela's moment, not mine. Only he would be able to calm his enraged followers. Any high-profile appearance by me – no matter how well intentioned – would probably have the opposite effect. Mandela rose to the occasion in a statesman-like manner. That evening – in a broadcast that was repeated three times – he said:

> Tonight, I am reaching out to every single South African, black and white, from the very depth of my being. A white man, full of prejudice and hate, came to our country and committed a deed so foul that our whole nation now teeters on the brink of disaster. A white woman, of Afrikaner origin, risked her life so that we may know, and bring to justice, the assassin . . . Now is the time for all South Africans to stand together against those who, from any quarter, wish to destroy what Chris Hani gave his life for – the freedom of all of us.

Unfortunately, neither he nor the ANC maintained this responsible approach for long. The alliance announced a six-week campaign of mass action. ANC demonstrations led to rioting and looting in several cities. The ANC had failed to exercise control over its followers and it seemed as though we might return to the volatile days of August 1992. Once again, the country had been plunged into crisis. I quickly convened a special meeting of the State Security Council on 14 April to consider the situation and to take steps to maintain law and order. That evening it was my turn to reassure my supporters and all South Africans who, in the wake of the serious riots throughout the country, were deeply concerned about the future. I announced measures to control mass demonstrations and to deploy an additional 3,000 members of the security forces. I said that solutions could not be found in slogans shouted in the streets. They had to be pursued in the calm and reasoned atmosphere of peaceful negotiations. I also warned the ANC against trying to exploit Mr Hani's assassination to pressure parties to the negotiations to accept positions inconsistent with approaches and timetables which had already been established.

We balanced this with a positive initiative and mandated Roelf Meyer to hold out a carrot to the ANC two days later. In a conciliatory statement he said that the government supported the rapid conclusion of an agreement on the Transitional Executive Council – the multiparty body which, in terms of the agreements we had reached, would be established to ensure fair play in the run-up to the elections. This would give the parties in the multiparty negotiating forum a limited form of power-sharing with the government.

On 19 April, at Hani's funeral, Mandela was back to his old form. He implied that the government had created the climate of violence in which Hani had been assassinated. He made ludicrous charges that we were spending nine billion rand a year on secret projects to foment violence. He tried to create the impression that I was not concerned about Hani's death. He said that my first action had been to call a meeting of the State Security Council and to mobilize 23,000 troops to protect whites. He said nothing of our phone call and the condolences that I had immediately expressed. He said nothing of our willingness to send a government representative to Hani's funeral (our offer was turned down). Mandela went on to say that he and the ANC were militants and radicals. It was not a question of armed struggle or negotiations. Armed struggle had brought about negotiations. He warned 'those who sought to impose endless negotiations' that any further delay would place on the national agenda the need for change by other means. He claimed that we had passed the Further Indemnity Act to protect people like Waluz and Derby-Lewis. As was often his style, he was no doubt expressing views and emotions that he thought would suit the angry mood of his immediate audience.

The next day I dealt with some of Mandela's more outrageous statements in Parliament. I said that the reason we came to – and remained at – the negotiating table was because negotiations offered all South Africans the only reasonable hope of building a peaceful and prosperous future. I emphasized that we had worked for a peaceful solution to our problems, not because we were weak, but because we were strong in our conviction that this would be in the best interest of all South Africans.

Fortunately, Hani's death did not cause the general conflagration for which extremists on the left and right had perhaps hoped – and even worked. Instead, cooler heads prevailed and after a few weeks we were able to pick up the reform process where we had left off before Hani's assassination.

On the basis of the extensive framework that had already been agreed in the run-up to Codesa II and subsequent talks, the negotiations made rapid progress. The one major interruption of their deliberations occurred on 25 June 1993. Several thousand right-wing demonstrators had gathered around the World Trade Centre to protest against the process which was continuing inside the building. They forced their way into the terrain and suddenly, an armoured van was driven through the plate-glass windows into the entrance foyer, followed by hundreds of khaki-clad followers of the neo-fascist AWB (Afrikaner Weerstandsbeweging). For a couple of hours they took over the building, causing mayhem before dispersing. During their occupation of the World Trade Centre they manifested the worst forms of hooliganism and naked racism. The incident demonstrated just how boorish and repulsive the far right really were. All decent Afrikaners, including those on the right, like General Constand Viljoen, were ashamed to be associated in any way with these thugs.

However, the far right could not stop the progress that was being made with the negotiations. A week later, on 2 July, the great majority of the parties were able to announce a definite date for our first fully democratic elections – 27 April 1994. Five of the parties, the Conservative Party, the IFP and representatives of the Ciskei, Bophuthatswana and KwaZulu governments walked out of the negotiations, because they did not agree with the proposed election date. Until then, decisions in the negotiations had been taken according to the vaguely defined notion of sufficient consensus. They believed that without their parties, there was not sufficient consensus and that the decision on the election date was accordingly invalid. In fact, in a sense, they were probably right. We realized that an election without the IFP and the representatives of conservative Afrikaners would not only lack representativeness – it would also be fraught with danger. Much of our time between then and the election would be spent in trying to lure them back into the process.

26

Progress Towards the Interim Constitution

At the beginning of July 1993, Nelson Mandela and I travelled separately to the United States to receive the Philadelphia Peace Medal. After a short official visit to Austria, I arrived well before schedule at Andrews Airforce Base. We were immediately whisked away, through the muggy afternoon, past leafy woods and wooden houses into the city. As we drove, I just caught a glimpse of our ambassador, Harry Schwarz, driving in the opposite lane on his way to Andrews Airforce Base for my arrival. No one had told him that our flight was early!

The next day, 2 July 1993, I made a lunch-time speech to the Washington Press Club. I reminded the Washington press corps that three years before I had given them a commitment that we would negotiate a new constitution for South Africa that would establish a multiparty democracy with regular elections, the protection of minorities, an independent judiciary and a free market system. I was proud to be able to report on the substantial progress that we had made in honouring that commitment. I described the major constitutional agreements that we had already reached at the World Trade Centre, including a decision on the date of our first fully democratic election. At the same time, I made it clear that after the election neither the National Party nor I intended to disappear from the scene. I said that I was not a colonial governor about to relinquish his post and sail away into the sunset. I was an African and a descendant of a people who fought the first freedom war of this century against colonialism in Africa. I did not represent whites only and looked forward to a time when the main determinant of political affiliation would no longer be race – but political conviction and values.

That afternoon I paid my first visit to the new American president, Bill Clinton, at the White House. We were first ushered through to the Cabinet Room and were then taken into the Oval Office. Clinton was taller and more gangly than I had expected. He was accompanied by

Vice-President Al Gore; the secretary of state, Warren Christopher; US ambassador to South Africa, Princeton Lyman; and the assistant secretary of state for African affairs, George Moose. My team included Pik Botha and our ambassador in Washington. President Clinton and Al Gore expressed genuine – and almost incredulous – admiration for what we had so far achieved in South Africa. I briefed them on the status of constitutional negotiations and the problems that we were experiencing with violence and with the latest walk-out by the IFP and the right-wing parties. Clinton and Gore asked us all the appropriate questions and promised us their support in our endeavours. When we finished our talks, the White House staff led us out of the president's suite by a rather circuitous route. We later discovered that they did not want us to bump into Nelson Mandela and his delegation, who had also come to call on President Clinton. Mandela had flatly refused to appear with me before the photographers who had gathered on the lawn outside the entrance to the West Wing. I shrugged off his snub and faced the photographers together with Pik Botha.

We finally met the ANC delegation the following evening at a reception offered by the hosts of the Liberty Medal ceremony in an exclusive restaurant at the top of one of Philadelphia's tallest buildings. I exchanged some pleasantries with Mandela and found him stiff, but courteous. Later that evening, from our magnificent vantage point, we watched a fireworks display over the Delaware River to mark the eve of Independence Day.

The next day was blisteringly hot and humid. Mandela and I both addressed a lunchtime gathering in Philadelphia's massive new convention centre. There must have been at least a thousand guests seated for lunch. There was all the razzmatazz, spot lights and brass bands associated with American conventions. Both Mandela and I made ten-minute speeches. I spoke about the relevance of Philadelphia – the city of brotherly love and the cradle of the American democracy – to the process that we were at that very time conducting at the World Trade Centre in South Africa. My speech went down extremely well and was interrupted several times by lengthy applause. Mandela's speech, by contrast, did not strike the right chord and consequently did not receive quite the same level of applause. I think this must have annoyed him, because later, at a joint press conference, he launched a broadside against me over my refusal to hand the South African Broadcasting Corporation (SABC) over to the ANC on a plate. It wasn't the right place to squabble about our domestic disputes and it did not create a good impression. This was not the first time that this had happened. His public attacks on me at functions where we were co-guests was becoming an embarrassment to our hosts.

The presentation ceremony took place on a platform that had been specially erected for the purpose outside Philadelphia's historic Independence Hall. While we were waiting inside the hall for all the guests to assemble, I once again had an opportunity of exchanging a few words with President Clinton before joining him and the other guests on the platform outside. In front of us, in a wide and leafy mall stretching into the distance, there was a crowd of several thousand people, most of them black Americans. The sun was extremely hot and the proceedings were long and drawn out – a situation which often creates special discomfort for bald, hatless people like myself. One of the participants was the Revd Leon Sullivan, a black American clergyman who had for many years been a prominent anti-apartheid leader. Judging by his contribution and his vitriolic attack on the South African government, he had hardly noticed the changes that had taken place in South Africa since his anti-apartheid days. Before presenting us with the medals, Clinton made an appropriate speech – but one which was clearly directed more to his local constituency than to the situation in South Africa. When we finally were released from the platform, I made a point of shaking hands with the Revd Sullivan. When I tackled him about his excessively aggressive speech, he nervously wiped his brow and apologized. 'Sorry,' he said, 'those were just some things that I had to say.'

When we returned to South Africa, the negotiations at Kempton Park had entered their final crucial phase. We had reached broad agreement on the transitional and electoral procedures and mechanisms. On 23 September, Parliament adopted the Transitional Executive Council Act which made provision for the establishment of a multiparty Transitional Executive Council which would monitor the government during the run-up to the election to ensure that none of its actions favoured or harmed any of the political parties. In essence its task would be to create a climate for free and fair elections. However, we had still not reached consensus on a number of key issues, including education, language, local government, property rights, affirmative action, amnesty, and the crucial question of the degree to which the new South Africa would have a federal system. As always, the tendency had been to leave the most difficult questions until last.

Also, we were still working hard to bring the IFP and the other parties that had walked out of the Multiparty Negotiating Forum back on board. At the end of August, Chief Minister Buthelezi had sent me letters which revealed the depth of his suspicions. He accused me of pandering to public opinion and running behind the ANC and serving their interests. He still seemed to believe that there was a special relationship between the ANC and the National Party based on secret agreements. In my reply I assured him that we had always regarded the ANC as our main adversary and would continue to do so until such time as they changed central elements of their policy; until they unequivocally renounced violence, not only in their words but in their deeds; and until they abandoned their alliance with the South African Communist Party.

Our exchange of letters led to a marathon meeting between the IFP and the government at Tuynhuys on 16 September 1993. Buthelezi and his delegation started the meeting with a two-hour harangue, during which they once again attacked the Record of Understanding and articulated their deep suspicions that the National Party and the ANC had concluded a secret bilateral deal. Slowly, during the next six hours, my colleagues and I patiently managed to address the IFP's concerns and to turn the meeting around. In the end, we were able to make substantial progress. (Or, at least, we thought we had.) We agreed to work together to achieve five common constitutional objectives: a constitutional state; a constitutional court; universal fundamental rights; comprehensive constitutional principles; and the powers, functions and boundaries of the states/provinces/regions in a federal system. (We called them SPRs in the negotiations, because the terms states, provinces or regions already presupposed the degree of federalism that there should be in the final constitution.) We also agreed to stay in close communication with one another to prevent future misinterpretations of one another's views.

Despite this new-found understanding, Buthelezi soon reverted to his old approach. At the beginning of October, the IFP, the Conservative Party, the AVF (the Afrikaanse Volksfront, a coalition of twenty-one conservative Afrikaans groups) and the governments of Bophuthatswana, KwaZulu and Ciskei formed a new negotiating alliance, which they called the Freedom Alliance. The main objectives of the Freedom Alliance were to promote the right of the peoples of South Africa to self-determination; to draw up a new national constitution before elections; and to continue negotiations until a settlement was reached.

It was in pursuit of the latter goal that the Freedom Alliance agreed to hold talks with the government on 29 October 1993.

The meeting was held in the Union Buildings between my delegation and delegations led by Chief Minister Mangosuthu Buthelezi of the IFP, President Lucas Mangope of Bophuthatswana, Brigadier Oupa Gqozo of Ciskei, Dr Ferdi Hartzenberg of the Conservative Party and General Constand Viljoen of the AVF. At a preparatory *bosberaad* at D'Nyala a few days earlier, the Freedom Alliance and the government had narrowed their differences down to four main issues, relating primarily to the powers, funding and boundaries of SPRs and their ability to draw up their own constitutions. Roelf Meyer believed that the two sides would be able to reach agreement on three of these issues. The heart of the problem was, however, a fundamental difference of philosophy between us on the basic relationship between SPRs and the federal government. They wanted strong states and a weak central government. We supported a balance between the two levels of government: we favoured a strong central government in those areas that were reserved for it, and strong states in matters which fell within their jurisdiction. We accepted that in many areas, central government would have normative powers. They did not. In effect, what they wanted was much nearer to a confederation.

During the meeting I noticed that there was little real unanimity among the parties of the Freedom Alliance: Buthelezi was primarily concerned with the future of KwaZulu-Natal; the Conservative Party and the AVF wanted self-determination for Afrikaners in their own, as yet, undefined (and as far as I am concerned indefinable) homeland; and Mangope and Gqozo simply wanted to survive. The alliance's main goal at that time was to convene a meeting of leaders – between the ANC and its allies, the Freedom Alliance and the government. We had no objections to such a meeting but we knew that there was no real chance that the ANC would accept it. The Freedom Alliance also wanted to stop the election clock, which they realized had already begun ticking inexorably towards 27 April 1994.

I found listening to them somewhat depressing. Although I could understand their concerns, it appeared to me as though they were all living in a dream world. Buthelezi was despondent. He said that Mandela had given them an ultimatum that in a few months they would cease to exist: 'If he thinks the way to the future is by trampling over us, then so be it.' He complained again about the government:

'There are so many assurances that you have made which have been torn to shreds by your agreements with Mandela . . . Mr Mandela now threatens to obliterate us . . . We are in a very serious part of our history. Our king, who is a descendant of Dingane (the second Zulu king), cannot take the destruction of our country lying down.'

I felt sorry for Mangope. He had done a better job than any of the other leaders of the independent states in trying to improve the lot of his people (while allegedly enriching himself as well). He was a tall dignified man, quiet and courteous. On state occasions he still wore the black top hat, sash of office, and black tail-coat that previous National Party governments had believed were fitting clothes for heads of state. All this, together with his permanently doleful expression, created the impression of a rather lugubrious funeral director. He complained that he was being forced into a straitjacket that he had not chosen: 'The three of us [he, Buthelezi and Gqozo] are seen as being on death row. At the World Trade Centre it was decided that the laws in terms of which we gained independence will be repealed. We will resist with all the power that we have – even against the mighty ANC. We are being placed in a straitjacket and must co-operate with your decision to kill us without our being consulted. The decision at the World Trade Centre means that in a few months the TVBC countries [Transkei, Venda, Bophuthatswana and Ciskei] and KwaZulu will simply cease to exist. The president in waiting is talking about it everywhere. He thinks that he is God.'

I decided to be patient, but also to confront them with reality. With regard to the position of the independent states, I replied that their status should be changed only in a constitutional manner. I said that it would be necessary to have fundamental talks with them on how this could be achieved. We would do nothing behind their backs. We believed that it was in their best interest to become part of South Africa again. In fact, they would be faced with an impossible situation if they rejected and resisted re-incorporation. And so we fenced to and fro with one another; Buthelezi appalled by the prospect that the Kingdom of the Zulus might fall under the heel of the (Xhosa) ANC; Mangope, fatalistic and feeling betrayed by his former patrons; Gqozo, desperate; Hartzenberg, drawing maps in his mind of an illusory Afrikaner homeland; Constand Viljoen, no doubt, considering the number of soldiers that he would need if he were to choose the route of armed struggle; and our side, patiently trying to persuade the others to accept reality and to achieve as many of their goals as possible

A meeting of Codesa at the World Trade Centre, Kempton Park, December 1991.

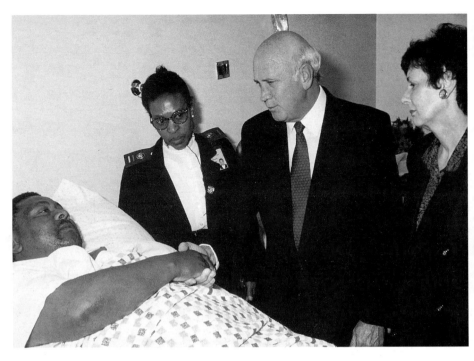

Visiting a victim of violence in Tembisa, 1 August 1993.

With Ambassador Henry Swarz, Marike and Dave Steward,
Director General of the Office of the State President, after receiving the
Philadelphia Peace Medal, Philadelphia, 4 July 1993.

With Baroness Thatcher during her visit to Cape Town in 1993.

In London meeting HM Queen Elizabeth II in December 1993.

Receiving the Nobel Peace Prize with Nelson Mandela in Oslo
on 10 December 1993.

In the run-up to the elections, meeting Dr Henry Kissinger with Pik Botha, the minister of foreign affairs, in Pretoria, April 1994.

My concession speech in Pretoria after the result of the general election on 27 April 1994, with Pik Botha, Roelf Meyer and Marike.

At the inauguration
of President Nelson
Mandela, Pretoria,
10 May 1994.

My brother Wimpie de
Klerk and my mother
Corrie de Klerk,
Pretoria, 10 May 1994.

With Hillary Clinton,
Vice President Al Gore
and the Revd Jesse
Jackson at the
inauguration of
President
Nelson Mandela,
10 May 1994.

Enjoying one of my favourite
pastimes.

With Elita, September 1998.

through negotiations. In reality, we and the Freedom Alliance were separated by a fundamental philosophical difference: none of them truly wanted to be part of the new South Africa, while we were convinced that it was the only option.

In the meantime, the sporadic violence continued to take its dreadful toll. On 25 July 1993, five masked APLA gunmen burst into a church service in Cape Town and opened fire on the congregation with machine guns and hand grenades. Twelve people were killed and fifty-six were injured. Among the dead was the sister of Fanie Pretorius, a senior official in my office. The next day I visited some of the injured in hospital. The irony is that many of those killed and injured had nothing at all to do with the conflict in South Africa: they were Russian seamen, whose ship happened to be docked in Cape Town harbour. A few days later I went to another hospital to visit the wounded of yet another brutal attack, which had taken place in Tembisa, east of Johannesburg. Thirty people had been killed and scores more injured when 200 hostel dwellers had attacked people in the surrounding community. The wounded that I had visited in different parts of the country within the space of a week had more in common than one would imagine. The first group had been middle-class whites – the second working-class blacks. They were, however, united by their pain and their incomprehension of the reasons that would drive other people to commit such terrible acts. After the Tembisa incident the ANC issued an irresponsible statement in which it insinuated that there was some kind of link between my meetings with Chief Minister Buthelezi and incidents of violence such as those at Boipatong, and most recently in Tembisa.

On 9 September twenty-four more people were brutally and mind-lessly murdered at Wadeville near Johannesburg. Twelve days later another thirty-nine people were killed in a series of incidents in areas east of Johannesburg. In each case we issued statements deploring the violence and commiserating with the victims. We also did what we could to stabilize the situation. We launched investigations and offered rewards for information on the culprits. We reinforced the police and deployed the SADF in greater numbers. We activated the mechanisms of the National Peace Secretariat to try to restore calm in the com-munities involved. We held urgent talks with the ANC and the IFP and we urged them to get together to put a stop to the violence between their followers. Where we succeeded in arresting perpetrators, they were prosecuted. But still the violence continued.

At the beginning of October, the South African Defence Force informed me and the security ministers that they had located an APLA house in Umtata that was used for the storage of weapons and for APLA soldiers in transit. The defence force said that they had had the house under surveillance for several days and had corroboration that it was being used by APLA for terrorist purposes. They had no doubt that it was a legitimate target. They warned me that if the government did nothing to stop the threat, the house and the weapons that it contained would certainly be used in more terrorist attacks against South African citizens across the Transkei border. The South African police advised me that the SADF information had been corroborated by two separate informants who had provided them with the same information. It was an extremely difficult decision to take and, because it would involve military action in a country that South Africa regarded as independent, it was a decision that I, as head of the government, would have to take. In my mind I was satisfied that we had tried all the peaceful options at our disposal to persuade Holomisa to prevent APLA from using Transkei as a base for cross-border terrorist attacks. Holomisa had not responded satisfactorily to any of our pleas or threats. I was sure that if we confronted him again with the information that we had now obtained, he would find a way to get APLA to move to some other safer place. I accordingly authorized the Defence Force to raid the house, but stipulated that minimum force should be used and that care should be taken to avoid serious injuries and casualties. Soon afterwards, in the early morning of 8 October, troops of the SADF burst into the house. Five people, later identified as teenagers who were sleeping in the house, were killed. If there had previously been any weapons in the house, they had already been removed, because none were found. When I later confronted the SADF with their failure to carry out my instructions that minimum force should be used, they explained that the troops involved had thought that the occupants of the house were reaching for their weapons so they opened fire, believing that they were in a combat situation. There was a furore. The media castigated the government and the ANC were furious. I deeply regretted the incident, and later in the Government of National Unity supported the ample settlement of the ensuing civil damages.

And so we lurched from security crisis to security crisis, from one incident of violence to the next until the end of the year by which time 3,706 people had died in political violence – several hundred more than the year before. I was deeply concerned about the implications which the escalating violence held for the prospect of being able to hold free and fair elections.

In the meantime, our negotiating teams continued to whittle away at the issues that still separated the parties in the negotiating forum. They did so with great skill and great tenacity, sometimes stretching the meaning of words so broadly, and contorting phrases so intricately, that it was thoroughly confusing for anyone without legal training. However, there was sufficient give and take and reasonable compromises to encompass the bottom lines of all the main parties on all but a few outstanding issues. On language we agreed that there would be eleven equal official languages in the new South Africa – but accommodated the concerns of Afrikaners by adding that 'rights relating to language and the status of languages existing at the commencement of this constitution shall not be diminished . . .' Minority concerns regarding education were addressed in one of the articles of the Bill of Rights which was contained in the constitution: 'Every person shall have the right . . . to establish, where practicable, educational institutions based on common culture, language or religion, provided that there shall be no discrimination on the ground of race.'

We won a titanic struggle with regard to the protection of property rights in terms of which private property could be expropriated only for public purposes. Lawful expropriation would be subject to the payment of agreed compensation which would take all the relevant factors into account, including 'the use to which the property is being put, the history of its acquisition, its market value, the value of investments in it by those affected and the interests of those affected'. We had insisted on the inclusion of market value and had finally achieved success.

The agreements that we negotiated regarding the powers and status of the SPRs were even more complex. However, they culminated, in our opinion, with the recognition of provinces which had powers and autonomy that were more consistent with a federal system than a unitary system. Other parties, most notably the IFP, vehemently disagreed with us. The federal nature of the new South Africa would be further strengthened by constitutional amendments that would be adopted by Parliament just before the election. In the same manner, we also reached agreement on transitional arrangements for local government.

Another key issue that was unresolved until shortly before the adoption of the interim constitution, was the question of amnesty and how we would deal with the conflict of the past. Throughout the negotiations, it had been accepted as one of our basic points of departure that there should be a comprehensive process of amnesty for all those, on all sides, who had been involved in the conflict of the past. The South African government had not been defeated in battle and the ANC was not in a position to dictate terms to it. Thousands of ANC members – including many who had committed heinous crimes that did not comply with the Norgard principles – had already been granted indemnity under the 1990 Indemnity Act and the Further Indemnity Act of 1992.

Minister Kobie Coetsee, in his capacity as minister of justice, continued to be involved in negotiations on the delicate question of amnesty. At the same time, Roelf Meyer, as our main negotiator, had an overall responsibility for all aspects of the negotiating process. Unfortunately, co-operation between them was bedevilled by a serious difference of opinion at the time of the Record of Understanding on the very issue of amnesty. The ANC, on the other hand, played a delaying game, regularly raising hopes for a breakthrough, but then finding excuses for repeated delays. As a result, there was little progress. As the date for the adoption of the interim constitution approached, senior members of the government, particularly those involved with the security departments, became anxious to learn what progress had been made. Minister Coetsee, who was renowned for playing his cards close to his chest, repeatedly assured them, on the basis of the assurances that he himself had received from the ANC, that agreement could still be reached.

However, the question of amnesty was not resolved. In the end, the best that our negotiating team could do was to reach agreement on the inclusion of a paragraph at the end of the interim constitution that stipulated that 'amnesty shall be granted in respect of acts and omissions and offences associated with political objectives and committed in the course of the conflicts of the past'. Amnesty was to be dealt with 'in a spirit of reconciliation, on the basis that there is a need for understanding but not for vengeance, a need for reparation but not for retaliation, a need for *ubuntu* (traditional African humanism) but not for victimization'.

This wording – although guaranteeing that amnesty would be granted for politically motivated acts – provided little or no indication of how the process would be managed in practice. It soon became clear that the ANC was determined to delay the clarification of this question until after the election, when it would be able to enforce its will through its majority in Parliament. They later did exactly this through the adoption of the Promotion of National Unity and Reconciliation Act of 1995, which led to the establishment of the Truth and Reconciliation Commission. By that time, all that the National Party could do was to fight a rearguard action and reach agreement on the best deal that was then possible. The manner in which we dealt with the question of amnesty was probably our greatest failure during the negotiating process.

On the evening of Sunday, 15 November, the cabinet went off for a final strategic conference before the adoption of the interim constitution. This time, we did not have sufficient time to fly off to D'Nyala or one of our other isolated meeting spots, so we met at Glenburn Lodge, a country hotel about 35 kilometres from Pretoria. The hotel was tucked into a little valley in a range of rocky hills just to the north of Krugersdorp, where I had gone to high school. We spent the night in chalets nestled along the banks of a little trout stream. It was a beautiful evening as we all gathered for sun-downers before dinner. We realized that this would be a crucial session. During our conference the next day we worked through the draft constitution, paragraph by paragraph – discussing and weighing each phrase and sometimes each word – deciding which elements we could live with and which we would have to try to renegotiate before 18 November.

By 17 November 1993, the text of our transitional constitution was virtually complete. There were still six important outstanding matters on which our negotiating teams had failed to reach agreement: the manner in which decisions would be taken in the Government of National Unity (GNU) cabinet; some outstanding matters related to the boundaries, powers and functions of the provinces; the right of provinces to adopt their own constitutions; aspects of the law governing the forthcoming elections; mechanisms to settle disputes; and the manner in which the Government of National Unity would function. Perhaps the most important of these were the functioning of the GNU and the process by which the multiparty cabinet would take its decisions – would it be by consensus or by a two-thirds majority? The latter option would conceivably give the minority parties a veto.

As had happened so often before during the negotiations, these questions were referred at the last moment to Mandela and me to resolve. Once again, the stories that the ANC leaked to the media about my private meeting with Mandela are misleading. They create the impression that I went into the meeting determined to force the ANC to accept the two-thirds option. Certainly, some of my cabinet colleagues very much wanted me to do so. However, I favoured a consensus model. By that time I had already presided over a cabinet for four years. In all that time, we had never voted on any decision. We had openly discussed matters and ministers had frankly expressed their views. In the end I had articulated what I thought was the general consensus. Sometimes, I personally did not agree with the consensus – but that then became the decision of the cabinet. I felt that an impossible situation would be created if the cabinet were to have to vote on every matter that came before it. If the minority parties consistently thwarted the will of the majority it might in the end cause intolerable strains on the whole constitutional edifice. On the other hand, if we were to adopt a non-confrontational, non-voting approach, all participants would probably be able to exercise real influence on decision-making. Mandela and I agreed that the GNU cabinet would take its decisions on the basis of the spirit of consensus underlying the concept of a government of national unity. In the end, this is how the Government of National Unity worked in practice – at least for the first two years of its existence.

We also reached a broad understanding on the other outstanding issues. On the basis of these discussions, our negotiating teams were able to thrash out detailed agreements. During the hours preceding the adoption of the draft constitution by the plenary of the multiparty negotiating forum, we also managed to reach agreement on two additional important issues: firstly, we secured confirmation that the Parliament and the Government of National Unity that would emerge from the elections on 27 April 1994, would continue for five years until 1999. There would be no new elections before this time, unless the government was defeated in a no-confidence vote. Secondly, and perhaps even more crucially, we reached agreement on the manner in which the members of the Constitutional Court would be appointed. The president would appoint the president of the court after consultation with the chief justice. However, instead of the government of the day being able to load the court with its own supporters, it was agreed that the president would have to appoint six of the eleven judges from a list submitted to him by a neutral Judicial Services Commission.

And so, early on the morning of 18 November 1993, we adopted the interim constitution. It was one of the major milestones on the road to the new South Africa. It was not exactly what we would have wanted when we set out at the beginning of the negotiation road: we would have liked to have seen something closer to the power sharing in the Swiss or Belgian models; we would have liked more clearly defined rights for the regions and minorities. But we were satisfied that we had substantially succeeded in achieving the total package that I had spelled out as our bottom line during the referendum the year before.

In my closing speech I said that despite all the setbacks and frustrations which we have endured; despite the walkouts and the boycotts; despite the terrible violence which continued to afflict so many of our people; despite the absence that day of important parties, we had shown that it was possible for people with widely differing views and beliefs to reach basic and sound agreements through compromise, through reasoned debate and through negotiation. I added that the transitional constitution was the distillation of the dreams of generations of disenfranchised South Africans. It offered a reasonable assurance of continuing security for others who had traditionally had the vote. It was capable of protecting individual and community rights. It would prevent the misuse of power and would uphold the rule of law. It established a fair division of powers between the pillars of good and orderly government.

It was also the product of compromise. As such it did not satisfy any of us completely. But it satisfied all of us sufficiently to meet our most pressing concerns and hopes. In so doing, it provided the basis for a new national consensus. I said that we would continue to work for broadening that base to include the significant parties that were not present at Kempton Park that day.

I concluded by predicting that when, in the future, South Africans looked back on the work which we had accomplished there that day they would say: Yes, it was on this day that we created a basis for good hope for this and for future generations of all our people.

The following month, on 22 December 1993, the interim constitution was adopted by Parliament. It was the end of an era. When I addressed Parliament I said that we had succeeded in bringing our country to this historic point through evolution – and not revolution. Parliament had supervised every step of the process which had led that day to the adoption of the interim constitution. There had throughout been the constitutional continuity for which I and my party had always worked – and not the revolutionary discontinuity that the ANC had always advocated. I said that the end of the old Parliament should not be regarded as a funeral, but as a birth. There would be a new Parliament, but this time it would be a Parliament without the legitimacy problem that we had always experienced. Parliamentary tradition would continue, but this time it would be without the albatross of injustice, discrimination and exclusion hanging about its neck.

27

The Nobel Peace Prize

Some three weeks after the adoption of the transitional constitution by the Multiparty Negotiating Forum I left for Oslo to receive the Nobel Peace Prize which I had been awarded jointly with Nelson Mandela.

I had heard that Mandela and I were to receive the prize on 15 October while I was taking a short break at Lekkerwater, the presidential retreat about 220 kilometres east of Cape Town. Lekkerwater means lovely water in Afrikaans. It is an apt description. The seaside home is situated in the Goode Hope Nature Reserve between the ocean and coastal hills. It is surrounded by fynbos – the natural vegetation of the Cape – which includes thousands of species of small heather-like bushes and wild flowers. Lekkerwater is completely isolated. It can be reached only by four-wheel-drive vehicle or by helicopter. The ocean is generally rough, forever crashing and surging onto the rocky coast and throwing up kelp onto the intermittent stretches of sandy beach. It is a wild, undisciplined and exhilarating place with strong prevailing winds from the south-east during the summer months and rain-bearing north-westerly gales during the winter.

The fishing is excellent, but because it is a nature reserve could be indulged in only by permit and for scientific purposes. This meant that every fish had to be carefully weighed and measured and recorded in an official logbook. My guests and I were issued with a permit which we used with great discretion and circumspection. On one occasion one of my bodyguards, duly authorized by me, caught an enormous fish – I think it was a kabeljou – in the course of his unselfish contribution to scientific research in the Goode Hope Nature Reserve. A photograph was taken with him, my grandson and namesake, and the fish. The photograph was subsequently published in our leading angling magazines and gave rise to heated correspondence and to much criticism. My use of the house – which had been built by anonymous donors under the direction of the late Louis Rive – was also the cause of much controversy and criticism, particularly by the handful of families that had owned cottages along the coast before the area had been included in the nature reserve. Something that I had thought was completely innocuous and above reproach was suddenly made to look sordid and irregular. I was so disgusted that I stopped using Lekkerwater a few years ago, even though I still had the right to do so. I subsequently learned that the donors were the Rupert family – one of South Africa's leading business families.

Until all this, I loved our occasional visits to Lekkerwater. They were the only times when Marike and I could truly relax and recharge our batteries. Everywhere else we were the subject of public scrutiny and the ever-present attention of our security personnel. Few people realize how tiring it becomes never to be able to escape these attentions, never to be able to slip down to the cinema without security people having to clear three rows of seats; never being able to drop into the corner store to buy a packet of cigarettes or go to a shopping centre without the visit becoming a publicity event; never being able to dine at one's favourite restaurant without half a dozen well-meaning people wanting you to sign their menus, or reminding you of the time that you met them at such and such an occasion or suggesting how the government should be run; and never even being allowed to drive one's own car. I love driving and while I was president acquired a new Mercedes. One day I could no longer resist the temptation. I pulled a cap low over my head, climbed into my new car, and to the immense consternation of my security team, took it for a spin all by myself. It was a wonderful experience. The best depiction of this presidential imprisonment that I have seen was in a movie called the *American President* in which the fictitious American leader caused immense disruption when he tried to make a phone call without the assistance of his secretary, or stopped to buy flowers for his girlfriend without previously notifying the Secret Service. Over the years, we got to know our bodyguards very well. They were seldom out of earshot and moved with us wherever we went and whenever we travelled abroad. They became almost like members of the family and I never blamed them for our lack of privacy.

On the morning of 15 October I was relaxing at Lekkerwater with some friends when the telephone rang. I picked it up to hear a voice say: 'This is the Norwegian Broadcasting Corporation. You have been awarded the Nobel Peace Prize together with Nelson Mandela. May we interview you?' I gulped a few times and then said yes in a wavering voice. To this day I cannot recall what I said to them. Next on the line was Dave Steward. Our Office was receiving numerous enquiries from the Norwegian press, wanting to know my reaction. Soon after that, the Nobel Committee called me and confirmed the report: Nelson Mandela and I had been jointly awarded the Nobel Peace Prize for 1993. Danie Hough, an old friend who was visiting Lekkerwater at the time, took a video of me while I was hearing the news on the phone. There is no sense in pretending to be blasé about these things: the fact is that Marike and I were absolutely thrilled by the news. I was delighted – not only for myself – but because this was somehow the ultimate recognition that my party and my people, the Afrikaners, after so many years of ostracism, were now at last part of the solution to the complex problems of our country.

And so, on the evening of 7 December 1993, I flew off to Europe on my way to receive the prize. We flew on the presidential aircraft that we affectionately called NAN, after the first three letters of its registration. It was a French Marcel-Dassault Falcon 900. On short trips it could carry about fifteen passengers. On long journeys it could transport five or six people in great comfort. Full-size beds could be made up for overnight flights and we could generally be sure of arriving at our destinations as fresh and relaxed as one can be after an intercontinental flight. NAN was indispensable for my non-stop agenda in South Africa – where I sometimes had to be in three different cities in the course of a single day – and it was extremely useful for overseas trips. It was a presidential perk that I thoroughly enjoyed, and the one that I most sorely missed when I left public office.

We stopped in London on our way to Oslo. I had finally received the British Foreign Office's ultimate stamp of approval – my first invitation to visit Queen Elizabeth. Marike and I were slipped into Buckingham Palace and had a pleasant meeting with the queen. She was well informed on South African affairs and was strongly supportive of the transformation process. I think she remembered her own visit to South Africa in 1947 with affection and looked forward to the day when South Africa would once again become a member of the Commonwealth.

I later called on Prime Minister John Major and Douglas Hurd, the British foreign secretary, at number 10 Downing Street. As always, John Major was well informed and extremely helpful. I always found him to be a thoroughly decent and reliable man. He was fair, impartial and supportive on all aspects of South African affairs – except for our occasional clashes against England at cricket and rugby. The previous day the Transitional Executive Council had come into being. All the parties represented in the Multiparty Negotiating Forum also participated in the TEC, whose main task, as already explained, was to create a climate for free and fair elections. Their first action – the following day – would be to approve a list of names for the Independent Electoral Commission, whose task it would be to administer the national election on 27 April 1994. I told Major that these initial stages of the TEC would be of fundamental importance. I predicted that there would be a move to try to turn the TEC into an interim government. However, its functions and responsibilities were related only to the election. It was an important body, and we would uphold its legitimate functions, but it was not responsible for the day-to-day government of the country. I said that I intended to make use of the TEC myself, to ensure that other parties did not take actions that were inconsistent with the establishment of a climate for free and fair elections.

We also discussed the importance of bringing the boycotting parties – and particularly the IFP – back into the negotiating process. Prime Minister Major asked me what I thought the chances were of their participating in the elections. I replied that I thought that the IFP would participate. About the Conservative Party I was less sure, but I expected that many of its followers would oppose an election boycott. They also did not want a civil war. People with good jobs would not put their futures on the line – although some might join underground movements. Major also asked me how my relations with Mandela were. I replied that they were generally satisfactory, but strained. I also assured him that I would not allow our differences to stand in the way of our working together to keep the negotiating process on track.

Major also asked me for an assessment of the threat of violence from the right. I shared with him my conviction that it could be contained, although the threat was serious. We discussed the risks of a *coup d'état* and I assured him that I did not believe that there was any chance that the SADF or the police would allow themselves to be co-opted into irresponsible far-right initiatives. We would nevertheless have to treat the security forces with discretion.

The next day we flew off on NAN across the grey North Sea, until in due course the snow-covered hills and pine forests of Norway came into view. We landed at Fornebu Airport where we were met by Pik Botha and Professors Francis Sejersted and Geir Lundestad, the chairman and the secretary of the Nobel Committee. We were then swept away in a convoy of Volvos toward the city, through a stark black and white landscape, quaint wooden buildings and incomprehensible traffic signs. We were accommodated at the stately Grand Hotel overlooking the Karl Johansgate, a broad mall leading to the Royal Palace on our right and the old Norwegian Parliament on our left. It was −10 degrees centigrade and had been snowing for most of the day. The mall and the trees in the centre of the Karl Johansgate were covered in snow.

That evening the Nobel Committee hosted a private dinner for Mandela and his daughter Zindzi and for Marike and me. It was pleasant and our hosts were courteous and considerate. But the atmosphere was stiff – particularly from Mandela's side. Before my arrival, he had chosen once again to attack me in interviews that he had given to the media. Apparently he was not pleased by the decision to include me in the award. In private conversations, Professor Sejersted had also let me know how controversial their decision to grant the peace prize to me as well as to Mandela had been. Although they had concluded, after lengthy consideration, that this would be the correct course, my reception was reserved by comparison with the effusive and unrestrained welcome that was accorded to Mandela. The fact is that for almost four decades South Africa had been a central preoccupation of the Norwegians. Whole generations of Norwegian schoolchildren had been raised on the premise that apartheid was the apotheosis of all evil and that Nelson Mandela and the ANC could do no wrong. Norway was one of the main contributors to the ANC and one of its most vociferous supporters in international campaigns to isolate South Africa.

*

The ceremony took place the next afternoon in the City Hall of Oslo. It is a large, rather angular brick building. The hall itself is like a huge box, several storeys high. One end is dominated by an enormous mural which depicted in vivid colour and angular lines the social progress of mankind. When we arrived, we walked up a broad aisle in the middle of the audience of several hundred people. We made our way to the front of the hall where the Nobel Committee had already taken their seats. Mandela and I sat on either side of the chairman, Professor Sejersted. On the day of the award, Mandela was much friendlier than he had been the previous night. I welcomed this because I felt that another of his regular displays of public animosity towards me would on that occasion have been very embarrassing for our country and for the cause of reconciliation.

The proceedings were interspersed with musical interludes, some provided by a string quartet and others by the South African pop group Ladysmith Black Mambazo. Professor Sejersted delivered the opening speech in which he explained the reasons for the committee's choice. He was effusive in his praise of Nelson Mandela but guarded when he referred to me. He almost created the impression that the jury was still out on the question of my motives for abandoning apartheid and my intention of seeing the process through to its conclusion. His summary of the recent history of South Africa was predictably one-sided and superficial. Still, he was a good man who had the courage to carry through with his conviction that our side also merited some recognition for the remarkable transformation that was taking place in South Africa at that very time.

In my speech I tried to avoid saying anything that was too contentious. Instead, I discussed what I believe were the forces that were helping to promote peace throughout the world – economic growth and democratization. I explained how these forces had also been at work in South Africa and how they had helped us to make impressive progress in negotiations for a new democratic constitutional dispensation. I conveyed my sincere congratulations to Mr Mandela and paid tribute to all those who were working for peace in South Africa.

I then quoted the poem by the Afrikaans poet N. P. van Wyk Louw, in which he had asked whether a deed would ever be wrought in South Africa which would resound over the earth and mock the ages in their impotence. I said that what was taking place in South Africa was such a deed. I concluded by saying that a new era was dawning in our country, beneath the great southern stars, that would lift us out of the silent grief of our past and into a future in which there would be opportunity and space for joy and beauty – and for real and lasting peace.

After me and after a further interlude by Ladysmith Black Mambazo, Nelson Mandela spoke. His speech was, for the most part, appropriate and conciliatory. He also congratulated me. The Nobel Peace Prize medals were then presented to us. Mandela smiled broadly; I reciprocated; we shook hands and dozens of cameras clicked and flashed.

That evening Professor Sejersted led Mandela and me onto a first-floor balcony at the Grand Hotel overlooking the snow-covered Karl Johansgate to witness a traditional Norwegian ceremony, what our programme described as a spontaneous torchlight procession. Although it was only 7 p.m. the northern winter night had already fallen and it was quite dark. I watched as a procession of several hundred people carrying candles filed up the avenue and gathered outside the hotel. It was very picturesque and quaint. Then they started shouting ANC slogans, praising Mandela while I was made to feel quite unwelcome. I heard some of the people shouting 'Kill the farmer, kill the Boer!' (the traditional name for Afrikaners was boer – or farmer) – an MK war cry. Others were shouting 'De Klerk, go home!' Mandela was smiling warmly and waving to the crowd below. For me and Marike, it was a very unpleasant situation. However, we stood our ground and faced the crowd, somewhat grimly. We felt quite isolated when the moving '*Nkosi Sikelel' iAfrika*' was sung, but with almost everybody raising their fists in the ANC salute. At the end of it, we slipped back into the hotel, quite upset by the hostility that we had experienced. It is untrue that we turned our backs on the crowd when '*Nkosi Sikelel' iAfrika*' was sung – as was subsequently rumoured.

Later that evening there was a reception at the Grand Hotel, followed by a gala dinner. Once again, our Norwegian hosts were charming – but decidedly and openly biased in favour of the ANC. I heard one snippet of conversation at the reception in which the wife of a former Norwegian prime minister asked a member of our delegation: 'And how is our vonderful Vinnie? Ve all think that she is the most marvellous person!' At the banquet later that evening, Mandela and I again had an opportunity to speak. I had recovered sufficiently from the unpleasant experience on the balcony to make a fairly light-hearted speech. Nevertheless, I managed to fit in a few friendly observations on how Marike and I had been treated. We had a good laugh when a member of our delegation, who had sat beside a very attractive Norwegian lady, told us how she had described her life-long devotion to the anti-apartheid cause and had even gone to work for the ANC in Tanzania. The member of our delegation asked her what she was going to do now that we had abolished apartheid. She looked quite dejected and replied: 'Well, I suppose there are always the whales' – referring, no doubt, to the determination of Norway's no-nonsense prime minister, Mrs Gro Harlem Brundtland, to continue with her country's whale fishing regardless of the negative international reaction.

The next day we flew to Stockholm, which we found to be quite different from Oslo. It had a much more sophisticated city atmosphere.

I attended a luncheon of leading Swedish businessmen, hosted by the prominent Swedish industrialist, Mr Peter Wallenberg. During the afternoon Mr Mandela and I paid a visit to King Carl Gustav XVI. That evening we were the guests of the Swedish prime minister, Mr Carl Bildt, at a banquet in the elegant Ministry of Foreign Affairs. Both Mandela and I had been asked to make short speeches. I made a few optimistic remarks about the constitutional progress that we were making in South Africa and thanked our Swedish hosts for their hospitality. Mandela then rose to speak and made a blistering personal attack on me and the National Party. He reminded the Swedes of all the sins of apartheid and blamed me for being involved in the on-going violence in the country. The Swedes were deeply embarrassed. While he was speaking some of them looked uncomfortably at the ceiling, while others examined their shirt-fronts. I was seething. It was only with the greatest self-control that I once again managed to bite my tongue and not shatter once and for all the illusion that there was a cordial relationship between me and Mandela. Afterwards some of the Swedes at my table came up to me and apologized for Mandela's behaviour.

That night we stayed at the Haga Palace, an old royal residence that the Swedish government now used for the accommodation of visiting heads of state. We enjoyed the dignified elegance of the lovely eighteenth-century building, set in a great snow-covered park with gaunt, black leafless trees. The next morning I had been asked to sign the Declaration on the Rights of Children, together with Mandela. I made it clear that I would not do so unless I could be assured that Mandela would not again abuse the opportunity by launching another unprovoked attack on me. I was given the assurance that I could speak second, and so decided to proceed with the ceremony. Mandela, true to form, once again made a few provocative and ill-informed remarks about the detention of children in South Africa. However, this time I spoke last and was able to refute his allegations in a reasonably calm and measured manner.

Later that day as I flew south across the silver Baltic Sea, I reflected on my relationship with Mandela. It was ironic that we had both travelled so far to be granted the world's highest accolade for peace and reconciliation – while the relationship between us was character-ized by so much vitriol and suspicion. I could honestly say that he was overwhelmingly responsible for the strain in our relationship. But I could not deny that I now found it increasingly difficult to dismiss or gloss over Mandela's continued and unwarranted attacks on me. I suspected that he was irritated by continuously being linked with me in the public's perception and begrudged me my share of international recognition. Nevertheless, I knew that I would have to continue to work with him. It was not a prospect that I greatly relished.

28

The Zulus Ask for Independence

During my visit to Europe for the Nobel Peace Prize, I confidently told the leaders with whom I spoke that I was optimistic that we would be able to hold the elections successfully. I said that there was still a good chance that the IFP and the more moderate right-wing parties would participate – but even if they did not, parties representing more than 80 per cent of the electorate would go to the polls. Nevertheless, I had no doubt about the importance of bringing the IFP and some of the leaders of the right on board. Their participation would give the election unquestionable legitimacy and would avert the destabilizing effect that their non-involvement might have on the whole process. Their participation was also essential to prevent the ANC from winning the two-thirds majority that it would need to impose a new constitution on the country.

As 1994 began there was great uncertainty in the country. Any group of experts that gathered at the beginning of the year to assess our chances would probably have come up with a negative forecast. Despite our repeated efforts, we were still experiencing enormous frustration in trying to persuade the parties of the Freedom Alliance to rejoin the process. The Independent Electoral Commission had started its task of organizing the national elections in December 1993. It had only four months to complete arrangements that would normally have taken at least a year to finalize. The commission was working with an entirely unknown process and nobody knew for sure whether it would really be able to complete its work in time. Its task was further hampered by the continuing refusal of Bophuthatswana and Ciskei to allow parties to campaign in their territories. The IFP and the ANC – despite protestations of disapproval from their leadership – were still making it practically impossible for other parties to campaign in many of the areas that they controlled. In addition, there were disturbing rumblings from the right and concerns, unfounded in my opinion, about the possibility of a *coup d'état*. And still the violence continued.

During the preceding months the main focus of violence had shifted from Natal to the townships of the East Rand (the metropolitan areas east of Johannesburg), where most of the conflict continued to take place between traditionalist IFP hostel dwellers and 'self-defence units' (SDUs) which had been set up in the neighbouring communities by the ANC and its allies. However, by this time many of the SDUs – which usually comprised revolutionary teenagers – were themselves out of control. Some were involved in criminal activities and others spent more time terrorizing their communities than in protecting them. On 10 January 1994, there was another flare-up of violence in the East Rand township of Kathlehong in which a journalist was killed and two others were wounded. The journalists had been accompanying political leaders, including Cyril Ramaphosa, who had also been at risk during the shooting. I referred the incident to the Goldstone Commission for immediate investigation, and discussed the situation with Nelson Mandela.

Now that the ANC was involved with the government in the Transitional Executive Council, I found Mandela's attitude a little more helpful. On 18 January, we held a meeting at the Union Buildings at which we received a report on the East Rand violence by a joint TEC team. The team included Mac Maharaj from the side of the ANC, and Mr Fanie van der Merwe, a senior civil servant and one of our most senior negotiators, from the side of the government. They had concluded that the problem of violence in the East Rand involved many factors, including depressed socio-economic conditions, lack of structured communication between the parties and mistrust of the police's Internal Stability Unit – which until then had borne the main responsibility for trying to maintain peace in the community.

Mr Mandela and I subsequently met on a number of occasions and agreed on the adoption of a comprehensive approach that would involve all interested parties. We persuaded the IFP to join the process of stabilizing the East Rand and finalized arrangements for the initiative within the framework of the TEC. The plan involved the appointment of a broadly representative task group under the chairmanship of General Jan van Loggerenberg, a former chief of the South African air force. It included representatives of the IFP, the ANC and the National Party, as well as individuals drawn from the civic structures, the trade unions, the peace/church structures and the private sector in the area. The task group was given the job of re-establishing proper administration and upgrading community services, of restoring stability and enabling people who had been displaced by the violence to return to their homes. The police's Internal Stability Unit was withdrawn from the area and the task of maintaining order was given to the South African Defence Force, which generally had a better image in the local communities than the police.

On 15 March, six weeks after we established the task group, I was able to make an inspection visit to the East Rand myself. I visited the task group's headquarters and flew by helicopter over the communities and hostels where the worst violence had occurred. It was a bleak vista of sprawling hostels, match-box houses – some of which had been burned down during the conflict – and crowded squatter camps. The task group had achieved considerable success. Normal services had been restored, communication between the previously warring factions had improved and incidents of violence had declined dramatically. The exercise showed that results could be achieved if we all worked together and adopted a holistic approach to the problem of violence. I could not help thinking what a great pity it was that we had not been able to launch a similar combined initiative to combat violence in the Natal.

While I continued these efforts to reduce the levels of violence, I was also doing everything in my power to try to persuade the parties of the Freedom Alliance to participate in the elections.

On 17 January 1994, I held a meeting at the Union Buildings with the Zulu king, Goodwill Zwelithini, Chief Minister Mangosuthu Buthelezi, several Zulu royal princes, IFP leaders and members of the Swazi royal family (the Zulu royal family had strong traditional and marital links with the royal family of the neighbouring independent kingdom of Swaziland). They were accompanied by some 35,000 Zulu warriors – dressed in their tribal regalia and bearing their traditional weapons – who had gathered peacefully on the lawns far below the Union Buildings. No doubt, they were meant to be a show of strength, but from where we sat and talked we could neither hear nor see them. The king and his delegation were deeply concerned that the transitional constitution contained no provision for the Zulu monarchy and that the name 'KwaZulu' would not appear in the name of their province, which would continue to be known simply as Natal. The ANC – and particularly Cyril Ramaphosa – had aggravated the situation by equating the Zulu king with the traditional leaders of the other tribal groups and by saying that the Transitional Executive Council was about to take over the administration of KwaZulu.

The IFP had reason to be worried. At that time many ANC leaders

– including Mandela – had begun to talk in terms of marginalizing or 'crushing' them. Their anxieties were expressed unambiguously during our meeting. One of the princes said that the Zulus were a long-established nation with their own king, and their own national terri-tory, KwaZulu. 'We tolerated British rule. We tolerated rule by you (the Afrikaners). We tolerated apartheid, but we will not tolerate rule by the Xhosas [many of the ANC leaders were from the Xhosa tribe]. We demand our sovereignty!' The princes were particularly contemp-tuous of Cyril Ramaphosa and his threats to impose rule by the Transitional Executive Council over KwaZulu. They said that it was inconceivable that 'that Venda [a reference to Ramaphosa's tribal affiliation] should dare to think that he could impose his will on the sons of heaven [the Zulus]'. On a less emotional level, the delegation was still unhappy with the powers and autonomy that the provinces would enjoy under the transitional constitution, as well as their dependence on the central government for their revenue. In addition, they wanted each voter to have two ballots in the election – one for the central parliament and one for the provincial parliament. As matters then stood, there would be a single ballot which meant that voters would be forced to support the same party for both levels of government.

I assured the king of the high consideration in which I held him, the Zulu monarchy and the kingdom of KwaZulu. I emphasized that adequate provision could be made for the entrenchment of these institutions in the envisaged provincial constitution of KwaZulu-Natal. We agreed to establish a working group to give urgent attention to ways and means of achieving these goals. However, during the delib-erations of the working group it became clear that the king and the IFP wanted more than mere amendments to the constitution. They had started to use the word independence.

On 1 February, I quickly convened a meeting to allow the king to clarify this new demand. He arrived at the Union Buildings accom-panied by senior Zulu princes. In response to my queries about the deadlock in the working group, he informed me quite blandly that he had come to see me in Pretoria to claim his right to his kingdom. He said that because the ANC had never accepted the idea of a genuine federation, the Zulus would have to make other arrangements to secure their right to self-determination. All the other nations of Africa had achieved their freedom, some through peaceful means and some through the barrel of a gun. Now it was the turn of the Zulus.

One of the princes, Prince Vincent, said that the key words were sovereignty and self-determination. The Zulus also wanted liberation. They had thought that they could achieve this through a federation – but it was clear that this was no longer possible. They were now about to be handed over from one government to another. The previous National Party government had offered them independence. Now they wanted to accept this offer – not simply for the homeland of KwaZulu – but for the whole of the king's ancient territories which included not only the whole of the province of KwaZulu-Natal but parts of the southern Transvaal and Eastern Cape as well. It emerged that what the king had in mind was a monarchy similar to the system in neighbouring Swaziland, where his relative, King Mswati II, was, in effect, the ruler of the country. (This, no doubt, explained the presence of members of the Swazi royal house in the delegation that had held talks with us on 17 January.)

I pointed out that a quarter of the people who lived in the area that the king was now claiming were not Zulus and would have a major problem with their inclusion in the proposed Zulu state. I said that there was a basic error in the delegation's thinking – that rule by the National Party government would simply be replaced by rule by an ANC government. There would be a provincial government within what I regarded as a system with at least strong federal elements. Zulus would also be able to participate in the central government.

Another of the senior princes, Prince Gideon, replied that it was a known fact that Natal belonged to his majesty, the king. The coming ANC government would not protect their interests. He added that Mandela had warned them not to negotiate with the National Party government because 'you are a dying horse. We can't wait until we are overcome by circumstances. We are glad that his majesty has decided to claim his rightful place.' I once again pointed to the impossibility of their proposal and urged them to continue with their efforts to achieve their objectives – some of which we, to a certain extent, shared – through negotiations aimed at suitable amendments to the transitional constitution.

Two weeks later, on 14 February, I travelled down to Durban for a third meeting with the king and Buthelezi. Because Buthelezi did not wish to break ranks with his partners in the Freedom Alliance, he attended these meetings, not in his capacity as the leader of the IFP, but as the traditional prime minister of the king. We met in the Durban City Hall – a magnificent imperial building with great porticoes and columns. We were a little disturbed when we arrived to see that the City Hall was surrounded by about 10,000 chanting and dancing Zulu warriors, decked out in their traditional dress and carrying *assegais*, *knobkerries* and cowhide shields. Some had ancient rifles which they discharged from time to time into the air. Thus besieged, we held our meeting in a committee room on one of the City Hall's upper floors.

It was clear from the beginning of the meeting that the king, the princes of the royal family and the king's traditional prime minister, Mangosuthu Buthelezi, had not diluted their demand for separate independence since our previous meeting. Once again they asked me to grant independence to KwaZulu-Natal. They cited the example of the Federation of Rhodesia and Nyasaland where the constituent states had received separate independence when the federation broke up. Once again I rejected their demands as being impossible to achieve. I assured them that they could achieve most of their more reasonable objectives by negotiating amendments to the 1993 constitution. I told them that there were many people within their proposed state who would not support their claims and who did not want to lose their South African citizenship. I emphasized that I simply did not have the constitutional power to accede to their request, even if I agreed with it – which I did not.

They reacted with anger and bitterness. They rejected the 1993 constitution with contempt and said that they had had no part in drawing it up (primarily, of course, because they had boycotted the proceedings). They criticized me for not having allowed the king to have his own delegation at Codesa I (ignoring the fact that membership of Codesa I had been limited to political parties) and repeated their belief that I was in league with their enemies. It was clear that they genuinely feared the prospect of being ruled by the ANC. Towards the end of our meeting King Goodwill said that he anticipated that things would go worse in the new South Africa than they had gone in other African countries. He said that he had nowhere to run to with his white and black brothers. 'I will pray to God and do my work. I am worried because communists never change. They are talking about nationalization again. My people will suffer. We can't run away. The people will be left to kill one another. Things are upside down. If all this happens, I will ask God not to allow me to go to Paradise and I will fight until my people are free!'

I replied that I was also an African and that I was just as concerned about the future as the king was. I said that if we had not taken the initiatives that we took in 1990, South Africa would have been engulfed in conflict. We wanted to avoid the fate of other African countries by negotiating a final constitution which would effectively prevent the misuse of power by any future government. I said that I would not rest until I had achieved this. The meeting broke up without any further progress. The Zulus were still intent on their demand for a separate independence and we were adamant that their more reasonable goals could be achieved only through negotiations and the amendment of the 1993 constitution.

By this time we had become strongly aware of the negative influence of two of Buthelezi's white advisers, Walter Felgate of the IFP, and Dr Mario Ambrosini, Buthelezi's American constitutional adviser. Time and again, when we appeared to be making progress, they would get into a huddle with Buthelezi and the whole process would once again freeze up. We found Buthelezi's senior black advisers far more approachable and reasonable.

29

The Collapse of the Freedom Alliance

By the middle of February – with only two months to go before the election – as in the case of the IFP, we were still confronted with a deadlock in our attempts to persuade the other members of the Freedom Alliance to participate in the process. Among them, I regarded two elements as being particularly important – the more moderate faction of the Afrikaner Volksfront, and President Lucas Mangope and his party, which ruled the relatively successful independent state of Bophuthatswana.

The Afrikaner Volksfront (the Afrikaner People's Front) was far from being a monolithic organization. It included a wide array of right-wing Afrikaans parties and groups, ranging from ultra-radicals and hardliners to those who were simply naive. Its largest component, the Conservative Party, was led by Dr Ferdi Hartzenberg, a hardline and politically astute veteran. Hartzenberg was a lean man, with an extravagant ginger moustache and a receding hairline. He was a true believer in the absolute right of Afrikaners to untrammelled self-determination within their own *volkstaat* – or national state. The only problem was that there was no area in South Africa in which white Afrikaners came near to being a majority. Afrikaans-speaking people were, indeed, a majority in the Northern Cape and Western Cape provinces – but these included large coloured populations who were not regarded as Afrikaners by the Conservative Party. The alternative of establishing an Afrikaner state in the uninhabited semi-desert areas of the western part of South Africa was simply not economically viable and had little attraction even for the most diehard Afrikaner ultra-nationalists. Accordingly, the suspicion was that what the Conservatives really intended was the establishment of a homeland in parts of the country which would still contain a non-Afrikaner majority. In the Conservative Party Volkstaat such non-Afrikaners would probably not enjoy full political rights – so, it would be back to apartheid.

However, a new personality had appeared on the stage of the Afrikaner Volksfront – General Constand Viljoen. I was sure that he did not fully share the dogmatic views of Hartzenberg and the diehard Conservatives. I accordingly identified him as the key player in the artificial and fragile Afrikaner Volksfront coalition. General Viljoen was widely admired and respected, not only by reasonable right-wing Afrikaners, but also by many white National Party supporters who had served under him as conscripts. He was a military hero who had personally led his troops into battle against pro-Communist forces in southern Angola. He was quite short and wiry. His hair was completely white and cut in a short back and sides military style. His face was lean and tanned and was dominated by piercing blue eyes. He had an identical twin brother, Braam, who in many respects was his opposite. Braam was a softer version of his brother. He was an academic and was a leading member of the liberal Democratic Party whose policies differed diametrically from those of the Freedom Alliance. (From this I could at least infer that Constand Viljoen's political attitudes were not hereditary and were, perhaps, amenable to reason.) After his retirement as chief of the South African Defence Force, General Viljoen had returned to his farm in the Eastern Transvaal. Like Cincinnatus he had been persuaded by his supporters to leave his agricultural pursuits and to become their leader in what they saw as their hour of national crisis. As a soldier he had been straightforward and direct. However, as a politician he was inexperienced and, at times, quite naive.

Nelson Mandela and his colleagues in the ANC also identified him as a key figure in the ranks of right-wing Afrikaners and decided to play on this naiveté. The ANC was far more concerned about the threat from the Afrikaner right than they were about the IFP. They felt that the IFP could, if necessary, be crushed – but they were worried about the military threat posed by right-wing Afrikaners. They feared the right-wing's influence in the SADF and the police and its supposed ability to call up hundreds of thousands of trained commandos. For decades, South Africa had had a system of national service which had required whites to complete two years' military training. After completion of their training, servicemen had been assigned to the country's military reserves – or commandos – which could be called up and armed within a matter of days. Nelson Mandela accordingly went out of his way to pay court to General Viljoen. His public references to the general were always much more polite and deferential than his often harsh and bitter attacks on me and Buthelezi. Perhaps he had some genuine appreciation for Viljoen's straightforward but simplistic military approach. More likely, Mandela was simply using his considerable charm to neutralize a person whom he regarded as a serious potential threat. For this reason he seemed to be prepared to offer Viljoen hope in respect of anything that he wanted – including impossible prospects for future Afrikaner self-determination through a geographically defined Afrikaner *volkstaat*. Viljoen seemed to believe him.

A curious situation began to unfold. General Viljoen, whom I had come to know well in different relationships over a number of years, preferred to deal with Mandela rather than with me. From a pragmatic point of view it made sense. Everybody expected that the ANC would win the elections. However, from an ideological point of view it made no sense at all. Viljoen's power base had an essentially racist approach. Mandela, in their eyes, was a communist and a terrorist. I decided to play along. If the ANC could woo Viljoen and his supporters into participating in the elections, I would not get in their way. At the same time, we continued to advocate a framework within the new constitution which would create room for the Buthelezis, Viljoens and Mangopes to save face and participate in the elections.

We believed that we could get General Viljoen, Chief Minister Buthelezi and President Mangope to move away from the negative boycott stance of the Freedom Alliance by addressing their concerns on five questions – by strengthening the powers and functions of the regions within the proposed federal system; by meeting Buthelezi's fears that the central government would undermine the regions after the elections; by giving more recognition to the Zulu monarchy; by strengthening the fiscal powers of the regions; and by promoting recognition of aspects of self-determination. Buthelezi had no natural affinity with the other parties in the Freedom Alliance. He rejected the racial policies of the Conservative Party and was in a completely different class from President Mangope of Bophuthatswana and Brigadier Gqozo of the Ciskei. I thought that if we presented him with a meaningful face-saving device by way of the strengthening of federalism and the Zulu monarchy there was still a chance that he would agree to join the process. If agreement could be reached with the ANC on a package to achieve this, there would still be time to reconvene Parliament to make the necessary amendments to the transitional constitution. Simultaneously, I believed that if we could get Buthelezi on board and if we, in our way, and the ANC, in theirs, could open a few doors for Constand Viljoen and his supporters, we would be able to ensure the highest possible participation in the coming elections. It would also break the back of the Freedom Alliance.

On 2 February, after weeks of intensive bargaining, the government's negotiating team made proposals to the ANC that could, in our opinion, resolve the deadlock. The ANC dropped its opposition to important aspects of our proposal and accepted a package that we believed could open the way for at least some of the parties of the Freedom Alliance to participate in the elections. In particular, the proposal included a constitutional principle providing for self-determination and a related mechanism for the consideration of the possibility of the establishment of a *volkstaat* for Afrikaner nationalists. I personally felt somewhat uncomfortable with this, since the National Party had consistently rejected the notion of a *volkstaat* in its own long-standing arguments with the Conservative Party. I was also sceptical about the ANC's real intentions regarding the expectations they were creating with all their vague promises to General Viljoen. Nevertheless, I decided not to be obstructive in the hope that the proposed amendments might persuade him to participate in the elections. The package also included provisions to strengthen the powers and functions of provinces and a constitutional principle that would ensure that these powers would in essence be maintained after the election. This, I hoped, would also help to open the door for Buthelezi.

As I had promised, I reconvened Parliament to adopt amendments to the transitional constitution which would give effect to the new package. I did so unilaterally, without any prior commitment from the parties of the Freedom Alliance that our new package would satisfy their demands. On 28 February, in a key speech, I pointed out that we had now addressed, what we believed to be, all their reasonable concerns.

The new constitution would bring into being provinces with genuine autonomous powers, based on federal principles. Those powers would be strongly entrenched and could not be arbitrarily diminished by the central government. Voters would have a double ballot as requested by the Freedom Alliance parties. The powers of the provinces would be further extended and clarified: they would have some independent taxation powers and would be able to adopt their own constitutions. This meant that the province of KwaZulu-Natal – which would now include the name KwaZulu – would be able to make their own provision for the Zulu monarchy. In addition, recognition would be given to the concept of self-determination and the door would be opened to continued negotiation around the concept of an Afrikaner *volkstaat*, however sceptical I might personally have felt about this.

I said that there could no longer be any reasonable excuse for non-participation in the elections. The Freedom Alliance parties could continue to exercise their legitimate option of boycotting the constitutional process. However, by boycotting the elections they would pointlessly exclude themselves and their followers from making their full contribution to the constitutional future of South Africa and to the peaceful promotion of their own values and ideals. At the same time, I stressed our determination to proceed with the elections on 27 April with or without them. I added that, although non-participation was a legitimate option, any attempt to prevent or disrupt the elections would be resisted with all the power of the state.

I ended my speech with a firm warning to parties that might be contemplating secession or the illegal seizure of power at national or municipal level. (At that time some town councils controlled by the Conservative Party in the rural areas were threatening that they would no longer recognize the authority of the National Party government.) They constituted a small minority of the total South African population. They could not even claim to speak on behalf of the Afrikaans people. They could expect support from neither the international community nor from the regular security forces. The South African Defence Force and the South African police had a key role to play in upholding the integrity of the new state and the new constitution and I was confident that they would play that role, notwithstanding the many difficulties that we had experienced with some elements which were opposed to the reform initiatives.

However, I do not believe that all our constitutional initiatives would by themselves have been sufficient to end the Freedom Alliance's intransigence. Unplanned events would soon dramatically change the political landscape. At the beginning of March 1994, the Bophutha-tswana government was still steadfastly refusing to allow parties to campaign for the elections in its territory or to make facilities available to the Independent Electoral Commission (IEC). During the first week of March this had led to serious unrest in Bophuthatswana as supporters of the ANC and other parties began to agitate to be allowed to participate in the elections. On 8 March we considered the deteriorating situation during a meeting of the cabinet committee dealing with security and intelligence affairs and decided to put the security forces on alert in case they might be required to restore order. We also made an urgent appeal to the Bophuthatswana government to become a full participant in the constitutional process, including the proposed election.

As the chaos in Bophuthatswana increased, Mangope called on paramilitary forces led by his Freedom Alliance ally, General Constand Viljoen, for assistance. The plan was that General Viljoen's force of about 3,000 men would gather at the airport near Mmabatho, the capital of Bophuthatswana. They would be issued with arms by the Bophuthatswana Defence Force and would then restore order. However, they were beaten to the mark by the ultra-rightist Afrikaanse Weerstandsbewing (AWB) of Eugene Terre'Blanche. Despite a specific request from the Bophuthatswana government that the AWB should not be involved in the operation, Terre'Blanche could not resist the opportunity of unleashing his much vaunted Iron Guard troops on the territory. In reality, they were a bunch of ill-disciplined and poorly organized racists. Hundreds of bearded and khaki-uniformed AWB soldiers rolled into Bophuthatswana in their family cars and bakkies (pick-up trucks). By this time the crowds in Mmabatho had begun to loot stores and there was general chaos in the town. The violence was further exacerbated when the AWB force began shooting people in the town at random.

The AWB invasion and the presence of General Viljoen's men triggered a mutiny in the ranks of the Bophuthatswana security forces. Two wounded AWB supporters were shot dead in front of international TV cameras by one of the Bophuthatswana soldiers. The pictures were carried on SABC TV that night and did much to expose the tragic farce of the AWB's invasion and to undermine support for right-wing violence. Faced with the chaotic intervention of the AWB, without the promised help and arms from the Bophuthatswana Defence Force and with the SADF standing at the ready to intervene, General Viljoen had little choice but to order his men to return to South Africa.

Throughout this period, I had been in constant communication with our embassy in Mmabatho, with the Bophuthatswana government and with the Transitional Executive Council. During his meeting with Judge Kriegler of the IEC at the beginning of the crisis, President Mangope had made it clear that he had no intention of giving up his country's sovereignty – although he did offer to convene the Bophuthatswana Parliament on 15 March to consider the IEC's request for co-operation in the holding of the elections. On Friday, 11 March 1994, I was involved in a last ditch effort to try to make Mangope see reason. One of his most trusted ministers, Rowan Cronje, spent most of the day in my office. We put together a package which we hoped would, at the last moment, make it possible for Mangope to participate in the election. At one stage Mangope indicated that he would accept our proposals. However, when he was pressed to give formal confirmation of his acceptance of the package and willingness to participate in the elections, he drew back and reverted to his former position of clinging to his country's independence. In fact, the independence of Bophutha-tswana was at that time an illusion. By the end of the day Mangope had lost control of his country. The following day, 12 March 1994, a delegation from the TEC was sent to see him at his country home at Motsoedi, to which he had retreated from the chaos in Mmabatho. The delegation was led by Foreign Minister Pik Botha. He informed Mangope bluntly on behalf of the South African government and the TEC that he was no longer in power. He was soon replaced by two administrators appointed by the TEC. After he returned to Pretoria, Pik Botha gave us a blow-by-blow account of the last hours of President Mangope's government. Despite his intransigence and sub-sequent allegations that he had enriched himself and his family during his presidency, I could not help feeling a twinge of sympathy for him and his doleful sense of abandonment. With his removal from power, the last remnants of Dr Verwoerd's elaborate edifice of grand apartheid came crashing to the ground.

At about the same time the government in Venda, another of the independent states, collapsed. The government of Brigadier Oupa Gqozo of the Ciskei followed suit – quickly and far less spectacularly than had been the case in Bophuthatswana. The TEC appointed administrators to run both territories and to facilitate the election process. Thus, by the middle of March, the Freedom Alliance had suddenly lost two of its members and the threat of right-wing violence had greatly diminished.

It was probably these factors – together with the constitutional package that we had steered through Parliament at the beginning of the month – that persuaded General Viljoen to join the constitutional process. On 16 March, almost at the very last minute, he broke ranks with the rest of the Afrikaanse Volksfront and the Freedom Alliance, established a new party called the Freedom Front and submitted a list of candidates for the election at the offices of the IEC. His decision to participate in the constitutional process was a major breakthrough. However, it had been a narrow escape. If General Viljoen's operation had not been sabotaged by the precipitate action of the AWB and if he had been able to re-establish order in Bophuthatswana at the invitation of a government to which we still gave legal recognition, we would have been confronted with a very serious situation. Under such circumstances would we have been prepared to send the SADF in to seize control of the country? And would they have been prepared to fire on their former comrades and their former commander?

I had personally never shared the concerns – often expressed by foreign visitors – regarding the loyalty of the security forces. I was always able to reassure them that the SADF and the police were professional organizations that would continue to accept the authority of constitutionally mandated governments. I pointed out that the security forces had a far higher success rate in tracking down and arresting right-wing terrorists than they had with left-wing terrorists. One of the main reasons for this was that the white community assisted the police with their investigations much more willingly than was the case with other communities. I had also been regularly briefed on the political mood of the security forces and had received numerous assurances from the top echelons of the police and the SADF regarding their loyalty.

At the same time, I did not discount the possibility that there could be elements within the security forces that might be working actively to undermine the government's reform policies.

On Sunday, 20 February 1994 Judge Goldstone came to see me and Mr Kobie Coetsee, the minister of justice and defence, at Libertas, my official residence in Pretoria. During our meeting he provided us with stark and disturbing confirmation of the existence of such activities. His revelations were based on the testimony of a former member of the police's notorious Vlakplaas Unit – which had been officially disbanded two years earlier. The informant – whose identity was originally kept secret by the commission – was subsequently revealed to be a Mr Chappies Klopper. He alleged that the Vlakplaas Unit – which had been exonerated by the Harms Commission – had been involved since 1989 in fomenting violence aimed at the destabilization of South Africa. Under the leadership of Colonel Eugene de Kock it had, according to Klopper, participated in the organization of train and hostel violence and had channelled arms to senior members of the IFP for use in their struggle against the ANC. Klopper also claimed that these operations were under the command of Lieutenant-General Basie Smit, then the deputy commissioner of the police and Major-General Krappies Engelbrecht, the head of the police's department of counter-intelligence. He alleged that another senior officer, General Johan le Roux, had also been aware of them. Klopper stated that after the Vlakplaas Unit had been disbanded, in the aftermath of the CCB exposé, its members had been transferred to other police units. Together with operatives such as Eugene de Kock, who had retired from the police, they had nevertheless continued with their hit squad and destabilization operations – allegedly with the support of senior officers within the police.

I was deeply shocked by Judge Goldstone's revelations – and particularly by information that he subsequently provided about many of the Vlakplaas Unit's horrifying activities and methods. I had until then been inclined to accept the earlier findings of the Harms Commission and the repeated assurances of General Johan van der Merwe, the commissioner of the South African police, that the charges against the unit were unfounded. I had supported the disbandment of the unit – which had been established to combat terrorists – because after 2 February 1990 it was no longer relevant. I had gone along with proposals by the police the previous year that special lump-sum payments should be made to former members of the unit in lieu of normal police pensions. The police had argued that many of the members of the unit – who were known as Askaris – were in a special position. Most of them had previously been members of the ANC and had been recruited to combat the organization during the period of conflict. They were worried about their position under a future ANC government and wanted to sever all links with the police. Some of the payments seemed to be very large and ranged from amounts of about R100,000–R200,000 that were paid to ordinary Askaris, to a sum of approximately R1.2 million that was paid to Colonel De Kock. The amounts had, however, been actuarially determined and were not out of line with packages that have since been paid – also by the ANC-led government – to officials of similar rank and with similar service who have exercised their option of taking early retirement. Nevertheless, the perception in the media and elsewhere was that the payments were intended to buy the silence of those involved.

During our meeting on 20 February, Judge Goldstone told me that he required additional technical assistance and advice to conclude his investigation. I immediately urged him to proceed as a matter of urgency. I asked him to conduct his investigation in such a way that, if corroborating evidence was found, it should form the basis upon which I would be able to take speedy and decisive action. As he confirmed in his subsequent report, Minister Coetsee and I made arrangements for him to receive all the assistance that he requested.

At 9.00 a.m. on 18 March, Judge Goldstone came to see me at the Union Buildings to discuss the publication of the report that he had drawn up as a result of his investigation. I had asked Hernus Kriel, the minister of law and order, and General Van der Merwe, the commissioner of the police to be present. Both of them – as well as Nelson Mandela – had already been briefed by Goldstone on the broad nature of the investigation. During their previous meeting General Van der Merwe had assured Judge Goldstone of his full co-operation in the investigation and had been given credit for this in Goldstone's report. However, as Judge Goldstone apprised the meeting of the main findings of the investigation, General Van der Merwe became progressively and visibly upset. In particular, he could not accept the allegations that had been made against his close colleagues, Generals Basie Smit and Johan le Roux – although he was less adamant in his defence of General Krappies Engelbrecht. He claimed that the evidence against them was unsubstantiated and objected strenuously to the inclusion of their names in the report. At 2.00 p.m. I met again with Judge Goldstone to discuss the finalization and release of his report. We decided that the best method of doing so would be to hold a joint press conference that evening. At 6.00 p.m. we gathered in the large wood-panelled circular conference room at the Union Buildings which we used for major press conferences. I was flanked by Judge Goldstone, Minister Hernus Kriel, General Van der Merwe and Dave Steward who, as government spokesman, introduced the proceedings. I announced that all those who had been implicated in the report – including the three generals – would be immediately placed on leave pending further investigations and that, where appropriate, cases would be referred to the attorneys-general for possible prosecution. After the press conference I returned to Libertas for drinks with a few friends and members of my family who had gathered there. It was my 58th birthday.

As expected, the media gave the Goldstone report massive coverage. It appeared at last to corroborate the long-held suspicions concerning the existence of a sinister third force within the security forces. In the meantime, General Van der Merwe had begun to show extreme reluctance to carry out my instruction that those implicated in the report should be placed on immediate leave. He informed me that he had received advice that he could not do so without first completing all the necessary formalities, which included consultations with the officers concerned. In fact, he had been deeply angered by the report and by what he regarded as unsubstantiated allegations against his close and senior colleagues, Generals Smit and Le Roux. He made little secret of his feelings or of his low opinion of Judge Goldstone. On 22 March I issued a statement in which I made it clear that if General Van der Merwe's consultations did not soon lead to a satisfactory outcome, the minister of law and order might have to intervene and suspend the officers concerned. Three days later the generals were temporarily withdrawn from service. In deciding my reaction to the Goldstone report, I had considered not only its contents, but also the national interest and the sound custom that police officers should be withdrawn from service – pending investigation – if serious allegations had been made against them.

March 1994 had been a tumultuous month. It had witnessed the disintegration of the right-wing threat, firstly as a result of the collapse of the far-right's intervention in Bophuthatswana and secondly as a result of General Viljoen's decision to participate in the elections. The cause of those seeking to disrupt the constitutional process had been further weakened by the Goldstone Commission's revelations concerning the reprehensible activities of the Vlakplaas Unit. Brutal and meaningless right-wing terrorism would continue to claim lives until the elections – but the threat of major disruption of the process from that quarter had significantly receded. By the end of March, with the demise of President Mangope and Brigadier Gqoso and the defection of General Viljoen, the Freedom Alliance had for all practical purposes ceased to exist as a credible factor on the political scene. The IFP, however, was still intransigent.

30

The IFP Comes on Board

As the governing party of an important second tier authority, Kwa-
Zulu, the IFP had an essential role to play in facilitating the holding of
the elections throughout KwaZulu. Toward the middle of March 1994,
Judge Kriegler of the IEC travelled to Ulundi, the KwaZulu capital, to
ensure that the KwaZulu government would co-operate with arrangements for the holding of the election. When Judge Kriegler addressed
the Legislative Assembly he encountered an outpouring of strongly
expressed IFP grievances. He was shaken and humiliated by the
treatment he received. As a result, he precipitately concluded that the
IFP government would not give the IEC the co-operation that it needed
to hold an election in KwaZulu. Mandela demanded that I should
depose Buthelezi and that the TEC should appoint an administrator in
his place. This would, of course, have been a prescription for disaster.
Once again we were faced with a crisis.

On 26 March, I flew down to Durban where I held talks with
Chief Minister Buthelezi and three of his ministers in the KwaZulu
government, Mr Joe Matthews, Dr Sipo Mzimela and Dr Ben Ngubane. I was accompanied by Ministers Roelf Meyer and Danie Schutte
– who was to become the leader of the National Party in KwaZulu-
Natal in June 1994. We met at King's House, the stately old Durban
residence of the former British governors of Natal and later of state
presidents when on official business in Natal.

Our meeting was, for once, a success. Chief Minister Buthelezi
assured us that his government would work with the Independent
Electoral Commission to create the circumstances for free and fair
elections in KwaZulu. We agreed to establish a mechanism involving
the KwaZulu government, the IEC and the South African government
to address the IEC's requirements and to remove any obstacles in the
way of the elections. I once again used the opportunity to implore
Buthelezi to participate in the elections. I had been advised – incorrectly, as it turned out – that it was too late for him to participate in
the elections at the national level, but that he could still enter the IFP

for the elections at the provincial level. Buthelezi was, however, still adamantly opposed to participation in any form – but did agree that he, Mandela, King Goodwill and I should meet as soon as possible to discuss the king's position and the self-determination of the Zulu nation. It was a major breakthrough.

During our talks, we had also discussed the ongoing violence and had expressed our support for measures to reduce tensions. Nevertheless, only two days later, on 28 March, the IFP mounted a provocative march through the centre of Johannesburg. The previous night Mandela phoned me to warn me that they expected the IFP march to lead to violence. I immediately instructed the head of my office, Dave Steward, to request General Johan van der Merwe, the commissioner of the police, to make special arrangements to control the situation. Despite the efforts of the police, the IFP marchers proceeded into the heart of Johannesburg. One of their objectives was apparently to mount a demonstration outside the ANC's headquarters at Shell House in the city. However, as they were approaching the building, ANC security personnel opened fire on the marchers. Several were killed. The ANC claimed that it had been acting in self-defence and that the IFP protesters had been shot while they were trying to storm the main entrance to the building. Journalists and eye-witnesses told a different story. Later, Nelson Mandela admitted that he himself had authorized the ANC guards to fire in self-defence if they had to. In the preceding and ensuing chaos and violence that erupted in and around Johannesburg, more than fifty people were killed. It was the worst violence that the city had witnessed for a long time and was a stark reminder of the volatility of the situation throughout South Africa.

The South African police obviously had to act. General Van der Merwe approached me to discuss the need to carry out investigations inside Shell House and to examine the weapons that had been used by the ANC guards. The situation was extremely sensitive. We were dealing with the head office of a major political party, which was expected to win the coming election in less than a month's time. The ANC had also been in the forefront of accusing the police of serious bias and of conducting a secret war against it. It also believed that the police themselves had connived in the IFP march to its headquarters. Under these circumstances, it would have been problematical, to say the very least, for the police to walk into Shell House with a warrant and demand to search the ANC's head office. I telephoned Mandela and discussed the situation with him. He promised to co-operate fully with the police and to make all the ANC weapons in the building available to them for their investigation. Under these circumstances, I told General Van der Merwe that I did not think that we should exacerbate tensions by sending the police into Shell House. We had also received the word of the man who would soon be president that he would co-operate with the investigation. However, Mandela did not deliver on his promise. The ANC weapons were not made available to the police in a manner which would have ensured a credible investigation and provided little or no co-operation to help establish the circumstances of the shooting. The question of what had happened in and around Shell House would hang over the heads of the ANC for many months to come – and would add to the already long list of the IFP's grievances and suspicions.

The violence in Johannesburg on 28 March and the further bitterness that it caused between the IFP and the ANC added to our concerns about the prospects for holding successful elections in Natal. After careful consideration of the security situation and consultations with the TEC, I concluded that our authorities would need special powers to manage the security situation in the province. On 31 March I accordingly decided to declare a state of emergency in Natal. On the one hand it was necessary to provide the security forces with the powers that they would need to maintain peace and order. On the other hand, the emergency regulations would have to be drafted in such a manner that they would not inhibit free political activity linked to the election. It was also critically important that they should not be construed by Buthelezi as being directed against the IFP. My first step was accordingly to telephone the chief minister to inform him personally of the background to my decision and the purpose of the State of Emergency. I stressed that the emergency regulations were not aimed at the IFP and that I had taken my decision in my capacity as head of state and not at the behest of any other party. I said that the State of Emergency would be implemented in an even-handed manner and would also help to protect IFP supporters from attack by their enemies.

The proposed meeting between the king, the IFP, the ANC and the government was made even more pressing by the publication of a report by a joint working group of the IEC, the KwaZulu government and the South African government that in the current political climate, elections could not be held in KwaZulu. I responded to the report by pointing to the action that the government had already taken to facilitate the holding of elections in KwaZulu – including the declaration of the State of Emergency in Natal. I added that the report underlined the importance of the scheduled talks on 8 April between King Goodwill Zwelithini, Mr Mandela, Chief Minister Buthelezi and myself.

The meeting took place at Jakkalsbessie, a secluded camp in the Kruger National Park. The camp comprised a number of guest lodges and a few larger buildings. The main building – where we held our talks – had a thatched roof and a wide verandah overlooking the chocolate brown Sabie River, meandering lazily in the late summer heat through the game reserve.

During the first part of the meeting before lunch, the four delegations held bilateral talks aimed at searching for common ground. Initial indications were positive and over lunch senior members of the IFP indicated privately that they thought that a breakthrough would be possible. However, each time that it seemed that progress was being made Buthelezi's advisers – particularly Dr Mario Ambrosini – would be seen in earnest discussion with the chief minister – and the IFP would return to its intransigent positions. One of the positive proposals that emerged from the morning's deliberations was the idea – which had already been discussed bilaterally between the IFP and the ANC – that their outstanding constitutional differences should be resolved by means of international mediation.

After lunch, the four delegations crammed together for a plenary meeting in the camp's largest conference room – which was still not nearly big enough to accommodate everyone. I stressed the critical importance of the meeting for the future of South Africa and tried to impress on the other parties the need to achieve success through meaningful discussions. However, it was clear from the opening statements of the king and Chief Minister Mangosuthu Buthelezi that the chances of success were limited. King Goodwill said that the time for discussion had come to an end. He accused the government of failing the take effective action against those who had been responsible for the Shell House massacre. He said that this failure and the government's unilateral decision to declare a State of Emergency in Natal spoke more strongly than its words. It was unacceptable to him that, in terms of the State of Emergency, his subjects could now be arrested without due process and had no rights. Buthelezi was equally negative. He said that it was difficult to see how the summit could resolve the deadlock. The failure of the constitutional talks had made it necessary for the king to call for a sovereign kingdom. Nevertheless, he promised to listen and to see if there was any hope of stopping the further slide towards the civil war.

Mandela, in his contribution, spoke in a careful and measured manner. His main interest was to make it absolutely clear that whatever happened with the negotiations, there could be no question of postponing the election. Even Cyril Ramaphosa was conciliatory and positive.

The meeting ended inconclusively without any real breakthrough having been achieved. But the door was kept open through the acceptance of the concept of international mediation and the establishment of a working group which would try to reach an agreement on the position of the Zulu monarchy.

At the conclusion of the meeting, the leaders of the four delegations held a joint press conference at the Skukuza Airstrip during which they attempted to put the best possible gloss on their deliberations. Night had fallen and the four of us sat beside one another at a table that had been hastily set up for the purpose. Although we could not announce the breakthrough for which the whole country had been hoping, we were able to inform the media of the limited progress that we had made, including the agreement on the principle of international mediation. We also announced that a follow-up meeting would be held within the course of the following week.

Thus began the short-lived and somewhat farcical efforts at immediate international mediation that preceded the election. It was an idea that had had its roots in bilateral discussions between the ANC and the IFP. The government was sceptical about the likely success of such a hasty exercise – particularly in the absence of clear terms of reference. We were, however, determined that if it was to succeed we would have to be part of it.

The former United States secretary of state, Dr Henry Kissinger, and the former British foreign secretary, Lord Carrington, were invited to play the role of international mediators. The government was not initially part of these arrangements which were made in a haphazard manner, without consulting all the parties involved. I had a problem with the whole exercise, not because of the mediators who had been proposed, but because there was no proper agreement on what their terms of reference should be. Within a few days they had arrived in South Africa and came to see me late in the evening of 12 April in the living room of Libertas, my residence in Pretoria. They looked a little travel weary and were clearly perplexed about the role that they were expected to play. I explained that the government had not been directly involved in the initiation of the mediation exercise. However, if it was to come to anything we would have to be included. I told them that I was worried that the IFP's real purpose was the postponement of the elections and that the terms of reference should make it clear that this would not be acceptable. One of the main issues would also be to include assurances that constitutional checks and balances would not be scrapped in the final constitution. The key question that Carrington and Kissinger put to me was whether Buthelezi really wanted to settle. My response was that he would do so only if he received something meaningful in return.

The parties subsequently failed to reach agreement on the terms of reference – particularly because of the IFP's view that the mediation process would necessitate a postponement of the election. As a result, Kissinger and Carrington left South Africa without ever having been put in a position where they could even begin with a meaningful mediation process.

And so the countdown to the election continued – with seemingly little or no prospect of IFP participation. Then within eleven days of the election there were two remarkable developments. The first came by way of the intervention of Professor Washington Okumu, an enormously corpulent Kenyan academic who had come to South Africa in the wake of the Carrington/Kissinger mission. He had requested an urgent meeting with his old friend Dr Buthelezi on 15 April. The meeting would not have taken place, except that Buthelezi's aircraft developed an engine fault and had to return to the airport where Okumu was waiting. The two men met and during their meeting the Kenyan persuaded Buthelezi to make a last-minute effort to find a solution which would enable the IFP to participate in the election. Buthelezi later described the circumstances of his remarkable meeting with Okumu as an Act of God.

The second unexpected development was the announcement by the IEC that, provided that Parliament amended the electoral act in time, it would still be possible for the IFP to participate in the elections at both the national and provincial levels. The IEC had concluded that it would still be able to print and distribute some eighty million IFP stickers which could be attached to the ballot papers and thus enable IFP supporters to cast their votes in favour of their party. The revelation that the IEC was still in a position – even at this late stage –

to include the IFP in the ballot came as a complete and extremely welcome surprise to me.

On 19 April – only a week before the elections were due to commence – Buthelezi, Mandela, the divinely opportune Professor Okumu and I met at the Union Buildings. We succeeded in reaching agreement on the IFP's participation in the elections for both the central Parliament and provincial Parliaments.

Part of the agreement was that provision would be made for the Zulu monarchy in the future provincial constitution of KwaZulu-Natal and that the transitional constitution would be amended before the election to recognize and protect the institution, status and role of the constitutional position of the king of the Zulus and the kingdom of KwaZulu. In a move that would return time and time again during the coming years and months to aggravate the relationship between the IFP and the ANC, we also agreed that any outstanding issues in respect of the king of the Zulus and the 1993 constitution would be addressed by way of international mediation as soon as possible after the elections.

There was only one outstanding question – where the IFP sticker would be affixed on the ballot papers? The choices were either at the top where there was most space, at the bottom, or on the reverse side. The top position had already been drawn by the PAC in a lottery organized by the IEC and it was unlikely that there would be sufficient time to persuade it to allow the IFP's name to appear above its own. The reverse side option was rejected by the IFP and other parties which felt that the inexperienced electorate might well overlook the IFP sticker if it did not appear on the front of the ballot. This left the position at the bottom of the ballot – which the National Party had drawn during the lottery. This was a good position from a marketing and communication point of view. Much of our campaign material had been based on the slogan that if voters wished to come out on top, they should vote for the bottom line. Once again I was faced with a difficult decision where I had to make a choice between the clear interest of my party on the one hand and of the country on the other. There was only one decision and that was to accept that the IFP sticker would be affixed at the bottom of the ballot paper, below the National Party. At the same time, I insisted that the National Party should be reimbursed for the expense of our campaign focusing on our position on the ballot paper and that due recognition should be given by the other parties to our gesture. Although we were reimbursed for most of these costs, we were never given much recognition by the other parties for our sacrifice.

What was far more important was that at the very last possible moment, we had made the breakthrough for which I had been working for months. The IFP's participation would mean that nearly all South Africa's political parties – except the Conservative Party and a few movements on the far-right – would participate in the elections. Somehow or other we had managed to pull it off with only days to spare. But, whether or not it was all due to the fortuitous intervention of Professor Okumu, the IFP election machine very quickly swung into action with an impressive last-minute campaign that included the appearance overnight of thousands of election posters and the launching of a sophisticated multimedia advertising blitz. I gained the impression that the IFP must have been planning their last-minute entry into the election campaign for some time. I could not exclude the possibility that for the past few months they had been playing games with us and the ANC.

On Monday, 25 April, two days before the election, Parliament met to adopt the agreed amendments to the constitution regarding the Zulu kingdom. Hundreds of MPs interrupted their election campaigns at a critical moment so that they could attend the special session. I heaved a sigh of relief, but could not help feeling irritated by the tremendous disruption and inconvenience that the IFP had, through its intransigence, caused to everybody else.

31

The Election and the End of National Party Rule

At the same time that I was dealing with the Bophuthatswana, IFP and Goldstone Commission crises, I also had to conduct the most important election campaign of my career.

I realized that the National Party's bargaining position in negotiating the final constitution would depend on how well we fared in this election. Our minimum objective was to ensure that the ANC did not achieve a two-thirds majority. The maximum objective – which I believed was not completely beyond our reach – was to try to get a third of the votes. This would assure us of a very strong position in the forthcoming constitutional negotiations without having to rely on other parties. I had no doubt that this would be a formidable task.

The election would be conducted on a proportional basis. Four hundred members of Parliament would be elected from lists drawn up by their parties. At the same time, voters would cast a second ballot to elect members of the provincial Parliaments. There had been insufficient time to compile a proper voters' register. Accordingly, anyone over the age of eighteen who was in possession of a South African identity document – including non-South African permanent residents and certain categories of prisoners – was eligible to vote. In the run-up to the election there had been a massive effort to ensure that as many inhabitants of the country as possible had been issued with ID documents. Those who were not in possession of IDs could, with very little difficulty or proof of identity, still apply for temporary voters' cards. In the period before the end of the election three and a half million temporary voters' cards were issued, constituting some 17.5 per cent of those who voted in the election. Of these, one and a half million were issued during the election itself. The haste and lack of control with which voters' cards were issued would prove to be one of the main causes for the irregularities which occurred during the election.

According to my calculations, we could be reasonably certain of achieving between 15 per cent and 20 per cent of the vote, based on our support in the white, coloured and Indian communities. The key to further success would be our ability to break into the black vote. We felt that we had considerable growth potential among black South Africans – particularly with the older and more conservative segments of the population, with the emerging black middle-class and with many black South Africans who had developed close personal relations with whites, either as domestic workers or as employees of small businesses. Reliable opinion polls indicated that 10 per cent of black voters might fall in this category. If we managed to win their support, we had a good chance of getting somewhere between 25 per cent and 30 per cent of the vote. If our support among black voters proved to be even stronger – in the range between 15 per cent and 20 per cent – we might even achieve the magical 33 per cent.

The great challenge would accordingly be to make a breakthrough to the black electorate. From the outset, we took great care to ensure that our candidates' lists included competent coloured, Indian and black members of our party. After the election, I wanted the National Party's representatives in the central Parliament, as well as in the provincial Parliaments, to reflect a healthy balance between the various population groups. There was a risk that white Nationalists would dominate the competitive struggle for places high on the candidates' list. Representatives of the other population groups were, at that stage, still not strongly enough established within the party structures at constituency level, so a little judicious pressure was sometimes required from me to redress the balance. In the final analysis most of the provinces succeeded in producing balanced lists and in placing suitable candidates from all of the population groups in favourable positions on the lists.

This was the first time that the National Party would participate in an election on a truly non-racial basis. However, our ability to campaign freely throughout the country was severely limited by the establishment by the ANC and the IFP of no-go areas in their traditional strongholds. In a publication which it produced after the election, the Independent Electoral Commission conceded that the National Party had not been able to campaign freely in urban black townships and the black homelands – where a very sizeable portion of the population lived.

From the security point of view, the election was a nightmare. Intimidation was rife throughout the country. Particularly where my actions were aimed at the coloured and black communities, we were regularly confronted by ANC intimidation and demonstrations. From time to time we had to cancel walkabouts or meetings on the advice of the police, because of the risk of violence and consequent casualties and damage to property. As far as I was personally concerned, the confrontational style of the ANC reached its climax during a visit to Kimberley in the Northern Cape. As I was riding on the back of a pick-up truck to a point where I was due to address a meeting with a hand-held megaphone, someone in the crowd threw a stone at me which hit me behind the ear. I was not seriously injured, but my supporters were furious. Fortunately, this incident made the ANC leadership realize that they would have to ensure greater discipline among their followers. Nelson Mandela took firm action after which the situation improved somewhat. Nevertheless, there was still widespread intimidation, particularly of black NP members.

Our second great challenge was to collect sufficient funds to be able to fight an imaginative campaign. The ANC had an enormous election budget and apparently experienced no problem in raising funds. With the support of a handful of colleagues within the party, I worked extremely hard to raise sufficient funds for our election campaign. Fortunately, the private sector also realized how important it was that the power of the ANC should be limited. Some of our regular donors gave a great deal more than usual, while we also received large donations from companies that had until then never previously given money to the National Party. We ultimately collected sufficient funds to mount a reasonably imaginative – but not lavish – campaign.

We made use of the services of two public relations and advertising companies – one from overseas and one from South Africa. After careful analysis of a series of opinion surveys, it was decided that I should be the main focus of our campaign. All of the opinion surveys had indicated that my personal popularity was higher than that of the party – particularly among non-white voters. My speech of 2 February 1990 and the enormous publicity that it had generated were largely responsible for this. Apart from this, the photos of party leaders would appear on the ballots.

I was somewhat embarrassed by this personalization of the campaign. Throughout my career, I had marketed the party and its policy and had never accentuated my own role. However, I had no choice. I had to fall in with strategic planning which placed F. W. de Klerk strongly in the limelight. Naturally, I was not the only focal point. The

National Party's policy, principles and value system were also strongly marketed and contrasted with those of the ANC. However, in the opinion of many analysts, the personal factor was ultimately of fundamental importance.

This was not good for the medium- and long-term prospects of the National Party. There are great risks in over-emphasizing the personality of a leader in political campaigns. His subsequent retirement or death must of necessity then have an excessively detrimental effect on the party's prospects. However, despite all my best efforts, this was the course that the party chose – and it is today paying the price for that decision.

Since the 1989 election – and especially during the 1992 referendum campaign – the National Party under my leadership had drastically changed its style and approach to elections. We moved away from the stereotyped formal public meetings of past campaigns to making personal contact with as many voters as possible by means of walkabouts, short impromptu speeches in public places and on street corners and mass gatherings coupled with extravaganzas, music and entertainment. Effective multimedia advertising had also become a central aspect of our campaign strategy. We decided to adopt this approach in the 1994 election as well – although we still planned to reach our more traditional supporters by means of old-style public meetings. In its campaign the ANC hammered on two broad themes: the National Party's association with apartheid, and wild and irresponsible promises about what it would do for the people – in providing jobs, houses, education and social programmes – once it had taken over the government. Although Mandela subsequently tried from time to time to put a damper on the expectations that his party was generating, they had by the election reached completely unrealistic levels. One of the ANC's main problems in the 1999 elections will be to explain to many of its disillusioned supporters why these promises were not kept.

A highlight of the election campaign was a one-on-one TV debate with Nelson Mandela. It was inevitable that at some point during the campaign we would be involved in a public debate. Election campaigns in South Africa had since the eighties begun to include TV and radio debates and it was logical that the leaders of the two strongest political parties would conduct a TV debate with one another. My previous experience with TV debates was that unless one of the participants made a fatal error, they never produced an outright winner. One could generally score a victory on points, but a knockout punch was very rare. With this in mind, and in view of the media's tendency to treat Mandela with kid gloves, I decided in consultation with my advisers that I would not try to plant a knockout punch. From the outset we were looking for a points victory. The preparation was thorough. My advisers and I tried to anticipate the line that Mandela would take and thoroughly prepared appropriate responses. We also developed our own plan of attack by targeting the ANC's weaknesses.

The debate finally took place on 14 April 1994 on the stage of a little auditorium in the Civic Theatre complex in the heart of Johannesburg. It was conducted within the framework of procedures and rules that had been hammered out in tough discussions between our parties. The rules ensured rapid interaction between Mandela and myself and prevented long speeches. Everything had been set up for a truly dynamic debate. When I finally found myself alone, powdered and made-up, in a small dressing room a few minutes before the debate, I was fairly calm. The adrenalin was pumping, but I was sure that I would not be caught off guard. I knew what I wanted to say and was mentally well-prepared.

Initially Mandela was quite aggressive and did not hesitate to launch personal attacks on me. I preferred to stick to the issues. The ball was hit this way and that across the net. Both sides attacked and defended and it was soon clear to me that my opponent was also well prepared. As the debate developed, I had the feeling that I was building up a reasonably good points advantage. Shortly before the end of the debate I was confident that I had forced Mandela onto his back foot. However, he suddenly took me by surprise by leaning across to me and taking me by the hand. 'In spite of my criticism of Mr De Klerk,' he said, looking at me, 'Sir, you are one of those I rely on . . . I am proud to hold your hand for us to go forward.' His single gesture of apparent goodwill probably counted for as much as all my reasoned replies. Suddenly, what had been a certain points victory had been converted into a draw. It was a masterful stroke and I mentally tipped my hat to the strategic planning ability of Mandela and his advisers. However, in retrospect, I do not think the TV debate made the slightest difference to the outcome of the election.

It took everything I had to keep up with my crippling election schedule. We had planned our campaign to peak in the weeks immediately preceding the election. However, this was precisely the time when

I was most preoccupied with negotiations with the IFP and King Goodwill, and with arrangements to ensure that the transition to the new dispensation would run as smoothly as possible. I nevertheless managed to make a gruelling series of public appearances throughout the country. It was not at all uncommon for me to make up to ten public appearances in a single day, often with long travelling distances in the rural areas in between.

I found it difficult to play the hand-shaking, baby-kissing, crowd-pleasing role that our strategists had choreographed for me. I had to fight against my inclination to be too analytical and logical in speeches and did not enjoy the slogan-style statements that our game plan demanded of me. Nevertheless, I did what was expected of me and was reasonably successful in concealing my embarrassment. Our approach worked well. Turnouts were good and we succeeded in generating genuine enthusiasm among many of our supporters. Coloured voters, in particular, were delighted by our new-style politics. In the process, I developed a very warm relationship with them. It was as though a bond had been established between us that was typified by the nickname that they gave me – Papa.

I was greatly relieved when the day of the election arrived. I was exhausted and felt like an orange that had been squeezed absolutely dry. I was also satisfied that we had run a good campaign and that our basic approach to the election – despite the mistakes that we made – was the best that we could have followed under the circumstances. I was confident that we would do well.

Altogether, some 19.5 million South Africans voted – including about 3 million whites, about 2 million coloureds, half a million Asians and around 14 million blacks. More than 9,000 polling stations had been established throughout the country – from the centres of South Africa's first-world cities to the remotest third-world tribal villages. On 26 April the elderly and the sick were able to cast special ballots. The election itself was scheduled for 27 and 28 April. Throughout the country millions of South Africans streamed to the polls – most of them for the first time in their lives. I voted at a primary school in Arcadia, a Pretoria suburb close to the Union Buildings. Mandela made a special point of voting in Natal.

It soon became clear that at many polling stations – particularly in the rural areas – there were major logistical problems. Many electoral officers complained that they had received no election material. Others soon ran out of ballots. The IEC quickly made arrangements to print an additional 3 million ballots. In many areas, voters patiently queued from dawn to sunset without being able to cast their ballots. In the Pretoria–Witwatersrand–Vereeniging area, the country's most populous region, 30 per cent of the polling stations were inoperative on the first day. In KwaZulu-Natal the figure was 25 per cent. When, by the end of the next day, the situation had still not been rectified in all parts of the country, the IEC urgently approached me to extend the election by another day in the old black homelands of Ciskei, Gazankulu, Lebowa, KwaZulu, Transkei and Venda. I immediately granted their request.

Because of the chronic disorganization of the election process, it took days for the final results to be announced. After two days, it became clear at some counting stations that there was simply no possibility of reconciling the ballots in boxes with the number of ballots that had been issued to presiding officers. Judge Kriegler, the chairman of the IEC, described his personal horror when the whole counting process ground to a halt. When it became clear that there was no way that all the votes could be reconciled, he asserted rather lamely that it was the reconciliation of people, not of ballot papers that the elections were all about. According to the IEC itself, chaos reigned at several counting stations and panic mounted.

There was, of course, never any possibility that the National Party would win the election. By Monday, 2 May initial information from the IEC and other sources had confirmed this. I had been monitoring the process from the National Party's headquarters in Pretoria and at 5.30 p.m. decided to concede defeat. It was an emotional moment. With Marike at my side, and surrounded by my closest supporters, I said that the election – and the interim constitution in terms of which it had been held – represented the realization of the vision that I had spelled out in Parliament on 2 February 1990. I congratulated Mr Mandela and said that I was looking forward to working with him in the Government of National Unity. Despite our differences, we had proved that we could work together. Mr Mandela would soon assume the highest office in the land with all the awesome responsibility which it bore. He had walked a long road, and now stood at the top of the hill. A traveller would sit and admire the view. But the man of destiny knew that beyond that hill lay another and another. The journey was never complete. As he contemplated the next hill, I said that I was holding out my hand to him – in friendship and in co-operation.

As far as my own position was concerned, I believed that my

political task had not been completed. Everything that we had done until then – the four years of difficult and often frustrating negotiations, the problems and the crises – had been simply a preparation for the work that lay ahead. The greatest challenge that the Government of National Unity would face would be to defend and nurture our new constitution. Our greatest task would be to ensure that our young and vulnerable democracy took root and flourished.

When I finished my speech I had tears in my eyes. I was later told that many South Africans who watched it on TV had also been very moved by the occasion and by my words. It was apparently also a critical moment for many ANC supporters. Quite a number of them never fully believed that we would really hand over power when the moment arrived. They thought that we would try to pull some trick; that we would reject the election result or that we would engineer a right-wing coup. For such people my concession speech was a major event.

When the results were finally announced by Judge Kriegler of the IEC on Friday, 6 May we learned that we had won 20.6 per cent of the vote. The ANC received 62.6 per cent; the IFP 10.5 per cent; the Freedom Front 2.2 per cent; the Democratic Party 1.7 per cent; the PAC 1.2 per cent and the African Christian Democratic Party 0.5 per cent. To this day I believe that the National Party actually did much better than the formal result of 20 per cent indicated. The fact is that there were enormous irregularities. I am convinced that as many as a million illegal votes might have been cast and allocated to other parties. The parties which benefited from these irregularities were, in particular, the ANC throughout the country and, to a lesser extent the IFP in KwaZulu-Natal. An enormous number of double ballots were cast, despite the measures that the IEC had taken to try to prevent this. We also had reason to believe that towards the end of the election people were being issued with temporary voters' cards virtually on request. The fact that one and half million such cards were issued during the election is in itself an indication that there could have been very little scrutiny of applicants. Many young people under the age of eighteen voted. In many of the voting locations in the heartland of the ANC's then most important power bases, such as the Transkei, there was no real control. In a number of ballot boxes the ballots were neatly arranged in piles and had clearly not been inserted by voters through the slot above. There was also some humour in all of this. One of our black supporters told me that he had wanted to vote at a rural polling station in one of the old homelands. As he walked into the polling station he was asked for whom he was going to vote. When he replied Mr F. W. de Klerk, he was summarily told that he should go to another polling station because that one was for Nelson Mandela!

The irregularities were so serious that some of my senior colleagues in the National Party wanted us to challenge the result of the elections in the courts. We certainly had sufficient juridical grounds to do so. The decision not to challenge the result was an extremely difficult one. After consultation with the provincial leaders, I decided, however, that despite all the irregularities, we had little choice but to accept the outcome of the election in the interest of South Africa and all its people. The fact is that although we were allocated a smaller percentage of the vote than that to which we were entitled, the result met the bottom-line requirements of all the main parties and of the country itself: the ANC emerged with less than the two-thirds majority they needed to impose a final constitution on the other parties, but won seven of the nine provincial elections; we received the 20 per cent that we needed to establish ourselves firmly as the second largest party with a constitutional right to appoint one of two executive deputy presidents and won the provincial election in the Western Cape; and the IFP achieved its primary objective of winning a majority of the votes in Natal. Thus, although it was not necessarily an accurate result, it was a result with which we all could – and did – live. This led to allegations that, confronted with the virtual collapse of the vote counting process, the major parties had secretly agreed on a result by sufficient consensus. There is no truth in these allegations. What can, however, be said is that ours had not been an election of the super realist school. It was definitely an impressionist election. The picture that it produced of the South African election was not minutely accurate, but in its broad brush strokes produced an acceptable likeness of the general wishes of all our people.

The National Party – the party that had created and then dismantled apartheid – also emerged from the election as the most multiracial of all South African parties. More than half our votes came from people of colour. We secured a majority of the votes from the white, coloured and Indian communities and, according to our estimates, we received between 500,000 and 600,000 votes from black South Africans. Although we had not made the breakthrough to the black community for which we had planned and worked, we did emerge as the third largest black party after the ANC and the IFP. Indeed, we received almost three times as many black votes as the much vaunted PAC.

The party that did best out of the elections did not even participate in them under its own name. In no reliable national opinion survey had the South African Communist Party ever been credited with more than one or two per cent support. However, through their alliance with the ANC they were granted fully 12.5 per cent of the seats in Parliament. The agreement enabled them to continue to play a key role in the alliance's political and strategic leadership.

In the weeks preceding the election, the government spent much of its time preparing for the transition from the National Party government to the Government of National Unity. I asked cabinet ministers to instruct their departments to prepare status reports on all their programmes, so that members of the new government could be properly briefed on where they stood. This was a new experience for our administration – since there had not been a change of government for almost forty-six years. At one of the cabinet meetings in the weeks before the election, a representative of the Bureau for Heraldry showed us the design that they had developed for the new South African flag. It contained the black, green and gold of the ANC and the red, white and blue that had traditionally been associated with the white communities. Afrikaners would probably have preferred orange, white and blue to the red, white and blue with which English-descended South Africans would have identified – so the colour chosen for the flag was actually a pepper red, half way between orange and red. Most of the members of the cabinet immediately liked the new flag, which was soon also approved by the Transitional Executive Council as the country's new interim flag. After the election, the flag became such a powerful symbol of national unity and was so popular with most segments of the population that it was subsequently adopted as the country's permanent flag.

*

As we approached the election, we still had very little idea of how the government would function in practice after the transition. We did not know how the new president would want to run his office, whether he would want the staff of the existing office of the state president to stay on in their posts to assist him, and how he would want the cabinet system to function. In the end, my own office took the initiative in discussions with the ANC and made proposals for the functioning of the presidency and the cabinet after the transition. In essence, they recommended that the president and the two executive deputy presidents for whom provision had been made in the interim constitution, should each have their own separate offices. They also suggested that the ANC should take over the very effective cabinet system that we had developed during the preceding decade.

In further discussions with the ANC and the Department of Public Works, they also reached agreement on where the offices of the president and the deputy presidents should be situated. The new president would naturally move into the suite of offices in the west wing of the Union Buildings in Pretoria and Tuynhuys in Cape Town that I was then occupying. The executive deputy president from the majority party – who was widely expected to be Thabo Mbeki – would also have offices in the west wing of the Union Buildings and Tuynhuys, while the executive deputy president from the largest minority party – whom everybody assumed would be me – would move to offices in the east wing of the Union Buildings which were a mirror image of those of the president in the west wing. In Cape Town, I would move to the suite on the top floor of the (soon to be renamed) Hendrik Verwoerd Building which had previously been occupied by P. W. Botha while he had been prime minister – and which I had occupied when I had been chairman of the Council of Ministers in the House of Assembly. The new president would, of course, decide which of the official residences he wished to occupy. To start with Mandela considered moving into the Presidency – the stately old residence of South Africa's former governors-general and ceremonial state presidents.

Soon after the election he was taken to view the Presidency by Dave Steward, the head of my office. Dressed in one of his characteristic Madiba shirts, he was accompanied by Barbara Masekela – who was later appointed as South Africa's ambassador to Paris – and by one of his grandchildren – a two-year-old toddler. The elderly leader, who for many of his twenty-seven years in prison had been accommodated in a tiny cell, was conducted through the echoing halls of the sprawling mansion that had for decades been the residence of South Africa's heads of state. Mandela seemed to be quite happy with the Presidency. He initially indicated that he would use the Presidency as his residence and told me that Marike and I would then be able to remain at Libertas, the residence where we had been living since I became president. However, Mandela later came back to me and said that he was under great pressure from the ANC to move into Libertas, because it had traditionally been the residence of the head of government in Pretoria. He said that Marike and I would be to able move into the Presidency. No sooner had we become used to this idea, than he informed me that he was now under pressure from his senior colleagues to use the Presidency for other purposes. We were then allocated Overvaal, the residence of the former administrators of the Transvaal. Overvaal was a delightful residence but, in our view and in the view of the Department of Public Works, needed extensive refurbishing.

The final humiliation that I had to endure in the saga of the official residences, was when President Mandela insisted on personally inspecting Overvaal, to satisfy himself that the refurbishment was, indeed, necessary. One winter Saturday morning, he joined me and the Public Works architect at Overvaal. Together we walked through the house, while the architect explained why a new fridge was needed here and repainting and redecoration was needed there. As far as I personally was concerned, I would have been just as happy to move back into our own fairly modest home in Pretoria. It was a matter of supreme indifference to me whether we stayed at Libertas, at the Presidency, at Overvaal or wherever. But not for Marike. She was deeply distressed by all the chopping and changing, which she interpreted as a calculated effort by Mandela himself to humiliate us. She could not forget his public and personal attacks on me – at Codesa I, in Philadelphia, in Stockholm, and from platforms all over South Africa. This latest humiliation was too much for her to swallow. She became very critical of Mandela and did not hesitate to voice her criticism. This, I believe, was a very real factor in the growing tension between Mandela and me, particularly in the years after the election. Ironically, Marike and I loved our stay at Overvaal. It proved to be a delightful home and, in the end, we preferred it to any of the other official residences in which we stayed over the years. In Cape Town, Mandela decided that he would prefer to live in Westbrook, the residence that P. W. Botha had used while he had been president. This meant that Marike and I could continue to live in the historic Groote Schuur while we were in Cape Town.

On Wednesday, 4 May 1994, we held the last cabinet meeting of the old dispensation. We gathered as usual around the long table in the elegant Cabinet Room, adjacent to my suite in the Union Buildings. The room was semicircular at one end and was panelled in light wood to a height of about three metres. Above us, the roof was vaulted and was reminiscent of a European chapel. The french doors leading to the balcony overlooking the amphitheatre at the other end of the room were permanently closed and shuttered for security reasons. In the panelling of the semicircular wall behind my chair there were two small alcoves, which held bronze statuettes of two Voortrekker women by Anton van Wouw, one of our foremost sculptors. They were models for the statues that stood at the Vrouemonument in Bloemfontein, the monument that commemorated the deaths of Afrikaner women and children in the internment camps that the British had established during the Anglo-Boer War. Elsewhere the walls of the Cabinet Room held landscapes by J. H. Pierneef and Tinus de Jongh, two of our most famous artists.

It was an historic occasion. Our meeting was the last manifestation of white rule – not only in South Africa – but on the whole continent of Africa. It signalled the end of a process that had begun with the first council meeting convened by Jan van Riebeeck, the Dutch founder of the Cape, three hundred and forty-two years earlier. We began our proceedings, as always, with a prayer. On this occasion, it was the turn of Mr Jac Rabie, the coloured minister of population development. Despite the fact that this was the end of an era, the cabinet continued with its work much as though this was just another ordinary meeting. It considered the reports of the cabinet committees and approved their recommendations on such mundane matters as the granting of subsidies to bus companies in the former Bophuthatswana and the need for expenditure cuts in various government departments. It also dealt with a number of issues related to the transition and to the election the week before and gave approval for the stock of old South African flags in the possession of government departments to be disposed of at half their book value. One of the flags still hung behind me. At the end of the proceedings I thanked my team for their support and dedication during the tumultuous transformation of the country. Pik Botha, the most senior minister, replied and thanked me for my leadership during the preceding four and a half years and reflected on the historic process that we had managed together. Most of the ministers found it hard to hold back a tear or two. Afterwards, we gathered in an adjacent lounge for a buffet lunch as we had always done after, or during, cabinet meetings. For the first time that I could recall we served drinks and wine with the lunch. However, even the wine could not quite dispel the feeling that we were attending a wake.

On Monday, 9 May the newly elected Parliament convened for the first time in Cape Town to formally elect Nelson Mandela as the country's new president. Mandela and I entered the chamber together, shook hands and then took our places, he to the right of the Speaker, and I, for the first time, on the left of the Speaker, in the places traditionally reserved for the opposition. It was clear from the outset that Parliament as an institution had undergone a radical change. The old sense of gravity and decorum had been replaced by a new informality and boisterous exuberance. The traditional ranks of grey- and blue-suited men had been replaced by multi-coloured African dresses and traditional robes. The number of women MPs had increased dramatically, particularly in the ranks of the ANC representatives. The subdued tones of the old Parliament had been replaced by the laughter, shrill interjections and spontaneous applause of the new order.

And so the last trek had ended. We all stood at the threshold of a new beginning.

32

The Government of National Unity

The constitution prescribed clear procedures for the formation of the Government of National Unity. The first practical task was the composition of the new cabinet. The number of ministers to which each party would be entitled in the Government of National Unity was determined by the percentage of votes that it received in the election. According to this formula, the ANC was entitled to eighteen ministers; we would have six and the IFP, three. According to the constitution, the president could decide which portfolios would be allocated to which parties. He was required to consult with the executive deputy presidents both on the division of portfolios between the parties and also on the people who would be appointed to the various portfolios. In the event of a disagreement, the president would decide on the allocation of portfolios, but the leader of the relevant party would have the final say in deciding who should be appointed to the portfolios that had been allocated to his party. Consultation between the president and the executive deputy presidents in the spirit underlying the concept of a Government of National Unity was, according to the constitution, a key requirement.

I was accordingly shocked on 6 May 1994 when Nelson Mandela announced the names and some of the portfolios of the eighteen cabinet ministers to which the ANC was entitled without making the slightest effort to consult me beforehand. It was the first instance of the ANC riding roughshod over the constitution when it suited them and was a foretaste of the many difficulties that we would encounter with them in the Government of National Unity. Later Mandela did, indeed, consult me with regard to the portfolios that would be assigned to the National Party. I had wanted the have one National Party minister in each of the four main areas of government – security, social, economic and administrative. However, it very soon became apparent that the ANC wanted to reserve the whole security sector for itself. Although there was originally some talk that we would be given responsibility for the National Intelligence Service, this possibility very quickly evaporated. The most that the ANC was ultimately prepared to concede on the security front was that I could be the chairman of the cabinet committee that dealt with security and intelligence affairs. Instead, the ANC cleverly weighted our portfolios in the economic area. We were given the ministries of finance, mineral and energy affairs, environment, agriculture, welfare and population development, and provincial affairs and constitutional development.

*

I knew that in filling these portfolios, I was bound to disappoint a majority of my former colleagues in the old cabinet who had served so loyally with me during the preceding years. There just simply were not enough senior posts to go around. I appointed Pik Botha – who was also the leader of the National Party in the Gauteng Province – to the mineral and energy affairs portfolio; Dawie de Villiers – the leader of the National Party in the Cape – to tourism and environmental affairs; Kraai van Niekerk, the leader of the National Party in the Northern Cape, to the agriculture portfolio that he had held in the previous government; Abe Williams – the most senior coloured member of the National Party, to social welfare; Roelf Meyer, our chief negotiator, to provincial affairs and constitutional development; and Derek Keys would remain as minister of finance. It was agreed from the outset that Keys, who had never had a high political profile, would play a non-party-political role. Keys had made an enormous contribution to the formulation of our economic strategy and was also respected and accepted by the ANC. However, I knew that – under pressure from his family – he was reluctant to remain in the government for longer than the bare minimum that it would require to oversee the transition and to pilot the new government's first budget through Parliament.

The new cabinet also included three IFP ministers, Mangosuthu Buthelezi himself – whom President Mandela had, at my suggestion appointed to the senior portfolio of home affairs; Dr Ben Ngubane, the minister of arts, culture, science and technology; and Mr Sipo Mzimela, the minister of correctional services.

The ANC had agreed to take over the existing cabinet system – comprising the cabinet and its three main cabinet committees virtually without change. It soon became clear that the new president did not wish to play a hands-on role in the cabinet. Although he attended meetings, he was frequently absent and appointed the two deputy presidents to chair cabinet meetings on a rotational basis. Thabo

Mbeki chaired the cabinet committee on economic affairs, while I chaired the committees on security and intelligence affairs and social and administrative affairs.

*

For the first year or so the new cabinet functioned surprisingly smoothly. The ANC and IFP ministers seemed to accept my authority as chairman of the meetings over which I presided without any difficulty. I sometimes found myself in the strange position of having to adjudicate in disputes between ANC members themselves. I also established a good working relationship with Thabo Mbeki. I found him to be a good listener who gave thoughtful consideration to all the matters that were presented to him. He was a pragmatist with sound insights into the economy and soon gained a good grasp of the essential realities of modern government. To start with, the ANC ministers seemed prepared to make use of the experience in government which the NP ministers and I brought to the cabinet.

During the first year, we were able to make good progress in reaching common approaches to a number of critical issues. In particular, I felt that we exercised a positive influence in ensuring that the government's Reconstruction and Development Programme – the centrepiece of its social planning – would be funded in a responsible manner. It was important for me that the RDP should not be regarded as simply an ANC policy but, in its improved form, as an initiative of the whole Government of National Unity and all three parties that served in it. I went out of my way to ensure that the programme would be funded according to sound budgeting procedures and that the ANC would not be able to claim sole ownership of the RDP.

We also made positive contributions to the development of the government's economic strategy – the Growth, Employment and Reconstruction strategy – known as GEAR. While I was still president during the period of negotiations, the government had already developed its own economic model known as the Normative Economic Model in 1993. This economic model had provided the framework for economic and financial policy during the rest of my administration. I was deeply aware of the fact that our challenge was not only to negotiate a new constitution, but also to ensure that, after the election, the ANC would implement the right economic and financial policies. With this in mind, I gave Derek Keys the task of entering into discussions on the economy with key people in the ANC. Such discussions were, in any case, necessary because just after the election a budget would have to be adopted which would have been drawn up by the National Party government. We had to ensure that the ANC, with its expected majority, would support the draft budget so that the administration of the country could continue. Derek Keys did wonderful work and succeeded in winning the confidence of the ANC, possibly because he had no party-political agenda and possibly also because of the clarity of his thought. He regularly reported back to the cabinet on his discussions with the ANC.

At the same time, a good foundation for greater economic realism was also being laid within the National Economic Forum, in which the government, the trade unions and the employers had for some time been discussing important aspects of national economic policy.

The result was that the ANC accepted a broad framework of responsible economic principles, not only with regard to the first budget, but finally as the basis for its own economic Growth, Employment and Reconstruction model. The strategy's central objective was to cater to the needs of the poorest segments of the population and to help to narrow the gap between rich and poor in the country. It planned to do so in a manner that would be fiscally responsible and in line with global economic principles. We accordingly supported GEAR. In my opinion, the National Party's greatest contribution in the Government of National Unity was to promote the adoption of a balanced economic policy framework which could assure growth and progress and which would steer a course away from the socialist tendencies which the ANC had espoused for the whole of its existence, as a result of its close alliance with the Congress of South African Trade Unions and the South African Communist Party.

We were also able to bring about important amendments to the Government of National Unity's new education policy which would ensure the right of pupils to be educated in the language of their choice, where this was feasible, and which would also strengthen the role of parents in the management of schools. This was not an easy process and involved lengthy discussions, and even clashes, within the cabinet. On one occasion I had to adjourn the social and administrative affairs cabinet committee for a quarter of an hour to give myself an opportunity to try to convince the minister of education, Professor S. Bengu, of the seriousness we attached to mother-tongue education and to parental control of schools. It was a critical point and, in my opinion, if our proposals had not been accepted, we would probably have considered leaving the Government of National Unity even at that early stage. However, the amendments which the ANC made to their original proposals were sufficient to enable us and the broader educational community which supported the National Party to live with the result. The battle over education policy would be continued in the negotiations on the final constitution.

However, in most of the cases where we were able to influence legislation positively, the result of our effort was often still short of what we by ourselves would have wanted. In such cases, because some of our recommendations had been accepted we were morally bound to vote in favour of the resultant legislation. We then frequently found it difficult to explain to our caucus and our rank and file members why we supported legislation that, on balance, seemed to suit the ANC's agenda better than our own. This created a constant tension within the party which I had to manage as best I could.

*

The first months of the new South Africa were often euphoric. After so many years of estrangement, South Africans of all races revelled in our new-found national unity. We proudly displayed our new multi-coloured flag and learned to twist our tongues around the Xhosa or Zulu words of '*Nkosi Sikelel' iAfrika*'. With equal enthusiasm, former ANC activists sang the Afrikaans words of our old national anthem '*Die Stem*' which had also been incorporated into the new anthem. President Mandela became the leading symbol of national unity. He had an unfailing ability to make just the right gesture at just the right time. When he donned our national team's green and gold rugby jersey after our fairytale victory in the rugby World Cup competition, he won the hearts of millions of white rugby fans.

During those early months, President Mandela seemed in many respects to be the embodiment of the spirit of reconciliation. He immediately established excellent relations with the mostly white staff of the office of the state president that he had kept on after his inauguration. One evening he invited the two middle-ranking Afrikaans women in charge of the office's logistics section to dine with him at his official residence. He had an exceptional ability to make everyone with whom he came into contact feel special – whether they were the gardeners at the Union Buildings, or the white policemen who continued to protect him, or schoolchildren of any race or age.

The interim constitution had created room for the president to give his deputies special responsibilities. Mandela never chose to involve me in any function outside the immediate role that the constitution had determined for me. I was never asked to represent the country at international meetings or to carry out any other task of national importance. Neither did Mandela ever ask me to act as president during his frequent overseas visits. He always ensured that Thabo Mbeki remained in South Africa on such occasions to play this role.

In the absence of any such specific role, I had to carve one out for myself. I continued to be overwhelmed by invitations from overseas organizations to address them on the transformation of South Africa and likely future developments. These invitations provided me with an excellent opportunity of making a contribution by marketing the new South Africa to the international community. I made a number of successful visits to Europe, North America and the Far East in which I painted a positive picture of our future prospects. In particular, I tried to persuade foreign companies and individuals to invest in South Africa. Unfortunately, my efforts received little recognition or encouragement from my ANC colleagues in the Government of National Unity. As a matter of courtesy, I always informed President Mandela of my overseas visits – but I did not request his permission as cabinet ministers were required to do. The way that I looked at it, I had been elected to the position of executive deputy president. Because I had not been appointed by the president it was my view that I did not require his permission to travel overseas. No doubt, this was yet another source of contention for him.

As time went by, our differences on policy issues became increasingly evident in cabinet discussions. These debates soon began to reveal the flaws and anomalies in the unnatural constitutional coalition within which we found ourselves. Coalition governments are formed elsewhere in the world because no single party has a majority in Parliament. This leads to the formation of natural coalitions and the acceptance by the participating parties of a common policy framework. The parties often spend weeks hammering out the details of their common policy approach – which then constitutes the cast-iron foundation of the coalition. Despite repeated requests that we should do so, the ANC, with its 62 per cent majority, refused to negotiate such a framework with us and the IFP. The result was that we were increasingly confronted with majority government positions with which we disagreed and with which we did not want to be associated. We accordingly insisted on the right to oppose publicly policies which had been adopted in the cabinet – despite our opposition. This led to the untenable position where we were at one and the same time part of the government, as well as being the government's main opposition, attacking it in public.

The inevitable result was that both our roles suffered. The ANC was increasingly unhappy when we criticized their policies – and were less inclined to allow us to play our proper role within the Government of National Unity. On the other hand, our ability to play an effective opposition role was seriously hampered by our co-responsibility for most of the policies of the Government of National Unity.

One of the first indications that the ANC was beginning to deviate from the spirit of reconciliation, was the avidity with which an ANC-appointed police task force sought to press murder charges against the former minister of defence, General Magnus Malan and two former chiefs of the SADF, General Jannie Geldenhuys and General Kat Liebenberg; as well as several other senior members of the security forces. There was speculation that the attorney-general of KwaZulu-Natal, Mr Tim McNally, had initiated the prosecutions because of enormous pressure from ANC members of the parliamentary Justice Portfolio Committee. He, however, assured me that he had decided himself to proceed with the prosecutions because of the prima facie evidence that had been presented to him by the police task force.

The charges arose from the involvement of the accused in a decision to train a special IFP unit to protect Chief Minister Mangosuthu Buthelezi and other IFP leaders from ANC attacks. The contention was that they were accordingly responsible for murders which members of the unit subsequently committed in the course of the bitter struggle between the IFP and the ANC. Although I was very disturbed by this development, I had to be careful to avoid the perception that I wished to interfere with the normal process of the law. I nevertheless felt obliged to come to the defence of General Malan and the senior officers of the old SADF who had served during my presidency. Accordingly, Roelf Meyer and I discussed the matter one evening with President Mandela at his home in Johannesburg. He had called Mr Sidney Mufamadi, the minister of law and order, to be present during the discussion. I recall Mufamadi kicked off his shoes and was barefoot throughout the meeting.

I was convinced that the case would not result in a guilty verdict and felt that taking the matter to court would be a travesty of justice.

However, my ability to pursue the matter was also limited by Magnus Malan's insistence that I should not try to stop the prosecution. He said that he preferred to put his case in court so that he could expose the ANC. In any case, President Mandela had refused to intervene and had taken refuge behind the universal principle that heads of government should not interfere in legal processes. Against this background, I decided that the National Party's approach should be to exert pressure for the reinstitution of the prosecution of prominent members of the ANC which had been suspended during the negotiations while I was president. We launched a whole campaign to achieve this. However, in one way or another, the ANC minister of justice and the South African Police Service managed to find ways of delaying the process, despite assurances that such prosecutions would continue. Finally, the whole question was overtaken by the Truth and Reconciliation Commission's amnesty process. After a lengthy and costly trial General Malan and all his co-defendants were acquitted.

My first serious clash with President Mandela occurred at a cabinet meeting on 18 January 1995. One of the items on the agenda was the functioning of the Government of National Unity. I had been pressing for such a discussion because of the National Party's problem of being simultaneously part of the government, but nevertheless also being the official opposition. The proceedings started with a sharp attack on me by several ANC ministers. Shortly before the cabinet meeting I had been very critical of the ANC in public statements. The ANC ministers had worked out a strategy to call me to account for these attacks. Their argument was that, as executive deputy president, I did not have the right to criticize government decisions and that I had gone beyond the limits in my actions as leader of the National Party when I had attacked and discredited the ANC. President Mandela initially did not participate in the attack. In the course of my reply, I strongly defended the National Party's right to criticize and oppose decisions that had been taken by the government despite our opposition to them in the cabinet. At first, it seemed that the ANC ministers had been swayed by my arguments and I thought that I had succeeded in defusing the crisis. It was at that point that President Mandela joined the attack, saying that he would not let me get away with my debating abilities. Then he let loose.

His main points of criticism related to the application for indemnity that had been submitted just before the election on behalf of some 3,500 members of the South African police. Mandela claimed that this had been a deceitful and underhand attempt by the former government to grant indemnity to perpetrators of gross violations of human rights just before the new government came into power. The fact is that the government had neither been aware of, nor involved in, the initiation of the applications, which had been lodged by the legal representatives of the policemen involved. In any event, the legislation under which their applications had been made did not provide for the granting of indemnity to perpetrators of serious crimes. Thousands of ANC members had already made use of the same legislation and there was no reason why the police should not have the same right. Mandela also criticized me for not supporting the Reconstruction and Development Programme – also a charge for which no factual basis existed. On the contrary, everywhere I went, I enthusiastically supported the RDP – although I was critical of the ineffective manner in which it was being implemented. I was also accused of opposing affirmative action. This was also not true. The National Party at all times supported the judicious application of affirmative action, but not the implementation of policies which constituted blatant reverse racial discrimination or which placed inexperienced people in jobs for which they were not yet qualified. The most bizarre criticism was that during a visit to Germany the previous year I had persuaded the German government to channel its aid away from officially sanctioned recipients in South Africa to National Party organizations. I was flabbergasted. During my visit, Carl-Dieter Spranger, the German minister who dealt with overseas aid, had asked me to recommend an organization in South Africa that was helping farm workers. I immediately thought of the Rural Foundation, which had for many years been doing excellent work in that area. As far as I was aware, the Rural Foundation had absolutely no links whatsoever to the National Party.

By the end of Mandela's tirade I was furious. I reacted very briefly and said that the National Party members of the cabinet and I were going to withdraw, because we had been left with no alternative but to reconsider our continued participation in the Government of National Unity. I went straight to my office and seriously considered resigning there and then and leading the National Party out of the Government of National Unity. The National Party ministers and I then held a lengthy discussion on the crisis. Some of them also spoke with a few influential ANC ministers, who were quite alarmed because they had not intended to drive us out of the Government of National Unity, but merely to try to intimidate us. In the end I decided not to take any immediate drastic action, but rather to adopt a strategy of trying to force the ANC to accept publicly the view that the National Party was entitled to criticize decisions to which we had not been party.

The next morning I briefed the Executive Council of the National Party on the situation. That evening I told the Congress of the National Party that was meeting at the World Trade Centre in Kempton Park that the attack had been so severe, and so uncalled for, that we were seriously thinking of withdrawing from the GNU. My statement caused unexpected national and international consternation and resulted in a sharp drop on the Johannesburg stock market.

The following morning I met Mandela in his office at the Union Buildings. He must have realized that he had gone too far and was his old charming self again. During our discussion, I stood by my position, which now had the support not only of the NP ministers, but also of the Federal Executive. I insisted that our concerns could not simply be dismissed with a smile and a handshake. I demanded a commitment from him to clarify our right as a party to public opposition. That right should be incorporated in a clear agreement on the functioning of the Government of National Unity. I also reminded him that during his outburst he had accused me, among other things, of speaking to black people as though I was their superior. I told Mandela that I regarded this as an extremely unfair insult because it simply was not true. I said that he should accept my style just as I accepted his, and that I did not speak to him or other senior people in the ANC in a manner that was any different from the manner in which I had spoken to my own father when he and I had argued over matters.

President Mandela was conciliatory and assured me that he wanted us to continue to work together in the Government of National Unity in the best interest of the country. That afternoon we issued a joint statement at an impromptu press conference on the back lawn of Libertas. We said that we had cleared up the misunderstandings and that we accepted one another's good faith and integrity. We agreed that the relevant ministries would remove without delay the uncertainty surrounding the indemnity applications which had been lodged by members of the police. We would also continue discussions on the functioning of the Government of National Unity with urgency and would give special attention to the rights and duties of parties within the Government of National Unity. Pictures of our handshake at the end of the meeting dominated the news. The stock market quickly recovered – but the ANC never honoured its undertakings to continue our discussions on the GNU or to resolve the uncertainty about the legality of the indemnity applications by members of the police.

For me, the incident once again highlighted two disturbing tendencies of President Mandela: firstly, his habit of flying off the handle without properly checking his facts beforehand; and secondly, his tactic of papering over problems with charm and promises, without taking effective remedial action. However, Mandela's attack had gone beyond politics. There had been a definite personal edge to it. The source of his growing irritation could probably be found in the nature of our new institutional relationship. At the best of times, it is hardly ever possible for a former chief executive officer to serve on the same board as his successor. No matter how sensitively he conducts himself, the former CEO will always wish to provide the new board with the benefit of his experience. No matter how sound that advice might be, his successor will nearly always resent it.

By now, there was little possibility of concealing the deterioration in our relationship. During a speech that I delivered in Johannesburg in September 1995 I said that everyone had probably read of the domestic tensions between the ANC and the NP within the GNU. I said that it was true. Ours had never been a marriage of love. We had come from very different backgrounds and our families didn't get on very well with one another. We had been forced together to legitimize the new South Africa. Now the honeymoon was over. We greeted each other politely; we ran the household jointly, and tried to keep up appearances. We only remained together for the sake of our joint offspring.

*

Another issue which caused growing friction between the National Party and the ANC within the Government of National Unity was the the ongoing violence in KwaZulu-Natal, which continued to be a running sore in the body of the new South Africa. After the election, the ANC refused to take steps to honour the unambiguous undertaking that it had given on 19 April 1994 to submit the IFP's constitutional concerns to international mediation. In September 1994 Cyril Ramaphosa announced that the ANC had received legal advice that it was no longer bound by the agreement. The ANC's lack of action incensed Buthelezi and drove him to make irresponsible statements in which he called on his supporters to rise and resist the central government and to fight for freedom, even if their lives depended on it. After having subsided following the elections, violence once again began to flare up in the province. Mandela made conciliatory gestures to Buthelezi. He embraced him in public and referred to him by his princely title Shenge – but as was so often the case with him, his gestures were not necessarily a reflection of his true intentions, nor were they followed up by any appropriate action. Strangely, although Mandela, Buthelezi and I sat together, week after week, at cabinet meetings, the serious tensions in KwaZulu-Natal were never discussed in that forum – probably because within the context of the cabinet we were not equal partners.

It became more and more clear to me that the ANC was toying with the idea of resolving the problems of KwaZulu-Natal by force, rather than through peaceful negotiations. During a discussion with President Mandela in August 1995, I gained the impression that he was trying to draw me into a common strategy against the IFP. He said that he wanted to crush Buthelezi. I rejected the idea and on 20 September 1995 wrote a letter to the president in which I suggested that the best way to address the violence in KwaZulu-Natal would be to call a meeting between himself, Deputy President Mbeki, myself and Chief Minister Mangosuthu Buthelezi to discuss international mediation and political initiatives to lessen the tensions and political violence in the province. I made it clear that I did not want to score political points on this issue. Something had to be done urgently and a constructive political initiative was required. In his acrimonious reply to my letter of 20 September, President Mandela dismissed my proposal and rejected the idea that the National Party should mediate between the ANC and the IFP – a suggestion which I had not made – because 'the historical part played by your party, and the government which it formed, in that conflict totally disqualifies you from performing that role'.

On 14 October I again wrote to Mandela and pointed out that we had not proposed the meeting to mediate between the ANC and the IFP, but because we had a direct interest as one of the parties to the agreement of 19 April 1994 to promote international mediation on the IFP's outstanding constitutional concerns as soon as possible after the election. President Mandela responded by once again sharply rejecting my proposal, and declaring that, 'rather than suggesting pointless meetings, I would appreciate your input on how we can deal with the legacy of the inhumane system of apartheid, of which you were one of the architects'. This time I did not bother to reply. His view that a meeting between the leaders of the three largest parties in the country to consider one of its greatest problems was pointless was beyond comprehension. His accusation that I was an architect of apartheid also bordered on the irrational.

Mandela's reply might have been influenced by another public clash that I had had with him only two weeks earlier. On 29 September 1995, I attended a function in Johannesburg to mark the opening of the renovated headquarters of Gencor, one South Africa's largest mining houses. President Mandela had been invited to preside over the opening ceremony, after which there would be a banquet. The ceremony itself was held outside in an open square where a marquee had been set up. In a speech which he delivered from the steps of the building, President Mandela launched a vicious attack against the National Party, which he worded in such a manner that it was clear that he had targeted me personally as the leader of the party. I was not the only member of the audience who felt that he had gone too far. Many of the other guests were also shocked. Mandela and I had greeted one another on his arrival. He was due to leave after his speech and offered his excuses for not being able to attend the banquet. As he left, I said to Pik Botha, who was standing beside me, that it would be better if I were to avoid Mandela, because I was angry and did not want to argue with him in front of the assembled guests. I accordingly withdrew to a corner, away from the route that Mandela would follow to his car. Brian Gilbertson, the managing director of Gencor, then came to me and told me that the President wanted to take his leave of me. I was very direct with him and said that I thought that it would be better if I did not say goodbye to the President and asked him to offer my excuses. The next moment a member of Mandela's staff came to me with a direct message that the President had requested to see me. Pik Botha and I walked across to where he was waiting on the sidewalk beside his car. Most of the other guests had already moved into the banquet. When we came together I told President Mandela that I was very upset. I said that I thought that he had made an unwarranted attack on me and the National Party at an unsuitable occasion. He had been invited to attend the function in his capacity as head of state and it was totally inappropriate for him to abuse the occasion with party-political attacks. Mandela also lost his temper and we ended up shaking our fingers at one another in a heated argument. Our altercation on the sidewalk was captured by a photographer and dominated the news the next day. That evening Mandela had shown a side of his character which indicated that he was, in fact, far more bitter than he had until then revealed.

33

The New Constitution, Withdrawal from the Government of National Unity, Opposition and Retirement

By this time it was clear to me that the Government of National Unity was not working. President Mandela clearly had no intention of allowing me and the National Party to play a constructive role. Our anomalous position within the GNU was also beginning to have a very negative effect on our party. Most of the members of our caucus and most of our grass-roots supporters wanted the party and its leaders to play a more vigorous and unambiguous opposition role. They were unhappy with the performance of National Party ministers in the GNU – who, they felt, were being dragooned into carrying out ANC policy. On the other hand, most of the ministers believed that the NP could continue to exert much more positive influence behind the scenes within the power structures of the GNU than they would be able to from the opposition benches. The reality was that, because of the lack of a proper coalition agreement, individual ministers had only a limited ability to determine policy, even within their own departments. Increasingly, it was their task simply to operate within the framework of the broad policies that had been dictated by the ANC majority.

I was deeply concerned by this problem. I had repeatedly urged our ministers and deputy ministers to play a more unambiguous and assertive role in the cabinet in support of National Party principles and policies. I had also encouraged them to brief the caucus properly on the background to our decisions to support particular legislation and the compromises that had been reached in the cabinet. Apart from their own portfolios, I divided the ANC portfolios between the NP ministers and deputy ministers and gave them special responsibility to deal with discussions relating to these portfolios in the cabinet and in subsequent caucus briefings. However, this system never worked particularly well. The ministers were, in general, too busy and had no real appetite to inform themselves in detail on portfolios other than their own. Perhaps most of them were too senior and had lost their hunger to accept additional responsibilities.

The growing internal tensions between the caucus and the ministers took their toll on me in the cabinet itself. Although there were some heartening exceptions, the majority of our ministers and the deputy ministers often failed to tackle the ANC as I would have wanted them to in the cabinet. They did well enough with regard to their own portfolios, but did not fare so well when it came to making a fighting stand against the ANC in opposing decisions which were irreconcilable with National Party policy. The result was that I quite often felt compelled to join the debate myself – sometimes even while I was acting as chairman of the cabinet – to confront the ANC on issues on which we disagreed. I believe that this role, that I so often had to play, was a major cause of the growing tension between myself and President Mandela and certain key ANC ministers. The ideal would have been for my ministers and deputy ministers to take the lead in confronting the ANC and that, I as executive deputy president and leader of the party, should then have played the role of peacemaker. Unfortunately, this happened rarely in practice. No doubt, some of the ministers whom I am now criticizing felt that I was sometimes too difficult and that I acted wrongly by so often making a stand.

I do not wish to detract from the good work that the National Party ministers and deputy ministers nevertheless did. But in retrospect I am sorry that I did not give younger and hungrier MPs a chance at an earlier stage to strengthen the National Party's opposition role in the cabinet.

On the party political front I, for some time, had felt that, after the realization of its vision of the democratic transformation of South Africa, the National Party should accept a new forward-looking vision – one that would be suited to the challenges of the new South Africa. On 2 February 1996 – exactly six years after my speech of 2 February 1990 – I spelled out such a vision. The occasion was the opening of the National Party's new headquarters in Pretoria. I said that we were confronted by two great questions: was the new South Africa going to establish a vital multiparty democracy or were we going to be caught in the trap of one-party domination? Were we going to be trapped in ethnic politics or were we going to establish a non-racial, value-driven party-political system? The vision that I spelled out for the party, after consultation with my colleagues, was that the National Party was going to play a leading role in the realignment of South African politics by bringing together a majority of all South Africans in a dynamic new political movement based on proven core values and Christian norms and standards.

I appointed Roelf Meyer – our chief constitutional negotiator – to take the lead in managing our initiatives to realize our new vision. He would be responsible for negotiations with other like-minded parties and groups with a view to forming a new, more broadly based opposition grouping which would be able to mount a formidable challenge to the ANC at the polls. I regarded his new function as being so important that Roelf Meyer resigned as minister of provincial affairs and constitutional development and took up a full-time position as secretary-general of the National Party – a new post that had been created especially for this purpose. Meyer's new position gave him an unprecedented status within the party – which soon resulted in his generally being regarded as the party's crown prince.

One of our main concerns since the elections was the negotiation of the final constitution, which had to be adopted within two years of the inauguration of the GNU – that is, before 10 May 1996. Our negotiating team succeeded in reaching successful compromises on a large number of contentious issues. However, in the closing stages of the negotiation process, we reached a deadlock on a small number of questions of fundamental importance. The most significant of these was the ANC's flat refusal to include any aspect of power-sharing at the executive level in the final constitution. The National Party had, since the inception of the negotiating process, attached the greatest importance to achieving consensus between the major political role players on key issues and had made this a central element in its undertakings to its own supporters. During the negotiations, we had made proposals that we felt would promote a spirit of consensus and joint decision-making, without, at the same time, granting inordinate influence or power to significant minority parties. We had finally suggested the establishment of a special consultative council which would be composed along similar lines to the GNU. The idea was that important minority parties should be able to participate in the con-sideration of a limited number of special issues, such as the preparation of the annual budget, foreign policy, matters of deep national interest, and any matters that might be of special concern to cultural minorities. We made it clear that this council would not be able to prescribe to the cabinet, but would serve as a vehicle to achieve consensus on issues of national importance and to lift them out of the confrontational party political arena. The ANC had rejected these proposals out of hand. I had warned President Mandela during the negotiating process that failure to include any such provision could lead to our withdrawal from the government. Mr Roelf Meyer had also conveyed the same message on a number of occasions to Cyril Ramaphosa.

We later learned from a number of sources that Mandela and the ANC believed that we were so attached to the status of our positions in the GNU and the accompanying privileges, that we would never leave the GNU. However, the fact is that their refusal to accommodate our modest proposal placed us in an untenable position. Our dilemma was further complicated by the fact that, while we could count on the support of the other minority parties on most of the other issues, none of them was prepared to cause a deadlock over the question of power-sharing at the executive level and the adoption of a consensus model. We would thus not be able to muster the required one-third support on this issue in Parliament.

There were also a whole number of other matters of key import-ance with which we wrestled right up to the end of the negotiations. On some of them – such as the death penalty – consensus was impossible. There was a fierce struggle over others, including the wording of the clause on the protection of private property; the definition of the rights of trade unions and employers in balance with one another; the powers and capacities of the provinces and the right to mother tongue education. The National Party sought the co-operation of the smaller minority parties on these issues and we went to a great deal of trouble to consult interest groups from the private sector and professional organizations in our preparations for the negotiations. We ultimately agreed to compromises on all these important issues, which, although not entirely satisfactory, neverthe-less enjoyed the support of key figures and spokesmen from the private sector, teachers' organizations, the agricultural community and employers' organizations.

On 5 May 1996, only three days before the constitution was due to be adopted, we were still unsure whether we would vote in favour of it. The Executive Committee of the Federal Council of the National Party met the next morning, 6 May, to consider our position and to determine our strategy. We decided that, despite our dissatisfaction with a number of important clauses, we would not vote against the new constitution. We did not want to subject the country to the trauma of holding a national referendum to break the deadlock, nor did we want to run the risk of unravelling the many positive aspects that we had negotiated in the final constitution. We decided instead to convene a special meeting of our Federal Council to consider the impact of the new constitution on our future strategies – and in, particular, our future involvement in the GNU.

The new constitution was duly adopted on 8 May. When my turn came to speak in Parliament I rose and explained our reasons for voting in favour of it. I expressed our deep reservations regarding some aspects, particularly the absence of any provision for future power-sharing and consensus-seeking at the executive level. I also mentioned, almost in passing, that the Federal Council would be meeting the following week to consider our position in the GNU.

The media immediately seized on this aspect of my speech and speculated, quite correctly, that the Federal Council would consider withdrawing the National Party from the Government of National Unity. My speech had been made late that morning. Only a few hours later, while Dave Steward, Frik Schoombee – my media secretary – and Noël Basson, my private secretary, were having lunch at a nearby restaurant, their cell phones were almost jammed by incoming calls from the national and international media asking for clarifications and statements. There were also quite a few anxious calls from the Johannesburg Stock Exchange. While they had been having their lunch the value of the rand had tumbled several cents.

I realized that I had a responsibility to minimize any damage to our economy. Clearly, we could not wait until the following week before clarifying our position on the GNU. After consulting with senior members of the party that afternoon, I convened a meeting of the smaller Federal Executive Committee of the National Party the next morning.

When the meeting began there was an almost tangible tension in the air. I knew that there were strongly divergent views on the question of our continued role within the Government of National Unity. One group was convinced that the time had arrived for us to leave the GNU. The other felt very strongly that we should not leave. I made it clear from the outset that I would be open to arguments from all sides, but that my own basic feeling was that we could not simply go on and that we would have to give serious consideration to withdrawal. One by one, I asked everyone around the table to give their views. The strongest supporters of continued participation were Pik Botha, Roelf Meyer and Chris Fismer. Dawie de Villiers, on the other hand, was in favour of withdrawal. His position was not a surprise to me but it clearly was to many of the others around the table. As soon as it became clear that the meeting was deeply divided, those who were in favour of our staying in the GNU tried to find a compromise. They suggested that we should stay on provisionally and then consider withdrawing about a year before the election.

After everyone around the table had had an opportunity of stating their views, I summed up the discussion and clearly stated my own position. I said that we owed it to the country not to behave in an opportunistic manner on this important issue. I totally rejected the idea of staying on and then later withdrawing because such a decision would not be based on principle. We would not be able to link later withdrawal to the fact that the new constitution did not contain any form of power-sharing at the executive level. It would mean that we would have to manufacture an incident ourselves, if one did not arise, to justify our withdrawal and might lead to our walking out of the GNU in a destructive and unworthy manner. Such a step might cause the country serious damage. The choice, I said, was thus between staying on until the 1999 election or withdrawing immediately on principled grounds and with as little drama as possible. I expressed myself clearly in favour of immediate withdrawal and of justifying our decision on the basis of the new constitution, the necessity of developing our opposition role and the interests of the party with regard to the 1999 election. I concluded by saying that I did not wish to inhibit the meeting and that it was free to vote on the question. However, they would have to bear in mind that I had decided, in my individual capacity, to resign as executive deputy president to enable myself to lead the party from the opposition benches in Parliament. I thus gave them the option of taking a decision that the National Party should remain in the government, and choose someone else to act as executive deputy president while I continued to lead the party from outside of the government.

For a moment a deathly silence descended on the meeting. Then Pik Botha said that if that was my view then there was no further argument and we should leave the GNU. This concluded the matter – but it was to have far-reaching repercussions. Chris Fismer was deeply unhappy, and despite my efforts and those of others to dissuade him, he announced his retirement from politics. Shortly afterwards Pik

Botha followed the same route – and one year later Dawie de Villiers. In this manner, our decision to withdraw from the GNU also resulted in the renewal and rejuvenation of the National Party.

After briefing the caucus – most of whom strongly supported our decision – I held an international press conference. I confirmed that we had decided to withdraw from the GNU with effect from the end of the following month. I explained that our decision should be seen as an important step in the growing maturity and normalization of our young democracy and that it should in no way be interpreted as a lack of confidence in the new South Africa. I said that we believed that the development of a strong and vigilant opposition was essential for the maintenance and promotion of a genuine multiparty democracy. Since the new constitution did not provide for the continuation of any form of joint decision-making in the executive branch of government, we had decided that the time had come for us to play our full role as the main opposition party. I added that our continued participation in the GNU had also become an obstacle to the realization of the new vision that our party adopted on 2 February 1996. My statement did much to restore confidence and the value of the rand strengthened. Once again it showed the importance of clear and timely communication.

*

So at the end of June 1996 – after almost eighteen years in the cabinet – I left the government. I found it, personally, quite difficult to adapt to my new role as full-time leader of the opposition. From 1978 until 1996 I had been a member of the government. I had been able to make a direct contribution because I was deeply involved in the formulation of policies and in a position to ensure that they were implemented. It was very difficult for me suddenly to have to make Parliament my main focus again with very little real ability to influence policy other than through debates inside, and outside, Parliament. I still found my task of promoting the National Party's interests at political meetings and through contact with the public both challenging and enjoyable. But I had lost my appetite for the infighting in Parliament and for the often futile debates. The ANC government developed a style of showing little respect to Parliament and even less to the opposition. Whenever our darts struck home, they fell back on the strategy of accusing us of being racists and of wanting to return to apartheid. It was becoming difficult for me to motivate myself and I quickly realized that I no longer had sufficient enthusiasm for the role that the leader of the official opposition had to play in Parliament.

The main political crisis with which I had to deal during the last years of my political career did not relate to developments outside the party, but to tensions that had begun to develop within our own ranks regarding the manner in which the party should pursue its new vision of transforming itself and playing a leading role in the creation of a new broadly based movement. Roelf Meyer, who was given responsibility for driving and developing the initiative, began to move further and further away from the rest of the party in the manner in which he sought to achieve our vision. Ultimately, it became clear that he actually favoured the early dismantling of the party before 1999 and its replacement by a new party. He advocated this irrespective of the fact that he had not succeeded in producing acceptable partners who would be willing to join us in the formation of such a new party. In a sense he wanted the National Party to dissolve without knowing what we would get in return. The great majority of the party leaders – including myself – rejected this notion. After a number of Executive Committee meetings at which harsh words were exchanged, I made it clear that our first objective was a new political movement of which the National Party would be part, but with the retention of its identity. I also stressed that from that could naturally grow a new party as a second step, which could then at a later stage result in the dissolution of the National Party as such.

Meyer ostensibly accepted this, but continued to cause tension. It was clear to me that he was leading up to a serious split in the party and that I would have to stop him from doing so. I stripped him of his special role and disbanded the committee which had assisted him. I urged him to remain in the party and continue to work with the rest of us in our efforts to build a more broadly based and dynamic opposition grouping. But I was not surprised when he informed me of his decision to resign from the party and when he later decided to create the United Democratic Movement, together with Bantu Holomisa, the former military ruler of the Transkei. Holomisa had also fallen foul of his former party, the ANC, because of his populist views and attacks on the integrity of his leaders. Meyer and Holomisa made a very odd couple.

Meyer's departure sent shockwaves through the National Party, but the damage was much less than it would have been in a later serious split. After I had restored a reasonable degree of unity within the party, I decided that the time had come for me to announce my retirement from active politics. I did so on 26 August 1997. I had, for some time, been resolved not to remain in politics after the next election in 1999. I felt that the National Party should fight the election campaign under a new leader and that the new leader should be given adequate time to establish his position in the party, the country and in Parliament. I emphasized that it was clear to me that our opponents would continue to campaign against the National Party on the basis of the apartheid baggage of the past. Despite the role that I had played in the transformation of South Africa, the ANC and other parties would continue to make me a symbol of the National Party's apartheid past on the basis of my long service in consecutive governments. I believed that by resigning I would enable the National Party to further change its image and to switch the debate away from the past to the pressing issues of the present and the future. I also hold the view that in any party or business there should be regular renewal in the top management. I felt that after eight and a half years as leader of the National Party – and after I had achieved the main goals that I had set for myself at the beginning of my term of office – the time had come for me to step down.

After I had made my announcement, I paid a courtesy call on President Mandela at his home in the exclusive suburb of Houghton in Johannesburg. He received me with warmth and courtesy. As we drank coffee, we discussed some of the problems that faced the country. I urged him to use his still great influence to counteract the hardening of racial attitudes. It was as if we again had something in common. I had retired. He had already announced that he would retire as president of the ANC at the end of 1997 and as president of South Africa after the next national election in 1999. Both of us were on our way out. Our meeting went well, without the rancour that had characterized so many of our other encounters. I still wonder to what extent the strains in our relationship were caused by the fact that we were political opponents; to what extent they were based on misunderstandings or on genuine antipathies. I would like to think that, in our retirement, in some way or other we will be able to work together as elder statesmen to nurture and protect the young democracy which both of us had the privilege of helping to create. And so, after twenty-six years, I left active politics. I was soon replaced as leader of the National Party by one of our brightest and most articulate young stars – Marthinus van

Schalkwyk. He was only thirty-seven years old. The baton had been passed on to a new generation of leaders, unencumbered by the baggage of the past.

*

My retirement from politics was, however, not the only major change in my personal circumstances. I also arrived at a crossroads in my personal life. My marriage was in a crisis. After many years of, first, denying it to myself and then later fighting against it, I had reached a stage where I had to do something.

It will serve no purpose to dwell on the nature of and the reasons for the stresses and strains in my marriage which had developed since the middle eighties. The fact is that they were there and that I then met and fell in love with Elita Georgiadis.

I met Elita together with her husband Tony in 1989 in London. Dawie de Villiers, who had become friends with them while he served as ambassador in London, arranged the meeting. The De Klerks and the Georgiadises soon became good friends. We saw one another regularly; we stayed over in one another's homes; we spent weekends and later a longer yachting holiday in Greece together. Elita attracted me right from our first meeting. She was not only beautiful, but also had a sparkling personality. We found that we had much in common, notwithstanding the difference in our cultural backgrounds. Before long, we became involved in animated discussions. Slowly but surely I felt myself increasingly drawn to her. She later told me that she had the same experience. But neither of us gave any indication to the other of this growing attraction.

At first I struggled against my feelings and tried to suppress my emotions. I did not want what was happening. I tried very hard to apply the mind over matter rule which I had used relatively successfully throughout my life. But it was to no avail. For once in my life my heart took control.

By October 1993 I could no longer suppress my inner feelings. With trepidation, because of the potentially enormous consequences, I created an opportunity to openly discuss what was happening between us with Elita. It ended with both of us admitting the strong attraction that had developed between us. We were simultaneously elated and apprehensive.

From then onward our relationship developed fairly rapidly. By the end of July 1994 at the end of the yachting holiday in Greece both of us realized that we had reached a crossroads. We could no longer hide our feelings, from each other or from our spouses, and realized that the situation as it was could not continue. Something had to happen. We parted on that note. Marike and I returned to South Africa and in due course Elita and Tony returned to England. We would meet again towards the end of August when she and Tony would be our guests for a weekend at Lekkerwater.

On the morning of their arrival in Cape Town, Tony came to see me. He informed me that he had become aware of the love between me and Elita. A painful yet friendly and civilized discussion followed. I had great respect for the dignified way in which he dealt with a very difficult situation. I was also open and direct and did not try to hide my feelings. Later that day I met Elita with the knowledge of her husband. After a long discussion we decided to end our relationship and to try to save our marriages. It was one of the most painful decisions that I have ever taken.

I went home and confided in Marike who was deeply shocked. However, she rallied valiantly and I have the greatest respect for the way in which she handled an extremely difficult situation.

For the next two years Elita and I broke off all communication. I really tried to forget her, to make amends to my wife and family and to put my marriage back on track. So did Elita. In the end we failed; what had grown between us was too strong. Towards the end of 1996 I initiated the resumption of our relationship.

Finally, Elita and I came to the conclusion that we could not continue living a lie. We could no longer bear the ignobility of conducting a clandestine relationship with all the attendant deceit and subterfuge. We discussed our predicament and decided to inform Tony and Marike of our situation, of our continuing love for one another and of our need to have time to sort things out. We also agreed to give each other space. Should either of us decide to turn back in an effort to save our marriages, the other would accept and respect the decision. However, neither of us could bear the thought of breaking up again. We were deeply in love and strongly committed to each other.

In my case, I confided in Marike at the end of November 1997. We separated on 19 February 1998 after months of painful discussions and honest interaction with each other and also with our children. At the end of April I initiated divorce proceedings in the face of Marike's efforts to persuade me to turn back. Once again it was one of the most painful decisions I have ever taken.

I accept my full part of the blame for the breakdown of our marriage. We had a good marriage for many, many years. I loved Marike and retain the highest regard for her. She was a good wife and mother as well as a loyal partner. She and our children made tremendous sacrifices for which I will forever remain indebted to them. And I am deeply sorry for my role in the hurt and pain that all of us have had to endure.

In addition, I had to consider my responsibility to my church, party and society. There were tremendous – and mostly well intended – pressures on me to turn back. Friends in my church appealed to me to take a moral stand akin to the political stand that I had taken on 2 February 1990. Powerful religious, political, moral and personal arguments were advanced – all of them related to my religion, place in history and the fact that I had become an important role model in more than just politics.

I had struggled with all these arguments within myself long before anybody else knew about my love for Elita. In the end I came to the conclusion that I had to make a choice. What had occurred by then I could not undo. There was also a new reality in my life that I could not and did not want to alter – the reality of the strong, deep and multi-faceted love that had grown between Elita and me.

I had to choose between moving forward on the basis of the truth of my love for Elita or backward to living a lie behind a façade of conventional respectability. I chose to move forward, to accept public exposure, censure and humiliation – and to seek God's forgiveness and that of all those affected.

My decision was exacerbated by my high political profile. From the moment that the news leaked out in January 1998, the media mercilessly hounded all of us – Elita and me, Marike and Tony. Particularly Marike and I were forced to deal publicly with our emotions, our attitudes and decisions. Marike chose to do so fairly extensively. I preferred to say the minimum.

My relationship with Elita did not impact in any significant way on the major decisions I took during my term of office as president or deputy president. The transitional constitution was finalized before my involvement with Elita gathered momentum. The final constitution was negotiated and adopted during the period when I had no contact with Elita. The same is true of the National Party's decision to leave the Government of National Unity which followed within days. Even my decision to retire from politics, which I announced in August 1997, was not directly related to my personal life. For all the reasons I then advanced, I would have retired in any event irrespective of my relationship with Elita. However, because I was fully aware that my relationship with Elita was likely to develop further, I included personal reasons in my statement.

Throughout my political career I sincerely tried to separate my personal problems from my political responsibilities. I always tried to put the cause first and subordinate my own personal interests. However, public figures are also human beings and are subject to the same crises in their intimate relationships as other people. I pray that history will judge me kindly in this respect.

34

Truth and Reconciliation

One of my main concerns during my last years in public life was the increasingly controversial role of the Truth and Reconciliation Commission.

I was originally in favour of the establishment of an appropriate process to deal with the conflict of our past. I believed – and still believe – that South Africans should come to terms with our troubled history. I never thought that it would be possible to achieve complete consensus on the past – our basic points of departure were simply too different. What I thought was necessary and possible would be to find some basis to put an end to the destructive and aggressive debates and recriminations about the past. We needed a mechanism which would prevent endless witch hunts; which could promote mutual understanding of one another's motives; which could close the book on the past. We needed reconciliation and mutual forgiveness to be able to make a new start with a reasonably clean slate. The essence of our approach was to establish the truth with a view to such reconciliation and not as the basis for further recrimination, demonization and persecution.

We were, however, shocked by the nature of the ANC's proposals for the Truth and Reconciliation Commission which the minister of justice tabled at the end of July 1994. The ANC wanted the TRC to have draconian powers, including powers of arbitrary search and seizure of private documents. Those who would be called before the commission could be forced to give incriminating testimony against themselves. Unlike most similar commissions in other parts of the world, testimony would be heard in public and hearings would be open to the media. The commission would not function as a court – so those who were called to appear before it would have no recourse to due legal process. In addition to all this, the ANC proposed two different tests for amnesty – a very easy one for those who had been opposed to the government and a much more stringent one for members of the security forces.

There was no way in which the National Party could accept the

ANC's original proposals for the TRC. I immediately appointed a team of National Party MPs with legal backgrounds, under the leadership of Danie Schutte, to negotiate with the ANC behind the scenes regarding our objections to the draft legislation. Chris Fismer also played a prominent role in this process. In the course of the tough negotiations that ensued we proposed alternatives to all those aspects of the legislation to which we objected. After a hard struggle, and heated debates in the cabinet during which I was sometimes involved in head-on confrontations with the minister of justice, Mr Dullah Omar, and with President Mandela himself, we finally came up with draft legislation with which we could live. All the serious shortcomings were addressed, either by amending or scrapping the formulations to which we had objected. Apart from a number of general improvements, the final product placed far greater accent on reconciliation; it included a test for amnesty which was equally applicable to all sides; it greatly limited the powers of the commission by comparison with the original proposal; it enhanced the rights of witnesses and imposed an obligation on the commission to provide advance notice to people who might be implicated in hearings.

Clearly, one of the main factors that would determine the success of the TRC would be the impartiality of its members. The TRC Act made provision for a special panel which would nominate a list of twenty-five candidates from which the president would appoint the seventeen commissioners, in consultation with the cabinet. The president was also required to consult me. I was deeply concerned when I was shown the list. I had considerable respect for Archbishop Desmond Tutu whom President Mandela wished to appoint as chairperson. The diminutive prelate, with his impish wit and brush of grey hair, had proved his integrity and independence on a number of occasions. However, he could hardly be regarded as impartial or as having a low political profile as the Act required. The archbishop made no pretence of being unbiased when it came to the conflict of the past – much of his own career had, after all, been dedicated to opposing the former government. I nevertheless decided that we could live with him.

I had more serious reservations regarding the proposed vice-chairperson, Dr Alex Boraine. Dr Boraine, a tall man with sandy grey hair and a florid complexion, was a former Methodist minister who had for many years been a leading member of the liberal Progressive Federal Party and its predecessors. He had left Parliament some years earlier to join the Institute for a Democratic South Africa – an organization established in the late eighties to promote the democratic transformation of South Africa. He had then established his own organization, Justice in Transition, specifically to make proposals regarding the manner in which South Africa should come to terms with its own past. He studied the reconciliation experiences of other divided societies and developed his own unambiguous ideas on the subject. He even began to draw up his own database of people who, in the South African context, had been guilty of gross violations of human rights. It was clear from Boraine's writings that he viewed the complex human saga of South Africa in the starkest black and white terms. Beneath an urbane and deceptively affable exterior beat the heart of a zealot and an inquisitor.

On perusing President Mandela's list, I was further shocked to note that it did not contain a single National Party member. It included Mr Chris de Jager, a former member of Parliament of the Afrikaner Volksunie (who subsequently resigned from the commission) and Wynand Malan, who had left the National Party several years earlier to help found the Democratic Party. One of the main reasons for the relative success of the Chilean Truth Commission had been that it had comprised an equal number of representatives from the old and new orders. As a result, its report represented a shared truth that was broadly acceptable to most sections of the Chilean political spectrum and its findings could make a genuine contribution to national reconciliation. It seemed most unlikely that President Mandela's commission would be able to achieve a similar result in South Africa.

Together with Danie Schutte and a number of key people in the party, I analysed the list and prepared alternative proposals. I realized that any attempt to reject the list in its totality would simply result in all our recommendations being ignored. Despite my serious misgivings about many of the nominations, I decided to request that only a limited number of names be scrapped and replaced by people whom I thought would at least be able to ensure a modicum of balance in the commission. When I went to discuss the list with President Mandela, I found that he was not in a mood for negotiation. Early in our discussion, he said that the list also contained names which he did not like at all, and that if I insisted on the removal of some names, he would also insist on the removal of others. The implication was that he would ensure that the TRC's composition would be even more unbalanced than it already was. He had already made up his mind. I told him that I had taken note of his attitude and suggested that we end our discussion so that I could consult my advisers.

After intensive consultation, I informed President Mandela that the National Party and I could not accept his list as it was. If he kept it as it was, it would be his commission and would not enjoy the support of the National Party. I also reserved my and the National Party's right to criticize the composition of the commission and its members.

Despite my growing misgivings, I decided to give the commission my full co-operation. When the commission subsequently approached me for information on the activities of the Kahn Committee – one of the organs that I had appointed to vet the government's secret projects during my presidency – I had a special report prepared, at the expense of the National Party, containing all the information that they had requested.

While I was still executive deputy president, a group of generals from the former security forces suggested to me that all the parties that had been involved in the past conflict should assist the commission by preparing detailed statements on their involvement in the struggle. General Johan van der Merwe, the former commissioner of the South African police, was the spokesman of the group, which also included other former commissioners and chiefs of the South African Defence Force. They suggested that all the parties involved in the struggle should consult on the form in which they would prepare and present their submissions. They thought that this would facilitate the TRC's task and reduce the likelihood that parties would simply use their submissions to attack one another. Part of their proposal was that the submissions and investigations should be limited to an agreed list of incidents, since they foresaw that the commission would never be able to deal with all the potential incidents in the limited period that it had at its disposal. Finally, they proposed that an inter-party committee should liaise with the commission on a day-to-day basis. I arranged a meeting between myself, Deputy President Mbeki and the generals to discuss their proposals. Mbeki and I then organized a multiparty meeting at Tuynhuys of all the parliamentary parties which had a direct interest in the TRC, which was also attended by Mangosuthu Buthelezi, Constand Viljoen and Clarence Mkwetu (from the PAC). We reached broad consensus that there was some merit in the generals' proposal, and after consultation with our parties, Mbeki and I discussed their initiative with Archbishop Tutu and Dr Boraine. However, they were opposed to anything that might be construed as a limitation of the scope of their investigation and also to the idea of liaising with an inter-party committee. However, they accepted the suggestion that all the parties should be given an opportunity of making initial submissions to the commission which could serve as departure points for the commission's investigations.

I also took the initiative in seeing whether we could prepare a common submission on behalf of the former government and security forces. After a few meetings, it became clear that the police and the Defence Force from the former era were uncomfortable about the explanations and motivations of political policies that such a submission would have to include. They said that they were apolitical and wished to be seen as such. We agreed that the National Party would draw up its own submission and make it available to them, but that they would prepare their own separate submissions from the non-party political perspectives of the former Defence Force and police.

I furthermore wanted to involve P. W. Botha in the preparation of the National Party's submission. I felt that he could, in particular, make critically important contributions about his own presidency. I flew to the southern Cape to see him at his lagoon-side home at the Wilderness. He received me politely but coolly and took me to his study. I noticed that there was a pile of books on his desk with bookmarkers at various places. I explained that we were preparing our submission for the TRC and wanted to offer him the opportunity of working with us – particularly because the submission would also cover the period when he had acted as minister of defence, as prime minister and as state president. At that point we were served *koeksusters* (traditional Afrikaans treacle pastries), snacks and coffee. His reaction was totally dismissive. He did not want to have anything to do with the commission and had no interest whatsoever in co-operating with the National Party and me. He accused me, by implication, of not having stood by the security forces. He then immediately changed the subject and said that there was something else that he wished to discuss with me, namely, what he called my membership of the New World Order. He picked up some of the books on his desk and began to read me passages, here and there, to the effect that there was an evil conspiracy in the world called the New World Order. He said that Pik Botha was a member of this conspiracy and that I had allowed him to manipulate me into joining it as well. He then referred to the joint press conference that I had held with President Bush in the rose garden of the White House during my official visit to the United States in 1990 while I was state president. He said that when we had announced the new spirit of co-operation between the United States and South Africa which had flowed from our discussions, I had been bound into this evil conspiracy by President Bush who, according to him, was a leading figure in the New World Order. Botha then began to pepper me with aggressive questions. I became extremely annoyed and told him that I had not come to visit him to be insulted and cross-examined. I said that he had really treated me very badly and that I saw no sense in continuing with our discussion. Without becoming involved in a lengthy argument, I strongly rejected his ludicrous allegations about the New World Order. Suddenly, his attitude changed and he looked taken aback. He said that it was unfair of me to say that I had been treated badly, after all, his wife had given me coffee and *koeksusters*. I almost fell off my chair. I stood up and said that I now had to go. He called out to his wife to join us and once again said, 'Mamma, Mr De Klerk says that we have treated him badly, and didn't we give him coffee and *koeksusters*.' I left him with two emotions – concern and anger over his insults, but also pity for a sick old man.

I presented the National Party's first submission to the TRC in Cape Town on 21 August 1996. In it I tried to explain the central role that the struggle for national self-determination had played in the history of the Afrikaner people. I set out the historic changes through which the National Party had gone during the preceding fifty years – from being the party that established apartheid, to the party that finally dismantled it. I described our perception of the nature of the conflict and made suggestions regarding criteria that should be adopted in assessing responsibility for the actions that had taken place during the struggle. I accepted overall responsibility for the period of my leadership and, together with the cabinet and the State Security Council, accepted joint responsibility for all the decisions that we took and the instructions that we gave, including all authorized actions and operations executed in terms of a reasonable interpretation of such instructions. I also reiterated the public apology that I had already made for the pain and suffering caused by the former policies of the National Party. I noted that my apology had been accepted and publicly acknowledged by the chairperson of the commission, Archbishop Tutu. My submission appeared to be quite well received by the commission.

My first serious problem with the TRC arose on 16 January 1997.

Even though I had been co-operating fully with the TRC and was in regular contact with them, Dr Boraine saw fit to hold a press conference, without giving me any prior notice, to issue a statement which called into question my integrity regarding the manner in which I had dealt with the findings of General Pierre Steyn at the end of 1992. Almost triumphally, the commission claimed that General Steyn had presented me with a written report, and not a verbal one, as I had repeatedly stated. (When I later checked this with General Steyn, he denied that he had ever told the commission this.) The commission went on to criticize the manner in which I had dealt with the crisis, claiming that I had acted precipitately in taking action against officers whose names had been mentioned by General Steyn and that I had not given Steyn's subsequent investigations sufficient support.

I immediately refuted these allegations. I repeated that General Steyn had given me an oral briefing, during which he had shown me a staff report addressed to him, which he had taken with him at the end of the briefing. Frankly, it would have made no difference whether or not he had given me a written report. The only relevance of this question was that I had truthfully stated in Parliament that he had not done so and that I was not in possession of such a report. I also listed the instructions that I had given for the further investigation of General Steyn's allegations. I said that the fact that neither General Steyn, nor the attorneys-general, nor the Goldstone Commission, nor the South African police had been able to find further evidence that would lead to prosecutions was highly unsatisfactory and frustrating, not only for General Steyn but also for myself.

The real relevance of Boraine's statement was that I had evidently become a target of the commission. In subsequent correspondence, Dr Boraine expressed his sincere dismay at any impression I may have gained that 'the press conference we held was an attempt to discredit yourself or the National Party'. His statement was a little disingenuous in the light of the critical tone of his press statement and the ensuing media headlines proclaiming that 'F.W. might have been involved in a cover-up' and 'De Klerk ignored recommendations to probe generals'.

In the meantime, I had been preparing my second submission to the TRC in response to a long list of increasingly hostile questions from the commission. I sent the submission to the TRC toward the end of March 1997 and at the same time released it to the media. I said that the National Party was deeply concerned that the commission was losing its credibility among a large majority of NP members. This was due to perceptions that the TRC's composition was hopelessly one-sided; that its hearings were beginning to create a skewed perception of the conflict; and that it was becoming increasingly involved in the domestic party political process.

I said that this situation had arisen because of the basically flawed nature of the commission's mandate and composition and warned that immense resentment would be aroused if the commission applied a harsher standard in granting amnesty to applicants from the security forces than had been applied to the hundreds of members of the ANC who had been granted indemnity by the former government under the Further Indemnity Act of 1992.

I added that the overwhelming majority of NP members had also been shocked by the revelations of human rights abuses committed by some elements within the security forces during the conflict. They also want to know who was responsible for the abuses; how they could have happened and why they were not detected long before their public exposure.

In reply to written questions from the commission, I rejected the contention that one side had been morally superior to the other during the conflict. I said that those who fought on the government side were motivated by a number of factors, including their wish to maintain their right to national self-determination; their commitment to resist the expansion of global Communism; and their duty to defend individuals and the state and to uphold law and order. All these factors were legitimate and had nothing to do with racism or apartheid per se.

I repeated my view that the ANC's armed struggle had been unnecessary and counter-productive. Although I could understand the motivation of those who took up arms, there was a very real question as to whether this was an effective or correct option. Undoubtedly, it had contributed to the spiral of violence and to the intensity of the conflict. It was a great pity that the ANC and its allies had opposed all the reform measures that the government had adopted from the end of the 1970s. (In fact, they stepped up their armed struggle after the National Party had already accepted its new vision of a united South Africa with one-man, one-vote.) In response to another question, I said that I had no intention of providing a moral defence of apartheid. My own presidency had been dedicated primarily to continuing the abolition of apartheid and to the democratic transformation of South Africa.

During its hearings the TRC successfully uncovered many of the brutal deeds that had been perpetrated during the conflict. Most of the revelations related to abuses committed by the security forces, although some hearings – such as those that dealt with Winnie Madikizela Mandela and the Mandela United Football Club – also examined the actions of revolutionary movements and opponents of the government. However, the TRC pursued its investigations of gross violations of human rights perpetrated by the security forces with a vigour and zeal that was quite lacking in its investigations of necklace murders, black on black violence, and the assassination of members of the IFP. The commission's hearings on incidents involving the security forces far outnumbered the hearings relating to those who had suffered at the hands of the revolutionary movements – and received much wider media coverage.

The hearings often had a cathartic effect. Nobody who listened to them could fail to be moved by the testimony of people who had been abused or tortured or of families who had lost a son, a daughter, a brother, a sister, a husband or a wife. Neither could anyone fail to be shocked by the testimony of perpetrators who often, in subdued tones, described in matter-of-fact terms how they had tortured and murdered their victims. These hearings certainly had a therapeutic effect on many of those involved, perpetrators and victims alike. In some cases they led to genuine reconciliation between victims and perpetrators.

The fact that the hearings were widely covered by TV, radio and the press, in my opinion, had a less healthy influence. The coverage given to the disproportionate number of hearings relating to security force victims created the impression that the security forces – and not the revolutionary movements themselves – had been responsible for the great majority of deaths and gross violations of human rights. Many whites, and particularly Afrikaners, were ashamed and confused by what they witnessed. The mass communication of the hearings created an unhealthy self-image among many whites, and particularly among many Afrikaners. Among many black South Africans I believe that it probably created feelings of anger and stirred sentiments for revenge. Neither of these emotions would be conducive to healthy national reconciliation.

The mass coverage of the hearings did not contribute to the balance or perspective so necessary for a genuine attempt to find the truth. Without wishing to detract in any way from the enormity of the suffering that occurred, the fact remains that South Africa emerged from its transition with much less loss of life than has been the case in most other divided societies that have undergone radical transformation. According to our assessment, only a relatively small portion of the approximately 22,000 people who died in political violence were killed by the security forces. Only a small number of whites were involved, or even aware of, gross violations of human rights – but nevertheless the perception was often that the whole community was being placed collectively in the dock.

The state-controlled SABC let no opportunity slip by to put its particular spin on the testimony of security force victims. Security force perpetrators were almost invariably identified with the National Party, regardless of what their personal party affiliation might have been. This continuous stream of vilification had an extremely negative effect on the image of the new National Party – despite the fact that the party's policy, leadership and composition had changed diametrically since the conflict of the eighties when most of the abuses had been perpetrated. The ANC did not hesitate to exploit the anti-National Party atmosphere created by the TRC hearings for its own party-political advantage. Willingly or unwillingly, the TRC process had become a significant and contentious factor in the democratic political process – to the considerable detriment of a legitimate non-racial political party.

On 14 May I was invited to attend TRC hearings in Cape Town at which, I was led to believe, the commission would seek further elucidation on the written replies that I had given them in my second submission. The hearings were held in a rather cramped conference room in the TRC headquarters. The room was packed with representatives of the media, my supporters and the public. My advisers sat with me at a narrow table facing the commission. Archbishop Tutu acted as the chairperson and was accompanied by Dr Alex Boraine, a number of other commissioners and Advocate Glen Goosen who, as it turned out, had been chosen to play the role of chief inquisitor.

I began my presentation with a brief statement in which I sought to clarify a number of key points. I repeated, in more impassioned terms than ever before, my apology for apartheid.

I said that apartheid was wrong. On my own behalf and on behalf of the National Party I apologized to the millions of South Africans who had suffered the wrenching disruption of being arbitrarily deprived of their homes, businesses and land because of forced removals; who over the years, had suffered the shame of being arrested for pass law offences; who over the decades – and indeed, centuries –

suffered the indignities and humiliation of racial discrimination; who were prevented from exercising their full democratic rights in the land of their birth; who were unable to achieve their full potential because of job reservation; and who received inadequate and unequal social, medical and educational services.

The second point that I made was that since the National Party's reform policies began – at first tentatively, and later with increasing boldness and vigour – we had been part of the solution, and not part of the problem. The new South Africa was just as much our creation as it was the creation of any other party. We refused to allow any party or any organ to deprive us of our rightful place in our new society.

I said that we, like the ANC and all the other parties of South Africa, were the product of a complex and tormented history. We did not regard ourselves as being morally superior – or inferior – to any other party. The glory of the past seven years had been that, together, we had been able to overcome the divisions and bitterness of our history and, together, we had been able to create the basis for a better and more peaceful future for all our people.

It was soon clear that the TRC had little interest in such sentiments. It had already determined its agenda – and its agenda was to discredit and humiliate me.

As soon as I had completed my introductory statement the TRC slapped a 90-page document in front of me containing a bewildering array of papers and correspondence, most of which I had never seen before. I had been given no prior opportunity to study the document – and yet I was expected to reply to hostile questions based on the document while the TV cameras were broadcasting the proceedings live. Advocate Goosen began to question me on my opinion of whether various gross violations perpetrated by the security forces had been authorized or not. He expected me to make judgements on the spur of the moment based simply on his version of the facts. We objected to this procedure and demanded that the chairperson allow us to study the document thoroughly before I replied to questions relating to its contents. After a number of appeals, Archbishop Tutu accepted our request and instructed Advocate Goosen to conduct his cross-examination accordingly. Advocate Goosen nevertheless continued quite unabashed with his line of attack. At one stage, I told the TRC that General Van der Merwe had assured me that he did not know of the real nature of the operations of the notorious Vlakplaas

Unit. Goosen then incorrectly stated that General Van der Merwe had, himself, applied for amnesty in respect of the deeds of which I was saying he had no knowledge. I was astounded and refused to accept Goosen's version. I subsequently was informed by General Van der Merwe that Goosen's allegation was indeed untrue, that my version was correct and that he had written to the TRC to that effect.

It soon became clear from Goosen's questions that the purpose of the hearings was not to discuss my second submission at all, but to try to harry me into admitting that the former government and I had been involved in authorizing gross violations of human rights. The TRC's case centred on a discussion that took place in the State Security Council on 12 May 1986 during which the establishment of a 'third force' was discussed. The question had been whether we, like many other countries, should create a paramilitary third force – between the Defence Force and the police – to deal with riot control, the maintenance of public order and revolutionary threats. The discussion was introduced by a memorandum drawn up by the SADF on the pros and cons of such a force, based on the experience of a number of Western democracies. The memorandum was, in fact, completely innocuous. There was no question of a sinister underground third force. At issue was a proposal for the creation of an overt specialist paramilitary force, alongside the two other forces, the SADF and the South African police.

The TRC based its case that the State Security Council had issued instructions to security forces to commit atrocities on statements that President P. W. Botha had made during the discussion, that

> The Third Force must be mobile and must have a well-trained ability to wipe out terrorists ... It must be prepared to be unpopular and even to be feared ... and the security forces must co-operate in the establishment of the Third Force so that the subversives could be engaged by using their own methods ...

Botha's words were robust – as could be expected from a leader confronted with a bitter revolutionary struggle. However, they could not, in my opinion, in any way be interpreted as authorizing the security forces to assassinate or murder its opponents. Under certain operational circumstances, the security forces were legally empowered to use force against terrorists and, in legally defined situations, to kill them. After all, the ANC had declared war against the state and had sent heavily armed terrorists into the country, often with orders to kill members of the security forces. Ironically, the minutes of the following meeting of the State Security Council reveal that the council, in any event, did not approve the recommendations in the memorandum.

Regardless of what the security forces were later revealed to have done, I certainly did not interpret Botha's words as authorizing illegal action. If I had I, and other members of the State Security Council, would have objected. In fact, I had completely forgotten about this particular discussion until it was brought to my attention eleven years later. This single reference was apparently all the TRC could come up with, after poring for months over all the cabinet and State Security Council documents in their possession, to support the contention that these bodies had authorized gross violations of human rights. One wonders what they would have discovered had they had similar access to all the innermost documents of the ANC and its allies. In any event, the decision ultimately taken by the State Security Council was that such a third force should not be established, and that the SADF and the police should retain their respective responsibilities for combating the revolutionary threat.

I, too, would also like to know the answers to these questions. Clearly, at some time and in some manner, someone must have given some authorization for the activities of units such as the Civilian Co-operation Bureau, the Directorate of Covert Collection and the Vlakplaas Unit. However, that authorization did not emanate from meetings of the cabinet or the State Security Council. I am convinced that the great majority of the members of both bodies remained unaware of such operations until they were finally exposed by the Goldstone Commission or by the media.

When I left the meeting with my colleagues, we were furious. I felt that far from participating in a discussion that would help to promote reconciliation and mutual understanding, we had walked into an ambush. The situation was further aggravated the next day by remarks made by Tutu and Boraine at a TRC press conference. Archbishop Tutu, close to tears, said that he had been devastated by my failure to accept that the former National Party government's policies had given the security forces a licence to kill. Tutu said he himself had told me about allegations of security force involvement in the Boipatong massacre – forgetting for the moment that I had immediately instructed the Goldstone Commission to investigate such allegations and that it had not been able to find any evidence to support them; and that the guilty were apprehended, charged and sentenced.

The statements made by Tutu and Boraine carried a clear message that they had already decided that I was implicated in gross violations of human rights. In fact, during the hearings Boraine had said that I had made a mistake by not applying personally for amnesty. I was angry and felt aggrieved. There seemed to be very little that I could do to satisfy the TRC short of making a false confession that I had been aware of – and thus condoned – the reprehensible actions of groups like the CCB and the Vlakplaas Unit, despite the fact that I had not been aware of these activities; despite everything that I had done to normalize the role of the security forces and to prevent violations of human rights; despite all the steps that I had taken to investigate all allegations of serious wrongdoing; and despite the fact that many of the actions of these elements were aimed at undermining my own reform policies.

My colleagues in the National Party were also incensed by the TRC's behaviour. We decided to withdraw our voluntary co-operation from the TRC and to approach the courts to demand that the commission carry out its mandate in accordance with the TRC Act. We presented a strong case to the court and in the end Tutu and Boraine agreed to apologize for their behaviour.

It was, however, an empty victory.

The pity is that Archbishop Tutu and I – and the essentially decent communities that we respectively represent – are still so deeply divided by our different perceptions of the truth of our country's troubled past. At the time of writing, the TRC has not yet produced its report. My fear is that, judging by its performance thus far, it will attempt to impose its own one-sided version of the truth on all South Africans, based on those aspects of the truth that fit its preconceived notions of our history. How can the result be otherwise, when those who share our truth lack any reasonable representation on the commission? My fear is that if the commission fails to produce a report which takes into account the perspectives and good faith of all the parties to our conflict, their efforts will lead neither to truth nor to reconciliation. Instead, our country will continue to be deeply divided by its different perceptions of the past.

The tragedy of the many atrocities committed by all sides during the years of conflict will continue to throw a shadow over our country. I had hoped that the TRC would become an instrument which would help to lighten this burden of pain and shame. I sincerely hope that I will be proved wrong in my fear that they will fail to achieve this.

We need to reach consensus about the past – but consensus by definition cannot be imposed by one side alone. Neither can it be determined proportionally – that those who have 62 per cent of the votes should have 62 per cent of the truth. We need a view of the past which takes into account all our truths, those that are painful and unpalatable for us, as well as those that are unacceptable to others. We need to acknowledge the deep injustices of apartheid; but we must also acknowledge the historical dilemma in which Afrikaners, as a separate nation with their own right to independence, found themselves. We need to acknowledge the suffering caused by apartheid, and particularly by forced removals, the pass laws and the so-called Immorality Act, but at the same time we must acknowledge the undeniable progress that many black South Africans made during this period and the many sincere efforts that former governments made to improve their circumstances. We need to acknowledge the atrocities committed in the name of former governments, but we must also acknowledge the brutalities committed in the name of the revolution. We may criticize the time it took for former governments to introduce fundamental reform, but we must also accept the validity of their concerns, particularly those arising from the influence of the SACP within a Soviet-supported ANC. In short, we must cease to see one another through the lens of our own propaganda and demonology, and try to see one another as we really are. Above all, we must sit around a table together to reach consensus on the past and present realities of our country. If we continue to work from our different maps of the past and the present it is unlikely that we will ever find one another.

There is no doubt that the Truth and Reconciliation Commission has caused my own personal image much harm. Hardly a week passes without some new and dramatic revelation of something or other, giving rise to renewed speculation about who knew what and who authorized what. Quite often the source of such accusations is the public testimony of the very people who were closely involved in the clandestine perpetration of atrocities. Naturally, it is in their interest to try to implicate those higher up the chain of command in their actions, leading ultimately to the person who had final authority – irrespective of the fact that the truth might have been carefully concealed from him. Most of these people were bitterly opposed to my reform policies and naturally revel in the opportunity of trying to damage my reputation. They, no doubt, also have a very strong interest in ingratiating themselves with the TRC and with the ANC and are thus inclined to give testimony that they think will please them.

Against this background, it is once again necessary for me to state my position. Neither I – nor I am sure the great majority of my colleagues in former cabinets – were involved in, or aware of, the gross violations of human rights committed by some operatives of the former security forces which have since come to light as a result of investigations which I myself initiated or which were subsequently initiated by the TRC. We deny responsibility for actions of which we were not informed; which we would not have approved; which were often diametrically opposed to the reform initiatives that my government and I had launched; which were not the policy of the National Party; and which we – and the vast majority of National Party supporters – find utterly repulsive and unacceptable.

*

I deeply regret the suffering and injustice that such activities have caused, just as I regret the immense suffering of all the victims on all sides during the conflict of the past. In so far as any bona fide actions or omissions on my part directly or indirectly contributed in any way to this suffering, I am deeply sorry. Since the time that I became president and before, the primary response of myself and the National Party to the gathering conflict in South Africa was to work for a peaceful resolution to our problems. We accepted that this would require the transformation of our country into a fully representative democracy – despite the immense risks that this entailed, and continues to entail. In this, I was supported in the referendum of 1992 by 69 per cent of the white electorate, who I believe were also casting their ballots for justice and reconciliation with all their fellow South Africans.

I am not trying to exculpate myself. I have accepted my responsibility and the responsibility of the old National Party with regard to the suffering caused by apartheid, as well as for all the actions and decisions in which I was involved, including the declaration of the States of Emergency in 1985 and 1986 and the cross-border raid which led to the tragic deaths of a number of youths in Umtata. I have stood by the security forces in all the actions that they took in the implementation of our policies and any reasonable interpretation of such policies. I have unreservedly apologized for these and other actions and policies where they caused suffering, hardship or humiliation to anyone in our country.

There is more involved in all this than my reputation alone. For better or worse, I have come to symbolize the efforts of the great majority of white South Africans who over the years have made the difficult trek from the past to the new South Africa. We believe that the role that we have played in conceiving and giving birth to our new democracy has been our proudest achievement. Those who are trying to drag us down to the sordid level of the murder squads of the CCB and Vlakplaas are robbing us of our right to stand with honour as the co-founders of our new nation.

35

With the Advantage of Hindsight

One of the most common questions I nowadays have to deal with is: what would you have done differently, if you were given the opportunity? And by many white South Africans I am asked whether, in the final analysis, I took the right course on 2 February 1990.

I have reflected deeply on this. Such questions confront everyone at the end of a career or a specific phase in their lives – questions which require deep self-analysis and honesty. Without such honesty, the result is usually self-serving rationalization. In the full awareness of this pitfall, I nevertheless remain convinced that all the most important decisions that the National Party and I took since 1989 were necessary and in the best interest of all South Africans – including my own people. I would once again accept co-responsibility for the National Party's decision to make a total break with the policy of separate development and to accept a new vision. I would still have worked for a united South Africa with a single citizenship, a one-man-one-vote franchise, and the abolition of all forms of discrimination on the grounds of race or colour. I would still have tried to negotiate a constitution which would seek a balance between equal rights for all and a fair form of protection for cultural and religious minorities; which would contain a strong and justiciable Charter of Basic Human Rights; and which would find a reasonable balance between the proper powers of central and provincial governments. I would once again repeat my speech of 2 February 1990 and, in the end, would once again say yes to both the interim and final constitutions. I would do so despite the clear shortcomings which exist in both constitutions with regard to the full realization of the goals for which the National Party and I strove in the negotiations. I would once again call a referendum, again decide that the atom bombs that we possessed should be dismantled, again repeal all discriminatory legislation before the election of April 1994, again accept the result of the 1994 election despite the many irregularities, again lead the National Party out of the

Government of National Unity and again decide to retire from active politics on the date on which I did.

Naturally, I must also admit to mistakes with regard to these and many other matters. In particular, I should have managed the negotiations on the TRC process differently. In retrospect I should have insisted much more strongly on guarantees for an even-handed process, in which all the parties to the conflict of the past would have been equal owners of the process – even if that would have caused a crisis of major proportions. In fact, it would in all probability have hastened the break-up of the Government of National Unity. I should also have tried even harder to ensure the inclusion of more effective power-sharing mechanisms in the final constitution – although it is difficult to see what more we could have done in the absence of support from the IFP, the DP and the Freedom Front. If I had known then what I know now, I would certainly have exercised greater vigilance within the State Security Council during the P. W. Botha period – although in those days the ability of outsider ministers to influence the decisions of the security departments was distinctly limited. I would also have started at the inception of my presidency to install a more reformist leadership within the SADF and the police – but here, again, my ability to dent the long-established cultures in both organizations was limited. In Afrikaans, the words for 'if' and 'ash' are the same – 'as'. We have a saying that *As is gebrande hout* – 'If is burned wood'.

The most important focal point that emerged in the debate about the rights and wrongs of my presidency relates to the constitutional negotiations. I am regularly accused of not having kept my referendum promises and of having made too many concessions. Simultaneously the ANC is also criticized by some of its followers for making too many concessions. Our negotiators – and specifically Roelf Meyer – have been bitterly, and often unfairly, criticized for not having achieved more than they did. There is a perception, strongly promoted by the ANC itself, that they out-manoeuvred and out-negotiated us at critical points. As I have pointed out in this book, I do not agree with this. Our negotiating team was professional and handled their brief with distinction. However, we had severe disadvantages: we could not afford to brag about our successes, knowing that this would only strengthen the hand of the anti-negotiation radicals in the ANC. As the custodians of the process, we could also not indulge in the brinkmanship, threats of mass action and boycotts to support our bargaining position – as the ANC, the IFP and other parties did whenever it suited them. We were also regularly left in the lurch by the smaller parties like the IFP and the DP, which often preferred to score points in building their own images even if it meant that we could not present a united front in respect of important principles. Despite all this, I still believe that the final package – a liberal constitutional state with reasonable minority guarantees, and the main elements of federalism and a free market economy – was much closer to our opening positions than it was to those of the ANC. The truth of the matter is that the skill and cunning of our respective negotiators probably did not play so decisive a role as the objective circumstances within which the negotiations took place. Given the population ratios in the country and the heritage of the past our new constitution could not, and should not, have been manipulated to thwart the will of the majority – although it should have included more reasonable power-sharing mechanisms. However, given the indispensable role that minority communities play; the need to maintain inter-group harmony and the influences of the international community and the global economy, the new constitution could hardly have given individuals and minorities fewer rights than those that they now enjoy in terms of our new constitution. In one area the negotiation process seriously failed to produce what South Africa urgently needs. The greatest shortcoming of our transformation process was the refusal of the ANC majority to accept a constitutional model that would contain strong provisions to accommodate our complex multicultural society – specifically, acceptance of the kind of balanced power-sharing mechanisms at the executive level which the National Party and I advocated throughout the process. Mandela – and some commentators – interpreted our wish to build in some form of power-sharing at the executive level as a crude attempt to maintain a white minority veto and to thwart the will of the majority. This has always been absolute nonsense. It was never my intention to deprive the majority of the right to implement its chosen policies. It was rather that we should have a forum where we would be able to identify our many common problems, goals and objectives and develop, together, a vision and policies – and strategies for their implementation – which would have the enthusiastic support of all our communities. The failure of other opposition parties to align themselves with such a consensus-seeking model will to my mind remain a charge against them.

In the end we succeeded in achieving to some extent limited forms of power-sharing, albeit not at executive level. However, I do not believe that the federal characteristics of our constitution and the supremacy of the constitution as amplified by the fairly extensive limitation of the powers of the president, the government and even Parliament, go far enough. In retrospect, my greatest disappointment in the constitutional field relates to our lack of success in producing a power-sharing model suited to the needs of our complex nation. It is widely accepted that in deeply divided societies such as ours, it is essential that all the major components of society should feel that they are meaningfully represented and included in the processes by which they are governed. The alternative is exactly the kind of alienation, division and mounting rage which now threatens our future success. The majoritarian reality which has now, to a certain extent, been thrust on us contains the clear threat of the kind of racial domination which must be avoided at all costs.

Those who criticize the result of negotiation now, forget how hopeless our situation seemed in 1988 – or how perilous it was in the months before the election in 1994. Anyone who would have predicted then that we would be able to bring the IFP and the Freedom Front into the elections; that we would be able to defuse the threat of right-wing violence; that we would be able to hold the elections with reasonable success; that the ANC-led government would adopt responsible economic policies and that the country would be broadly at peace with itself four years after the transformation, would have been accused of hopeless optimism. The reality is that despite all our problems we are in a far better position now than we would have been had we failed to act as we did.

I maintain that we have substantially delivered on our referendum promises. Those who say that we did not are generally speaking people who either voted 'no' in the referendum and/or people who incorrectly expected that we would achieve a white minority veto. This we never advocated.

Simultaneously, those who are critical should also not underestimate the remarkable progress that we have all made during the past ten years, nor our historic achievement in creating the new South Africa. They should constantly remind themselves of the tremendous gains that the new South Africa has brought them – and the perils that they have avoided by resolving centuries of division and bitterness in a reasonably peaceful and sensible manner.

After three centuries of struggle black, coloured and Indian South Africans have at last been liberated from the restrictions, powerlessness and injustices of the past. That liberation has brought with it all the rights and privileges which they were, to a greater or lesser extent, denied for generations. And with those rights have come the corresponding responsibilities. They are now, together with all their fellow South Africans, in charge of their own destiny.

We have avoided the racial cataclysm that so many observers believed was unavoidable. We have proved that even the most intractable and complex problems can be resolved through compromise, negotiations and goodwill. By so doing we have become an inspiration for other divided societies throughout the world.

We have established a free and truly democratic society with a constitution and a charter of fundamental rights that can compare with the best in the world.

It is not only black, coloured and Indian South Africans who have been liberated. After generations, whites have been freed from the defensive *laager* in which they had for centuries been confined.

Many of the national symbols with which I grew up in the old South Africa had exclusive and defensive connotations. They reflected the historic determination of Afrikaners to hold at bay the perils of a sometimes hostile and threatening continent. The first such symbol was the castle that the Dutch had built in 1666 in Cape Town – the five-pointed plan of which was adopted in the insignia of the SADF. Another of our symbols was the *laager* of the Voortrekkers – the circled ox-wagons which served as a kind of mobile fortress within which they could protect their women and children and cattle. The powder horn – the source of the power with which the Voortrekkers conquered and defended the wild interior – also became one.

By the middle of this century we could no longer accommodate our families and property within defensive *laagers*. Faced with the influx of millions of black South Africans from the rural areas our people then began to construct a *laager* of legislation around our communities to hold at bay the threatening realities of Africa. This book is, in essence, the story of how we, at last, confronted those realities and dismantled the *laager* of apartheid. It is the story of the great trek that most of my people have undertaken, particularly during the last twenty years, to the new South Africa. It has not been a trek in space – but a trek of the spirit. It required us to leave long-cherished ideals behind; to confront our fears and doubts and to press onward until at last on 2 February 1990 we finally crossed the Rubicon. As with the first Great Trek, there were those who chose to stay behind, there were stragglers and there were arguments between the leaders about which direction we should take and the haste with which we should make it.

And so we have at last arrived at our destination – the new South Africa. It is sometimes frightening, but always exciting and exhilarating. We no longer view our continent from behind defensive positions – of stone or ox-wagons or discriminatory laws. But we are not without protection. Our new constitution now gives all South Africans a reasonable degree of security. We can now confront the challenges of our country together with all our fellow South Africans. We can share common aspirations and work for common goals unencumbered by the baggage of discrimination – with no greater nor lesser rights than any of our fellow countrymen. I believe that we have at last come to terms with the realities of our continent. We have completed a great spiritual trek. We are ready for a new beginning.

Conclusion

Recently, I returned to Pretoria. I drove up to the Union Buildings and parked in the broad roadway beneath its sandstone ramparts, overlooking the gardens and the city to the west. There were a few tourist buses – many more than there used to be – standing near the monument to South African servicemen who died during the First and Second World Wars. The terraced gardens were past their summer splendour and the early winter lawn below was almost the colour of straw.

Superficially, little seemed to have changed since the day of President Mandela's inauguration, a little more than four years earlier. The hustle and bustle of the city below continued as it always had. The economy was still growing at only about 3 per cent per annum – still not fast enough to meet the needs and aspirations of all our people. In the office blocks of the city below businessmen, lawyers and bankers still continued with their busy schedules. They were no longer hobbled by sanctions and the distortions caused by a siege economy, but now they had to contend with an increasingly rigid labour system and interventionist government policies.

Behind me, the process of government continued within the Union Buildings as it had for decades. The cabinet and its committees met; foreign ambassadors presented their credentials; bullet-proof Mercedes-Benz and BMWs swept up to the porte cochère at the back of the west wing – as they had when I was president. Young ministers jockeyed for position. Old ministers clung on to office. Secretaries and clerks still scurried down the echoing hallways in search of files. The same black worker, dressed in brown Public Works overalls, still patiently swept the brick paving outside the back entrance, his hair now whiter with the passage of time.

But now the voices and cadences were different. The incumbents of the cars had changed. Most of the people working inside the Union Buildings were members of a rapidly emerging and self-confident black governmental and civil service elite. A new order had arrived.

Across the valley, much the same people lived in the elegant suburbs of Muckleneuk, Brooklyn and Waterkloof, except that many more homes were occupied by diplomats from the scores of new embassies which had opened in the city. In busy suburban malls housewives continued to do their weekly shopping. The government schools were more integrated. Generally there were few problems, but the waiting lists for private schools had grown longer. The golf courses remained busy with peak activity on Wednesday afternoons and over the weekends. In the country-club lounges the ladies continued to play bridge and sip tea and sometimes gin and tonic. Beyond the fringes of the city, new middle-class housing developments were mushrooming, clustered around golf courses and surrounded by electrified walls.

Breaking the horizon on the opposite ridge of hills, the stark form of the Voortrekker Monument – half church, half fortress – remained as a reminder of the ideals which had inspired me when I was a young man. The intervening years had showed that they were ideals which could be clung to only by withholding justice from other South Africans and by denying the economic and demographic realities of our country. Elsewhere in the city and throughout the country Afrikaners wrestled with the problems of disempowerment. The feelings of most remained ambivalent, relieved that their daily lives had thus far changed so little; happy to be rid of the burden and guilt of apartheid; anxious about the future of their schools, their communities and their jobs; hurt and confused that the euphoria and goodwill of the first months of the new South Africa had dissipated in the recriminations and revelations of the Truth and Reconciliation Commission.

In the predominantly white suburbs they still gathered on Saturday evenings after rugby for a *braai* (barbecue) – but now the conversation frequently centred on the latest car hijacking or burglary or how they would invest the packages they would receive after their retrenchment from the public service. The next morning, they would, as always, still go off to church and still hope that their dominee would be able to make some moral sense of their bewildering and changing world. Before lunch, while reading their Sunday newspapers, their eyes would stray from the reports of the previous day's rugby matches, the latest government scandals and brazen crimes to discreet advertisements offering emigration services to Australia or New Zealand. If you spoke to them now, most of them would still grudgingly admit that we had little choice in transforming the country as we did. Many would be critical, after the event, of how we managed the process. Most, I know from experience, would still remember me with some kindness. Some would think, incorrectly, that I must have known about the activities of the CCB and Vlakplaas and would accuse me of having left the security forces in the lurch. Many would have been upset and disappointed by my decision to divorce Marike.

If little has changed in the white suburbs of Pretoria, it is also true that almost as little has changed in its sprawling black townships. Workers still rise before dawn and pile into minibus taxis, buses and commuter trains to make their way to their jobs in the city, those who are lucky enough to have jobs. They return in the evenings to their crowded match-box houses, those who are lucky enough to have houses. There has been some progress. There are more houses – but not nearly as many as the ANC promised. More people have access to electricity and telephones, and a lucky minority is beginning to benefit from their greater access to public service jobs. But apart from that, most of the old problems – crime, poverty, inadequate services, poor education and unemployment – remain.

It was considerations such as this which led Deputy President Thabo Mbeki to make a speech in Parliament at the end of May 1998 in which he said that four years after the birth of the new South Africa, whites and blacks were still two separate nations. He accused whites of having done nothing to redress the situation. He repeated an earlier warning that much of what was happening in the country was 'producing rage among millions of people to which we must respond seriously'. He quoted the African-American poet Langston Hughes who had asked – 'what happens to a dream deferred?' His conclusion was that it explodes. There can be no doubt that among black South Africans there is a growing sense of disillusionment and discontent based on unfulfilled expectations. The ANC promised them heaven and earth. They expected to see a substantial improvement in their quality of life and are deeply frustrated because of what they perceive as non-delivery. The socialist trade unions and populist black politicians are beginning to ask how they can use this disillusionment to upset the delicate balance which has been achieved in our new constitution.

It is not only among black South Africans that discontent is growing. Among white South Africans the discontent and disillusionment is at this stage disjointed and unarticulated, but with each year that passes it is becoming more focused and more immediate. There is growing anxiety over the intolerable levels of crime in the country;

there is anger over the apparently systematic murder of white farmers; there is a sense of deep injury over the downgrading of Afrikaans, particularly in the SABC and government institutions; there is alarm over the decline in services and standards; there is a sense of grievance over the reverse racial discrimination in unfairly applied affirmative action; there is deep concern over the perception that whites are now being made the scapegoats for all the ills of our society and that, in the future, the ANC will blame us for their failure to deliver on the promises that they made to their supporters; there is disillusion over the perceptions that whites are no longer really welcome in the new South Africa unless they conform with the ANC's model; and there is growing indignation and anger over the role that has been played by the Truth and Reconciliation Commission and by its denigration of former leaders. The 69 per cent of whites who voted for reform in the 1992 election also had a dream – a dream of a South Africa free from racial discrimination and domination, where all our peoples would be able to coexist with mutual respect and dignity and work together to achieve our pressing national goals; a dream of a new South Africa in which there would be an honourable place for everyone. The question might be asked: what happens should this dream disintegrate?

Likewise there is growing disillusionment among other minority groups, such as the coloureds and Indians. They also feel sidelined in many respects and they share in the concerns about crime, reverse racial discrimination, unemployment and the decline in service and standards. They feel threatened by the ANC's growing emphasis on race and colour and they fear a return to a new form of apartheid which will lead to suppression and deprivation.

In this growing disillusionment and discontent among all South Africans lies our biggest challenge. How then, should we respond to this challenge? There are a number of major areas in which all South Africans need to work together to achieve our common goals of building a peaceful, prosperous, safe and free society.

We must do everything in our power to maintain peace and harmonious relations in our complex multicultural country. Our experience, and the experience of many other multicultural societies around the world, shows that there are some basic ground rules for the maintenance of healthy inter-communal relations. These include the need to safeguard the reasonable cultural, economic and security interests of all our communities, without introducing new forms of racial discrimination. We must strictly enforce non-discrimination and promote a culture of toleration, mutual respect and pride in our rich diversity. In particular, we should create circumstances in which all our cultural communities should be recognized, welcomed and included in the institutions of our broader society. We must find alternatives to simple majoritarianism, in terms of which significant minorities are excluded from meaningful participation in the processes by which they are governed. At the same time we must work together to establish a new and inclusive overarching national identity.

The key to the solution of the problem of discontent and disillusion is rapid and sustained economic growth. Experience has shown that the more quickly the economy grows, the more quickly a fairer distribution of income takes place. To achieve this we must apply the lessons to be learned from countries that have achieved sustained economic growth, while avoiding the mistakes which have led to the economic crises in East and South-East Asia. However, the basic recipe for success remains much the same: we need to maintain fiscal discipline and continue our successful struggle against inflation; we must encourage domestic and foreign investment; we must continue with privatization; we must open our economy in a responsible manner to domestic and global competition; and if we wish to create jobs, we must above all develop a more flexible and productive labour system.

We should furthermore insist on cost-effective, efficient and honest government. Because of the limited resources available, we must ensure that appropriate services are delivered in the most cost-effective possible manner. This will require a lean, highly professional, non-political and dedicated public service. We should also strive as rapidly as possible to ensure that the public service is representative of the population as a whole – but not at the cost of efficiency or the implementation of new forms of racial discrimination and exclusion.

Finally, we must promote and strengthen a functioning multiparty democracy in South Africa. At the moment there is a very real danger of too much power being concentrated in the hands of a single self-perpetuating and ethnically based majority party. We need a dynamic and vibrant political system in which the voters are presented with credible alternatives, where they can vote according to their values, rather than according to their ethnic affiliation. A great responsibility accordingly rests on the present opposition parties to strengthen themselves, to improve their performance and co-operation and to make themselves more attractive to voters from all communities. A democracy without strong competing parties often ends up with no democracy at all. It was accordingly for this reason that, on 2 February 1996, I spelled out a new vision for the National Party that one day, by ourselves or together with others, under our present name or under some other, we would once again form the majority. That majority would not then be based on race, but on common values and a shared vision of how the country should be governed.

We need a fundamental realignment of political forces within South Africa. The time is ripe to break away from the dangerous and sterile political situation in which we now find ourselves. The ANC's attempts to hold its old anti-apartheid alliance together are impeding its ability to provide good government and to set a clear vision for the country. Instead of making clear choices, the ANC is trying to be everything to everyone – because they fear that clear choices might lead to a loss of support and the possible breakaway of the more radical elements.

*

In our new constitution, I, together with all other South Africans, committed myself to the transformation of South Africa into a non-racial society in which there will be no form of discrimination on the basis of race or colour. This is a high ideal, but I have no illusions that it is an ideal that will be difficult to achieve. Only if we can free party politics from the chains of the past and break out of the overall racially determined pattern will we be able to succeed in placing the overwhelming majority of moderate South Africans from all population groups in charge of affairs. Only then will we be able to control the dangerous radical elements on the left and on the right and marginalize them sufficiently to ensure that South Africa will be stable and progressive.

To sum up in a single concept: we must break away from race-based politics to value-based politics. I am proud that my last bequest as leader of my party was, in fact, this – the transformation of the National Party into a truly non-racial party, within which blacks, whites, coloureds and Indians can join hands and work together to protect and promote their shared values.

I have no doubt that the party-political realignment that South Africa needs will occur within the foreseeable future, although in all probability only after the 1999 election. The ANC alliance will split. It is difficult to say what the aftermath of such a split might be. Certainly, the most healthy outcome would be a broad, moderate coalition of the centre. Whether such a coalition will ever become a reality will depend on the moderate leaders within the ANC and the moderate parties such as the National Party, the Inkatha Freedom Party, the Democratic Party and the new United Democratic Movement. The new South Africa calls for all leaders of goodwill to rise above their, and their supporters', selfish short-term interests; old battle axes will have to be buried and clear and creative thought will be required. A further paradigm shift is needed.

I have no doubt that we have the capacity as a nation to avert the danger of the country slipping back into racial tension, unrest, disruption and conflict. Nearly all South Africans dearly wish to work together to make a success of the new South Africa. Threats and recriminations are neither necessary nor productive. Consultation, inclusion and mutual acceptance are. We must find ways within appropriate forums of continuing the type of process of negotiation and the search for consensus which so successfully created the new South Africa. Only now it must be aimed at building consensus on how we can together tackle the challenges that confront our country and which constitute the basis for discontent and new tensions between our various peoples. Perhaps the answer may lie in adapting the traditional consensual basis of African politics to the needs of our complex multicultural society. In addition to the confrontational and competitive politics of Parliament – which are necessary for successful modern states – we need an ongoing *indaba* of the people where the voices of all can be heard and weighed in the search for consensus.

If we can do all this, we will be able to achieve our national goals. We will be able to improve the lives of millions of our people who still live in conditions of unacceptable poverty and deprivation; we will be able to develop a successful and prosperous economy; we will be able to create a new multicultural nation, unified, but proud and strong in its rich diversity. The new beginning that our country has made presents us all with a wonderful opportunity. It is up to all South Africans and their leaders to grasp this opportunity and to meet the challenges that confront us.

Index

SOUTH AFRICA BEFORE THE 1994 ELECTION

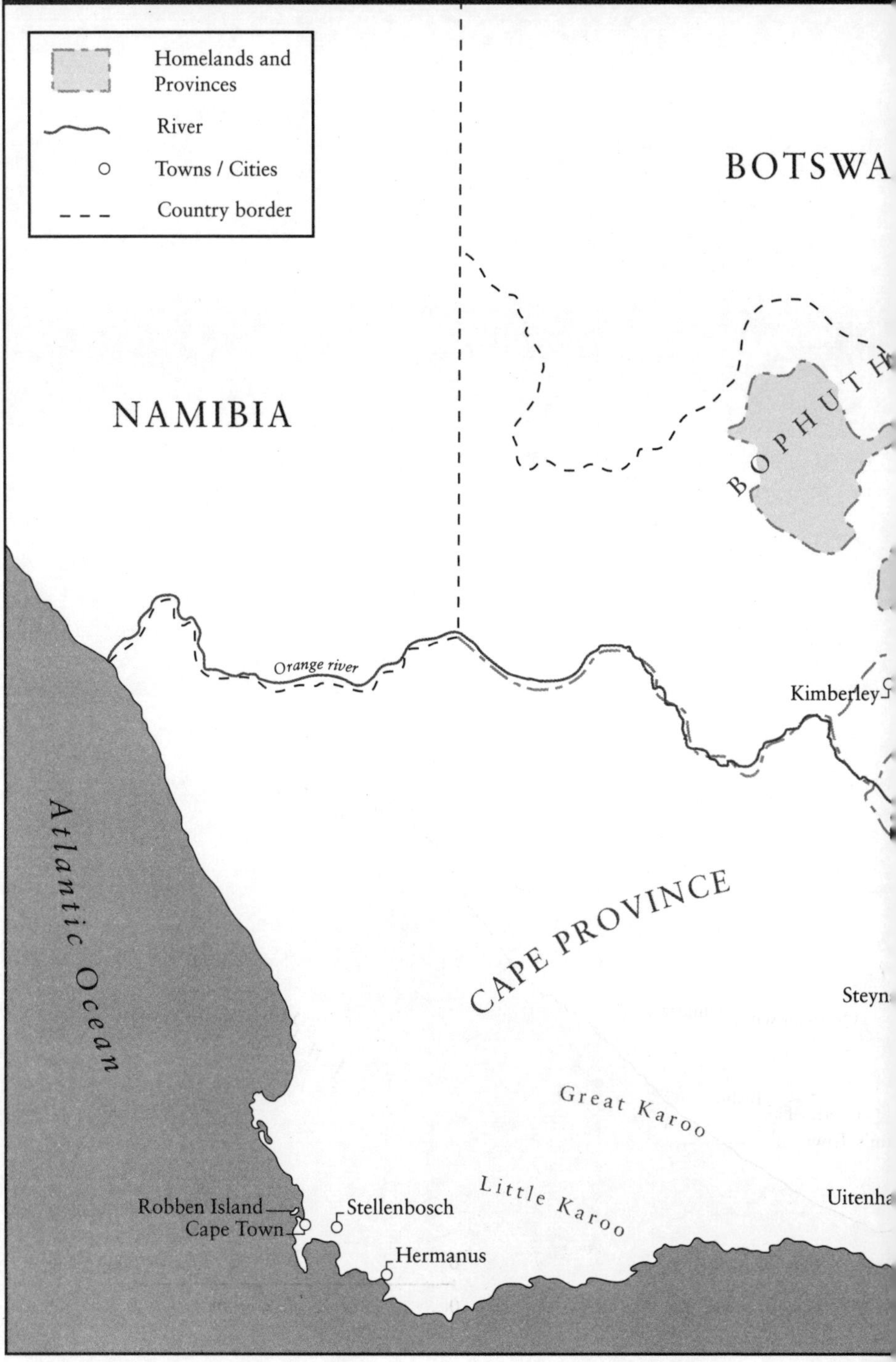

	Homelands and Provinces
	River
○	Towns / Cities
- - -	Country border

BOTSWA

NAMIBIA

BOPHUTH

Atlantic Ocean

Orange river

Kimberley

CAPE PROVINCE

Steyn

Great Karoo

Little Karoo

Uitenha

Robben Island
Cape Town
Stellenbosch
Hermanus